OXFORD GREEK AND LATIN COLLEGE COMMENTARIES

Suetonius' *Life of Augustus*

OXFORD GREEK AND LATIN COLLEGE COMMENTARIES

The Oxford Greek and Latin College Commentaries series is designed for students in intermediate or advanced Greek or Latin at colleges and universities. Each volume includes, on the same page, the ancient text, a running vocabulary, and succinct notes focusing on grammar and syntax, distinctive features of style, and essential context. The Greek and Latin texts are based on the most recent Oxford Classical Text (OCT) editions whenever available; otherwise, other authoritative editions are used. Each volume features a comprehensive introduction intended to enhance utility in the classroom and student appreciation of the work at hand.

The series focuses on texts and authors frequently taught at the intermediate or advanced undergraduate level, but it also makes available some central works currently lacking an appropriate commentary. The primary purpose of this series is to offer streamlined commentaries that are up-to-date, user-friendly, and affordable. Each volume presents entire works or substantial selections that can form the basis for an entire semester's coursework. Each commentary's close attention to grammar and syntax is intended to address the needs of readers encountering a work or author for the first time.

Series Editors

Barbara Weiden Boyd
Bowdoin College

Stephen Esposito
Boston University

Mary Lefkowitz
Wellesley College

Ovid, Ars Amatoria Book 3
Commentary by Christopher M. Brunelle

Selected Letters from Pliny the Younger's *Epistulae*
Commentary by Jacqueline Carlon

Aristophanes' *Wasps*
Commentary by Kenneth S. Rothwell, Jr.

Sophocles' *Electra*
Commentary by Hanna M. Roisman

Suetonius' *Life of Augustus*
Commentary by Darryl A. Phillips

OXFORD GREEK AND LATIN COLLEGE COMMENTARIES

Suetonius' *Life of Augustus*

Commentary by
Darryl A. Phillips

Oxford University Press is a department of the University of Oxford. It furthers
the University's objective of excellence in research, scholarship, and education
by publishing worldwide. Oxford is a registered trade mark of Oxford University
Press in the UK and certain other countries.

Published in the United States of America by Oxford University Press
198 Madison Avenue, New York, NY 10016, United States of America.

© Oxford University Press 2023

All rights reserved. No part of this publication may be reproduced, stored in
a retrieval system, or transmitted, in any form or by any means, without the
prior permission in writing of Oxford University Press, or as expressly permitted
by law, by license, or under terms agreed with the appropriate reproduction
rights organization. Inquiries concerning reproduction outside the scope of the
above should be sent to the Rights Department, Oxford University Press, at the
address above.

You must not circulate this work in any other form
and you must impose this same condition on any acquirer.

CIP data is on file at the Library of Congress
ISBN 978–0–19–939238–4 (pbk.)
ISBN 978–0–19–767608–0 (hbk.)

Paperback printed by Marquis Book Printing, Canada
Hardback printed by Bridgeport National Bindery, Inc., United States of America

CONTENTS

Acknowledgments ix

INTRODUCTION 1
Augustus' Lifetime and the *Life of Augustus* 1
Suetonius' Life and Works 2
Suetonius and the Biographical Tradition 3
Structure and Content of the *Life of Augustus* 4
Suetonius' Latin Style 5
This Volume 8
Outline of the *Life of Augustus* (including major Latin rubric headings) 9
Further Reading 10
Commentary Abbreviations 11
Frequent Vocabulary 15
The Family of Augustus as Mentioned by Suetonius 27

LIFE OF AUGUSTUS WITH COMMENTARY 29

ACKNOWLEDGMENTS

WELL OVER TWO decades ago Jim Franklin and Barbara Weiden Boyd encouraged me to write up notes on the *Life of Augustus* to use with my students; those notes have grown into the present volume. I am grateful to them both for planting the seed. I offer my sincere thanks to the many Latin students at Connecticut College who have worked through sections of the commentary with me in more recent years, including Kaavya Antony, Michelle Chapman, Dominique D'Onofrio, Mikela Karaiosifoglou, Aly Young, Stephan Boodlal, and especially Bailey Mertz; to my colleagues and friends Melissa Huber, Sharon Portnoff, Sue Shapiro, and Noelle Zeiner-Carmichael, for their support and encouragement; and to the Susan Eckert Lynch '62 Faculty Research Fund at Connecticut College. The editors at Oxford University Press and the anonymous readers offered suggestions that improved this volume in more ways than I can count. Most of all, I owe special thanks to my husband Mark McConnel, who graciously welcomed Suetonius and Augustus into our home, not quite realizing how long they would stay.

INTRODUCTION

AUGUSTUS' LIFETIME AND THE *LIFE OF AUGUSTUS*

The lifetime of Augustus (63 BCE–14 CE) was an era of remarkable change in the Roman world. Following decades of civil war, Gaius Julius Caesar Octavianus emerged as the leading man in the state and in 27 BCE was honored by the Senate with the new cognomen Augustus. In the decades that followed, the traditional government of the Roman Republic evolved to include a leading role for Augustus. Peace at home was balanced with wars of expansion and consolidation on the frontiers. Literature and the arts flourished. A building boom transformed the city of Rome. The period is recognized as one of the key moments of transition for the Mediterranean world, when the foundation was laid for two centuries of the Pax Romana and an imperial monarchy in the form of an emperor operating within the structure of a "republican" system. Augustus was at the center of it all, and thus the lifetime of Augustus and the life of Augustus himself have attracted keen interest from antiquity up to the present day.

Gaius Suetonius Tranquillus' *Life of Augustus* is arguably our most important surviving Latin prose source for the period. Velleius Paterculus, who came of age in the last decades of Augustus' lifetime, offers only a condensed history of the period in a partisan narrative that reflects contemporary culture under Tiberius. The great Roman imperial historian Tacitus, writing almost a century later, begins his *Annals* with a critical summary of Augustus' accomplishments, turning to a full narrative only with the death of Augustus and the accession of Tiberius in 14 CE. Cassius Dio, who wrote in Greek some two centuries after the era, provides our most detailed chronological account, but Dio often reads back into the Augustan period characteristics and concerns of his own time. Augustus' own account of his public achievements, the so-called *Res gestae divi Augusti*, written for display in front of his tomb in Rome and surviving in inscriptions from Asia Minor, is a uniquely valuable source, but lacks the scope and depth of a literary account. Given the dearth of in-depth and reliable histories, our understanding of the period and of Augustus himself leans heavily on Suetonius' biography, written in the early second century CE.

Suetonius offers a comprehensive and nuanced view of Augustus, drawing upon a wide variety of sources, both favorable and critical, as well as the words of Augustus himself. The *Life of Augustus* is largely accurate in its details; the errors that we detect are more often of generalization than of fact. Furthermore, Suetonius' interests range far beyond those of Roman prose chroniclers. In his biography of Augustus,

Suetonius surveys not only the major political, military, and civic accomplishments of his subject, but also such diverse topics as Augustus' family lineage, spouses, offspring, and personal characteristics such as appearance, leisure activities, intellectual pursuits, and style of living. As the discipline of history has evolved in our own age to include much more than the political and military topics that occupy a central place in the Roman historical tradition, Suetonius' work has received new attention and appreciation. We find in the *Life of Augustus* a detailed biography of a leading figure at a pivotal historical moment, as well as the material for political, social, and cultural history that offers a wide range of approaches to the Augustan age.

SUETONIUS' LIFE AND WORKS

We are well enough informed about the life and literary output of Suetonius to offer a broad reconstruction. Details come from Suetonius himself (as he inserts occasional autobiographical references into his work), a number of letters of Pliny the Younger (letters to Suetonius and letters about him sent to others), and notices about Suetonius from later writers. The outline of his career in service to the emperor is also recorded in an inscription from Hippo Regius in Roman North Africa (possibly the place of Suetonius' birth).

Born into a wealthy equestrian family, Gaius Suetonius Tranquillus was the son of a military commander who had served during the civil wars following the reign of Nero. His cognomen Tranquillus suggests that Suetonius may have been born in 69 or 70 CE, in the period of calm following the end of the conflict. Suetonius chose not to follow a military career, but instead rose through the ranks of the civil service under the emperors Trajan and Hadrian, holding in turn the posts of *a studiis* (head of imperial research), *a bibliothecis* (library commissioner), and finally the important post of *ab epistulis* (director of the emperor's correspondence). Suetonius was holding the latter appointment when he completed (at least some of) the *Lives of the Caesars*, of which the *Life of Augustus* is the second book. He is said to have dedicated the work to C. Septicius Clarus, the praetorian prefect at the time (the dedication itself is missing, along with the opening chapters of the biography of Julius Caesar). According to the biography of Hadrian in the *Historia Augusta*, Suetonius and Septicius were both dismissed from their positions working for the emperor for being overly casual in their relations with Hadrian's wife Sabina (the event likely dates to 122 CE). The dismissal provides a *terminus ante quem* for the completion of the *Life of Augustus*. How long Suetonius lived after his dismissal is not known; his death is placed as late as 141 CE.

The patronage of Pliny the Younger was an important factor both in Suetonius' rise to prominence in the imperial service and in his literary pursuits, since Pliny encouraged Suetonius to publish his work. Suetonius was a prolific writer. The works of Suetonius that survive for us are all biographies: a set of biographies of famous men of letters (*De viris illustribus*, of which a selection survives) and his lives of the twelve Caesars (*De vita Caesarum*, which includes the *Life of Augustus*). Other works attributed to Suetonius, most now known only by title or through passing references by other authors, reveal his wide-ranging antiquarian interests. His works include studies of Greek games, Roman spectacles, the Roman year, customs, public offices, names of seas and rivers, names and types of clothes, names of winds, physical defects, and weather signs, as well as studies of kings and famous courtesans (perhaps from literature) and a work on Cicero's *Republic*. It is for his biographies of the Caesars, and especially the *Life of Augustus*, that Suetonius has been remembered by people in later ages.

SUETONIUS AND THE BIOGRAPHICAL TRADITION

The Romans had long celebrated the deeds and characters of leading men. Funeral orations extolled the major accomplishments and virtues of the deceased and his ancestors. Wax portraits of the dead, along with concise summaries of their achievements, were displayed in the houses of their descendants. Tomb inscriptions listing offices held and wars waged became increasingly elaborate over time. Public speeches, delivered in the courts or in front of assemblies of the people, scrutinized the character and deeds of others. These orations might be intensely personal in their portrayal of the virtues and vices of allies and rivals. Leading Romans also presented their own accomplishments and defended their actions in writing. Julius Caesar's third-person narrative of his own role in the Gallic Wars is one surviving example of a tradition that included such works as the dictator Sulla's memoirs and a poem by M. Tullius Cicero about his own consulship, neither of which survive intact. The Roman culture of political competition motivated these works, as each generation would hope to follow in the footsteps of their forefathers, competing with their peers to reach the top offices in the state.

In the Greek world, biographical writing had its own development. Greek biography grew out of a tradition of encomium and monographs focused on the deeds of great men such as Alexander the Great. Philosophical interest in ethics influenced the development of biographical writing, since details from the lives of individuals might illustrate virtues and vices and reveal character. A scholarly tradition also developed of introducing edited texts and commentaries with short biographies of the authors, often using information gleaned from references within the authors' own works. Lives of poets compiled in Latin by M. Terentius Varro in the first century BCE (now lost) as well as those written by Suetonius (surviving in part) picked up this Hellenistic Greek tradition.

With all of these influences, biography did not develop into a narrowly defined genre in antiquity. Traces of these diverse traditions can be seen in the biographies that survive today. Our knowledge of the development of biographical writing in the Roman world is limited by the chance survival of the works themselves. Writing in the first century BCE, Cornelius Nepos produced some four hundred short biographies of famous Romans and foreigners (*De viris illustribus*), of which only a small number survive. Nepos' longest surviving work, a biography of T. Pomponius Atticus, reveals a eulogistic style and focus on ethics. Suetonius' older contemporary, the Greek writer Plutarch, wrote matched pairs of biographies of Greeks and Romans. These *Parallel Lives*, of which we have twenty-three pairs, explore the lives of leading men, paying close attention to their upbringing and the development and revelation of their character, reflecting Greek traditions. Another contemporary of Suetonius, the Roman historian Tacitus, wrote a monograph about his father-in-law Cn. Julius Agricola that combines panegyric, a narrative of Agricola's years in Britain, ethnography and geography, and invective against the emperor Domitian. Both Tacitus and Plutarch take a chronological approach to their subjects, thus presenting biographical works that share key traits with historical writing.

Suetonius' own work also shows some of the range of the genre, as his biographies include brief surveys of literary figures as well as in-depth examinations of leading politicians that contain extensive quotation of source materials and attention to minute details, as we see in the lives of Julius Caesar and Augustus. For his *Lives of the Caesars*, Suetonius chose to eschew the chronological narrative that we see employed by Plutarch and Tacitus in favor of a topical approach that facilitates direct comparison between his subjects within topics. Suetonius' *Lives of the Caesars* was influential, and the biographies of Rome's later emperors collected in the so-called *Historia Augusta* continued Suetonius' work, although they never approach the fullness or quality of Suetonius' *Life of Augustus*. In the ninth century CE, the Frankish courtier and scholar Einhard would also turn to Suetonius as a model for his *Life of Charlemagne*.

STRUCTURE AND CONTENT OF THE *LIFE OF AUGUSTUS*

In the modern age biography regularly takes the form of a chronological narrative; not so for Suetonius. Although chronological accounts are found at the beginning of the work, where Suetonius explores the ancestors and upbringing of Augustus, and again at the end, where Suetonius recounts Augustus' final days, death, and burial, the body of the biography—the vast majority of the life—is arranged not chronologically but by categories, as Suetonius informs his reader in chapter 9 (*neque per tempora sed per species exsequar*). Suetonius employs a similar organizational scheme in his other biographies of the Caesars, arranging the bulk of the material by topics framed by chronological book-ends treating the early years and death of each Caesar.

Categories (*species*) provide the structure of the *Life of Augustus*, and Suetonius signals the shift to a new category by introducing the chapter or section with a key word or phrase, a rubric or heading marker. Chapters 9–60 explore the public life of Augustus, with sections devoted to civil and foreign wars and his administration of Rome, Italy, and the provinces. Examples of his citizen-like behavior are presented, as well as evidence that reveals the high regard in which he was held. Augustus' personal and family life are presented in chapters 61–93. Here Suetonius discusses women and children in Augustus' family, along with his friends, freedmen, and slaves. Examples of his personal behavior are presented, highlighting both disgraceful acts and examples of self-restraint. Other sections explore such categories as Augustus' physical appearance, health, exercise regimen, intellectual pursuits, and religious customs.

Within categories information is often presented in chronological order, as we see, for example, in chapters 9–18, which discuss civil wars (*bella ciuilia*). Here Suetonius proceeds in order from Mutina (43 BCE) to Actium (31 BCE). Chronological order within a category is also seen in the section devoted to signs foretelling Augustus' greatness (ch. 94–96). However, a strict chronology is not always followed. We find in the discussion of uprisings and conspiracies against Augustus (ch. 19) that Suetonius saves for his final example an assassination attempt by a camp follower during Augustus' Illyrian campaigns, an event that predates the notable senatorial conspiracies with which he began the chapter. Here Suetonius breaks the chronology to emphasize the lowly status of the conspirator.

In the use of categories as an organizing scheme, the contrast between biography and history is perhaps most striking. Annalistic history, a year-by-year chronological account of events, had long been a standard form of historical narrative in the Roman world. The political structure of the Roman state, which centers on the annual election of magistrates, makes annalistic history an ideal fit. The consuls who give their names to the year are also the chief magistrates whose actions will be of interest throughout the year. For Suetonius the biographer, however, Augustus' magistracies are not employed as chronological markers; instead, magistracies form just one of the many categories that are explored in discrete sections of the life (they are covered in chapters 26–28, introduced by the rubric *magistratus atque honores*, "magistracies and elective offices"). Throughout the biography, the actions of Augustus are presented without any connection to the position he held. Suetonius is focused on presenting the life of a man topic by topic, not a year-by-year history of the period.

By setting out Augustus' offices in a discrete section separate from the discussion of Augustus' actions, Suetonius leaves his reader uncertain as to the basis of Augustus' power. In the case of Augustus' successors, who were granted a host of imperial powers upon their accession, this structure poses few problems. As we know from other sources, however, Augustus' powers changed and evolved over time. A reader interested in the political history of the period needs to be aware of Suetonius' structural choices, for in the biography Augustus' actions appear out of chronological context and everything seems to be done by fiat. Although Suetonius presents a multifaceted view of Augustus, the image we see is largely static, not dynamic. Taken on its own terms, however, Suetonius' *Life of Augustus* is a remarkable work, providing a comprehensive exploration of the public and personal life of a leading political figure, one which brings together sources that both criticize and praise its subject.

SUETONIUS' LATIN STYLE

Although Suetonius' work has often been mined for information, relatively little attention has been paid to Suetonius' style of writing. Suetonius has a distinctive prose style characterized by the seemingly contradictory traits of great concision and a rich vocabulary. Understanding key characteristics of his style will aid in reading and interpreting the work.

Most distinctive is Suetonius' habit of leaving Augustus unnamed. The name Augustus appears only twenty-one times in the biography: eleven times in the opening sections that treat Augustus' ancestry and his name (ch. 1–7) and seven times in the concluding sections of the biography that discuss signs of his greatness and his death and burial (ch. 94–101). In the main body of the work (ch. 8–93), Augustus is named only three times (in ch. 58–59). When not named directly, Augustus is regularly the unexpressed subject of the third person singular verb. Throughout the text, we also find pronouns, adjectives, and participles that refer to Augustus; in such cases the reader should understand that Augustus is the point of reference (e.g., ch. 6.1: *nutrimentorum eius . . . locus*, "the place of his [Augustus'] upbringing"; ch. 7.1: *infanti cognomen Thurino inditum est*, "the name Thurinus was given to him [Augustus] as an infant"). Where confusion might otherwise arise, notes in the commentary point out instances of this practice. On those occasions when Suetonius does name his subject, he always refers to him as Augustus and does so consistently throughout the biography, although "Augustus" was not adopted as a name until 27 BCE. In characteristic fashion, Suetonius presents all of the names used by Augustus throughout his life in a single chapter devoted to the category of "names" (ch. 7). Suetonius' practice of employing Augustus as the unexpressed subject can lead to imprecise presentation of historical details. Nevertheless, the focus on Augustus as the subject (the "doer" of the vast majority of verbs) is a natural feature of a work that aims to explore the man and his actions. This feature of Suetonius' style should be kept in mind when interpreting the text.

To give just one example, in a chapter devoted to Augustus' actions as pontifex maximus, Suetonius includes an account of reforms he made to the Roman calendar. Following Julius Caesar's work to regularize the calendar, Augustus made a further adjustment to bring the system into proper alignment. To mark this reform, the month of Sextilis was renamed August. Suetonius' wording is illustrative of his style as he writes (ch. 31.2): *Sextilem mensem e suo cognomine nuncupauit*, "he [Augustus] renamed the month of Sextilis after his own name." Here Augustus is the unexpressed subject, and the reflexive possessive adjective *suo* makes this point clear. In contrast to Suetonius' account, information about the naming of the month of August is conveyed more directly, and more accurately, in the epitome of Livy (*Per.* 134), where it is said: *et mensis Sextilis in honorem eius appellatus est*, "the month of Sextilis was renamed in his [Augustus'] honor." Here the month is the subject, and Augustus appears in the form of the genitive of the personal pronoun, *eius*. A full account of the event by Macrobius (*Sat.* 1.12.35) reports that the Senate passed a decree changing the name of the month as an honor to Augustus, and that a law to the same effect was sponsored by a tribune of the plebs, Sextus Pacuvius. Suetonius succinctly captures the main idea and keeps the focus squarely on Augustus himself, even at the expense of the procedural details that might be of concern to the historian. The reader must recognize these stylistic choices or else risk misinterpreting the evidence.

Another characteristic of Suetonius' style is the regular use of rubric or heading markers as an organizing feature. These headings allow for easy navigation between sections, but often require a subversion of the usual word order. Suetonius places the key word or rubric heading at the start of a section in whichever case the sentence requires. For example, chapter 75, discussing how Augustus spent holidays, begins with the rubric *festos et sollemnes dies* (acc.

dir. obj.); chapter 76 on Augustus' diet starts with *cibi* (gen. of quality); and chapter 77 on Augustus' drinking habits is introduced with *uini* (objv. gen.). Each section or chapter begins with a rubric or heading marker that presents the category.

Through the use of categories and the persistent placement of Augustus as the subject of sentences Suetonius is able to explore systematically the actions, accomplishments, and habits of his subject, and thus he successfully fulfills his goals as a biographer. Throughout, Suetonius keeps a tight focus on Augustus himself, examining how Augustus handled different situations, exploring Augustus' personal role in affairs, and noting the impact of events on Augustus himself. Suetonius' treatment of the civil wars exemplifies this point. Lacking here is a developed narrative of the battles and the strategies of warring parties. Instead, we learn that Augustus spent the night on board ship after the battle of Actium, weathered two storms on his way to Egypt, and had hoped to bring Cleopatra back to Rome for his triumph. Suetonius intends to have us better understand Augustus' character and behavior, not the civil wars.

Writing more than a century after Augustus' lifetime, Suetonius had a wealth of sources to draw from, most of which do not survive today. Furthermore, he is more transparent in his use of sources than was the practice for writers of "high style" prose. Unlike historians, Suetonius very often names his source (e.g., M. Antonius in ch. 2.3; the minutes of the senate in ch. 5; the inscription on a statue in ch. 7.1) and he quotes directly from a wide variety of material (e.g., the words of a letter of Cassius of Parma in ch. 4.2; a popular epigram that is critical of Augustus in ch. 70.2; sections of Augustus' own letters in ch. 76). He makes frequent use of indirect discourse and often presents a belief or rumor (not necessarily untrue) in a subordinate subjunctive clause introduced by *tamquam* or *quasi* (AG #524, BG #602n4). Causal clauses are found in great number as Suetonius explores the motives and meanings behind actions. A distinction is made between a reason that is given on Suetonius' own authority (expressed in the indicative) and an explanation offered on the authority of another (using the subjunctive) (AG #540).

Perhaps more than any other writer, Suetonius makes frequent use of participles. Participles are used as adjectives, substantively, and in participial phrases, especially in the ablative absolute. Suetonius often uses participial phrases in place of temporal, causal, concessive, and conditional clauses (AG #420, 496). As an aid to the reader, these particular uses of participial phrases are noted in the commentary, and may often best be translated into English with a subordinate clause.

A few other stylistic points should be kept in mind. Suetonius frequently uses the imperfect and pluperfect subjunctive with *quotiens* to refer to repeated or customary actions in past time (iterative subjunctive), a construction akin to a past general condition (AG #518c, BG #567n). Suetonius draws on specialized vocabulary, both high and low, that is not often found in other writers (e.g., ch. 2.3: *restionem*, "rope-seller"). He is fond of using a general noun with an adjective where a single word might have been substituted (e.g., ch. 1.1: *rem diuinam = sacrificium*). Compound forms of verbs are used much more frequently than the root forms themselves (this is true of compounds of *mitto*, for example). Pleonasm is quite often found, as two synonymous words are employed seemingly for emphasis rather than to draw a fine distinction (e.g., ch. 31.2: *annum . . . conturbatum atque confusum*; ch. 42.2: *turpitudinem et impudentiam . . . exprobrauit*; ch. 71.1: *simpliciter et palam*). Asyndeton, the omission of conjunctions, is very common, especially in brief sentences (e.g., ch. 8.1) and cases of enumeration (e.g., ch. 9). Finally, like other writers, Suetonius regularly contracts verb tenses formed on the perfect system (AG #181) and omits forms of the verb *esse*.

THIS VOLUME

The *Life of Augustus* ranks among the longest single books of Latin prose. The entire work is presented here, but the reader may well choose to focus on particular sections or topics of interest. We are fortunate to have a new critical edition of the text produced by Robert Kaster in 2016 for the Oxford Classical Texts series. David Wardle's comprehensive historical commentary on the *Life of Augustus*, published by Oxford in 2014, provides detailed and up-to-date discussions of the content of each section of the biography. The aims of the present volume are rather more modest: to provide notes on grammar, vocabulary, and content to make the Latin text of the *Life of Augustus* accessible to readers at all levels, and especially for use in intermediate and advanced Latin classrooms. Historical commentary is kept to a bare minimum in the present volume, offering enough context to comprehend a particular passage. When appropriate, references are provided to the *Oxford Classical Dictionary* (*OCD*) so that the reader can seek out additional information. For further details about the content of the biography, the reader should turn to Wardle's work, as I myself have done time and time again.

The Latin text and commentary are presented together on the same page. Definitions of words are provided in the order that the words appear in the text. When a word appears multiple times in a single section, the definition is given only at the first appearance. Some common words and words that appear five or more times in the text are included in the Frequent Vocabulary list; these words are not glossed in the commentary except in cases of unusual meaning or special use. Compound verbs, verbs that include prefixed particles, are especially common in Suetonius. The components of compound verbs are presented as an aid to identification and acquisition of vocabulary. For points of morphology and syntax, numbered references to *Allen and Greenough's New Latin Grammar* (AG) are provided so that the reader can quickly access more detailed discussions by consulting the print or online edition. Within the explanatory notes, italics are used to present Latin words in the form in which they appear in the text. Words that have been omitted have been supplied in the notes in square brackets—[ ]—to aid comprehension. A full list of other symbols and abbreviations used in this commentary is included below.

The text of the *Life of Augustus* presented here is from Robert Kaster's critical edition (*C. Suetoni Tranquilli De vita Caesarum libri VIII et De grammaticis et rhetoribus liber*, Oxford: Oxford University Press, 2016) with one minor change (ch. 83: *segestri* for *segresti*).

OUTLINE OF THE *LIFE OF AUGUSTUS* (INCLUDING MAJOR LATIN RUBRIC HEADINGS)

1–2	Ancestors (*gentem Octauiam*)
3–4	Augustus' father (*C. Octauius pater*)
5–6	Birth of Augustus (*natus est Augustus*)
7	Names (*cognomen*)
8	Summary of life
9	Suetonius' statement of organizing principles
9–18	Civil wars (*bella ciuilia*)
19	Disturbances (*tumultus*)
20–22	Foreign wars (*externa bella*)
23	Military disgraces and defeats (*graues ignominias cladesque*)
24–25	Other military matters (*re militari*)
26–28.2	Magistracies and public offices (*magistratus atque honores*)
28.3–31	Rome: buildings and religion (*urbem*)
32–45	Administration in Rome
34	Laws (*leges*)
35–38.2	Senators (*senatorum*)
38.3–40.1	Equites (*equitum turmas*)
40.2–40.5	The common people (*populi*)
41–45	Acts of generosity (*liberalitatem*)
46–50	Administration in Italy and the Empire
46	Italy (*Italiam*)
47	Provinces (*prouincias*)
48	Client-kingdoms (*regnorum*)
49–50	Military arrangements (*militaribus copiis*)
51–56	Acts of clemency and citizen-like behavior (*clementiae ciuilitatisque*)
57–60	Love for Augustus (*quanto opere dilectus sit*)
61	Transition to the personal life (*referam nunc interiorem ac familiarem eius uitam*)
61.2–65	Family
61.2	Mother (*matrem*) and sister (*sororem*)
62	Fiancée and wives (*sponsam*)
63	Daughter (*Iuliam*)
64	Grandchildren (*nepotes*)
66	Friendships (*amicitias*)
67	Role as patron and master (*patronus dominusque*)
68–71	Disgraceful acts (*uariorum dedecorum infamiam*)

72–78	Examples of self-restraint (*continentissimum*)
79–80	Physical appearance (*forma*)
81–82	Illnesses and health (*graues et periculosas ualitudines*)
83	Exercise regimen (*exercitationes*)
84–89	Intellectual interests and habits (*eloquentiam studiaque liberalia*)
90–93	Religious customs and superstitions (*religiones*)
94–96	Transition to ending: signs foretelling his greatness and good fortune
97–100	Death and burial (*mors eius*)
101	Augustus' will (*testamentum*)

FURTHER READING

Texts and Commentaries on the *Life of Augustus*

Adams, Michael. *C. Suetonius Tranquillus. Divi Augusti vita*. London: Macmillan, 1939.

Carter, John Marshall. *Suetonius. Divus Augustus*. Bristol: Bristol Classical Press, 1982.

Ihm, Maximilian. *C. Suetoni Tranquilli Opera*. Vol. 1, *De vita Caesarum libri VIII*. Leipzig: Teubner, 1907.

Kaster, Robert A. *C. Suetoni Tranquilli De vita Caesarum libri VIII et De grammaticis et rhetoribus liber*. Oxford: Oxford University Press, 2016.

Louis, Nathalie. *Commentaire historique et traduction du "Divus Augustus" de Suétone*. Brussels: Collection Latomus, 2010.

Shuckburgh, Evelyn S. *C. Suetonius Tranquillus. Divus Augustus*. Cambridge, UK: Cambridge University Press, 1896.

Wardle, David. *Suetonius. Life of Augustus*. Oxford: Clarendon Press, 2014.

Suetonius and His Work

Bradley, Keith R. "The Imperial Ideal in Suetonius's 'Caesars.'" *Aufstieg und Niedergang der römischen Welt*. Vol. 2. Part 33.5 (1991): 3701–3732.

Garrett, Phoebe. "Structure and Persuasion in Suetonius' *De vita Caesarum*." *Ramus* 47, no. 2 (2018): 197–215.

Lewis, R. G. "Suetonius's 'Caesares' and Their Literary Antecedents." *Aufstieg und Niedergang der römischen Welt*. Vol. 2. Part 33.5 (1991): 3623–3674.

Lounsbury, Richard C. *The Arts of Suetonius*. New York: Peter Lang, 1987.

Power, Tristan. *Collected Papers on Suetonius*. London and New York: Routledge, 2021.

Power, Tristan, and Roy K. Gibson, eds. *Suetonius the Biographer*. Oxford: Oxford University Press, 2014.

Wallace-Hadrill, Andrew. *Suetonius: The Scholar and His Caesars*. London: Duckworth, 1983.

Augustus and the Augustan Age

Cooley, Alison E. *Res gestae divi Augusti: Text, Translation, and Commentary*. Cambridge, UK: Cambridge University Press, 2009.

Galinsky, Karl. *Augustan Culture: An Interpretive Introduction*. Princeton, NJ: Princeton University Press, 1996.

Lacey, Walter Kirkpatrick. *Augustus and the Principate: The Evolution of the System*. Leeds, UK: Cairns, 1996.

Richardson, John S. *Augustan Rome, 44 BC to AD 14: The Restoration of the Republic and the Establishment of the Empire*. Edinburgh: Edinburgh University Press, 2012.

Severy, Beth A. *Augustus and the Family at the Birth of the Roman Empire*. New York and London: Routledge, 2003.

Syme, Ronald. *The Roman Revolution*. Oxford: Oxford University Press, 1939.

Wiseman, Timothy P. *The House of Augustus: A Historical Detective Story*. Princeton, NJ: Princeton University Press, 2019.

Zanker, Paul. *The Power of Images in the Age of Augustus*. Ann Arbor: University of Michigan Press, 1988.

Edited Collections about Augustus and the Augustan Age

Galinsky, Karl., ed. *Cambridge Companion to the Age of Augustus*. Cambridge, UK: Cambridge University Press, 2005.

Morrell, Kit, Josiah Osgood, and Kathryn Welch, eds. *The Alternative Augustan Age*. Oxford: Oxford University Press, 2019.

Raaflaub, Kurt A., and Mark Toher. *Between Republic and Empire: Interpretations of Augustus and his Principate*. Berkeley: University of California Press, 1990.

COMMENTARY ABBREVIATIONS

Reference Works and Sources

AG	*Allen and Greenough's New Latin Grammar*. Edited by Anne Mahoney. Newburyport, MA: Focus Publishing, 2001
BG	*Gildersleeve's Latin Grammar*. By Basil L. Gildersleeve and Gonzalez Lodge. 3rd ed. New York: Boston University Publishing Co., 1894
OCD	*Oxford Classical Dictionary*. 4th ed. Edited by Simon Hornblower and Anthony Spawforth. Oxford: Oxford University Press, 2012
OLD	*Oxford Latin Dictionary*. Edited by P. G. W. Glare. Oxford: Oxford University Press, 1982
RG	*Res gestae divi Augusti*

SYMBOLS IN TEXT

< > word(s) supplied by the editor
{ } word(s) considered by the editor to be spurious
† † word(s) considered by the editor to be corrupt, but not satisfactorily emended

SYMBOLS IN ENTRIES

< derived from
= equivalent to, identical with

ABBREVIATIONS USED IN THE GRAMMATICAL NOTES

(1)	first conjugation
1st	first
2nd	second
3rd	third
abbrev.	abbreviation/abbreviated
abl.	ablative
abs.	absolute
acc.	accusative
act.	active
adj.	adjective
adv.	adverb(s)/adverbial
alt.	alternate
anteced.	antecedent
apod.	apodosis
appos.	apposition/appositive
attrib.	attributive
b/w	between
cf.	*confer* = compare
ch.	chapter(s)
char.	characteristic
circumst.	circumstance/circumstantial
cl.	clause(s)
comm.	command(ing)
compar.	comparative/comparison
compd.	compound
compl.	complementary

conces.	concessive
condit.	condition(al)
conj.	conjunction(s)
constr.	construction
contr.	contracted
correl.	correlative
C-to-F	contrary-to-fact
dat.	dative
dbl.	double
decl.	declension
defect.	defective
deg.	degree
diff.	difference
dim.	diminutive
dir.	direct(ly)
e.g.	*exempli gratia* = for example
f.	feminine
ff.	following
FLV	future less vivid
FMV	future more vivid
frequent.	frequentative
fut.	future
gen.	genitive
gener.	general(ly)
ger.	gerund
gerv.	gerundive
Gk.	Greek
hort.	hortatory
i.e.	*id est* = that is (to say)
impers.	impersonal
impf.	imperfect
impv.	imperative
indecl.	indeclinable
indef.	indefinite
indic.	indicative
indir.	indirect
indir. disc.	indirect discourse
inf.	infinitive
interj.	interjection

interrog.	interrogative
introd.	introducing
irreg.	irregular
lit.	literally
locat.	locative
m.	masculine
n.	neuter
n. (in citations)	note
negat.	negative
nom.	nominative
obj.	object(s)
objv.	objective
opt.	optative
partit.	partitive
pass.	passive
pcl.	particle
periphr.	periphrastic
pers.	person(al)
pf.	perfect
phr.	phrase(s)
pl.	plural
plupf.	pluperfect
pos.	positive
poss.	possessive/possession
postpos.	postpositive
potent.	potential
ppp.	perfect passive participle
pred.	predicate
prep.	preposition
pres.	present
pron.	pronoun
prot.	protasis
ptc.	participle(s)/participial
purp.	purpose
quest.	question
ref.	reference
reflex.	reflexive
relat.	relative
s.	see

s.v.	*sub verbo* = under the word
separ.	separation
seq.	sequence
sg.	singular
specif.	specification
stmt.	statement
subj.	subject(ive)
subjv.	subjunctive
subord.	subordinate
subst.	substantive(ly)
superl.	superlative
term.	termination
tmp.	temporal
tr.	transitive
usu.	usual/usually
vb.	verb/verbal
voc.	vocative
w/	with
w/out	without
wd.	word(s)

FREQUENT VOCABULARY

absum, abesse, afui be absent, be away (w/ abl.) (<*ab-* + *sum*)

absumo, absumere, absumpsi, absumptum consume, waste, destroy, spend (money) (<*ab-* + *sumo*)

accipio, accipere, accepi, acceptum receive, acquire, accept, learn, hear (<*ad-* + *capio*)

ad (prep. + acc.) to, toward, at, for

addo, addere, addidi, additum attach, add (<*ad-* + *do*)

adeo (adv.) to such a degree, so much

adeo, adire, ad(i)i, aditum go to, visit, approach, engage in, incur, submit to (danger) (<*ad-* + *eo*)

adhuc (adv.) up to the present time, still

adicio, adicere, adieci, adiectum add, give in addition, contribute (<*ad-* + *iacio*)

adimo, adimere, ademi, ademptum take away, capture from (w/ dat.), deny (w/ acc. & dat.) (<*ad-* + *emo*)

administro (1) carry out, manage the affairs of, perform duties of (an office) (*OLD* 3) (<*ad-* + *ministro*)

admitto, admittere, admisi, admissum admit, let in, accept, grant access to (w/ acc. & dat.) (<*ad-* + *mitto*)

aduersus (prep. + acc.) against
aedes, -is (f.) temple, shrine; (pl.) house, dwelling-place
aeque (adv.) equally, similarly, likewise, as much as (w/ *quam*)
aerarium, -(i)i (n.) public treasury
aetas, -atis (f.) person's life, age, period of time
ager, agri (m.) land, fields, countryside
ago, agere, egi, actum do, drive, live, spend (time)
aliquanto (adv.) somewhat, to some extent
aliqui, -qua, -quod some, certain (for decl., AG #151e)
aliquis, -qua, -quid (pron.) someone, something; (pl.) some, a few (for decl., AG #151e)
aliter (adv.) in another way, otherwise (w/ *quam*)
alius, -a, -ud other, another (w/ *quam*); *alii... alii*: some... others (for decl., AG #113)
alter, -ra, -rum another, second; *alter... alter*: the one... the other (for decl., AG #113)
amicus, -i (m.) personal friend
amplius (compar. adv.) more
amplus, -a, -um abundant, great, impressive in size (compar. = *-ior*, superl. = *-issimus*)
animaduerto, animaduertere, animaduerti, animaduersum direct the mind toward, notice
animus, -i (m.) mind, spirit, attitude; (pl.) courage
annus, -i (m.) year
ante (adv.) in front, before; (prep. + acc.) before, in front of
Apollo, -inis (m.) the god Apollo
apud (prep. + acc.) at, near, among, in the writings of (an author)
aqua, -ae (f.) water, supply of water, aqueduct
ara, -ae (f.) altar
assidue (adv.) continually, regularly, constantly
atque (conj.) and, and even
auctor, -oris (m.) author, one who authorizes, originator, source
augeo, augere, auxi, auctum increase, extend
aureus, -a, -um made of gold, golden
autem (postpos. conj.) but, moreover, and indeed (AG #324j)
bellum, -i (n.) war, battle
bis (adv.) twice, on two occasions
caelum, -i (n.) the sky, heavens
capio, capere, cepi, captum take, take up, hold, obtain, capture
Capitolium, -(i)i (n.) the Capitoline Hill (in Rome); Temple of Jupiter on the Capitoline Hill
castra, -orum (n. pl.) military camp, base
caueo, cauere, caui, cautum decree, take care, provide guarantees, make legal provision
causa, -ae (f.) cause, reason, motive, case; *causa* (abl.): for the sake of (w/ gen.)
cena, -ae (f.) dinner

ceno (1) dine
certus, -a, -um fixed, firm, certain, unambiguous (superl. = *-issimus*)
ceterus, -a, -um the rest, the remaining, other
circa (adv.) round about, in the vicinity; (prep. + acc.) near, close to, concerning
ciuitas, -atis (f.) state, a town, independent city, citizenship; (pl.) gift of citizenship to single persons
classis, -is (f.) naval force, fleet
cognosco, cognoscere, cognoui, cognitum know, learn, study, investigate judicially, try (a case) (*<con- + nosco*)
cogo, cogere, coegi, coactum drive together, compel, convene (*<con- + ago*)
collega, -ae (m.) colleague, associate
comes, -itis (m./f.) companion, follower, staff member
comitium, -ii (n.) the Comitium, the place of assembly in the Forum Romanum; (pl.) a voting assembly
commodum, -i (n.) advantage, benefit, reward, convenience
complures, -a (pl. adj.) several, many
compono, componere, composui, compositum compose, write (*<con- + pono*)
concedo, concedere, concessi, concessum yield, concede, grant (*<con- + cedo*)
condo, condere, condidi, conditum found, establish, put away, bury, preserve, conduct (the *lustrum*) (*<con- + do*)
confero, conferre, contuli, collatum convey, carry, collect; (reflex.) take oneself, go over to (*<con- + fero*)
constituo, constituere, constitui, constitutum set up, erect, establish, set in order (*<con- + statuo*)
consul, -lis (m.) consul
consulatus, -us (m.) office of consul, consulship
consulo, consulere, consului, consultum consult
continuus, -a, -um uninterrupted, successive, unbroken
contraho, contrahere, contraxi, contractum draw together, draw in, assemble, collect (*<con- + traho*)
conuiuium, -(i)i (n.) dinner-party, banquet
copia, -ae (f.) abundance, number, amount, body of men; (pl.) forces, troops
corpus, -oris (n.) body, physique, physical appearance
cubiculum, -i (n.) bedroom, room
cubo, cubare, cubui, cubitum lie down, retire for the night, sleep
cura, -ae (f.) care, concern, attention, administration
curia, -ae (f.) meeting-place of the Senate, Senate house, meeting of the Senate
curo (1) see to, undertake, care for, look after
de (prep. + abl.) away from, down from, about, concerning

dedico (1) declare, dedicate (<*de-* + *dico*)
defungor, defungi, defunctus sum bring to an end, come to an end; (pf.) died (<*de-* + *fungor*)
deinde (adv.) afterwards, then, next
demum (adv.) only, eventually, in the end, at last
destino (1) fix one's mind on, designate, mark out, intend (w/ inf.)
deus, dei (m.) god (for decl., AG #49g)
dico, dicere, dixi, dictum talk, speak, say, declare, call
dies, -ei (m.) day
dimitto, demittere, demisi, demissum send away, dismiss, divorce (<*de-* + *mitto*)
diu (adv.) for a long time
diuido, diuidere, diuisi, diuisum divide, distribute
do, dare, dedi, datum give, grant
dominus, -i (m.) master, lord
domus, -us (-i) (f.) house, home, household, family (for decl., AG #93); *domi* (locat.) at home (AG #427.3a); *domum*: acc. place to which w/out prep. (AG #427.2)
dono (1) present, reward (with), honor, grant, excuse, let off
duco, ducere, duxi, ductum lead, conduct, draw, consider
dum (conj.) while, provided that (w/ subjv.)
duo, -ae, -o two (for decl., AG #134b)
dux, ducis (m.) leader, commander, general
edictum, -i (n.) proclamation, decree, edict
edo, edere, edidi, editum produce, put on, give birth to, carry out, publish (<*ex-* + *do*)
enim (postpos. conj.) for (AG #324j)
epistula, -ae (f.) letter, epistle
eques, -itis (m.) horseman, cavalryman, equestrian; (collective sg.) the equestrian order, the Roman knights
equester, -tris, -tre equestrian
etiam (conj.) still, yet, also, in addition, even
excipio, excipere, excepi, exceptum except, exclude, pick up, collect, take up, accept (<*ex-* + *capio*)
exerceo, exercere, exercui, exercitum train, exercise, run (a business), carry on, practice, perform (<*ex-* + *arceo*)
exercitus, -us (m.) military force, army
exigo, exigere, exegi, exactum force out, remove, exact, demand, require, call for, execute (a task) (<*ex-* + *ago*)
existimo (1) judge, consider, think (<*ex-* + *aestimo*)
exto, extare, extiti stand out, be conspicuous, exist, be on record (<*ex-* + *sto*)
extruo, extruere, extruxi, extructum erect, build up, heap up, construct (<*ex-* + *struo*)
facile (adv.) without difficulty, easily, readily (compar. = *-ius*; superl. = *-lime*)
facio, facere, feci, factum make, build, do, perform

fere (adv.) approximately, nearly, mostly, almost always

fero, ferre, tuli, latum carry, bear, report, record (a vote), be the father of (*OLD* 39); (refl.) make one's way, go

filia, -ae (f.) daughter

filius, -(i)i (m.) son

fio, fieri be made, be done, happen, occur (for conjugation & use, AG #204)

forte (adv.) by chance

forum, -i (n.) forum, public square

frequenter (adv.) frequently, on many occasions (compar. = *-ius*; superl. = *-issime*)

frequento (1) take part in, attend, visit often, fill with inhabitants, populate

fungor, fungi, functus sum perform, discharge, serve (+ abl.)

gens, -tis (f.) a race, nation, people, clan, family sharing the same *nomen* (mixed i-stem, AG #71–72)

genus, -eris (n.) stock, descent, birth, race, type, kind, class

gero, gerere, gessi, gestum bear, carry, carry on, perform, administer, wage (war) (*OLD* 8b)

Graecus, -a, -um Greek

gratia, -ae (f.) favor, goodwill, gratitude, charm, agreeableness

grauis, -e severe, harsh, serious, weighty, heavy, hard to bear (compar. = *-ior*; superl. = *-issimus*)

habeo, habere, habui, habitum have, hold, consider

homo, -inis (m.) human being, person, man

honor, -oris (m.) esteem, honor, an elective political office (*OLD* 5)

hora, -ae (f.) hour

hostis, -is (m.) foreigner, stranger, enemy (for i-stem decl., AG #66–67)

ibi (adv.) there, in that place, thereupon

idem, eadem, idem (pron., adj.) the same, the previously mentioned (for decl., AG #146)

igitur (conj.) therefore, so (usually postpos., AG #324j)

imperium, -(i)i (n.) supreme authority, command, empire

ingredior, ingredi, ingressus sum enter into, move forward, embark on (<*in-* + *gradior*)

initium, -(i)i (n.) start, commencement, beginning, origin

insequor, insequi, insecutus sum follow (<*in-* + *sequor*)

instituo, instituere, institui, institutum set up, establish, train, instruct (<*in-* + *statuo*)

insula, -ae (f.) island

inter (prep. + acc.) among, between, during

interdum (adv.) at times, from time to time, sometimes, meanwhile

interrogo (1) put a question to, interrogate (<*inter-* + *rogo*)

iocus, -i (m.) joke, jest, joking

ipse, ipsa, ipsum (pron., adj.) himself, herself, oneself (for decl., AG #146)

is, ea, id (pron., adj.) this, that, he, she, it (for decl., AG #146)

ita (adv.) so, thus

Italia, -ae (f.) Italy
item (adv.) in addition, similarly, likewise
iter, itineris (n.) journey, route, road
iterum (adv.) another time, again
iubeo, iubere, iussi, iussum order, direct (w/ acc. + inf.)
Iuppiter, Iouis (m.) Jupiter
ius, iuris (n.) law, legal decision, pronouncement, right, authority, jurisdiction
iuuenis, -e young; (m./f. subst.) a young man or woman
lectica, -ae (f.) litter, vehicle carried by porters
legatus, -i (m.) lieutenant, deputy, legate, envoy, ambassador
legio, -onis (f.) a legion, an army
lego, legere, legi, lectum select, choose, read, coast along (*OLD* 7b)
leuis, -e light, unsubstantial, trivial (compar. = *-ior*; superl. = *-issimus*)
lex, legis (f.) law, the law, rule
libellus, -i (m.) pamphlet, notebook, dispatch, report
liberi, -um/-orum (m. pl.) children
libertas, -atis (f.) freedom, independence
libertus, -i (m.) freedman, former slave
littera, -ae (f.) letter, letter of the alphabet; (pl.) epistle, piece of writing, writing
locus, -i (m.) place, position, opportunity (n. pl. *loca, -orum*, AG #106b)
loquor, loqui, locutus sum talk, speak, say
ludo, ludere, lusi, lusum play, play a role, make fun of
ludus, -i (m.) sport, play; (pl.) public games
magis (adv.) to a greater extent, more, rather, instead
magistratus, -us (m.) magistracy, public office, magistrate, officer of the Roman state
magnus, -a, -um great, eminent
maior, maius older, elder, greater (compar. of *magnus*); **maiores, -um** (m. pl. subst.): ancestors
maneo, manere, mansi, mansum remain, stay
manus, -us (f.) hand, band, armed force, gang
maxime (superl. adv.) very much, especially
medius, -a, -um central, middle (one), middle of, in the middle
memoria, -ae (f.) memory, remembrance, period of time covered by one's recollection
mensis, -is (m.) month
metus, -us (m.) fear, dread, apprehension
miles, militis (m.) soldier, foot-soldier
militaris, -e of the army, military
mille a thousand (indecl. adj.); **milia, -ium** (n. pl. noun; for use, AG #134d)
minor, minus less, smaller, younger (compar. of *paruus*; for irreg. compar., AG #129)
mitto, mittere, misi, missum send, let go, throw (dice)

modicus, -a, -um modest, moderate, undistinguished
modo (adv.) only, just; *non modo ... sed et*: not only ... but even; *modo ... modo*: first ... then (coordinate conj., AG #224)
modus, -i (m.) limit, end, quantity, manner, way
mors, -tis (f.) death
mos, moris (m.) established practice, custom, habit; (pl.) character
mox (adv.) shortly after, in the future, later on, next
multus, -a, -um much, numerous, many
munus, -eris (n.) function, service, duty, gladiatorial games (*OLD* 4b), gift
nam (conj.) for, because
nascor, nasci, natus sum be born, come into being, rise
nec (conj., adv.) not, and not, nor
nego (1) deny, say that ... not
negotium, -(i)i (n.) work, business, special assignment (*OLD* 5), lawsuit (*OLD* 9)
nepos, -otis (m./f.) grandson, granddaughter, descendant
neptis, -is (f.) granddaughter
nihil (n. indecl.) nothing
nisi (conj.) unless, except if
nomen, -inis (n.) name, the second (family) name of a Roman; *nomine* + gen.: in the name of, by the authority of; *sub nomine*: under someone's name
nonnullus, -a, -um some, not a few, a certain amount of
nonnumquam (adv.) on various occasions, sometimes
noto (1) mention, call attention to, notice, note, censure, mark
nouus, -a, -um new, made for the first time
nox, noctis (f.) the night, darkness, nightfall
nullus, -a, -um not any, no (for decl., AG #113)
numerus, -i (m.) number, sum, body (of persons), class
nummus, -i (m.) coin
numquam (adv.) never, at no time
nunc (adv.) now, at the present
ob (prep. + acc.) on account of, because of
obicio, obicere, obieci, obiectum throw or put before, lay as a charge against, cite (in disapproval), produce/bring (something) to someone (+ dat., *OLD* 4) (<*ob-* + *iacio*)
occido, occidere, occidi, occisum kill, slaughter (<*ob-* + *caedo*)
oculus, -i (m.) eye
offero, offerre, optuli, oblatum hold out, offer, supply, hand over; (refl.) put oneself forward (<*ob-* + *fero*)
officium, -(i)i (n.) service, duty, task, post, act of respect
olim (adv.) before the present time, formerly, once

omen, -inis (n.) omen, sign that foreshows an event or outcome
omitto, omittere, omisi, omissum let go of, discard, discontinue, disregard, leave out (<*ob-* + *mitto*)
omnino (adv.) entirely, altogether, in every respect, in all
omnis, omne the entire amount of, all, every
opera, -ae (f.) effort, work, activity
oppidum, -i (n.) town
opus, -eris (n.) work, activity, operation, a building (*OLD* 10); *opus est*: there is need for (+ abl.)
ordo, -inis (m.) social class, order, row of seats in the theater
ostendo, ostendere, ostendi, ostentum show, point out, hold out; (refl.) present oneself as a volunteer, come forward (*OLD* 1d) (<*ob-* + *tendo*)
ostentum, -i (n.) portent, prodigy
paene (adv.) almost, practically
par, paris equal, similar, fitting (for decl., AG #119)
pars, -tis (f.) part, portion, quarter (of a city), party, side (acc. sg. *partim*)
parum (adv.) not enough, too little
pater, -tris (m.) father; (pl.) senators
patior, pati, passus sum put up with, suffer, tolerate, allow
paulo (adv.) by a little, somewhat
pecunia, -ae (f.) wealth, money
per (prep. + acc.) through, along, in the course of, during (a time), by
periculum, -i (n.) danger, risk
permitto, permittere, permisi, permissum permit, allow (w/ dat. + inf.) (<*per-* + *mitto*)
perpetuus, -a, -um continuous, permanent
pes, pedis (m.) foot
peto, petere, petiui(-ii), petitum seek, request
plebs, -ebis (f.) common citizens of Rome (as distinct from the patricians)
plerusque, -aque, -umque the greater part of, most
plurimus, -a, -um very many, most (superl. of *multus, multi*; for irreg. compar., AG #129)
poena, -ae (f.) penalty, punishment
pono, ponere, posui, positum set up, erect, place, set aside, put down (in words)
populus, -i (m.) people, populace
possum, posse, potui be able (w/ inf.) (<*potis* + *sum*)
post (adv.) after, at a later time; (prep. + acc.) behind, after
postea (adv.) subsequently, thereafter, afterwards
posthac (adv.) from this time, from now on, thereafter
praebeo, praebere, praebui, praebitum put forward, show, expose, present, provide, sponsor (contr. form of *praehibeo*)
praecipue (adv.) peculiarly, especially, above all

praecipuus, -a, -um special, outstanding, foremost
praemium, -(i)i (n.) payment, reward, prize
praeter (prep. + acc.) past, beyond, besides, in addition to
praetor, -oris (m.) praetor, magistrate ranking second after consuls
primo (adv.) at first, originally
primum (adv.) first, for the first time
primus, -a, -um first, in front
princeps, -ipis (m.) leader, chief man (a title adopted by the emperor)
prius quam (conj.) before
pro (prep. + abl.) in front of, before, on behalf of, instead of, for
proelium, -(i)i (n.) armed encounter, battle, conflict
profiteor, profiteri, professus sum state openly, declare, promise, claim (<*pro-* + *fateor*)
pronuntio (1) proclaim, pronounce (<*pro-* + *nuntio*)
propono, proponere, proposui, propositum plan, set out, propose, expose (<*pro-* + *pono*)
prosequor, prosequi, prosecutus sum escort, accompany, honor, pursue (<*pro-* + *sequor*)
prouincia, -ae (f.) province, task assigned to a magistrate, governorship
proximus, -a, -um nearest, closest, adjacent, next (superl. lacking pos., AG #130)
publice (adv.) at public expense, in public, publicly
publicus, -a, -um belonging to the people, public
quamquam (relat. adv.) although
quamuis (relat. adv.) although, however much
quartus, -a, -um fourth
quasi (conj.) as, as if, as though, that
queror, queri, questus sum complain, express discontent, protest
qui, quae, quod (relat. pron.) who, that
quia (conj.) because, in view of the fact that, since
quidam, quaedam, quiddam (quoddam) (indef. pron., adj.) certain, particular
quidem (adv.) indeed; *ne . . . quidem*: not even (emphasizing extreme case)
quis, quid (interrog. pron.) who, what
quisquam, quicquam (quidquam) (pron., adj.) anyone, anything, any
quisque, quaeque, quidque (pron., adj.) each one, each
quod (conj.) that, because
quondam (adv.) formerly, once, on an occasion in the past
quoque (conj.) also, as well, too
quotiens (relat. adv.) as often as, whenever
rapio, rapere, rapui, raptum seize, snatch away, carry off from
ratio, -onis (f.) system, practice, calculation, reasoning, account, method
recipio, recipere, recepi, receptum accept, receive, recover, regain; (reflex.) turn back, withdraw, retire (<*re-* + *capio*)

recito (1) read aloud, recite (<*re-* + *cito*)
reddo, reddere, redidi, reditum give back, allot, render, repeat, reply, restore (<*re-* + *do*)
redeo, redire, redii, reditum come back, return, go back to (<*re-* + *eo*)
redigo, redigere, redegi, redactum drive back, reduce, return, restore (<*re-* + *ago*)
refero, referre, rettuli, relatum bring back, return, give back, assign, record, report, refer (<*re-* + *fero*)
relinquo, relinquere, reliqui, relictum leave, leave behind, disregard (<*re-* + *linquo*)
reliquus, -a, -um rest of, remaining
repente (adv.) suddenly
res, rei (f.) thing, matter, wealth; *res publica*: the state; *res nouae* (f. pl.): revolution, constitutional change (*OLD nouus* 10)
respondeo, respondere, respondi, responsum speak in answer, reply, respond (<*re-* + *spondeo*)
retineo, retinere, retinui, retentum hold fast, retain, maintain, restrain (<*re-* + *teneo*)
Roma, -ae (f.) Rome; *Romae*: locat. (AG #427.3)
Romanus, -a, -um Roman
rursus (adv.) back again, once again, again
saepe (adv.) often, frequently (compar. = *saepius*)
satis (indecl. subst.) enough, sufficient; (adv.) sufficiently
scribo, scribere, scripsi, scriptum write, mention, record
secundus, -a, -um favorable, second
sed (conj.) but, however
sedeo, sedere, sedi, sessum sit, be seated
semper (adv.) always, at all times
senator, -oris (m.) member of the senate, senator
senatus, -us (m.) senate
sequor, sequi, secutus sum follow, come next, observe (a practice)
sermo, -onis (m.) speech, talk, discussion, conversation, language
seruus, -i (m.) slave
sic (adv.) thus, in this way, so
similis, -e similar, like (w/ dat.) (superl. = *-limus*)
simul (adv.) together, at the same time as, simultaneously (w/ *cum* + abl.)
sine (prep. + abl.) without
singuli, -ae, -a (pl. adj.) each one, individual
siue, seu (conj.) or if, whether . . . or
sol, solis (m.) sun
soleo, solere, solitus sum be accustomed to, make a practice (w/ inf.) (semi-deponent, AG #192)
solus, -a, -um alone, single-handed, without a partner (for decl., AG #113)

soror, -oris (f.) sister
spectaculum, -i (n.) spectacle, performance
specto (1) look at, watch (entertainments)
spes, -ei (f.) hope, expectation, promise
statim (adv.) immediately, without delay
statua, -ae (f.) statue
sub (prep. + abl. or acc.) under, below, before, underneath, around
subicio, subicere, subieci, subiectum place under, lay before, put in (a remark) (<*sub-* + *iacio*)
summa, -ae (f.) amount of money, sum, summary, overview
sumo, sumere, sumpsi, sumptum take up, put on, undertake
super (adv.) over, above, in addition to, besides; (prep. + acc. or abl.) over, above
suscipio, suscipere, suscepi, susceptum take up, receive, take on, assume (a role) (<*sub-* + *capio*)
suus, -a, -um (reflex. poss. adj.) his, her, their own
tabula, -ae (f.) tablet; (pl.) records, documents
tamen (adv.) nevertheless, yet (often postpos., AG #324j)
tandem (adv.) after some time, at last
tantum (advl. < adj. *tantum*) to such an extent, only; *non tantum... sed etiam*: not only... but also
tantus, -a, -um so great, so many
temere (adv.) recklessly, without due care, casually; *nec/non temere*: scarcely
templum, -i (n.) temple, building consecrated to a god or gods
tempus, -oris (n.) time, period of time
teneo, tenere, tenui, tentum hold, reach (in a journey), bind, understand
terra, -ae (f.) land, mainland, ground
tertius, -a, -um third
testamentum, -i (n.) will, testament
theatrum, -i (n.) theater
toga, -ae (f.) toga, the formal outerwear of freeborn Roman men; *toga uirilis*: the adult toga, the assumption of which formally marked a young man's coming of age
trado, tradere, tradidi, traditum hand over, deliver, relate, pass on information (<*trans-* + *do*)
transfero, transferre, transtuli, translatum move across, bring over, transfer (<*trans-* + *fero*)
triumphus, -i (m.) triumph, the procession of a victorious general in Rome
tumultus, -us (m.) commotion, turmoil, sudden outbreak of disorder, uprising
tunc (adv.) then, at that moment, after that
turba, -ae (f.) crowd, disorderly mass of people
ualitudo, -inis (f.) health, good health, illness
uarius, -a, -um varied, different in each case, variable
ubi (interrog., relat., and indef. adv.) where, when
uel (conj. and adv.) even, or, especially (emphasizes an unlikely thought, OLD 5); *uel... uel*: either... or

uerbum, -i (n.) word, speech
uero (postpos. adv.) in fact, indeed (AG #324j)
uerum (conj.) but, however, but in fact, on the contrary (introd. qualification or contrasting idea)
uersus, -us (m.) line of poetry, line of writing
uestis, -is (f.) clothes, clothing
uetus, -eris old, long-standing (3rd decl. adj. of one term., AG #119) (superl. = *-rimus*)
uictoria, -ae (f.) victory
uideo, uidere, uisi, uisum see; (pass.) seem, appear
uir, uiri (m.) man, husband
uita, -ae (f.) life
uix (adv.) barely, scarcely, with difficulty, reluctantly
ullus, -a, -um any at all, any (for decl., AG #113)
umquam (adv.) at any time, ever
uniuersus, -a, -um the whole, entire; (pl.) all without exception
unus, -a, -um one, only, alone (for decl., AG #113)
uoco (1) call, summon, name
uolo, uelle, uolui want, wish (for conj., AG #199)
uox, uocis (f.) voice, spoken utterance, word (*OLD* 10)
urbs, -bis (f.) city, the city (Rome)
usque (adv.) as far as, all the way, up to
usus, -us (m.) use, means of enjoying, employment, right to make use of
uterque, utraque, utrumque each of two, each person (for decl., AG #113, 151g)
utor, uti, usus sum use, make use of (w/ abl.)
uxor, -oris (f.) wife

THE FAMILY OF AUGUSTUS AS MENTIONED BY SUETONIUS

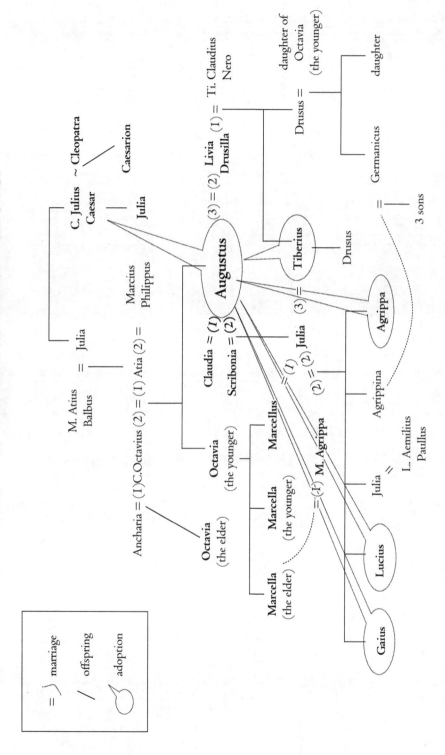

C. SVETONI TRANQVILLI
DE VITA CAESARVM
DIVVS AVGVSTVS
LIBER SECVNDVS

1 GENTEM Octauiam Velitris praecipuam olim fuisse multa declarant. nam et uicus celeberrima parte oppidi iam pridem Octauius uocabatur et ostendebatur ara Octauio consecrata qui bello dux finitimo, cum forte Marti rem diuinam faceret,

---

Ancestors (*gentem Octauiam*). The first word, *gentem*, serves as a rubric marker as the biography begins with several chapters exploring Augustus' ancestry. Suetonius focuses on the public life and political offices of the Octavii, and notes the family's connection with two leading figures of the mid-first century BCE, Julius Caesar and Pompeius Magnus.

1.
Gentem . . . fuisse indir. disc. (AG #580) ff. *multa declarant*; *gentem*: acc. subj.; Octauius, -a, -um: Octavius, of the Octavian clan (the name of Augustus' birth family); as adj. w/ *gentem* and (below) as m./f. noun to refer to members of the family (on the names of Augustus, s. introduction and ch. 7.1–2); Velitrae, -arum (f. pl.): modern Velletri, a town south of Rome; *Velitris*: locat. (AG #427.3); *fuisse*: pf. inf. (<sum) indicating past action in indir. disc. (AG #584)
multa "many things," n. nom. pl. subst.
declaro (1) reveal, declare
nam for, because (pcl. introd. reason or proof)
et . . . et "both . . . and" (AG #323e)
uicus, -i (m.) neighborhood, group of houses
celeber, -bris, -bre busy, populous (superl. = -berrimus)
parte abl. of place where w/out prep. (AG #429.1)
oppidi partit. gen. (AG #346a.1)
iam pridem long ago, well before now, for a long time past
uocabatur et ostendebatur impf. vb. suggests past practices that had fallen out of use by Suet.'s day
ara . . . consecrata ptc. phr., nom. subj. of *ostendebatur*; consecro (1): dedicate, make holy (<con- + sacro); *Octauio*: "by an Octavius," dat. of agent w/ pass. vb. (AG #375a); Suet. does not specify which ancestor of Augustus dedicated the altar
qui (relat. pron.) anteced. *Octauio*, subj. of *prosecuit* and *redit*
bello dux finitimo "as leader in a border war"; finitimus, -a, -um: involving neighbors
cum . . . faceret circumst. cum cl. (AG #546); Mars, Martis (m.): the god Mars (Roman god of war); *rem diuinam*: a sacrifice; divinus, -a, -um: divine, belonging to a god; Suet. uses res w/ adj. instead of the noun sacrificium (cf. ch. 24.1: *re militari*)

nuntiata repente hostis incursione semicruda exta rapta foco prosecuit atque ita proelium ingressus uictor redit. decretum etiam publicum extabat quo cauebatur ut in posterum quoque simili modo exta Marti redderentur reliquiaeque ad Octauios referrentur.

2   Ea gens a Tarquinio Prisco rege inter minores gentis adlecta in senatum, mox a Seruio Tullio in patricias traducta, procedente tempore ad plebem se contulit ac rursus magno interuallo

---

nuntiata ... incursione tmp. abl. abs. (AG #420.1); nuntio (1): announce; repens, -ntis: sudden; incursio, -onis (f.): attack, raid

semicruda exta rapta foco ptc. phr., obj. of *prosecuit*; semicrudus, -a, -um: half-raw, underdone; exta, -orum (n. pl.): organs of the upper torso of an animal; heart, lungs, and liver; focus, -i (m.): hearth, sacrificial altar; *foco*: abl. of separ. w/ *rapta* (AG #401)

proseco, prosecare, prosecui, prosectum cut off (a part of the body), sever (<pro- + seco); a technical wd. from Roman ritual, exta were cut off as offerings to the god, while the meat was shared by participants; the story is aetiological, explaining the origin of this peculiar form of sacrifice

ita proelium ingressus tmp. ptc. phr. (AG #496)

uictor, -oris (m.) victor, conqueror; *uictor*: pred. appos., "as victor" (AG #282); in this section, Suet. highlights qualities of Augustus' ancestors, such as military prowess and religious piety, for which Augustus himself was known

decretum, -i (n.) decree

quo (relat. pron.) anteced. *decretum*, abl. of means w/ *cauebatur*

caueo, cauere, caui, cautum beware, make a legal stipulation; *cauebatur*: impers. vb. introd. subst. cl. of purp. w/ subjv. (AG #563)

ut ... redderentur subst. cl. of purp. (AG #563); *in posterum*: "in/for the future"; *simili modo*: "in a similar way", abl. of manner (AG #412); *redderentur* is a technical term referring to the placing of exta on the altar

reliquiaeque ...... referrentur a second subst. cl. of purp. (AG #563); reliquiae, -arum (f. pl.): the remains, remnants

2.1

a Tarquinio Prisco ... adlecta in senatum ptc. phr. (AG #496) w/ *gens*; Tarquinius Priscus: Lucius Tarquinius Priscus, the fifth king of Rome (traditionally 616–579 BCE) (*OCD* 1431–1432); rex, regis (m.): king; *minores gentis*: acc. pl.; "lesser families" were added to the original senatorial families selected by Romulus (s. *OCD* s.v. patricians, 1091–1092); adlego, adlegere, adlegi, adlectum: elect, admit, appoint (for a duty/office) (<ad- + lego); the accuracy of Suet.'s account of the early history of the Octavian gens is doubted; only the transfer to the patriciate under Caesar is secure

mox ... in patricias [gentis] **traducta** ptc. phr. (AG #496) w/ *gens*; Seruius Tullius: sixth king of Rome (traditionally 578–535 BCE) (*OCD* s.v. Tullius, Servius, 1514); patricius, -a, -um: patrician; traduco, traducere, traduxi, traductum: move, transfer (<trans- + duco)

procedente tempore abl. abs. (AG #419); procedo, procedere, processi, processum: move forward, advance (w/ time: go by, pass) (<pro- + cedo)

plebem common citizens of Rome (as distinct from the patricians) (*OCD* 1161)

se contulit (reflex.) went over to

magno interuallo tmp. abl. abs. w/out ptc. (AG #419a, 420.1); interuallum, -i (n.): interval, intervening period of time

per Diuum Iulium in patriciatum redit. primus ex hac magistratum populi suffragio cepit C. Rufus.   **2.** is quaestorius Cn. et C. procreauit, a quibus duplex Octauiorum familia defluxit condicione diuersa, siquidem Gnaeus et deinceps ab eo reliqui omnes functi sunt honoribus summis, at C. eiusque posteri seu fortuna seu uoluntate in equestri ordine constiterunt usque ad Augusti patrem. proauus Augusti secundo Punico bello stipen-

---

per Diuum Iulium "by (the actions of) the Divine Julius"; per + acc. of agent (AG #405b); Suet. anachronistically refers to the "Divine Caesar" although Julius Caesar was not deified until after his death; the lex Cassia of 45 BCE granted Caesar the right to create new patricians (cf. Tac. *Ann.* 11.25.3)
patriciatus, -us (m.) patrician status, patriciate (an unusual wd. <patricius + -atus)
primus nom. sg. w/ *C. Rufus*
ex hac [gente] ref. is to the gens Octauia
suffragium, -(i)i (n.) vote, voting
C. Rufus Gaius Rufus (for abbrev., AG #108c); his magistracy must date to the third century BCE

2.2
quaestorius, -a, -um of quaestorian rank, one who held quaestorship but no higher office (*OCD* 1249); adj. used as appos. (AG #282b); the quaestorship was the lowest magistracy in the senatorial cursus honorum
Cn[aeum] et C[aium] "Gnaeus and Gaius" (for abbrev., AG #108c)
procreo (1) produce, beget (<pro- + creo)
quibus (relat. pron.) anteced. *Cn. et C.*, abl. of source (AG #403) w/ *defluxit*
duplex, -icis double, having two parts; 3rd decl. adj. of one term (AG #118); *duplex*: PROLEPSIS (AG #640)
familia, -ae (f.) family line
defluo, defluere, defluxi, defluxum flow down, descend (<de- + fluo)
condicio, -onis (f.) state of affairs, legal position or status (*OLD* 7)
diuersus, -a, -um opposite, differing
siquidem seeing that, inasmuch as; causal conj. introd. reason for the previous stmt. (AG #224f)
deinceps (adv.) in succession, in turn, then
functi sunt honoribus summis "held the highest political offices"; summus, -a, -um: highest; Cn. Octavius held the praetorship in 205 BCE; his descendants held praetorships and consulships
posteri, -orum (m. pl.) descendants
fortuna, -ae (f.) fortune, luck
uoluntas, -atis (f.) choice, wish
equester ordo "the equestrian order"; the social class b/w senate and plebs, originally serving as cavalry (*OCD* s.v. equites, 530–532)
constiterunt pf.: remain; pf. of consto, constare, constiti ("stop") and consisto, consistere, constiti ("remain motionless") are the same in form and meaning
Augustus Suet. refers to his subject as Augustus throughout the biography, although he did not receive this honorific name until 27 BCE; s. introduction and ch. 7
proauus, -i (m.) great-grandfather, (more gener.) a remote ancestor; for Augustus to have had a great-grandfather of military age at this time, each generation would have had to have spanned more than fifty years
secundo Punico bello "in the second Punic War"; abl. of time (AG #424d); war b/w Rome and Carthage fought in Italy, Spain, and Africa, 218–201 BCE (*OCD* 1239–1241)
stipendia facere "serve (in the military)"; stipendium, -(i)i (n.): salary

dia in Sicilia tribunus militum fecit Aemilio Papo imperatore,
auus municipalibus magisteriis contentus abundante patrimonio tranquillissime senuit.   3. sed haec alii, ipse Augustus nihil
amplius quam equestri familia ortum se scribit uetere ac
locuplete et in qua primus senator pater suus fuerit. M. Antonius
libertinum ei proauum exprobrat restionem e pago Thurino,
auum argentarium. nec quicquam ultra de paternis Augusti
maioribus repperi.

---

tribunus militum "as military tribune" (pred. appos., AG #282); six military tribunes served as the senior
  officers in a legion
Aemilio Papo imperatore abl. abs. w/out ptc. (AG #419a); Aemilius Papus, commander in Sicily in 205
  BCE; imperator, -oris (m.): commander
auus ... contentus ptc. phr.; auus, -i (m.): grandfather; *municipalibus magisteriis*: "local offices";
  municipalis, -e: local, municipal; magisterium, -i (n.): superintendency, office; contentus, -a, -um:
  content with, satisfied with (w/ abl.)
abundo (1) overflow, be plentifully supplied (<ab- + undo)
patrimonium, -(i)i (n.) private or personal possessions, estate
tranquille (adv.) calmly, quietly (superl. = -issime) (AG #218); Suet. commonly uses superl. adv.
senesco, senescere, senui grow old

2.3
sed haec alii, ipse Augustus ... scribit Suet. uses CHIASMUS (AG #598f, 641) and ASYNDETON
  (AG #323b, 640) to contrast what other sources report (*alii*) with the words of Augustus himself
  (presumably from his autobiography, s. ch. 85.1)
nihil amplius quam "nothing more than"
equestri ... ortum [esse] **se ... locuplete** indir. disc. (AG #580) ff. *scribit*; *equestri familia*: abl. of source
  w/ *ortum* [*esse*], here w/out prep. (AG #403a); orior, oriri, ortus sum: be born (ELLIPSIS of esse for pf.
  act. inf.); locuples, -etis: wealthy, rich
in qua ... fuerit relat. cl. in indir. disc. w/ subjv. (AG #580); *qua*: anteced. *familia*; *fuerit*: pf. subjv. (<sum)
M[arcus] Antonius Mark Antony, Augustus' one-time ally and later rival (*OCD* s.v. Antonius (2), Marcus,
  111–112); Suet. uses the writings of Antony as a source hostile to Augustus (s. ch. 7.1)
libertinum ei proauum ... auum argentarium "the fact that he had a freedman for a great-grandfather ...
  a grandfather who was a money-changer," acc. obj. of *exprobrat*; note use of CHIASMUS for emphasis;
  libertinus, -i (m.): freedman, former slave (alt. form of libertus); exprobro (1): bring up as a reproach;
  restio, -onis (m.): rope-seller (an unusual wd. <restis); *restionem*: appos. w/ *proauum*; pagus, -i
  (m.): country district, community; Thurinus, -a, -um: of/from Thurii (a city in southern Italy); auus,
  -i (m.): grandfather; argentarius, -(i)i (m.): banker, money-lender; in this condensed passage Suet.
  summarizes Antony's criticisms of Augustus' ancestry; cf. ch. 16.2 and 70.1 where Suet. uses the vb.
  exprobro w/ indir. disc. to present other criticisms raised by Mark Antony
quicquam ultra "anything further"; ultra (adv.): further, beyond
paternus, -a, -um paternal, ancestral
maiores, -um (m. pl.) ancestors (subst. use of maior)
reperio, reperire, repperi, repertum find, discover (<re- + pario); *repperi*: 1st pers. sg. pf. as Suet. inserts
  himself into the narrative (cf. ch. 9)

3 C. Octauius pater a principio aetatis et re et existimatione magna fuit, ut equidem mirer hunc quoque a nonnullis argentarium atque etiam inter diuisores operasque campestres proditum. amplis enim innutritus opibus honores et adeptus est facile et egregie administrauit. ex praetura Macedoniam sortitus fugitiuos, residuam Spartaci et Catilinae manum, Thurinum agrum tenentis in itinere deleuit, negotio sibi in senatu extra

---

Augustus' father (*C. Octauius pater*). Gaius Octavius, the father of Augustus, is the subject of the final two chapters that discuss Augustus' ancestry.

3.1
C[aius] **Octauius pater** Augustus' father (*OCD* 1031); father and son shared the same name
principium, -(i)i (n.) beginning, start
et re et existimatione magna abl. of quality (AG #415), "[a man] of both great wealth and reputation"; existimatio, -onis (f.): opinion, reputation
ut equidem mirer "with the result that, for my part, I am surprised"; result cl. (AG #537); *miror* (1): be surprised, amazed; *equidem*: indeed, for my part, pcl. used for emphasis; equidem has the same sense as quidem but is used w/ 1st pers. (AG #322e–f)
hunc ... proditum [esse] indir. disc. ff. *mirer* (AG #580); *a nonnullis*: abl. of agent (AG #405); argentarius, -(i)i (m.): banker, money-lender; *argentarium*: pred. acc. w/ *hunc*; diuisor, -oris (m.): agent employed to distribute bribes or gifts; *operas campestres*: "hired political henchmen"; by METONOMY, opera, -ae (f.) may mean "one who performs a task or service" (*OLD* 9b); campestris, -e: belonging to the Campus Martius, the place of assembly (*OLD* 4b); note the use of *etiam* to add emphasis to the second charge; prodo, prodere, prodidi, proditum: record, publish in writing (<pro- + do); Suet. is surprised that some claimed that Augustus' father was a common banker or, even worse, a political lackey
enim for (postpos. conj., AG #324j); Suet. here states the reasons why he doubts the reported criticisms
innutrio, innutire, innutriui (-ii), innutritum rear, bring up (+abl. *amplis opibus*) (<in- + nutrio)
ops, opis (f.) (pl.) wealth, financial resources (defect. noun, AG #103)
adipiscor, adipisci, adeptus sum reach, attain, win (<ad- + apiscor)
egregie (adv.) admirably well, excellently
praetura, -ae (f.) praetorship; *ex praetura*: "right after his praetorship" (AG #221.11c); Octavius was praetor in 61 BCE
Macedonia, -ae (f.) Roman province of Macedonia; Octavius was governor 60–59 BCE
sortior, sortiri, sortitus sum obtain by lot; sortition, the drawing of lots, was the regular Roman method of assigning provincial commands
fugitiuos ... tenentis ptc. phr. as obj. of *deleuit* where English might use relat. cl. (AG #496); fugitiuus, -i (m.): runaway slave, fugitive; *residuam ... manum*: "the leftover band of Spartacus and Catiline," appos. to *fugitiuos* (AG #282); residuus, -a, -um: leftover, remaining; Spartacus led a slave revolt in Italy, 73–71 BCE (*OCD* 1391–1392); L. Sergius Catilina, a Roman nobleman and senator, led an unsuccessful conspiracy against the state in 63 BCE (*OCD* 1353); Thurinus, -a, -um: of Thurii (a city in southern Italy)
in itinere "en route"
deleo, delere, deleui, deletum remove, wipe out, destroy completely
negotio ... dato abl. abs. (AG #419); negotium, -(i)i (n.): commission or special assignment (*OLD* 5);

ordinem dato.   2. prouinciae praefuit non minore iustitia
quam fortitudine, namque Bessis ac Thracibus magno proelio
fusis ita socios tractauit ut epistulae M. Ciceronis extent
quibus Quintum fratrem eodem tempore parum secunda
fama proconsulatum Asiae administrantem hortatur et monet
imitetur in promerendis sociis uicinum suum Octauium.

4   decedens Macedonia, priusquam profiteri se candidatum consulatus posset, mortem obiit repentinam, superstitibus liberis

---

extra ordinem: "beyond his regular assignment"; Octavius received from the senate a special, additional task to complete en route to Macedonia

3.2
praesum, praeesse, praefui be in charge of, command (compd. vb. w/ dat. *prouinciae*, AG #370) (<prae- + sum)

non minore iustitia quam fortitudine compar. w/ *quam* (AG #407); *non minore*: LITOTES (AG #641); iustitia, -ae (f.): justice, fairness; fortitudo, -inis (f.): strength, courage

Bessis ac Thracibus ... fusis tmp. abl. abs. (AG #420a); Bessi, -orum (m. pl.): the Bessi, an independent tribe on the borders of Thrace later conquered by Augustus; Thrax, -acis (m.): a Thracian; fundo, fundere, fudi, fusum: rout (*OLD* 11b)

socius, -(i)i (m.) ally

tracto (1) deal with, handle

ut ... extent result cl. (AG #537); Marcus Tullius Cicero, consul in 63 BCE (*OCD* s.v. Tullius Cicero (1), Marcus, 1514–1519); one such letter of Cicero's survives (Cic. *Q. Frat.* 1.2.7)

quibus (relat. pron.) anteced. *epistulae*, abl. of means w/ *hortatur et monet*

Quintum fratrem ... administrantem ptc. phr., obj. of *hortatur et monet*; Quintus Tullius Cicero, brother of Marcus (*OCD* s.v. Tullius Cicero (1), Quintus, 1519); frater, -tris (m.): brother; *parum secunda fama*: "with a rather unfavorable reputation" (LITOTES, lit. "too little favorable"); fama, -ae (f.): reputation, renown (*OLD* 7); proconsulatus, -us (m.): proconsulship; following his praetorship in 62 BCE, Quintus Cicero was proconsular governor of Asia from 61–58 BCE

hortor (1) urge to action, incite

moneo, monere, monui, monitum warn, advise

imitetur ... Octauium subst. cl. of purp. (= indir. comm.) w/out ut (AG #563, 565a); imitor (1): copy, follow; *in promerendis sociis*: "in winning over the allies," gerv. phr. (AG #507); promereo, promerere, promerui, promeritum: win over, gain the favor of (<pro- + mereo); uicinus, -a, -um: neighboring, neighbor (m./f. used as subst.)

4.1
decedo, decedere, decessi, decessum depart, go away from, leave office (technical term) (w/ abl. of separ. *Macedonia*, AG #402) (<de- + cedo)

priusquam ... posset tmp. cl. w/ *priusquam* (before) and impf. subjv. for unfulfilled action (AG #551b); *profiteri*: compl. inf. (AG #456); candidatus, -i (m.): candidate for office; *candidatum*: pred. acc. (AG #393); *consulatus*: objv. gen. (AG #348); Suet. uses the technical language of the *professio*, the formal declaration of candidacy

obeo, obire, obii, obitum meet with (<ob- + eo); mortem obire: die; Augustus' father Octavius probably died early in 58 BCE

repentinus, -a, -um sudden, without warning

superstitibus liberis abl. abs. (AG #419a); superstes, -itis: remaining alive; the children Octavia the elder (*OCD* s.v. Octavia (1), 1031), Octavia the younger (*OCD* s.v. Octavia (2), 1031), and Augustus are listed as an extension of the abl. abs.; s. introduction for family tree

Octauia maiore, quam ex Ancharia, et Octauia minore item
Augusto, quos ex Atia tulerat. Atia M. Atio Balbo et Iulia, sorore
C. Caesaris, genita est. Balbus, paterna stirpe Aricinus, multis in
familia senatoriis imaginibus, a matre Magnum Pompeium
artissimo contingebat gradu functusque honore praeturae
inter uigintiuiros agrum Campanum plebi Iulia lege diuisit.
2. uerum idem Antonius, despiciens etiam maternam Augusti

---

maior, maius older, elder, compar. of magnus (for irreg. compar., AG #129); as Roman daughters took the f. form of the family nomen as their own name, the compar. adjs. maior and minor were regularly used to distinguish b/w two daughters

Ancharia first wife of C. Octavius

quos (relat. pron.) anteced. *Octauia item Augusto*

Atia wife of C. Octavius (*OCD* s.v. Atia (1), 199)

fero, ferre, tuli, latum bear, be the father of (*OLD* 39)

M[arco] Atio Balbo et Iulia abl. of source w/ *genita est* (AG #403); Marcus Atius Balbus (*OCD* 199); Iulia (*OCD* s.v. Iulia (1), 753); it is through this Julia, his maternal grandmother, that Augustus is related to Julius Caesar

sorore in appos. to *Iulia* (AG #282)

C. Caesar Gaius Julius Caesar (*OCD* s.v. Iulius Caesar (2), Gaius, 757–760)

gigno, gignere, genui, genitum create, produce, give rise to; (pass.) be born (*OLD* 3)

stirps, stirpis (f.) family stock, ancestral race

Aricinus, -a, -um of Aricia, a town in Latium south of Rome on the Via Appia

multis in familia senatoriis imaginibus abl. of quality (AG #415); familia, -ae (f.): family; senatorius, -a, -um: of a senator, senatorial; imago, -inis (f.): image, likeness; imagines were portrait-masks of ancestors who had held higher magistracies in Rome (*OCD* 727)

a matre "on his mother's side"; Balbus' mother was Pompeia, paternal aunt of Pompey the Great

Magnum Pompeium Gnaeus Pompeius Magnus (Pompey the Great) (*OCD* s.v. Pompeius Magnus (1), Gnaeus, 1179–1180); Suet. here reverses the normal order (cf. ch. 86.3: Crispus Sallustius)

artissimo ... gradu "by the closest degree"; abl. of specif. (AG #418a); artus, -a, -um: close, tight (superl. = -issimus); gradus, -us (m): step, degree of relationship (*OLD* 7)

contingo, contingere, contigi, contactum be in contact with, be connected with (+ acc. *Magnum Pompeium*) (<con- + tango)

functusque honore praeturae ptc. phr., "and having held the office of praetor"; praetura, -ae (f.): the praetorship

uigintiuiri, -orum (m. pl.) a board or commission of twenty men

Campanus, -a, -um Campanian, of Campania (the region south of Latium)

Iulia lege "in accordance with the Julian law", abl. of specif. (AG #418a); a lex took the name of the magistrate who proposed the measure; the lex Iulia distributing land to the plebs in Campania was sponsored by Julius Caesar during his consulship in 59 BCE

4.2

idem the same man, the previously mentioned man (= Marcus Antonius, s. ch. 2.3); here *idem* is used in place of an adv. in English (AG #298b): translate as "also"

despicio, despicere, despexi, despectum look down on, despise (<de- + specio)

maternus, -a, -um maternal, of or belonging to a mother

originem, proauum eius Afri generis fuisse et modo unguenta-
riam tabernam modo pistrinum Ariciae exercuisse obicit.
Cassius quidem Parmensis quadam epistula non tantum ut pistoris, sed etiam ut nummulari nepotem sic taxat Augustum:
'materna tibi farina est ex crudissimo Ariciae pistrino: hanc
finxit manibus collybo decoloratis Nerulonensis mensarius'.

5   Natus est Augustus M. Tullio Cicerone C. Antonio conss. VIIII.
Kal. Octob. paulo ante solis exortum regione Palati ad Capita
bubula, ubi nunc sacrarium habet aliquanto postquam excessit

---

origo, -inis (f.) beginning, birth, ancestral line
proauum ... fuisse et ... exercuisse indir. disc. (AG #580) ff. *obicit*; *proauus, -i* (m.): great-grandfather (s. ch. 2.2); *eius* = Augusti; *Afer, Afra, Afrum*: African; provincial origin was despised by traditional elite Romans; *modo ... modo*: "first ... then" (*OLD* 6), coordinate conj. (AG #224); *unguentarius, -ia, -ium*: concerned with the production/sale of ointments; *taberna, -ae* (f.): shop; *pistrinum, -i* (n.): mill, bakery; *Ariciae*: "in Aricia," locat. w/ name of town (AG #427.3); *exerceo, exercere, exercui, exercitum*: run (a business) (*OLD* 7b) (<ex- + arceo)
obicio, obicere, obieci, obiectum lay as a charge against, cite (in disapproval) (<ob- + iacio); a favorite vb. of Suet. (cf. ch. 6.1, 7.1)
Cassius Parmensis Cassius of Parma, a conspirator against Julius Caesar (*OCD* 289); Pliny (*NH* 31.2) mentions his letters to Antony which included attacks on Augustus; Suet. first reports Cassius' criticisms (*taxat ...*), then quotes directly from his letter (*materna tibi ...*)
non tantum ... nepotem ... Augustum dbl. acc. ff. *taxat* (AG #393); *non tantum ... sed etiam*: "not only ... but also"; *ut pistoris ... ut nummulari nepotem*: ut followed by pred. acc. w/ vb. of praising or blaming "as being" (*OLD* 10); *pistor, -oris* (m.): baker; *nummularius, -i* (m.): money-changer, banker (an unusual subst. noun); *nepotem*: pred. acc.; *Augustum*: acc. dir. obj.
taxo (1) criticize, censure (frequent. vb. <tango, a vb. form favored by Suet.)
materna tibi farina ... mensarius Suet. quotes dir., "your mother's bread came from"; *farina, -ae* (f.): flour, bread; *crudus, -a, -um*: crude, rough, unrefined (superl. = -issimus); *fingo, fingere, finxi, finctum*: shape, form, knead; *collybus, -i* (m.): profit from money-changing, coin (a Gk. wd. w/ Latinized spelling); *decoloro* (1): discolor, stain (<de- + coloro); compd. vb. w/ abl. *collybo* (AG #402); *Nerulonensis, -e*: from Nerulum, a town in Lucania in southern Italy; *mensarius, -(i)i* (m.): money-changer, banker

Birth of Augustus (*natus est Augustus*). A prominent rubric heading marks the start of Augustus' life and the start of a new section of the biography focused on the date and place of Augustus' birth and upbringing.

5.
M. Tullio Cicerone C. Antonio cons[ulibu]s "in the consulship of Marcus Tullius Cicero and Gaius Antonius" = 63 BCE; the Roman year is designated by the names of the consules ordinarii using abl. abs. (AG #424g, 630)
VIIII. Kal[endas] Octob[res] "nine days before the Kalends of October" = September 22 by the Republican calendar; September 23 by the Julian (post-46 BCE) (AG #631)
exortus, -us (m.) rising, appearance
regio, -onis (f.) region, district; *regione*: abl. of place where w/out prep. (AG #429.1)
Palatium, -(i)i (n.) the Palatine Hill (in Rome)
ad Capita bubula "at the Ox Heads," a crossroads or neighborhood on the Palatine; "ox heads" may refer to a signpost, or perhaps Suet. is using a technical surveying term for the intersection of plots of land
nunc sacrarium habet "he now has a shrine"; Augustus is the subj.; *sacrarium, -(i)i* (n.): shrine, sanctuary

constitutum. nam ut senatus actis continetur, cum C. Laetorius,
adulescens patricii generis, in deprecanda grauiore adulterii
poena praeter aetatem atque natales hoc quoque patribus conscriptis allegaret, esse se possessorem ac uelut aedituum soli
quod primum Diuus Augustus nascens attigisset, peteretque
donari quasi proprio suo ac peculiari deo, decretum est ut
6 ea pars domus consecraretur. nutrimentorum eius ostenditur
adhuc locus in auito suburbano iuxta Velitras permodicus et

---

sacrarium ... constitutum ptc. phr. containing tmp. cl. *aliquanto postquam excessit* (AG #543);
   postquam: after; excedo, excedere, excessi, excessum: die (<ex- + cedo)
ut ... continetur (impers.) "as [it] is contained"; *ut* w/ indic. introd. case or example (*OLD* 6);
   senatus acta: the official minutes of meetings of the Roman senate; actum, -i (n.): act, deed (usu.
   pl.); contineo, continere, continui, contentum: contain (<con- + teneo); Suet. had access to the
   senate records although they had been made private by Augustus (s. ch. 36)
cum ... allegaret circumst. cum cl. (AG #546); adulescens, -ntis (m.): a young man; patricius, -a, -um:
   patrician; *in deprecanda ... poena*: "in pleading to avoid a harsher penalty for adultery," abl. of gerv.
   (AG #507); deprecor (1): try to avert by prayer, ask for pardon (<de- + precor); adulterium, -(i)
   i (n.): adultery (first made a state crime in 17 BCE by the lex Julia, s. ch. 34.1); *praeter ... natales*: "in
   addition to his age and [patrician] parentage"; natalis, -is (m.): birth, (pl.,) one's parentage, origins; *hoc*:
   n. acc. obj. of *allegaret* ("he also pleaded this, namely that"); the idea of *hoc* is taken up in indir. disc.
   (*esse se possessorem*); conscripti patres: the senators (lit., those enrolled as members of the senate);
   patribus conscriptis: dat. pl. indir. obj. of compd. vb. *allegaret* (AG #370); allego (1): plead, urge
   (<ad- + lego)
esse se ... soli indir. disc. (AG #580) ff. *allegaret*; possessor, -oris (m.): owner; uelut (adv.): as it were, so to
   speak; aedituus, -i (m.): temple-guardian; solum, -i (n.): the ground
quod ... attigisset relat. cl. in indir. disc. w/ subjv. (AG #580); *quod*: (relat. pron.) anteced. *soli*; attingo,
   attingere, attigi, attactum: touch, set foot on (<ad- + tango)
peteretque ... deo continuation of circumst. cum cl. (AG #546); dono (1): excuse, let off;
   donari: compl. inf. (AG #456); *proprio suo ac peculiari deo*: "out of regard for his own personal
   god," dat. of ref. (AG #376); proprius, -a, -um: one's own, belonging to one person; peculiaris, -
   e: private, personal
decretum est (impers.) "it was decreed"
ut ... consecraretur subst. cl. of purp. (AG #563d); consecro (1): dedicate (<con- + sacro)

6.
nutrimentum, -i (n.) nourishment, (pl.) upbringing; *eius* = Augusti
auitus, -a, -um of or belonging to a grandfather, ancestral
suburbanum, -i (n.) country house (n. of adj. used as a subst., *OLD* 2)
iuxta (prep. + acc.) in the vicinity of, close to
Velitrae, -arum (f. pl.) modern Velletri, a town south of Rome
permodicus, -a, -um very limited in size, rather modest (an unusual adj. <per- + modicus); *permodicus*
   w/ *locus*

cellae penuariae instar, tenetque uicinitatem opinio tamquam
et natus ibi sit. huc introire nisi necessario et caste religio est,
concepta opinione ueteri quasi temere adeuntibus horror
quidam et metus obiciatur, sed et mox confirmata. nam cum
possessor uillae nouus seu forte seu temptandi causa cubitum
se eo contulisset, euenit ut post paucissimas noctis horas extur-
batus inde subita ui et incerta paene semianimis cum strato
simul ante fores inueniretur.

---

cella penuaria a store room for food, pantry
instar (n.) equivalent, equal (defect. noun, found only in nom. and acc.), appos. (AG #282) w/ *locus*
uicinitas, -tatis (f.) neighborhood, vicinity, community
opinio, -ionis (f.) opinion, belief; the view presented here counters the claim (ch. 5) that Augustus was born on the Palatine Hill in Rome
tamquam et natus ibi sit "that he was even born there"; Suet. uses tamquam or quasi w/ subjv. to express a belief or rumor, not necessarily untrue (AG #524, BG #602n4)
huc (adv.) to this place
introeo, introire, introii(-iui), introitum go inside, enter; *introire*: inf. as subj. (AG #452) (<intro- + eo)
necessario (adv.) of necessity, as dictated by the needs of the situation
caste (adv.) with ceremonial purity, purely
religio, -onis (f.) that which is prohibited, taboo (*OLD* 1b)
concepta opinione ueteri abl. abs. (AG #419); concipio, concipere, concepi, conceptum: hold, conceive (<con- + capio); *ueteri*: adj. w/ adv. force (AG #290)
quasi ... obiciatur *quasi* w/ subjv. to express a belief or rumor (AG #524, BG #602n4); *temere adeuntibus*: "to those approaching recklessly"; *adeuntibus*: dat. pl. of pres. act. ptc. (<adeo), indir. obj. of *obiciatur*; horror, -oris (m.): bristling, dread; obicio, obicere, obieci, obiectum: produce or bring (something) to someone (*OLD* 4), w/ dat. *adeuntibus* (<ob- + iacio)
et mox confirmata abl. abs. (AG #419); confirmo (1): confirm, corroborate; *confirmata* w/ *opinione*
cum ... contulisset circumst. cum cl. (AG #546); possessor, -oris (m.): owner; uilla, -ae (f.): country estate; *temptandi causa*: "for the sake of testing"; tempto (1): test, try out; *causa* (abl.): "for the sake of" preceded by gen. of ger. to express purp. (AG #504b); *cubitum*: acc. supine used to express purp. after vb. of motion (AG #508–509); eo (adv.): there; confero, conferre, contuli, conlatum: (reflex.) take oneself (<con- + fero)
euenio, euenire, eueni, euentum come out, happen (<ex- + uenio); *euenit*: impers.
ut ... inueniretur subst. cl. of result (AG #568); paucus, -a, -um: few, a small number (superl. = -issimus); exturbo (1): drive out, expel, remove by force; inde (adv.): from that place, from there; *subita ui et incerta*: abl. of means; subitus, -a, -um: sudden; uis, uis (f.): force; *ui*: abl. sg. (AG #79 for irreg. decl.); incertus, -a, -um: uncertain, unpredictable; semianimis, -e: half-alive; stratum, -i (n.): a piece of bedding, coverlet; foris, -is (f.): door, doorway; inuenio, inuenire, inueni, inuentum: find, discover; *inueniretur*: impf. subj. used here by Suet. in place of pf. to express a single act

7   Infanti cognomen Thurino inditum est in memoriam maiorum
    originis uel quod regione Thurina recens eo nato pater Octauius
    aduersus fugitiuos rem prospere gesserat. Thurinum cognomi-
    natum satis certa probatione tradiderim nactus puerilem
    imagunculam eius aeream ueterem ferreis et paene iam exoles-
    centibus litteris hoc nomine inscriptam, quae dono a me
    principi data inter cubiculi Lares colitur. sed et a M. Antonio
    in epistulis per contumeliam saepe Thurinus appellatur, et

---

Names (*cognomen*). The names that Augustus held throughout his life are summarized in ch. 7. Augustus was born with the name Octavius, acquired the name Julius by adoption, and was awarded the new honorific Augustus in 27 BCE. Throughout the biography, Suetonius calls his subject Augustus, thus simplifying references but often obscuring the chronology.

7.1

infans, -ntis (m.) infant, small child; *infanti*: dat. indir. obj. of *inditum est*

cognomen, -inis (n.) the surname of a family or individual, the third part of the Roman tria nomina (AG #108); a Roman man might have multiple cognomina (*OCD* s.v. names, personal, Roman, 996–998)

Thurinus "Thurinus," derived from the name of the city Thurii; *Thurino*: dat. sg. agrees w/ *infanti*, not *cognomen*, w/ which it logically belongs

indo, indere, indidi, inditum put or place in, bestow, attach (a name or title) (<in- + do)

in memoriam "in memory (of)"

origo, -inis (f.) origin, place of birth

quod ... gesserat causal cl. w/ indic. (AG #540); *regione Thurina*: abl. of place where w/out prep. for noun qualified by adj. (AG #429.2); regio, -onis (f.): region; recens, -ntis: newly arrived, fresh; *recens* agrees w/ *pater Octauius*, adj. w/ adv. force (AG #290); *eo nato*: abl. abs. (AG #420.1), Suet. often uses the demonstrative pron. in place of Augustus' name; fugitiuus, -i (m.): runaway slave, fugitive (s. ch. 3.1); prospere (adv.): successfully

Thurinum cognominatum [esse] indir. disc. (AG #580) ff. *tradiderim*; cognomino (1): give a surname to, name

probatio, -onis (f.) proof, evidence

tradiderim "I would relate," potent. subjv. used for modest assertion (AG #447)

nanciscor, nancisci, nactus sum obtain; *nactus*: pf. act. ptc. of deponent vb. (AG #190a), Suet. is the subj.

puerilem imagunculam ... inscriptam ptc. phr., acc. obj. of *nactus*; puerilis, -e: of a boy, of a child; imaguncula, -ae (f.): a small statue (dim. <imago, a form favored by Suet.; cf. *forulis*, ch. 31.1; *auriculis*, 69.1); aereus, -a, -um: made of bronze; ferreus, -a, -um: made of iron; exolesco, exolescere, exoleui, exoletum: deteriorate, fade away (<ex- + olesco); inscribo, inscribere, inscripsi, inscriptum: inscribe (<in- + scribo)

quae (relat. pron.) anteced. *imagunculam*, subj. of *colitur*

dono ... data "given as a gift," ptc. phr. w/ *quae* (imaguncula); donum, -i (n.): gift; *dono*: dat. of purp. (AG #382); *principi* = the emperor Hadrian

cubiculi Lares "protective gods of his bedchamber"; Lar, -ris (m.): protective god (*OCD* s.v. Lares, 793–794); Suet. reports here that Hadrian kept small statues of past emperors and ancestors in a shrine in his private chambers

colo, colere, colui, cultum cultivate, worship

contumelia, -ae (f.) insulting language, insult, affront

appello (1) call, use the name; Augustus is the implied subj.; *Thurinus*: pred. nom. (AG #284)

ipse nihil amplius quam mirari se rescribit pro obprobrio sibi
prius nomen obici. **2.** postea {Gai} Caesaris et deinde Augusti
cognomen assumpsit, alterum testamento maioris auunculi,
alterum Munati Planci sententia, cum quibusdam censentibus
Romulum appellari oportere quasi et ipsum conditorem urbis
praeualuisset ut Augustus potius uocaretur non tantum nouo
sed etiam ampliore cognomine, quod loca quoque religiosa et

---

ipse ... rescribit "Augustus himself writes" (s. ch. 2.3, 85.1); rescribo, rescribere, rescripsi, rescriptum: write in reply, write back (<re- + scribo)
nihil amplius quam "nothing more than"
mirari se indir. disc. (AG #580) ff. *rescribit*; miror (1): be surprised
pro ... prius nomen obici indir. disc. (AG #580) ff. *mirari*; obprobrium, -i (n.): insult; *prius nomen*: "his former name" (i.e. Thurinus), acc. subj.; prior, prius: former (compar. adj.)

7.2
assumo, assumere, assumpsi, assumptum add, adopt, use (<ad- + sumo)
alterum ... alterum "the one ... the other"
testamento abl. of means; Augustus was adopted by provision of Julius Caesar's will and thus took the name of his adoptive father in accordance w/ Roman practice
maior auunculus great-uncle (= Gaius Julius Caesar)
Munatius Plancus Lucius Munatius Plancus, consul 42 BCE (*OCD* 972); in 27 BCE Plancus proposed the new name Augustus
sententia, -ae (f.) opinion, sentiment; *sententia*: "by a proposal of," abl. used in a technical sense to refer to a motion in the senate (*OLD* 3)
cum ... praeualuisset circumst. cum cl. (AG #546) immediately interrupted by an abl. abs.; *quibusdam censentibus*: conces. abl. abs. (AG #420.3) introd. indir. disc.: [*eum*] *Romulum appellari oportere*: "when certain people were recommending that he ought to be called Romulus"; censeo, censere, censui, censum: think, recommend; oportet, oportere, oportuit: (impers.) it is fitting, it is right (w/ acc. + inf., AG #565); *quasi et ipsum*: "as he himself also was"; conditor, -oris (m.): founder; *conditorem*: pred. acc.; praeualeo, praeualere, praeualui: prevail (<prae- + ualeo); *praeualuisset*: impers.
ut ... uocaretur subst. cl. of result (AG #569.2) ff. *praeualuisset*; potius (adv.): rather, more suitably, instead
quod ... dicantur causal cl. w/ subjv. indicating the authority of another (AG #540) interrupted by relat. cl.; Suet. here sets out various etymologies for the new name Augustus, ending with a quote from Ennius that connects the adj. "august" with the augury at Rome's founding; *quibus* (relat. pron.): anteced. *loca* ("places in which"); *augurato*: "after due observance of auguries," adv. abl. of impers. ppp.; formulaic one-wd. abl. abs. (AG #419c); quis, quid (indef. pron.): someone, something; consecro (1): dedicate, make holy; augustus, -a, -um: solemn, august; *augusta*: pred. nom. w/ *dicantur*; the religious connotations of the adj. augustus made it an extraordinary cognomen

in quibus augurato quid consecratur augusta dicantur, ab auctu
uel ab auium gestu gustuue, sicut etiam Ennius docet scribens,
   augusto augurio postquam incluta condita Roma est.

8   Quadrimus patrem amisit, duodecimum annum agens auiam
Iuliam defunctam pro contione laudauit. quadriennio post
uirili toga sumpta militaribus donis triumpho Caesaris Africano
donatus est, quamquam expers belli propter aetatem. profec-

---

ab auctu ... gestuue Suet. presents "increase" (auctus) and the "movement and pecking of birds" (auium gestu gustusue) as possible origins of the name Augustus; auctus, -us (m.): act of increasing, increase; auis, -is (f.): bird; gestus, -us (m.): movement or motion of the body; gustus, -us (m.): taking of food, tasting
sicut (conj.) just as, as indeed (<sic + ut)
Ennius Quintus Ennius, early Latin poet (239–169 BCE) who wrote *Annales*, an epic poem about the history of Rome (*OCD* 506–507); the line cited here is also quoted by Varro (*RR* 3.1)
doceo, docere, docui, doctum tell, instruct, demonstrate
augurium, -(i)i (n.) taking of auguries, augury, omen, portent
postquam (conj.) after
inclutus, -a, -um famous, renowned, celebrated

Summary of life. Suetonius ends the introduction with a chronological survey of key moments in Augustus' life: the death of his father, his first public appearance, first honors, acceptance of his inheritance under Caesar's will, and the periods of joint and sole rule.

8.1
quadrimus, -a, -um four years old; Augustus is understood as the subj.
amitto, amittere, amisi, amissum lose (<ab- + mitto)
duodecimum annum agens "at eleven years old," lit.: living his twelfth year; duodecimus, -a, -um: twelfth
auia, -ae (f.) grandmother; Julia was the sister of Julius Caesar (s. ch. 4.1)
pro contione "in front of an assembly"; contio, -onis (f.): public meeting, assembly
laudo (1) praise, deliver a funerary eulogy of (*OLD* 3); the honor of delivering a funeral oration (laudatio) regularly fell to a younger male relative
quadriennio post "four years later," abl. of deg. of diff. w/ post (AG #414); quadriennium, -ii (n.): period of four years
uirili toga sumpta abl. abs. (AG #419); sumo, sumere, sumpsi, sumptum: take up, put on; the assumption of the toga uirilis formally marked a young man's coming of age and entry into public life; the date is probably 48 BCE
dona militaria prize awarded to a soldier for distinguished service, military honor; donum, -i (n): gift
triumpho ... Africano abl. of time when (AG #424d); Caesar's African triumph was part of his quadruple triumph of 46 BCE
expers, -rtis having no share of, taking no part in, w/ gen. of specif. (AG #349d); *expers belli*: "taking no part in the war"
propter (prep. + acc) on account of
profectum ... auunculum ptc. phr., acc. dir. obj. of *subsecutus*; proficiscor, proficisci, profectus sum: start a journey, set out; Hispania, -ae (f.): the Spanish peninsula, (pl.) provinces of Spain; Pompey the Great's sons Gnaeus and Sextus were defeated by Caesar at the battle of Munda in 45 BCE; Sextus escaped and became a rival to Augustus

tum mox auunculum in Hispanias aduersus Cn. Pompei liberos
uixdum firmus a graui ualitudine per infestas hostibus uias
paucissimis comitibus naufragio etiam facto subsecutus
magno opere demeruit, approbata cito etiam morum indole
super itineris industriam.   **2.** Caesare post receptas Hispanias
expeditionem in Dacos et inde Parthos destinante praemissus
Apolloniam studiis uacauit utque primum occisum eum heredemque se comperit, diu cunctatus an proximas legiones

---

uixdum (adv.) scarcely yet, only just
firmus, -a, -um strong, in sound health
a graui ualitudine = post grauem ualitudinem
infestus, -a, -um infested with (+ abl.); *per infestas hostibus uias*: "through roads infested with the enemy"
paucissimis comitibus abl. of accompaniment w/out cum in military situations (AG #413a); paucus, -a, -um: a small number, few (superl. = -issimus)
naufragio ... facto abl. abs. (AG #419); naufragium, -(i)i (n.): a shipwreck, disaster
subsequor, subsequi, subsecutus sum follow close behind (<sub- + sequor); *subsecutus*: pf. ptc. of dep. vb. w/ sense of pres. (AG #491)
magno opere (adv.) to a great extent, especially (also as one wd.: magnopere)
demereo, demerere, demerui, demeritum earn, oblige, win the favor of (<de- + mereo)
approbata ... indole abl. abs. (AG #419); approbo (1): express approval of, commend (<ad- + probo); cito (adv.): quickly, readily; indoles, -is (f.): a person's nature, disposition
super itineris industriam "over and above the purposefulness he showed in undertaking the journey"; industria, -ae (f.): diligent activity, purposefulness; a much-condensed phr., BRACHYLOGY (AG #640)

8.2
Caesare ... destinante abl. abs. (AG #419); expeditio, -onis (f.): military operation; *in Dacos et inde Parthos*: Caesar had planned campaigns for 44 BCE against the Dacians (Daci) along the Danube and the Parthians (Parthi) in the east; inde (adv.): then
praemitto, praemittere, praemisi, praemissum send in advance, send ahead (<prae- + mitto)
Apollonia, -ae (f.) Apollonia, city on the southern Illyrian coast across the Adriatic Sea from Italy; *Apolloniam*: acc. of place to which w/out prep. (AG #427.2)
uaco (1) have leisure for (+ dat. *studiis*) (OLD 7); Augustus is the understood subj.; studium, -(i)i (n.): study, intellectual activity
utque ... comperit tmp. cl. w/ *ut* + indic. indicating when (AG #543); *occisum* [*esse*] *eum* (= Julius Caesar) *heredemque se* (= Augustus) [*esse*]: indir. disc. (AG #580) ff. comperit; heres, -edis (m./f.): heir; comperio, comperire, comperi, compertum: find out, learn (a fact)
cunctor (1) be slow in taking action, hesitate; here the hesitation is mental and is followed by an indir. quest.
an ... imploraret indir. quest. w/ deliberative subjv. (AG #575b); imploro (1): call upon for aid, appeal to

imploraret, id quidem consilium ut praeceps inmaturumque
omisit. ceterum urbe repetita hereditatem adiit, dubitante
matre, uitrico uero Marcio Philippo consulari multum dissuadente. 3. atque ab eo tempore exercitibus comparatis primum
cum M. Antonio M.que Lepido, deinde tantum cum Antonio per
duodecim fere annos, nouissime per quattuor et quadraginta
solus rem p. tenuit.

9 Proposita uitae eius uelut summa partes singillatim neque per

---

consilium, -(i)i (n.) plan, course of action (i.e., to appeal to the legions)
ut praeceps inmaturumque "as being rash and premature"; *ut* followed by pred. acc. w/ vb. of praising or blaming (AG #393); praeceps, -ipitis: impetuous, rash; inmaturus, -a, -um: premature, untimely; appealing to the legions stationed nearby in Macedonia would have been seen as instigating a military revolt
ceterum (adv.) moreover, in addition, however that may be
urbe repetita tmp. abl. abs. (AG #420.1); *urbe* = Roma; repeto, repetere, repetiui (-ii), repetitum: return to, go back to (<re- + peto)
hereditatem adiit "he accepted the inheritance," a technical expression (*OLD* adeo 10c); hereditas, -atis (f.): inheritance
dubitante matre abl. abs. (AG #419); dubito (1): be in doubt; mater, -ris (f.): mother
uitrico ... dissuadente abl. abs. (AG #419); uitricus, -i (m.): stepfather; L. Marcius Philippus (*OCD* s.v. Marcius Philippus (2), Lucius, 897) married Augustus' mother Atia in 58 BCE shortly after the death of C. Octavius; consularis, -e: of consular rank (Marcius Philippus had been consul in 56 BCE); multum (adv.): greatly, much; dissuadeo, dissuadere, dissuasi, dissuasum: advise against (<dis- + suadeo)

8.3
exercitibus comparatis abl. abs. (AG #419); comparo (1): prepare, raise, secure
cum M. Antonio M.que Lepido Marcus Antonius (*OCD* s.v. Antonius (2), Marcus, 111–112), Marcus Aemilius Lepidus (*OCD* s.v. Aemilius Lepidus (3), Marcus, 20), and Augustus were appointed tres uiri rei publicae constitutendae in November 43 BCE by the lex Titia; Lepidus was removed in 36 BCE (s. ch. 16.4); Suet. reckons twelve years of joint rule by counting from 43 BCE to the battle of Actium in 31 BCE
duodecim (indecl. adj.) twelve
nouissime (adv.) very recently, last (in time), superl. adv. of *noue*; Suet. commonly uses superl. adv.
quattuor et quadraginta four and forty = forty-four
rem p[ublicam] tenuit "he held control over the state," an unusual phr. indicating that Augustus maintained control over affairs but not pointing to an official position; for Augustus' formal offices and powers, s. ch. 26–27; res publica, rei publicae (f.): the state, the republic

Suetonius' statement of organizing principles. Suetonius sets out his organizational scheme: to explore Augustus' life not chronologically but by category. **Civil wars** (*bella ciuilia*) are introduced as the first category.

9.
proposita ... summa abl. abs. (AG #419); uelut (adv.): as it were, so to speak; *eius* = Augusti; summa, -ae (f.): summary, overview
singillatim (adv.) one by one, singly, separately; Suet. frequently uses adv. in -*tim* (cf. *prouinciatim*, ch. 49; *oppidatim*, ch. 59; for forms, AG #75a.3, 215.2)
neque ... sed "not ... but," establishes a strong contrast
per tempora "in chronological order"

tempora sed per species exequar, quo distinctius demonstrari cognoscique possint.

Bella ciuilia quinque gessit—Mutinense, Philippense, Perusinum, Siculum, Actiacum—e quibus primum ac nouissimum aduersus M. Antonium, secundum aduersus Brutum et Cassium, tertium aduersus L. Antonium triumuiri fratrem, quartum aduersus Sextum Pompeium Cn. f.

10 Omnium bellorum initium et causam hinc sumpsit: nihil conuenientius ducens quam necem auunculi uindicare tuerique

---

species, -ei (f) subdivision, category (*OLD* 10); see introduction for a discussion and an outline of the different topics

exequor, exequi, executus sum follow, pursue, enumerate (<ex- + sequor); *exequar*: 1st pers. sg. fut. act.

quo ... possint relat. cl. of purp. w/ compar. (AG #531.2a), "so that by this they may be able to be more clearly described and studied"; distincte (adv.): distinctly, clearly (compar. = -ius); demonstro (1): explain, describe; *demonstrari*: compl. inf. (AG #456); *cognosci*: compl. inf.; supply partes as subj. of *possint*

bella ciuilia "civil wars," acc. pl.; Suet. here introduces the first topic for discussion, civil wars, which are his focus through ch. 18; note the emphatic placement of the rubric heading at the start of the section

quinque (indecl. adj.) five

gero, gerere, gessi, gestum carry on, wage (war) (*OLD* 8b)

Mutinensis, -e of or belonging to Mutina (modern Modena), a town in N. Italy; supply bellum

Philippensis, -e of or belonging to Philippi, a town in N. Greece

Perusinus, -a, -um of or connected with Perusia (modern Perugia), a town in Etruria

Siculus, -a, -um Sicilian, of or belonging to Sicily

Actiacus, -a, -um of or connected with Actium, a promontory in W. Greece

e quibus (relat. pron.) anteced. *bella*, "of these wars" (AG #346c)

nouissimus, -a, -um last in order of time, final (superl. of nouus)

triumuir, -i (m) member of a board of three, "triumvir"; the triumvirate of Antony, Octavian, and Lepidus was established in 43 BCE (*OCD* 1510–1511)

Cn[aei] f[ilium] Sextus Pompeius (*OCD* 1180–1181) was the son of Gnaeus Pompeius Magnus (Pompey the Great)

The account of the civil wars begins with a discussion of Augustus' aim to uphold Caesar's acts and then turns to the campaign at Mutina (ch. 10–12). Augustus initially sided with the "optimates" in defense of Decimus Brutus, who was being besieged by Antony at Mutina, but later changed his allegiance after the senators failed to recognize the contributions made by Augustus and his troops.

10.1
hinc (adv.) from here, from this fact (expressing cause) (*OLD* 8a)

nihil conuenientius ducens quam ... acta ptc. phr. w/ cl. of compar. ff. *conuenientius*; conueniens, -ntis: appropriate, fitting (compar. = -ntior); duco, ducere, duxi, ductum: consider (*OLD* 30); nex, necis (f.): the murder, death; auunculus, -i (m.): (great) uncle (here = Julius Caesar); uindico (1): avenge;

acta, confestim ut Apollonia rediit Brutum Cassiumque et ui
necopinantis et, quia prouisum periculum subterfugerant,
legibus adgredi reosque caedis absentis deferre statuit. ludos
autem uictoriae Caesaris non audentibus facere quibus optigerat id munus ipse edidit. **2.** et quo constantius cetera quoque
exequeretur in locum tr. pl. forte demortui candidatum se

---

uindicare: inf. as noun (AG #452); tueor, tueri, tuitus sum: protect, preserve; *tueri*: inf. as noun; actum, -i (n.): act, deed (usu. pl.)

confestim (adv.) immediately, without delay

ut ... rediit "when he returned," tmp. cl. (AG #543); *Apollonia*: abl. place from which (AG #428g)

Brutum Cassiumque acc. obj. of *adgredi* and *deferre*; M. Iunius Brutus (*OCD* s.v. Iunius Brutus (2), Marcus, 765–766) and C. Cassius Longinus (*OCD* s.v. Cassius Longinus (1), Gaius, 289), the assassins of Julius Caesar

et ui ... et ... legibus "both by force ... and by laws"; uis, uis (f.): force; parallel structure interrupted by causal cl.

necopinans, -ntis unsuspecting, unaware; *necopinantis*: acc. pl. w/ *Brutum Cassiumque*

quia ... subterfugerant causal cl. (AG #540.1); prouideo, prouidere, prouidi, prouisum: foresee (<pro- + uideo); subterfugio, subterfugere, subterfugi: dodge, evade (<subter + fugio)

adgredior, adgredi, adgressus sum approach, attack (<ad + gradior); *adgredi*: compl. inf. (AG #457) ff. *statuit*

reosque ... deferre bring legal proceedings against, indict (+ gen. *caedis* of crime charged) (a technical legal expression); reus, -i (m.): defendant; *reos*: pred. acc. (AG #393); caedes, -is (f): killing, assassination; absens, -ntis: absent, not present; *absentis*: acc. pl. w/ *reos*; *deferre*: compl. inf. (AG #457) ff. *statuit*

statuo, statuere, statui, statutum decide, resolve (w/ inf.)

ludos uictoriae Caesaris "the games for Caesar's victory"; these annual games were instituted in 46 BCE

non audentibus facere "because those men did not dare to produce," causal abl. abs. w/ subst. use of ptc. (AG #420.2); audeo, audere, ausus sum: intend, dare (w/ inf.)

quibus optigerat ... munus "to whom that duty had fallen"; *quibus* (relat. pron.): anteced. *audentibus*; optingo, optingere, obtingi: (impers.) fall to one's lot (+ dat.) (<ob- + tango); munus, -eris (n.): a duty (applied to funeral games, *OLD* 4b); the games in July 44 BCE were formally in honor of Venus Genetrix and fell to the priestly college to produce, but they became associated with Caesar's victories and funeral

10.2

quo ... exequeretur "so that he might more firmly carry out," relat. cl. of purp. w/ compar. (AG #531.2a); constanter (adv.): firmly, resolutely (compar. = -tius); ceteri, -ae, -a (pl. pron.): the rest of, other; exequor, exequi, executus sum: carry out, execute (<ex- + sequor)

in locum ... demortui "in the place of a tribune who had by chance died"; *tr[ibuni] pl[ebis]* (gen. sg.): tribune of the plebs; tribunus, -i (m.): tribune, a Roman official who represented the interests of the plebeians; demorior, demori, demortuus sum: die (<de- + morior)

candidatus, -i (m.) candidate for office; *candidatum*: pred. acc. w/ dir. obj. *se* (AG #393)

ostendit, quamquam patricius necdum senator. sed aduersante
conatibus suis M. Antonio consule, quem uel praecipuum
adiutorem sperauerat, ac ne publicum quidem et tralaticium
ius ulla in re sibi sine pactione grauissimae mercedis impertiente, ad optimates se contulit, quibus eum inuisum sentiebat,
maxime quod D. Brutum obsessum Mutinae prouincia a Caesare
data et per senatum confirmata expellere armis niteretur.
3. hortantibus itaque nonnullis percussores ei subornauit ac
fraude deprehensa periculum in uicem metuens ueteranos

---

ostendo, ostendere, ostendi, ostentum (refl.) present oneself as a volunteer, come forward (*OLD* 1d) (<ob- + tendo)

patricius, -a, -um patrician; a candidate for the tribunate had to be a plebeian; Augustus' candidacy would have required special measures

necdum (conj.) and not yet

aduersante ... consule ... impertiente two abl. abs. (AG #419) interrupted by a relat. cl.; aduersor (1): oppose, resist, w/ dat. indir. obj. for compd. vb. (AG #370); conatus, -us (m.): effort, attempt

quem uel praecipuum adiutorem sperauerat relat. cl.: "whom he had hoped would be"; *quem* (relat. pron.): anteced. *Antonio*; uel (pcl.): even, especially (emphasizes an unlikely thought, *OLD* 5); adiutor, -oris (m.): helper, supporter (vb. subst. <adiuuo); spero (1): hope (to be) w/ dir. obj. *quem* and pred. acc. *adiutorem* (AG #393)

ac ... impertiente abl. abs. resumes; *ne ... quidem*: not even; tralaticius, -a, -um: usual, traditional; *ulla*: abl. w/ *re*; pactio, -onis (f.): agreement, pact (w/ objv. gen. *mercedis*); grauis, -e: substantial (superl. = -issimus); merces, -edis (f.): payment, bribe; impertio, impertire, impertiui (-ii), impertitum: provide, give a share of, present (<in- + partio)

optimates, -ium (m. pl.) the best class of citizens, the senatorial party (those who had supported Pompey and Cato in their struggles against Caesar)

confero, conferre, contuli, conlatum (reflex.) take oneself, go over to (<con- + fero)

quibus eum inuisum sentiebat relat. cl.: "by whom he (Augustus) was sensing that he (Antony) was disliked"; *quibus* (relat. pron.): anteced. *optimates*, dat. w/ *inuisum* (AG #384); *sentiebat* w/ dir. obj. *eum* (= Antonium) and pred. acc. *inuisum* (AG #393); inuisus, -a, -um: disliked, unpopular; sentio, sentire, sensi, sensum: perceive, sense

maxime quod ... niteretur causal cl. w/ subjv. indicating authority of another (AG #540); the animosity of the optimates toward Antony is here explained by Antony's siege of Decimus Brutus at Mutina; *maxime quod*: "especially because"; Decimus Iunius Brutus Albinus (*OCD* 766); obsideo, obsidere, obsedi, obsessum: besiege (<ob- + sideo); Mutina, -ae (f.): Mutina (modern Modena); *Mutinae*: locat. (AG #427.3); *prouincia* = "ex prouincia": Suet. regularly omits prep. w/ compd. vb.; data: abl. w/ *prouincia*; confirmo (1): confirm; *confirmata*: abl. w/ *prouincia*; expello, expellere, expuli, expulsum: drive out, expel (+acc. dir. obj. *Brutum*, +abl. of place from which *prouincia*); *expellere*: compl. inf. (AG #456); arma, -orum (n. pl.): military forces, troops; nitor, niti, nixus (nisus) sum: strive

10.3
hortantibus ... nonnullis abl. abs. (AG #419); hortor (1): urge to action, incite; itaque (adv.): and so, then

percussor, -oris (m.) an assassin

ei = Antonio

suborno (1) prepare, instruct (for a secret purpose) (*OLD* 3) (<sub- + orno)

fraude deprehensa tmp. abl. abs. (AG #420.1); fraus, -dis (f.): deceit, fraud; deprehendo, deprehendere, deprehendi, deprehensum: discover, detect (<de- + prehendo)

periculum in uicem metuens ptc. phr.; *in uicem*: in return; metuo, metuere, metui, metutum: be afraid of, fear

ueteranus, -a, -um mature, experienced, (m. subst.) veteran soldier; *ueteranos*: acc. obj. of *contraxit*

simul in suum ac rei p. auxilium quanta potuit largitione contraxit iussusque comparato exercitui pro praetore praeesse et cum Hirtio ac Pansa, qui consulatum susceperant, D. Bruto opem ferre demandatum bellum tertio mense confecit duobus proeliis. **4.** priore Antonius fugisse eum scribit ac sine paludamento equoque post biduum demum apparuisse, sequenti satis constat non modo ducis sed etiam militis functum munere atque in media dimicatione, aquilifero legionis suae grauiter saucio, aquilam umeris subisse diuque portasse.

11 Hoc bello cum Hirtius in acie, Pansa paulo post ex uulnere per-

---

in suum ac rei p[ublicae] **auxilium** "to help him and the state"; *auxilium, -(i)i* (n.): assistance, help, aid
quanta potuit largitione "with what funds he was able [to assemble]"; *quantus, -a, -um* (relat. adj.): of what size, of what amount; *largitio, -onis* (f.): a distribution of gifts, largess
iussusque ... praesse ... ferre ptc. phr.; *iussus* introd. subst. cl. of purp. w/ subj. nom. + inf. (AG #566c); *comparo* (1): prepare, raise, secure; *pro praetore*: indecl. phrs., "as a propraetor," a commander whose power was conferred by the senate; *praesum, praeesse, praefui*: be in charge of (<prae- + sum), compd. vb. w/ dat. *exercitui* (AG #370); *praeesse*: inf. ff. *iussus*; Aulus Hirtius (*OCD* 689–690), consul 43 BCE; C. Vibius Pansa Caetronianus (*OCD* 1550), consul 43 BCE; *qui* (relat. pron.): anteced. *Hirtio ac Pansa*; *ops, opis* (f.): aid, assistance; *ferre*: a second inf. ff. *iussus*
demandatum bellum "the war entrusted to him"; *demando* (1): entrust, lay (a duty upon a person)
tertio mense abl. of time when (AG #423.1)
conficio, conficere, confeci, confectum complete (<con- + facio)

10.4
priore [proelio] **... sequenti** [proelio] abl. of time when (AG #424d), supply *proelio*; *prior, prius*: former (compar. adj.); Suet. takes up each of the two battles in order, but w/out a conj. (ADVERSATIVE ASYNDETON, AG #640, 224b)
fugere eum ... apparuisse indir. disc. (AG #580) ff. *scribit*; *fugio, fugere, fugi*: flee, desert; *eum* = Augustus; *paludamentum, -i* (n.): military cloak; *equus, -i* (m.): horse; *biduum, -i* (n.): period of two days; *appareo, apparere, apparui, apparitum*: appear, be found (<ad- + pareo)
constat (impers.) "it is agreed" (AG #208c)
non modo ... functum [esse] **... subisse ... portasse** indir. disc. (AG #580) w/ three cl. ff. *constat*; Augustus is the unexpressed subj.; *non modo ... sed etiam*: "not only ... but also"; *fungor, fungi, functus sum*: perform (w/ abl. *munere*); *functum*: ELLIPSIS of *esse* for pf. act. inf.; *dimicatio, -onis* (f.): battle, fight; *aquilifero ... saucio*: abl. abs. w/ adj. in place of ptc. (AG #419a); *aquilifer, -eri* (m.): standard-bearer of a legion; *grauiter* (adv.): seriously; *saucius, -a, -um*: wounded; *aquila, -ae* (f.): eagle, image of an eagle used as the standard of a legion; *umerus, -i* (m.): shoulder; *subeo, subire, subii, subitum*: go underneath (<sub- + eo); *porto* (1): carry, convey; *portasse* = contr. form of portauisse (AG #181)

11
hoc bello abl. of time when (AG #424d)
cum ... perissent circumst. cum cl. (AG #546); *acies, -ei* (f.): battle line, battle; *paulo post*: "a short while later"; *paulo*: abl. of deg. of diff. (AG #414); *uulnus, -eris* (n.): wound, injury; *pereo, perire, perii, peritum*: die, perish (<per- + eo)

47

issent, rumor increbruit ambos opera eius occisos ut Antonio fugato, re p. consulibus orbata solus uictores exercitus occuparet. Pansae quidem adeo suspecta mors fuit ut Glyco medicus custoditus sit, quasi uenenum uulneri indidisset. adicit his Aquilius Niger alterum e consulibus Hirtium in pugnae tumultu ab ipso interemptum.

12 Sed ut cognouit Antonium post fugam a M. Lepido receptum ceterosque duces et exercitus consentire pro partibus, causam optimatium sine cunctatione deseruit ad praetextum mutatae

---

rumor, -oris (m.) rumor, unconfirmed report; throughout this ch., Suet. presents unconfirmed rumors attacking Augustus, reaching a climax with the claim that Augustus himself had killed Hirtius
increbresco, increbrescere, increbrui increase in degree, spread (<in- + crebresco)
ambos ... occisos [esse] indir. disc. (AG #580a) ff. *rumor*; ambo, -ae, -o: both; *ambos*: m. acc. pl. (for decl., AG #134); *eius* = Augusti
ut ... solus ... occuparet purp. cl. (AG #531.1) w/ two abl. abs.; *Antonio fugato*: abl. abs. (AG #419); fugo (1): cause to flee, frighten off; *re p[ublica] ... orbata*: abl. abs.; orbo (1): deprive of, rob (w. abl. of separ. *consulibus*); uictor, -oris (m.): victor, conquer, (w/ adjectival force) victorious (*OLD* 3); occupo (1): seize, take possession of
suspectus, -a, -um viewed with mistrust, suspected
ut ... custoditus sit result cl. (AG #537); Glyco, a freedman of Pansa; medicus, -i (m.): physician, doctor; custodio, custodire, custodiui (-ii), custoditum: imprison; *custoditus sit*: pf. subjv., frequently used in subord. cl. in secondary seq. (AG #485c)
quasi uenenum uulneri indidisset "on suspicion that he had introduced poison into the wound"; *quasi* w/ subjv. to express a belief or rumor (AG #524, BG #602n4); uenenum, -i (n.): poison; indo, indere, indidi, inditum: put in, introduce
Aquilius Niger an otherwise unknown source
alterum ... interemptum [esse] indir. disc. (AG #580) ff. *adicit*; pugna, -ae (f.): fight, battle; *ipso* = Augusto; interimo, interimere, interemi, interemptum: kill, do away with (<inter- + emo)

12
ut cognouit tmp. cl. w/ indic. (AG #543)
Antonium ... receptum [esse] **ceterosque duces ... consentire** indir. disc. (AG #580) ff. *cognouit* w/ two cl.; fuga, -ae (f.): flight, rout; *consentire pro partibus*: "were reaching an agreement in the interests of the party"; consentio, consentire, consensi, consensum: be in harmony, reach an agreement (<con- + sentio); pars, partis (f.): party, side (sg. or pl., *OLD* 16)
optimates, -atium (m. pl.) the best class of citizens, the senatorial party
cunctatio, -onis (f.) hesitation, delay
desero, desere, deserui, desertum part company with, leave, desert (<de- + sero)
ad praetextum ... calumniatus ptc. phr.; *ad praetextum*: "for a pretext," ad expressing function or purp. (*OLD* G), a frequent constr. in Suet.; praetextum, -i (n.): adornment, pretext, cloak; the wording here shows that Suet. was not convinced by Augustus' claims; muto (1): exchange, change; uoluntas, -tatis (f.): wish, disposition, sympathy; *mutatae uoluntatis*: objv. gen. (AG #348); *dicta factaque*: "the words and deeds"; calumnior (1): allege, misrepresent; *calumniatus*: pf. act. ptc.

uoluntatis dicta factaque quorundam calumniatus, quasi alii
se puerum, alii ornandum tollendumque iactassent neque
aut sibi aut ueteranis par gratia referretur. et quo magis paenitentiam prioris sectae approbaret, Nursinos grandi pecunia et
quam pendere nequirent multatos extorres oppido egit quod
Mutinensi acie interemptorum ciuium tumulo publice extructo
ascripserant pro libertate eos occubuisse.

13   Inita cum Antonio et Lepido societate Philippense quoque

---

quasi alii ... iactassent   *quasi* w/ subjv. to express a belief or rumor (AG #524, BG #602n4); *se puerum [esse] ... tollendum [esse]*: Suet. reports the wd. using indir. disc. (AG #580) ff. *iactassent*; *ornandum tollendumque*: 2nd (pass.) periphr. denoting necessity or obligation (AG #196, 500); orno (1): honor, give distinction to; tollo, tollere, sustuli, sublatum: raise, remove; iacto (1): hurl, utter with force (OLD 10) (frequent. <iacio, a vb. form favored by Suet.); *iactassent* = contr. form of iactauissent (AG #181); Suet. here echoes the famous quip about Augustus attributed to Cicero by D. Brutus (Cic. *Fam.* 11.20.1: laudandum adulescentem, ornandum, tollendum)

neque ... par gratia referretur   second cl. w/ subjv. ff. *quasi* expressing a belief or rumor (AG #524, BG #602n4); neque: "and not" (AG #328a); *par gratia*: nom. subj.; gratia, -ae (f.): thanks; after the battle of Mutina, the senate honored D. Brutus and his troops more highly than Augustus and his men

quo magis ... approbaret   relat. cl. of purp. w/ compar. (AG #531.2a), "so that he might better confirm"; paenitentia, -ae (f.): regret for one's action, change of mind; prior, prius: former (compar. adj.); secta, -ae (f.): course of action, behavior; approbo (1): confirm (<ad- + probo); the episode described here by Suet. is confused as it makes little sense for Augustus to punish the people of Nursia who fought on his side at Mutina; the episode might better belong to the Perusine War (cf. Dio 48.13.6)

Nursinos ... multatos   ptc. phr., dir. obj. of *egit*; Nursini: people of Nursia, a town in central Italy; grandis, -e: ample, large; *quam ... nequirent*: relat. cl. of char. (AG #535), "a fine which they were not able to pay"; *quam*: anteced. *pecunia*; pendo, pendere, pependi, pensum: pay out; nequeo, nequire (defect. vb.): be unable (AG #206d); multo (1): fine, punish

extorres oppido egit   a rare example of PROLEPSIS in Suet. (AG #640); extorris, -e: driven from one's home, exiled, banished; *oppido* = ex oppido (AG #428g)

quod ... ascripserant   causal cl. w/ indic. indicating a fact on the authority of the writer (AG #540); *Mutinensi acie*: "at the battle of Mutina"; interemo, interemere, interemi, interemptum: kill (<inter- + eo); *tumulo publice extructo*: dat. indir. obj. of compd. vb. *ascripserant* (AG #370); tumulus, -i (m.): burial mound; ascribo, ascribere, ascripsi, ascriptum: inscribe (<ad- + scribo)

pro libertate eos occubuisse   indir. disc. (AG #580) ff. *ascripserant*; occumbo, occumbere, occubui: die (<ob- + cumbo)

The second civil conflict, fought at Philippi in 42 BCE, is discussed in one chapter, with a single sentence describing Augustus' role in battle. The rest of the chapter focuses on Augustus' treatment of the conquered, and his settlement of veteran soldiers after the campaign.

13.1

inita ... societate   abl. abs. (AG #419); ineo, inire, iniui (-ii), initum: go into, enter into (<in- + eo); societas, -atis (f.): partnership; the agreement b/w Augustus, Antony, and Lepidus led to the formation of the Triumvirate in November of 43 BCE (s. ch. 27.1)

Philippense ... bellum   the war at Philippi, acc. sg. obj. of *transegit*

bellum, quamquam inualidus atque aeger, duplici proelio
transegit, quorum priore castris exutus uix ad Antoni cornu
fuga euaserat. nec successum uictoriae moderatus est sed capite
Bruti Romam misso ut statuae Caesaris subiceretur in splendidissimum quemque captiuorum non sine uerborum contumelia saeuiit, **2.** ut quidem uni suppliciter sepulturam precanti
respondisse dicitur iam istam uolucrum fore potestatem, alios,
patrem et filium, pro uita rogantis sortiri uel micare iussisse ut
alterutri concederetur ac spectasse utrumque morientem, cum

---

inualidus, -a, -um weak, infirm
aeger, -gra, -grum unwell, sick
duplex, -icis double, having two parts
transigo, transigere, transegi, transactum carry through, settle, complete (<trans- + ago)
quorum priore ... euaserat relat. cl., "in the first of these battles," abl. of time when (AG #424d); *quorum* (relat. pron.) agrees in gender and number w/ implied pl. anteced. *duplici proelio* (AG #306b); prior, prius: former (compar. adj.); *castris*: abl. of separ. ff. *exutus* (AG #401); exuo, exuere, exui, exutum: cut off, remove; cornu, -us (n.): wing of an army (*OLD* 8); fuga, -ae (f.): act of running away, flight; *fuga*: abl. of means; euado, euadere, euasi, euasum: escape (<ex- + uado)
successus, -us (m.) success, successful outcome
moderor (1) restrain, temper
capite ... misso abl. abs. (AG #419); caput, -itis (n.): the head; M. Iunius Brutus (*OCD* s.v. Iunius Brutus (2), Marcus, 765–766)), assassin of Caesar; *Romam*: acc. place to which w/out prep. (AG #427.2)
ut ... subiceretur purp. cl. (AG #531.1); *statuae*: dat. w/ compd. vb. (AG #370); Dio (47.49.2) reports that the head of Brutus was lost at sea
in splendidissimum quemque ... saeuit "he raged against each of the most illustrious of the captives"; splendidus, -a, -um: bright, splendid, illustrious (superl. = -issimus); captiuus, -a, -um: captured in war, (m. subst.): a captive; *non sine ... contumelia*: LITOTES (AG #641, 326.c); contumelia, -ae (f.): insult, affront; saeuio, saeuire, saeuii, saeuitum: rage, vent one's rage on (w/ in + acc)

13.2
ut quidem "as indeed"; Suet. gives three examples of acts that Augustus is said to have committed
uni ... precanti ptc. phr., dat. indir. obj. w/ *respondisse*; suppliciter (adv.): humbly, as a suppliant; sepultura, -ae (f.): burial; precor (1): pray for
respondisse dicitur ... iussisse ... spectasse "he (Augustus) is said to have responded," indir. disc. pers. constr. w/ pass. vb. (AG #582), each inf. introd. a cl.
iam istam uolucrum fore potestatem indir. disc. (AG #580) ff. *respondisse*, "now that will be left to the vultures to decide"; uolucris, -cris (f.): winged creature, bird; *fore* = futuram esse; potestas, -tatis (f.): right of decision
alios ... sortiri uel micare subst. cl. of purp. ff. *iussisse* w/ inf. and subj. acc. (AG #563a); rogo (1): ask; *rogantis*: acc. pl. w/ *alios*; sortior, sortiri, sortitus sum: obtain by lot, draw lots; mico, micare, micui: play "morra," a game involving guessing the number of fingers held up by oneself and one's opponent
ut ... concederetur purp. cl. (AG #531.1); alteruter, -tra, -trum: one or the other of two
spectasse = contr. form. of spectauisse (AG #181)
morior, mori, mortuus sum die, perish
cum ... occubuisset circumst. cum cl. (AG #546) w/ abl. abs.; *patre ... occiso*: tmp. abl. abs. (AG #420.1); *quia ... optulerat*: causal cl. (AG #540.1); offero, offerre, optuli, oblatum: (reflex.) put oneself forward,

patre, quia se optulerat, occiso filius quoque uoluntariam occubuisset necem. quare ceteri, in his M. Fauonius ille Catonis aemulus, cum catenati producerentur imperatore Antonio honorifice salutato hunc foedissimo conuicio coram prosciderunt.

3. Partitis post uictoriam officiis cum Antonius Orientem ordinandum, ipse ueteranos in Italiam reducendos et municipalibus agris collocandos recepisset, neque ueteranorum neque possessorum gratiam tenuit, alteris pelli se, alteris non pro spe meritorum tractari querentibus.

---

offer oneself (<ob- + fero); uoluntarius, -a, -um: voluntary; occumbo, occumbere, occumbui: meet with (<ob- + cumbo); nex, necis (f.): violent death, death

quare (relat. adv.) because of which, wherefore, hence

in his M. Fauonius ille Catonis aemulus PARENTHESIS; Marcus Favonius (*OCD* 571), like M. Porcius Cato (*OCD* s.v. Procius Cato (2), Marcus, 1189–1190), opposed Caesar and was among those captured at Philippi; aemulus, -i (m.): emulator, imitator

cum ... producerentur circumst. cum cl. (AG #546); catenatus, -a, -um: wearing chains, fettered; produco, producere, produxi, productum: bring forth, lead out (<pro- + duco)

imperatore ... salutato conces. abl. abs. (AG #420.3); imperator, -oris (m.): commander; *imperatore*: in appos. to *Antonio*; honorifice (adv.): with honor, honorably; saluto (1): salute, greet

hunc = Augustum

foedus, -a, -um foul, loathsome, obscene (superl. = -issimus)

conuicium, -(i)i (n.) angry noise, uproar, mockery

coram (adv.) openly, publicly

proscindo, proscindere, proscidi, proscissum flay with words, castigate (<pro- + scindo)

13.3

partitis ... officiis abl. abs. (AG #419); partio, partire, partiui, partitum: share, divide out, apportion

cum ... recepisset circumst. cum cl. (AG #546) in two cl. w/out conj. (ASYNDETON, AG #640) w/ subj. *Antonius* and *ipse* (= Augustus); *Orientem ordinandum*: "organizing the East," gerv. agreeing w/ obj. ff. *recepisset* to express purp. (AG #500.4); Oriens, -ntis (m.): the eastern part of the world; ordino (1): organize, manage; *ueteranos ... reducendos ... collocandos*: gerv. agreeing w/ obj. expressing purp. (AG #500.4); ueteranus, -a, -um: veteran, (m. subst.) veteran soldier; reduco, reducere, reduxi, reductum: bring back (<re- + duco); *municipalibus agris*: abl. of place where w/out prep. (AG #429.2); municipalis, -e: municipal, belonging to the local towns; colloco (1): settle (<con- + loco)

possessor, -oris (m.) possessor, one who holds or owns land

gratiam tenuit "he won the thanks"; Augustus is the subj.

alteris ... querentibus causal abl. abs. (AG #420.2) explaining the reactions of the landowners and veterans; *querentibus* introd. indir. disc.; *pelli se*: indir. disc. (AG #580); pello, pellere, pepuli, pulsum: eject, expel; [*se*] ... *tractari*: indir. disc.; meritum, -i (n.): due reward; tracto (1): deal with, treat, manage

14 Quo tempore L. Antonium fiducia consulatus, quem gerebat, ac
fraternae potentiae res nouas molientem confugere Perusiam
coegit et ad deditionem fame conpulit, non tamen sine magnis
suis et ante bellum et in bello discriminibus. nam cum spectaculo ludorum gregarium militem in quattuordecim ordinibus
sedentem excitari per apparitorem iussisset, rumore ab
obtrectatoribus dilato quasi eundem mox et discruciatum
necasset, minimum afuit quin periret concursu et indignatione
turbae militaris. saluti fuit quod qui desiderabatur repente
comparuit incolumis ac sine iniuria. circa Perusinum autem

The Perusine War, fought against Lucius Antonius in 41–40 BCE, is treated in ch. 14–15. The focus of Suetonius' narrative is again on the person of Augustus, relating the threats that Augustus faced and Augustus' treatment of those captured at Perusia.

14.
Quo tempore abl. of time when (AG #423.1) w/ relat. pron. as connector (AG #308f)
L[ucium] **Antonium ... molientem** ptc. phr., acc. subj. of subst. cl. of purp. (AG #563a) ff. *coegit*; Lucius Antonius (*OCD* 113), brother of Mark Antony, and consul in 41 BCE; fiducia, -ae (f.): trust, reliance; *fiducia*: abl. (w/ gen.) "trusting in," here w/ *consulatus* and *fraternae potentiae*; fraternus, -a, -um: of a brother, fraternal; potentia, -ae (f.): power, influence; res nouae (pl.): revolution; molior, moliri, molitus sum: set in motion, stir
confugio, confugere, confugi flee for safety (<con- + fugio); *confugere*: pres. act. inf. in subst. cl. of purp. (AG #563a)
Perusia, -ae (f.) Perusia, modern Perugia in central Italy; *Perusiam*: acc. of place to which w/out prep. (AG #427.2)
coegit Augustus is the subj.
deditio, -onis (f.) surrender, capitulation
fames, famis (f.) hunger, lack of food, famine
conpello, conpellere, conpuli, conpulsum compel, force (<con- + pello); *L. Antonium* is dir. obj.
sine ... discriminibus prep. phr.; discrimen, -inis (n.): a crisis, dangerous situation; Suet.'s focus turns to the dangers faced by Augustus
cum ... iussisset circumst. cum cl. (AG #546); *spectaculo ludorum*: "at a performance of the games"; *spectaculo*: abl. of time when (AG #424d); gregarius, -a, -um: rank-and-file; *in quattuordecim ordinibus*: "in the fourteen rows (reserved for equites)"; ordo, -inis (m.): a row (of seats); the lex Roscia of 67 BCE reserved the front rows of the theater for members of the elite; excito (1): dislodge, call out (<ex- + cito); *excitari*: inf. in subst. cl. of purp. ff. *iussisset* (AG #563a); apparitor, -oris (m.): a magistrate's attendant, lictor
rumore ... dilato abl. abs. (AG #419); rumor, -oris (m.): rumor; obtrectator, -oris (m.): detractor (vb. subst. <obtrecto); differo, differre, distuli, dilatum: spread, publish (<dis- + fero)
quasi ... necasset *quasi* w/ subjv. to express a belief or rumor (AG #524, BG #602n4); discrucio (1): torture (<dis- + crucio); neco (1): kill; *necasset* = contr. form of necauisset (AG #181)
minimum afuit quin periret "he almost died," lit.: "it lacked a little but that he perished"; *quin* w/ subjv (AG #558); absum, abesse (*OLD* 6a); pereo, perire, perii (-iui), peritum: die (<per- + eo)
concursu et indignatione abl. of cause (AG #404); concursus, -us (m.): attack, charge; indignatio, -onis (f.): anger, rage; HENDIADYS (AG #640)
salus, -utis (f.) personal safety, security; *saluti*: dat. of purp. (AG #382)
quod ... comparuit incolumis ac sine iniuria causal cl. w/ indic. on the authority of the writer (AG #540); *qui desiderabatur*: "the man who was missing," relat. cl. serving as subj. of causal cl.; desidero (1): long for, miss; compareo, comparere, comparui: appear, show oneself (<con- + pareo); incolumis, -e: unharmed, safe; iniuria, -ae (f.): an injury

murum sacrificans paene interceptus est a manu gladiatorum
quae oppido eruperat.

15   Perusia capta in plurimos animaduertit, orare ueniam uel
excusare se conantibus una uoce occurrens, moriendum esse.
scribunt quidam trecentos ex dediticiis electos utriusque
ordinis ad aram Diuo Iulio extructam Idibus Martiis hostiarum
more mactatos. extiterunt qui traderent conpecto eum ad
arma isse ut occulti aduersarii et quos metus magis quam

---

murus, -i (m.) city wall, defensive wall
sacrifico (1) perform a sacrifice
intercipio, intercipere, intercepi, interceptum catch, trap (<inter- + capio)
manus, -us (f.) band, gang; the band of gladiators was likely a special unit employed by L. Antonius
quae (relat. pron.) anteced. *manu*, f. nom. sg. subj. of *eruperat*
erumpo, erumpere, erupi, eruptum burst forth, break out (<ex- + rumpo)

15.
Perusia capta tmp. abl. abs. (AG #420.1); Perusia was captured in 40 BCE
animaduerto, animaduertere, animaduerti, animaduersum turn one's attention to, punish
   (w/ in + acc.)
orare ... excusare se conantibus ptc. phr., indir. obj. of *occurrens*; *orare ... excusare*: compl. inf.
   ff. *conantibus* (AG #456); oro (1): pray for; uenia, -ae (f.): forgiveness, pardon; excuso (1):
   excuse, justify, explain the conduct of; conor (1): try, attempt; *conantibus*: dat. pl. indir. obj. ff.
   occurrens
occurro, occurrere, occurri, occursum meet, confront, counter (w/ dat.) (<ob- + curro)
moriendum esse "they must die"; indir. disc. ff. *una uoce* (AG #580a); impers. n. of gerv. w/ esse in 2nd
   (pass.) periphr. (AG #500.3)
trecentos ... mactatos [esse] indir. disc. (AG #580) ff. *scribunt*; trecenti, -ae, -a: three hundred;
   dediticius, -a, -um: having surrendered; *dediticiis*: m. abl. pl. subst. adj. (AG #288); eligo, eligere, elegi,
   electum: select, choose (<ex- + lego); *utriusque ordinis*: "of each social class" (i.e., both senators and
   equites); *ad aram Diuo Iulio extructam*: "at the altar erected to the Divine Julius"; Diuus Iulius: "the
   Divine Julius": Julius Caesar had been formally deified in 42 BCE; *Idibus Martiis*: "on the Ides of March,"
   abl. of time when (AG #423.1); hostia, -ae (f.): sacrificial animal; macto (1): sacrifice, kill; Suet. here
   includes a tradition hostile to Augustus that characterizes the punishment of those captured at Perusia
   as a form of human sacrifice
exsto, exstare, extiti exist, be found (<ex- + sto)
qui traderent relat. cl. of char. (AG #535)
conpecto eum ad arma isse indir. disc. (AG #580) ff. *traderent*; conpectum, -i (n.): agreement, compact;
   conpecto: "by agreement" or "on purpose"; *eum* = Augustum; *ad arma*: "to arms" (to war); eo, ire, ii (iui),
   itum: go, proceed
ut occulti aduersarii ... detegerentur purp. cl. (AG #531); occultus, -a, -um: hidden, concealed;
   aduersarius, -(i)i (m.): adversary, opponent; *quos metus ... contineret*: relat. cl. of char. (AG #535);
   quos (relat. pron.): "those whom," anteced. omitted (AG #307c); *magis quam*: "more than";

uoluntas contineret, facultate L. Antoni ducis praebita, detegerentur deuictisque iis et confiscatis promissa ueteranis
praemia soluerentur.

16 Siculum bellum incohauit in primis, sed diu traxit intermissum
saepius—modo reparandarum classium causa quas tempestatibus duplici naufragio et quidem per aestatem amiserat,
modo pace facta flagitante populo ob interclusos commeatus
famemque ingrauescentem—donec nauibus ex integro fabrica-

---

uoluntas, -atis (f.): choice, will; contineo, continere, continui, contentum: hold together, contain; *facultate ... praebita*: abl. abs. (AG #419), "with the opportunity provided of having L. Antonius as a leader," an extremely condensed phr. (BRACHYLOGY, AG #640); facultas, -atis (f.): ability, opportunity; detego, detegere, detexi, detectum: uncover, disclose (<de- + tego)

deuictisque iis et confiscatis abl. abs. (AG #419); deuinco, deuincere, deuici, deuictum: defeat decisively, subdue (<de- + uinco); confisco (1): seize the property of (a person)

promissa ueteranis praemia soluerentur a second purp. cl. (AG #531); promitto, promittere, promisi, promissum: promise (<pro- + mitto); *praemia*: n. pl. subj.; soluo, soluere, solui, solutum: settle (a debt), pay

The heading *Siculum bellum* identifies the focus of chapter 16. Augustus' efforts to defeat Sextus Pompey in Sicily required the construction of a new port and fleet.

16.1
incoho (1) start, initiate
in primis [bellis] "among the first [wars]," *bellis* understood
traho, trahere, traxi, tractum drag, draw out
intermitto, intermittere, intermisi, intermissum interrupt, leave off temporarily (<inter- + mitto); *intermissum* is the first of ten ptc. in this sentence
modo ... modo "first ... then," coordinate conj. (AG #224); here Suet. has inverted chronological order
reparandarum classium causa gerv. w/ causa to express purp. (AG #504b); reparo (1): restore, repair
quas ... amiserat relat. cl.; *quas* (relat. pron.): anteced. *classium*; tempestas, -atis (f.): storm; duplex, -icis: double; naufragium, -(i)i (n.): shipwreck, disaster; aestas, -atis (f.): summer; *et quidem per aestatem*: "and what is more, even during the summer" (summer was considered a safe season for sailing); amitto, amittere, amisi, amissum: lose (<ab- + mitto); the shipwrecks date to 38 or 36 BCE
pace facta tmp. abl. abs. (AG #420.1); pax, pacis (f.): pact, peace; a settlement had been negotiated with Sextus Pompey in 39 BCE
flagitante populo ... ingrauescentem abl. abs. replacing causal cl. (AG #420.2); flagito (1): press with demands, clamor for; intercludo, intercludere, interclusi, interclusum: block, cut off (<inter- + claudo); commeatus, -us (m.): supplies, provisions; fames, famis (f.): hunger, famine; ingrauesco, ingrauescere: grow worse (<in- + grauesco)
donec (conj.) until, until such time as, w/ pf. indic. to denote a fact in past time (AG #554)
nauibus ... fabricatis abl. abs. (AG #419); nauis, -is (f.): ship, warship; integer, -gra, -grum: fresh; *ex integro*: "afresh, anew" (*OLD* 3a); fabrico (1): build, construct

tis ac uiginti seruorum milibus manumissis et ad remum datis
portum Iulium apud Baias inmisso in Lucrinum et Auernum
lacum mari effecit. in quo cum hieme tota copias exercuisset,
Pompeium inter Mylas et Naulochum superauit, sub horam
pugnae tam arto repente somno deuinctus ut ad dandum
signum ab amicis excitaretur. **2.** unde praebitam Antonio
materiam putem exprobrandi ne rectis quidem oculis eum
aspicere potuisse instructam aciem, uerum supinum, caelum

---

uiginti ... milibus manumissis ... datis abl. abs. w/ two ptc. (AG #419); uiginti (indecl. adj.): twenty; milia, -ium (pl.): thousands; manumitto, manumittere, manumisi, manumissum: emancipate, free (<manus + mitto); remus, -i (m.): an oar; ad remum dare: "to assign as an oarsman"

portus, -us (m.) a harbor, port; *portum Iulium*: "the Julian harbor," dir. obj. of *effecit*

Baiae, -arum (f. pl.) Baiae, a resort on the bay of Naples

inmisso ... mari abl. abs. (AG #419); inmitto, inmittere, inmisi, inmissum: send, direct (flow of water) (<in- + mitto); lacus, -us (m.): lake; the Lucrine Lake and Lake Avernus were connected to the sea by newly constructed channels

efficio, efficere, effeci, effectum make, construct (<ex- + facio)

in quo cum ... exercuisset circumst. cum cl. (AG #546), "when he had trained his forces in this port"; *quo* (relat. pron.): anteced. *portum*, the relat. belongs inside the cum cl.; *hieme tota*: "for the whole winter," abl. instead of acc. to express duration of time (AG #424b); hiems, -mis (f.): winter; copiae, -arum (f. pl.): forces, troops

Pompeium Sextus Pompeius (*OCD* 1180–1181), son of Pompeius Magnus and commander of the enemy fleet

inter Mylas et Naulochum the decisive naval battle of 36 BCE took place on the northeast coast of Sicily b/w Augustus' camp at Mylae and Pompey's base at Naulochus

supero (1) overcome, defeat

sub horam pugnae "just before the hour of battle"; sub (prep. + acc): just before (*OLD* 23); pugna, -ae (f.): fight, battle

tam arto ... somno deuinctus ptc. phr.; artus, -a, -um: close, deep; somnus, -i (m.): sleep; deuincio, deuincire, deuinxi, deuinctum: bind, hold fast (<de- + uincio); *deuinctus*: nom. sg. ppp.; Augustus is the subj.

ut ... excitaretur result cl. (AG #537); *ad dandum signum*: gerv. w/ ad to express purp. (AG #506); signum, -i (n.): sign for action, signal; excito (1): rouse (<ex- + cito); *excitaretur*: impf. subjv. used by Suet. in place of pf. to express a single act

16.2

unde praebitam [esse] Antonio materiam putem exprobrandi indir. disc. ff. *putem* (AG #580); puto (1): think, suppose; *putem*: "I (Suet.) should think," potent. subjv. in cautious assertion (AG #447); unde (relat. adv.): from which source, whence; materia, -ae (f.): material; exprobro (1): bring up as a reproach; *exprobrandi*: obj. gen. ger. (AG #504), "for reproaching"

ne ... eum ... potuisse ... naues indir. disc. (AG #580) is used to report Antony's criticism of Augustus; *eum* = Augustum, acc. subj; *potuisse, cubuisse, surrexisse, uenisse*: pf. inf. in indir. disc. to indicate past time (AG #584), each marking a cl.; *ne ... quidem*: not even (emphasizing extreme case); rectus, -a, -um: (of eyes) facing directly; aspicio, aspicere, aspexi, aspectum: look at, gaze upon (<ad- + specio); *aspicere*: compl. inf. (AG #456); instruo, instruere, instruxi, instructum: draw up in battle order,

intuentem, stupidum cubuisse nec prius surrexisse ac militibus in conspectum uenisse quam a M. Agrippa fugatae sint hostium naues. alii dictum factumque eius criminantur quasi classibus tempestate perditis exclamauerit etiam inuito Neptuno uictoriam se adepturum ac die circensium proximo sollemni pompae simulacrum dei detraxerit.   3. nec temere plura ac maiora pericula ullo alio bello adiit. traiecto in Siciliam exercitu, cum partem reliquam copiarum <ex> continenti repeteret, oppressus ex inprouiso a Demochare et Apollophane praefectis

---

arrange (<in- + struo); acies, -ei (f.): battle line; supinus, -a, -um: lying flat on one's back; intueor, intueri, intuitus sum: fix one's gaze upon, watch (<in- + tueor); stupidus, -a, -um: physically dazed, spellbound; surgo, surgere, surrexi, surrectum: get up, rise from bed (<contr. form of subrigo); *militibus*: dat. of ref. (AG #378); conspectus, -us (m.): sight, view; *prius ... quam ... fugatae sint*: tmp. cl. (AG #551) in indir. disc; *prius ... quam*: "before" (AG #434); M. Vipsanius Agrippa (*OCD* 1554–1555), a skilled military commander and the lifelong friend of Augustus; *fugatae sint*: pf. pass. subjv. in subord. cl. in indir. disc. (AG #580), Suet. frequently uses pf. subjv. in place of impf. or plpf.; fugo (1): drive away, frighten off

dictum, -i (n.) saying, remark

factum, -i (n.) deed, action

criminor (1) denounce, accuse, complain of

quasi ... exclamauerit ... detraxerit   *quasi* w/ subjv. to express a belief or rumor (AG #524, BG #602n4); *classibus ... perditis*: abl. abs. (AG #419); perdo, perdere, perdidi, perditum: destroy, lose (<per- + do); exclamo (1): exclaim; *etiam ... se adepturum* [*esse*]: indir. disc. (AG #580) ff. *exclamauerit*; *inuito Neptuno*: abl. abs., "against Neptune's wishes"; *inuitus, -a, -um*: unwilling; adipiscor, adipisci, adeptus sum: obtain, win (<ad- + apiscor); *die ... proximo*: abl. of time when (AG #423.1); circenses, -ium (m. pl.): circus games; sollemnis, -e: solemn, ceremonial; pompa, -ae (f.): procession, parade; *solemni pompae*: dat. of separ. w/ compd. vb. (AG #381); simulacrum, -i (n.): image, statue; detraho, detrahere, detraxi, detractum: pull down, remove (<de- + traho); the episode is especially meaningful as Sextus Pompey associated himself closely with Neptune

---

16.3

nec temere   (adv.) "and scarcely"

plus   (irreg. compar. adj.) more (for decl., s. AG #120)

ullo alio bello   "in any other war," abl. of time when (AG #424d)

traiecto ... exercitu   abl. abs. (AG #419); traicio, traicere, traieci, traiectum: transfer, transport (<trans- + iacio)

cum ... repeteret   circumst. cum cl. (AG #546); continens, -ntis (f. as subst.): mainland; repeto, repetere, repetiui (-ii), repetitum: return to, go back for (<re- + peto)

opprimo, opprimere, oppressi, oppressum   overwhelm, catch unawares (<ob- + premo)

ex improuiso   (adv. phr.) unexpectedly, suddenly

a Demochare et Apollophane praefectis Pompei   Demochares and Apollophanes, freedmen of Sextus Pompey who commanded his fleet; praefectus, -i (m.): commander, captain

Pompei uno demum nauigio aegerrime effugit. iterum cum
praeter Locros Regium pedibus iret et prospectis biremibus
Pompeianis terram legentibus suas ratus descendisset ad litus,
paene exceptus est. tunc etiam per deuios tramites refugientem
seruus Aemili Pauli comitis eius, dolens proscriptum olim
ab eo patrem Paulum et quasi occasione ultionis oblata, interficere conatus est. **4.** post Pompei fugam collegarum alterum
M. Lepidum, quem ex Africa in auxilium euocarat, superbien-

---

nauigium, -(i)i (n.) a ship, boat
aegre (adv.) with difficulty (superl. = -rime)
effugio, effugere, effugi flee, slip away, escape (<ex- + fugio)
cum ... pedibus iret "when he was going on foot," circumst. cum cl. (AG #546); Locri, -orum (m. pl.): Locri, a Greek settlement on the toe of Italy; Regium, -(i)i (n.): Regium, a town in southernmost Italy on the straits of Messina; *Regium*: acc. of place to which w/out prep. (AG #427.2); pes, pedis (m.): foot, emphasizing land travel (*OLD* 6a); eo, ire, ii (iui), itum: go
et ... descendisset continuation of circumst. cum cl. (AG #546); *prospectis ... legentibus*: abl. abs. (AG #419); prospicio, prospicere, prospexi, prospectum: see in front (<pro- + specio); biremis, -is (f.): bireme, a ship with paired oars; lego, legere, legi, lectum: coast along (*OLD* 7b); *suas ratus*: "having believed that they were his own ships," abbrev. ptc. phr.; reor, reri, ratus sum: think, believe; descendo, descendere, descendi, descensum: descend, come down (<de- + scando); litus, -oris (n.): seashore, coast
excipio, excipere, excepi, exceptum catch, intercept (<ex- + capio)
deuius, -a, -um remote, out of the way
trames, -itis (m.) footpath, track
refugio, refugere, refugi turn back and flee, run away (<re- + fugio); *refugientem* [*Augustum*]: dir. obj. of *interficere*
seruus nom. sg. subj.; Suet. adds emphasis to this episode by making the slave the subject
Aemilius Paulus Paullus Aemilius Lepidus (*OCD* 20–21), nephew of the triumvir Lepidus
comitis appos. w/ *Aemili Pauli*; *eius* = Augusti
doleo, dolere, dolui, dolitum grieve, feel pained
proscriptum ... Paulum ptc. phr., obj. of *dolens*; proscribo, proscribere, proscripsi, proscriptum: proscribe, publish the name in a list of outlaws (s. *OCD* s.v. proscription, 1223) (<pro- + scribo); *patrem Paulum* = Lucius Aemilius Lepidus Paullus (*OCD* s.v. Aemilius Paullus (3), Lucius, 21), the brother of the triumvir Lepidus; the father Paulus had been included in the proscriptions list of 43 BCE
quasi occasione ... oblata abl. abs. (AG #419); occasio, -onis (f.): opportunity; ultio, -onis (f.): revenge
interficio, interficere, interfeci, interfectum put to death, kill (<inter- + facio); *interficere*: compl. inf. (AG #456)
conor (1) make an effort, try, attempt

16.4

fuga, -ae (f.) flight, rout; Sextus Pompey fled after the battle of Naulochus but was caught and executed in 35 BCE
collegarum alterum M[arcum] Lepidum ... superbientem ... uindicantem ptc. phr., dir. obj. of *spoliauit*; collega, -ae (m.): colleague, associate (s. ch. 8.3); *quem* (relat. pron.): anteced. M. Lepidum; *in auxilium*: "for assistance"; euoco (1): call out, summon (<ex- + uoco); *euocarat* = contr. form of euocauerat (AG #181); *superbientem uiginti legionum fiducia*: "arrogantly trusting in his twenty legions"; superbio,

tem uiginti legionum fiducia summasque sibi partes terrore et
minis uindicantem spoliauit exercitu supplicemque concessa
uita Cerceios in perpetuum relegauit.

17   M. Antoni societatem semper dubiam et incertam reconcilia-
tionibusque uariis male focilatam abrupit tandem et quo magis
degenerasse eum a ciuili more approbaret testamentum quod
is Romae etiam de Cleopatra liberis inter heredes nuncupatis

---

superbire: show pride or disdain on account (of) (w/ abl.); fiducia, -ae (f.): trust; *fiducia*: "trusting in,"
abl. w/ gen. *legionum*; *summasque sibi partes*: "the greatest part for himself," obj. of *uindicantem*; terror,
-oris (m.): terror, extreme fear; minae, -arum (f. pl.): threats, menaces; uindico (1): assert one's title
to, lay claim to; Lepidus made an unsuccessful play to place himself over Augustus after the defeat of
Sextus Pompey

spolio (1) strip, disarm, despoil (w/ abl. of separ. *exercitu*)
supplex, -icis making humble entreaty, (subst.) a suppliant
concessa uita abl. abs. (AG #419)
Cerceii, -orum (m. pl.) Circeii, a town in Latium; *Cerceios*: acc. place to which w/out prep. (AG #427.2)
in perpetuum permanently, for an indefinite period; Lepidus died at Circeii in 13 BCE
relego (1) banish to a specified place (<re- + lego)

The fifth and final civil war, fought against Mark Antony, is taken up in chapters 17–18. The struggle ends with
the battle of Actium in 31 BCE and Augustus' capture of Egypt.

17.1
societas, -atis (f.) a partnership, alliance; Antony was Augustus' colleague in the triumvirate (s. ch. 8.3)
dubius, -a, -um uncertain, wavering, doubtful
incertus, -a, -um unpredictable, not dependable, faltering
reconciliatio, -onis (f.) reconciliation
male (adv.) scarcely, barely, hardly
focilo (1) restore to health, revive, keep alive
abrumpo, abrumpere, abrupi, abruptum put an end to, break off (<ab- + rumpo)
quo magis ... approbaret relat. cl. of purp. w/ compar. (AG #531.2a); *degenerasse eum ... more*: indir. disc.
(AG #580) ff. *approbaret*; degenero (1): fall away from, decline from (w/ *ab*); *degenerasse* = contr. form
of degenerauisse (AG #181); ciuilis, -e: civil, suited to a citizen; approbo (1): confirm (<ad- + probo);
after having cited some of Antony's attacks against Augustus, Suet. here shifts the focus to charges leveled
against Antony of un-Roman behavior
testamentum ... aperiundum recitandumque [esse] subst. cl. of purp. w/ inf. and acc. subj. (AG #563d)
ff. *curauit*, interrupted by relat. cl., "he saw to it that the will be opened and read"; *quod* (relat. pron.):
anteced. *testamentum*, obj. of *reliquerat*; *Romae*: locat. (AG #427.3); Antony had deposited his will with
the Vestal Virgins in Rome; *etiam ... liberis ... nuncupatis*: abl. abs. (AG #419); heres, -edis (m./f.): heir;
nuncupo (1): declare, appoint; *etiam* emphasizes that the inclusion of Antony's children from Cleopatra
was surprising, especially given that Antony also had legitimate children (and heirs) from his legal
Roman marriages to Fulvia and Octavia; Cleopatra = Cleopatra VII (*OCD* 333), queen of Egypt;

reliquerat aperiundum recitandumque pro contione curauit.
2. remisit tamen hosti iudicato necessitudines amicosque omnes atque inter alios C. Sosium et T. Domitium tunc adhuc consules. Bononiensibus quoque publice, quod in Antoniorum clientela antiquitus erant, gratiam fecit coniurandi cum tota Italia pro partibus suis. nec multo post nauali proelio apud Actium uicit, in serum dimicatione protracta ut in naue uictor pernoctauerit.
3. Ab Actio cum Samum in hiberna se recepisset, turbatus

---

aperiundum recitandumque [*esse*]: inf. of 2nd (pass.) periphr. (AG #563d, n3) with ELLIPSIS of *esse*; aperio, aperire, aperui, aperiitum: open
contio, -onis (f.) a public meeting, assembly; *pro contione*: "in front of an assembly"

17.2
remitto, remittere, remisi, remissum send back, let go (<re- + mitto)
hosti iudicato [Antonio] "after Antony had been declared an enemy," tmp. abl. abs. (AG #420.1); iudico (1): judge, declare formally
necessitudo, -inis (f.) a bond, connection; (by extension): a relative, a person bound by close ties
C. Sosium et T. Domitium Gaius Sosius (*OCD* 1386) and Gnaeus Domitius Ahenobarbus (*OCD* s.v. Domitius Ahenobarbus (4), Gnaeus, 473) were consuls in 32 BCE; the manuscripts of Suet. incorrectly list Titus as Domitius' praenomen
Bononiensis, -e of Bologna; (m. subst.): an inhabitant of Bologna
quod ... erant causal cl. (AG #540.1); clientela, -ae (f.): clientship, the relationship of a town to their Roman patron; antiquitus (adv.): from of old, long ago; supply Bononienses as subj. of *erant*
gratiam facere grant an exemption to a person (+ dat. *Bononiensibus*) from an obligation (+ gen. *coniurandi*) (*OLD* 1b)
coniuro (1) join in taking an oath (<con- + iuro); *coniurandi*: gen. of ger.; the communities of Italy, except for Bologna, swore an oath of allegiance to Augustus in 32 BCE
totus, -a, -um whole of, entire, all
nec multo post "not much later"; the break with Antony occurred early in 32 BCE, leading to the battle of Actium in September of 31 BCE
naualis, -e naval, of or belonging to a ship
apud Actium "at Actium"; Actium was a promontory in western Greece (*OCD* 10)
uinco, uincere, uici, uictum gain victory, prevail
in serum dimicatione ... protracta abl. abs. (AG #419); serus, -a, -um: late; (n. sg. subst.): a late hour; dimicatio, -onis (f.): a battle, fight; protraho, protrahere, protraxi, protractum: drag out, prolong (<pro- + traho)
ut ... pernoctauerit result cl. (AG #537) w/ pf. subjv. (AG #485c); nauis, -is (f.): a ship, warship; uictor, -oris (m.): victor; pernocto (1): to spend the night; the detail is noteworthy since warships were usually beached at night as it was dangerous to remain at sea

17.3
cum ... se recepisset circumst. cum cl. (AG #546); Samos, -i (m.): Samos, an island in the eastern Aegean; *Samum*: acc. place to which w/out prep. (AG #427.2); hiberna, -orum (n. pl.): winter quarters; recipio, recipere, recepi, receptum: (reflex.) withdraw, retire (<re- + capio)
turbo (1) agitate, stir up, disturb, rouse

nuntiis de seditione praemia et missionem poscentium quos
ex omni numero confecta uictoria Brundisium praemiserat,
repetita Italia tempestate in traiectu bis conflictatus, primo
inter promunturia Peloponnensi atque Aetoliae, rursus circa
montes Ceraunios utrubique parte liburnicarum demersa,
simul eius in qua uehebatur fusis armamentis et gubernaculo
diffracto. nec amplius quam septem et uiginti dies, donec
ad desideria militum <omnia> ordinarentur, Brundisii com-
moratus Asiae Syriaeque circuitu Aegyptum petit obsessaque

---

nuntius, -(i)i (m.) message, report

de seditione ... poscentium "about the sedition of those demanding," prep. phr. as attrib. modifier of *nuntiis*; seditio, -onis (f.): rebellion, mutiny; missio, -onis (f.): discharge from service; posco, poscere, poposci: ask for, demand; *poscentium*: pres. act. ptc., "of those [soldiers] demanding"; the identity of the soldiers is explained in the relat. cl. that follows

quos ... praemiserat relat. cl.; *quos* (relat. pron.): "the soldiers whom," the anteced. is the subst. ptc. *poscentium*, obj. of *praemiserat*; *confecta uictoria*: tmp. abl. abs. (AG #420.1); conficio, conficere, confeci, confectum: accomplish, achieve (<con- + facio); Brundisium, -(i)i (n.): Brundisium, a town on the southeast coast of Italy; *Brundisium*: acc. of place to which w/out prep. (AG #427.2); praemitto, praemittere, praemisi, praemissum: send in advance, send ahead (<prae- + mitto)

repetita Italia abl. abs. (AG #419); repeto, repetere, repetiui (-ii), repetitum: return to, go back to (<re- + peto)

tempestas, -atis (f.) a storm

traiectus, -us (m.) act of crossing over; *in traiectu*: abl. of time which does not ordinarily require prep. (AG #424a)

bis (adv.) twice; the two near disasters are explored in order: *primo ... rursus*

conflicto (1) strike frequently, buffet, distress; *conflictus [est]*: ELLIPSIS

promunturium, -(i)i (n.) promontory, spur of mountain projecting into the sea; the exact location of these sites in the Peloponnese and Aetolia is uncertain

montes Ceraunii the Acroceraunian mountains in Epirus, modern Albania

utrubique (adv.) in both places (<uterque + ubi)

parte ... demersa abl. abs. (AG #419); liburnica, -ae (f.): Libernian galley, a fast-sailing warship; demergo, demergere, demersi, demersum: sink (<de- + mergo)

eius [libernicae] **in qua uehebatur** *eius*: poss. gen. w/ *armamentis et gubernaculo*; ueho, uehere, uexi, uectum: carry, convey; Suet. explains the damage "of that ship" in which Augustus was carried

fusis armamentis et gubernaculo diffracto dbl. abl. abs. (AG #419) w/ CHIASMUS (AG #641); fundo, fundere, fudi, fusum: scatter; armamenta, -orum (n. pl.): tackle, rigging (of a ship); gubernaculum, -i (n.): steering-oar, rudder; diffringo, diffringere, diffregi, diffractum: break up, shatter (<dis- + frango)

nec amplius quam ... dies "for not more than twenty-seven days," acc. of extent of time (AG #423.2) w/ compar.

donec ... omnia ordinarentur tmp. cl. implying expectancy (AG #553); donec: until; desiderium, -(i)i (n.): desire, expressed request; *omnia*: n. nom. pl. subj.; ordino (1): organize, manage

Brundisii "at Brundisium," locat. (AG #427.3)

commoror (1) delay, stay on, remain (<con- + moror)

circuitus, -us (m.) path, orbit; w/ gen. (*Asiae Syriaeque*): a passing along the edge of, skirting

obsessaque Alexandria abl. abs. (AG #419); obsideo, obsidere, obsedi, obsessum: besiege, assail (<ob- + sedeo)

Alexandria, quo Antonius cum Cleopatra confugerat, breui
potitus est.

4. Et Antonium quidem seras condiciones pacis temptantem
ad mortem adegit uiditque mortuum, Cleopatrae, quam seruatam triumpho magno opere cupiebat, etiam psyllos admouit
qui uenenum ac uirus exugerent, quod perisse morsu aspidis
putabatur. ambobus communem sepulturae honorem tribuit ac
tumulum ab ipsis incohatum perfici iussit.   5. Antonium iuue-

---

quo Antonius . . . confugerat relat. cl.; quo (relat. adv.): in which place, where; confugio, confugere, confugi: flee for safety, take refuge (<con- + fugio)

breuis, -e short, small; *breui*: (n. subst.) "after a short time" (*OLD* 6)

potior, potiri, potitus sum take possession of, control, possess; Augustus captured Alexandria in August of 30 BCE, less than a year after Actium

17.4

Antonium . . . temptantem ptc. phr., obj. of *adegit*; serus, -a, -um: late, not taking place until after the proper time; *seras*: adj. w/ adv. force (AG #290); condicio, -onis (f.): agreement; *condicio pacis*: truce, pact; tempto (1): try to attain

adigo, adigere, adegi, adactum drive, compel (<ad + ago)

mortuus, -a, -um dead; to view the body of one's enemy was unusual and considered cruel

Cleopatrae dat. indir. obj. of *admouit* (AG #370); Cleopatra VII (*OCD* 333), queen of Egypt

quam seruatam [esse] *triumpho* subst. cl. of purp. ff. *cupiebat* (AG #563b.2); *quam* (relat. pron.): anteced. *Cleopatrae*; seruo (1): preserve, save; *seruatam*: ELLIPSIS of esse for pf. pass. inf.; *triumpho*: dat. of purp. (AG #382)

magno opere (adv.) greatly, strongly, especially

cupio, cupere, cupiui (-ii), cupitum wish for, desire

Psylli, -orum (m. pl.) the Psylli, a people of N. Africa skilled at curing snake bites

admoueo, admouere, admoui, admotum bring up, call upon (<ad- + moueo)

qui . . . exugerent relat. cl. of purp. (AG #531.2); uenenum, -i (n.): poison; uirus, -i (m.): venom, a poisonous secretion or fluid; exugo, exugere, exuxi, exuctum: suck out, draw out (<ex- + sugo)

quod . . . putabatur causal cl. (AG #540.1) w/ indir. disc. pers. constr. w/ pass. vb. (AG #582), "because she was thought to have perished"; pereo, perire, perii (-iui), peritum: die, perish (<per- + eo); morsus, -us (m.): bite; aspis, -idis (f.): asp, a venomous snake of N. Africa; puto (1): think, suppose; *putabatur*: Cleopatra is the subj.

ambo, -ae, -o (pl.) two of a pair, both; *ambobus*: dat. (decl., AG #134b)

communem sepulturae honorem "the honor of burial together," HYPALLAGE (AG #640); communis, -e: shared, joint; sepultura, -ae (f.): burial

tribuo, tribuere, tribui, tributum grant, bestow

tumulum . . . perfici subst. cl. of purp. ff. *iussit* (AG #563a); tumulus, -i (m.): burial mound, tomb; incoho (1): start, initiate; perficio, perficere, perfeci, perfectum; complete, finish (<per- + facio)

17.5

Antonium iuuenem . . . abreptum ptc. phr., obj. of *interemit*; *Antonium iuuenem*: "the young Antonius," M. Antonius Antyllus (*OCD* 112); Fulvia (*OCD* 593), wife of Mark Antony, who had been besieged

nem, maiorem de duobus Fuluia genitis, simulacro Diui Iuli ad quod post multas et irritas preces confugerat abreptum interemit, item Caesarionem, quem ex Caesare patre Cleopatra concepisse praedicabat, retractum e fuga supplicio adfecit. reliquos Antoni reginaeque communes liberos non secus ac necessitudine iunctos sibi et conseruauit et mox pro condicione cuiusque sustinuit ac fouit.

---

at Perusia w/ L. Antonius (s. ch. 14–15); *Fuluia*: abl. of source (AG #403a); gigno, gignere, genui, genitum: (pass.) be born; simulacrum, -i (n.): image, statue; *simulacro*: dat. of separ. (AG #381) w/ *abreptum*; Diuus Iulius: "the Divine Julius"; Julius Caesar had been formally deified in 42 BCE and Cleopatra had begun construction of a temple in Alexandria; *ad quod . . . confugerat*: relat. cl.; irritus, -a, -um: empty, ineffectual; prex, -ecis (f.): entreaty, prayer; confugio, confugere, confugi: flee for safety, take refuge (<con- + fugio); abripio, abripere, abripui, abreptum: remove by force, drag away (<ab- + rapio)

interemo, interemere, interemi, interemptum kill, destroy (<inter- + emo); Augustus ignored Antyllus' claim to a right of asylum

Caesarion nickname of Ptolemy XV Caesar (*OCD* 1236)

quem . . . concepisse indir. disc. (AG #580) ff. *Cleopatra praedicabat*, acc. subj. omitted (AG #581n1); *quem* (relat. pron.): anteced. Caesarion; concipio, concipere, concepi, conceptum: conceive (<con- + capio)

praedico (1) proclaim, declare (<prae- + dico)

retraho, retrahere, retraxi, retractum drag back, bring back by force (<re- + traho)

fuga, -ae (f.) flight; Caesarion had fled toward Ethiopia for safety

supplicio adfecit lit., "he visited with punishment" = "he killed"; supplicium, -(i)i (n.): punishment; adficio, adficere, adfeci, adfectum:
affect, cause to suffer (w/ abl. *supplicio*) (<ad- + facio); Caesarion posed a special threat to Augustus' position as Caesar's heir

reliquos . . . liberos regina, -ae (f.): queen (here = Cleopatra); communis, -e: shared, joint; Antony and Cleopatra had twins, Alexander Helios and Cleopatra Selene, and a third child, Ptolemy Philadelphus; the two boys drop out of the historical record, but Cleopatra Selene went on to marry Juba of Mauretania

non secus ac necessitudine iunctos sibi "just as if they were joined to him by a close tie"; *non secus ac*: not otherwise than, exactly as if; necessitudo, -inis (f.): a bond or tie; iungo, iungere, iunxi, iunctum: join; the family relationship here is complex as Antony had been married to Augustus' sister Octavia (although this point is not mentioned in Suet.'s biography of Augustus); no mention is made of Antony's other son by Fulvia, Iullus Antonius, who was raised in Octavia's household along with Antony and Octavia's two daughters, Antonia the Elder and Antonia the Younger

conseruo (1) preserve, keep unharmed (<con- + seruo)

pro condicione "in accordance with the status"; condicio, -onis (f.): status, condition

sustineo, sustinere, sustinui support, raise (<sub- + teneo)

foueo, fouere, foui, fotum protect, watch over, nurture

18 Per idem tempus conditorium et corpus Magni Alexandri, cum
prolatum e penetrali subiecisset oculis, corona aurea imposita
ac floribus aspersis ueneratus est consultusque num et
Ptolomaeum inspicere uellet, regem se uoluisse ait uidere, non
mortuos. **2.** Aegyptum in prouinciae formam redactam ut
feraciorem habilioremque annonae urbicae redderet fossas
omnis in quas Nilus exaestuat oblimatas longa uetustate mili-

---

18.1

per idem tempus "during this same time"

conditorium, -(i)i (n.) tomb, sepulchre (an unusual wd. <condo + -torium); *conditorium et corpus*: acc. dir. obj. of *ueneratus est*

Magnus Alexander Alexander the Great (*OCD* s.v. Alexander (3) III, 56–58), Macedonian king and conqueror of Egypt in fourth century BCE

cum ... subiecisset circumst. cum cl. (AG #546); profero, proferre, protuli, prolatum: bring forth, carry out (<pro- + fero); penetrale, -is (n.): inner shrine; *subiecisset*: compd. vb. w/ acc. dir. obj. *prolatum* and dat. indir. obj. *oculis*

corona aurea imposita ac floribus aspersis tmp. abl. abs. (AG #420.1) or abl. of means (AG #409); corona, -ae (f.): crown; impono, imponere, imposui, impositum: place on (<in- + pono); flos, -oris (m.): flower; aspergo, aspergere, aspersi, aspersum: sprinkle (<ad- + spargo)

ueneror (1) pay homage to, venerate

consulto (1) consult; *consultus*: ppp. introd. indir. quest.

num ... uellet indir. quest. (AG #574); num (interr. pcl.): whether; Ptolemaeum, -i (n.): the tomb of the Ptolemies, the Macedonian dynasty of Cleopatra that had ruled Egypt for three centuries; inspicio, inspicere, inspexi, inspectum: look at, see (<in- + specio); *inspicere*: compl. inf. w/ *uellet* (AG #456)

regem se uoluisse ... non mortuos indir. disc. (AG #580) ff. *ait*; note CHIASMUS emphasizing the antithesis b/w the two dir. obj. *regem* and *mortuos*; rex, regis (m.): king; *se uoluisse*: acc. subj. + inf. in indir. disc.: "he wished"; *ait*: "he said" (for forms, AG #206a); *uidere*: compl. inf. w/ *uoluisse* (AG #456); mortuus, -a, -um: dead; *mortuos*: (subst.) "dead people" (AG #288)

18.2

Aegyptum ... redactam ptc. phr., obj. of *redderet*; forma, -ae (f.): form, configuration; redigo, redigere, redegi, redactum: convert, reduce (<re- + ago); Egypt was annexed to the Roman empire, but was not a typical province as it was governed by an equestrian prefect appointed by Augustus

ut ... redderet purp. cl. (AG #531.1); ferax, -acis: fertile, fruitful (compar. = -acior); habilis, -e: easy to handle, adaptable, fit (compar. = -ior); *feraciorem habilioremque*: pred. acc. (AG #393); annona, -ae (f.): the supply of grain; *annonae*: dat. of purp. (AG # 382); urbicus, -a, -um: urban, belong to the city (Rome); reddo, reddere, reddidi, redditum: render, cause to turn out (w/ pred. acc., *OLD* 17) (<re- + do)

fossa, -ae (f.) canal, channel

in quas Nilus exaestuat relat. cl.; *quas* (relat. pron.): anteced. *fossas*; Nilus, -i (m.): the river Nile; exaestuo (1): surge up (<ex- + aestuo)

oblimo (1) cover or fill with mud, silt up, clog (<ob- + limo)

uetustas, -atis (f.) age, old age

militari opere "by military labor"; Suet. uses opus w/ adj. instead of the noun militibus

tari opere detersit, quoque Actiacae uictoriae memoria celebratior et in posterum esset urbem Nicopolim apud Actium
condidit ludosque illic quinquennales constituit et ampliato
uetere Apollinis templo locum castrorum quibus fuerat usus
exornatum naualibus spoliis Neptuno ac Marti consecrauit.

19 Tumultus posthac et rerum nouarum initia coniurationesque
complures, prius quam inualescerent indicio detectas, com-
pressit alias alio tempore Lepidi iuuenis, deinde Varronis

---

detergeo, detergere, detersi, detersum clean away, clean (<de- + tergeo)
quoque ... memoria ... esset relat. cl. of purp. (AG #531.2); Actiacus, -a, -um: of or connected with
   Actium; celebratus, -a, -um: famous, celebrated (compar. = -ior); *celebratior*: pred. nom. w/ *memoria*
   (AG #272); *in posterum*: "in/for the future"
Nicopolis "Victory City" (*OCD* s.v. Nicopolis (3), 1015–1016)
illic (adv.) at that place, over there
quinquennalis, -e occurring every five years (in the Roman system of inclusive reckoning; every four years
   in modern terms)
ampliato ... templo abl. abs. (AG #419); amplio (1): increase the size of, extend; the temple to Apollo at
   Actium dated back to the sixth century BCE
locum ... exornatum ptc. phr., dir. obj. of *consecrauit*; *quibus* (relat. pron.): anteced. *castrorum*, abl. obj.
   of *usus fuerat*; *usus fuerat* = usus erat, a form common in Suet.; exorno (1): equip, furnish with (w/ abl.
   naualibus spoliis) (<ex- + orno); naualis, -e: naval, of or belonging to a ship; spolium, -ii (n.): (pl.) spoils
   of war, equipment taken from the enemy
Neptuno ac Marti new dedications to Neptune and Mars were added to the expanded temple of Apollo
consecro (1) dedicate, consecrate (to gods) (<con- + sacro)

Disturbances (*tumultus*). Revolts and conspiracies against Augustus are the next topic, forming a bridge
between discussions of civil and foreign wars. Suetonius lists conspiracies led by senators that must have been
well known as well as attempts made by men of the lower classes.

19.1
res nouae, rerum nouarum (f. pl.) revolution, constitutional change (*OLD* nouus 10)
coniuratio, -onis (f.) conspiracy, plot
complures ... alias " several ... others"; Suet. divides the insurrections into two groups based on when
   they were detected and suppressed
prius quam inualescerent tmp. cl. w/ impf. subjv. denoting action that did not take place (AG #551b);
   inualesco, inualescere, inualui: grow strong (<in- + ualesco)
indicium, -(i)i (n.) disclosure of a secret, information
detego, detegere, detexi, detectum uncover, expose, disclose (<de- + tego); *detectas*: ppp. w/ *complures*
comprimo, comprimere, compressi, compressum suppress, check, put down (<con- + premo)
Lepidi iuuenis "the plot of the young Lepidus"; Suet. presents a list of conspirators in the gen. case linking
   back to *coniurationes*; the son of Lepidus the triumvir (*OCD* s.v. Aemilius Lepidus (4), Marcus, 20), the
   plot dates to 30 BCE; Suet. offers no details for the senatorial conspiracies as they were likely well known
   to his readers
Varronis Murenae et Fanni Caepionis Aulus Terentius Varro Murena (*OCD* 1443) and Fannius Caepio
   (*OCD* 567) led a conspiracy, probably in 22 BCE

Murenae et Fanni Caepionis, mox M. Egnati, exin Plauti Rufi
Lucique Pauli progeneri sui, ac praeter has L. Audasi falsarum
tabularum rei ac neque aetate neque corpore integri, item Asini
Epicadi ex gente Parthina hybridae, ad extremum Telephi,
mulieris serui nomenculatoris. nam ne ultimae quidem sortis
hominum conspiratione et periculo caruit.   2. Audasius atque
Epicadus Iuliam filiam et Agrippam nepotem ex insulis quibus

M. Egnati Marcus Egnatius Rufus (*OCD* 491) led a conspiracy in 19 BCE

exin (adv.) thereafter, next

Plauti Rufi Lucique Pauli the conspiracy of Plautius Rufus and L. Aemilius Paullus (*OCD* s.v. Aemilius Paulus (4), Lucius, 21) dates to late in Augustus' life, perhaps 5–8 CE

progener, -eri (m.) a granddaughter's husband; Paullus was married to Augustus' granddaughter Julia, s. introduction for family tree

praeter has [coniurationes] "in addition to these conspiracies"; Suet. follows his primary list of nobles who plotted against Augustus with the plots of others, including an old and infirm man, a foreigner, and a slave; the arrangement seems to be hierarchical by social class rather than chronological

L. Audasi Lucius Audasius; the details of Audasius' plot are recorded only here

falsarum tabularum rei "for a matter of forgery"; *rei*: gen. of charge (AG #352)

neque aetate neque corpore integri "impaired by both old age and an infirm body"; LITOTES is used for emphasis; integer, -gra, -grum: unimpaired (w/ abl.); Suet. comments on the range of people who plotted against Augustus, including even the old and infirm

Asini Epicadi Asinius Epicadus

Parthinus, -a, -um Parthinian (an Illyrian tribe)

hybrida, -ae (m.) a person of mixed parentage (Roman and foreign); *hybridae*: gen. appos. (AG #282) w/ *Asini Epicadi*

ad extremum lastly, in the end (pointing to the final item of a list or the last item chronologically)

Telephi, mulieris serui nomenculatoris "[the plot] of Telephus, a slave name-prompter owned by a woman"; mulier, -eris (f.): woman; nomenculator, -oris (m.): monitor, slave who informs his master of people's names

ne ... quidem not even (emphasizing an extreme case)

ultimae ... sortis "of the lowest status"; gen. of quality (AG #345); ultimus, -a, -um: lowest; sors, -rtis (f.): fortune, social position, status (*OLD* 9)

conspiratio, -onis (f.) a conspiracy

careo, carere, carui, caritum lack, be without, be free from (w/ abl.)

19.2

Audasius atque Epicadus ... Telephus nom. subj. of *destinarant*; note shift in subj. as Augustus is the target of the plots and is referred to in the acc. (*ipsum*) and gen. (*eius*)

Iuliam Julia (*OCD* s.v. Iulia (3), 753–754), Augustus' only child, Julia had been exiled to Pandateria, but was transferred to Rhegium in 3 CE (s. ch. 65.3)

nepos, -otis (m.) grandson; on Augustus' grandson Agrippa Postumus (*OCD* s.v. Iulius Caesar, Agrippa, 756–757), s. ch. 64.1; Agrippa was held on Planasia (s. ch. 65.4)

quibus (relat. pron.) anteced. *insulis*; *quibus*: abl. of place where w/out prep. (AG #427.3) w/ *continebantur*

continebantur rapere ad exercitus, Telephus quasi debita sibi
fato dominatione et ipsum et senatum adgredi destinarant.
quin etiam quondam iuxta cubiculum eius lixa quidam ex
Illyrico exercitu, ianitoribus deceptis, noctu deprehensus est
cultro uenatorio cinctus, imposne mentis an simulata dementia
incertum: nihil enim exprimi quaestione potuit.

20 Externa bella duo omnino per se gessit, Delmaticum adulescens

---

contineo, continere, continui, contentum confine, detain (<con- + teneo)
rapere compl. inf. w/ *destinarant* (AG #456)
quasi debita sibi fato dominatione "believing that absolute power was owed to him by fate," abl. abs. in place of causal cl. (AG #420.2); debeo, debere, debui, debitum: owe; fatum, -i (n.): fate; dominatio, -onis (f.): absolute power
ipsum = Augustum
adgredior, adgredi, adgressus sum attack, confront (<ad- + gradior); *adgredi*: compl. inf. w/ *destinarant* (AG #456)
destino (1) intend, determine on (w/ inf.); *destinarant* = contr. form of destinauerant (AG #181)
quin etiam "and furthermore"
iuxta (prep. w/ acc.) in the vicinity of, next to, beside
eius = Augusti
lixa, -ae (m.) a camp follower, attendant; *lixa*: nom. subj.
Illyricus, -a, -um Illyrian; the reference to the Illyrian army dates the event to 35–33 BCE
ianitoribus deceptis abl. abs. (AG #419); ianitor, -is (m.): door-keeper; decipio, decipere, decepi, deceptum: deceive (<de- + capio)
noctu (adv.) at night
deprehendo, deprehendere, deprehendi, deprehensum catch, seize, discover, detect (<de- + prehendo)
cultro ... cinctus ptc. phr. w/ *lixa*; culter, -tri (m.): knife; uenatorius, -a, -um: hunting, used by hunters; cingo, cingere, cinxi, cinctum: equip (w/ abl. *cultro*)
imposne ... an ... incertum "it is uncertain whether ... or", disjunctive quest. ff. adj. (cf. ch. 28.1); *impos mentis*: out of one's mind; impos, -otis: not having control (w/ gen. *mentis*); *impos* = non compos; -ne ... an: whether ... or; *simulata dementia*: "with feigned madness"; abl. of quality (AG #415); simulo (1): pretend; dementia, -ae (f.): madness
exprimo, exprimere, expressi, expressum extract, extort (<ex- + premo); *exprimi*: compl. inf. w/ *potuit* (AG #456)
quaestio, -onis (f.) examination, interrogation

Foreign wars (*externa bella*). The focus of chapters 20–22 shifts to foreign wars waged by Augustus throughout his life. Emphasis is once again placed on Augustus' personal actions and experiences during the conflicts, especially his treatment of the enemy.

20.
externus, -a, -um external, foreign
per se by his own efforts, by himself (*OLD* per 15b)
gero, gerere, gessi, gestum carry on, wage (war) (*OLD* 8b)
Delmaticus, -a, -um of or concerning Dalmatia, a region on the east coast of the Adriatic Sea; Augustus campaigned in Dalmatia in 35 and 34 BCE
adulescens, -ntis (m.) a young man; the term applies to those in their teens and twenties; Augustus was in his late twenties

adhuc et Antonio deuicto Cantabricum. Delmatico etiam
uulnera excepit, una acie dextrum genu lapide ictus, altera et
crus et utrumque brachium ruina pontis consauciatus. reliqua
per legatos administrauit, ut tamen quibusdam Pannonicis
atque Germanicis aut interueniret aut non longe abesset,
Rauennam uel Mediolanium uel Aquileiam usque {ab urbe}
21 progrediens. domuit autem partim ductu partim auspiciis suis
Cantabriam, Aquitaniam, Pannoniam, Delmatiam cum Illyrico
omni, item Raetiam et Vindelicos ac Salassos, gentes Inalpinas.

Antonio deuicto tmp. abl. abs. (AG #420.1); deuinco, deuincere, deuici, deuictum: defeat decisively (<de- + uinco)

Cantabricus, -a, -um of the Cantabri, a people of the north coast of Spain; Augustus led campaigns against the Cantabri in 26–25 BCE

Delmatico [bello] "in the Dalmatian war"; abl. of time when (AG #424d)

uulnus, -eris (n.) wound, injury

excipio, excipere, excepi, exceptum receive (a wound) (*OLD* 11) (<ex- + capio)

una acie ... ictus ptc. phr.; *una acie*: abl. of time when (AG #424d); acies, -ei (f.): a battle, battle line; *dextrum genu*: acc. denoting the part affected (Gk. acc., AG #397b); dexter, -tra, -trum: right; genu, -us (n.): knee; lapis, -idis (m.): stone, pebble (used as the bullet of a sling); icio, icere, ici, ictum: strike (with a weapon)

altera [acie] **... consauciatus** ptc. phr.; *et crus et utrumque brachium*: acc. denoting the part affected (Gk. acc., AG #397b); crus, -uris (n.): leg; brachium, -(i)i (n.): arm; ruina, -ae (f.): fall, collapse; pons, -ntis (m.): bridge; consaucio (1): wound severely, injure (<con- + saucio)

reliqua [bella]

legatus, -i (m.) lieutenant, deputy, legate; in charge of multiple provinces, Augustus was granted the right to govern through legates

ut ... interueniret ... abesset purp. cl. (AG #531) ff. *progrediens*; *quibusdam Pannonicis atque Germanicis*: dat. (AG #370) or abl. (AG #401) ff. *interueniret* or *abesset*; Pannonicus, -a, -um: Pannonian, of or concerned with Pannonia, a province south and west of the Danube; Germanicus, -a, -um: German; longe (adv.): far, at a distance; interuenio, interuenire: intervene (<inter- + uenio); Augustus moved to northern Italy to be closer to the battle lines

Rauennam uel Mediolanium uel Aquileiam acc. of place to which w/out prep. (AG #427.2); Ravenna, Mediolanium (modern Milan), and Aquileia all lie in the north of Italy, closer to the Rhine and Danube frontiers

progredior, progredi, progressus sum go forward, advance (<pro- + gradior)

21.1

domo, domare, domui, domitum subdue, subjugate

partim ductu partim auspiciis suis "partly as leader, partly under his auspices"; partim (adv.): in part, partly; *ductu ... auspiciis*: abl. of manner w/out cum (AG #412); ductus, -us (m.): military leadership, command; auspicium, -(i)i (n.): auspices; Augustus' legates fought under his authority, thus the victories accrued to Augustus even when he was not present for the campaigns

Cantabriam ... gentes Inalpinas Suet., here and below, lists campaigns and conquests taking place over four decades, starting under the Triumvirate in the late 40s BCE; the edited list draws upon Augustus' own account (*RG* 26–30), but the organizing scheme employed within the section is unclear; Cantabria, -ae (f.): country of the Cantabri on the north coast of Spain; Aquitania, -ae (f.): country of the Aquitani, the

coercuit et Dacorum incursiones tribus eorum ducibus cum
magna copia caesis Germanosque ultra Albim fluuium summouit, ex quibus Suebos et Sugambros dedentis se traduxit in
Galliam atque in proximis Rheno agris conlocauit. alias item
nationes male quietas ad obsequium redegit.

2. Nec ulli genti sine iustis et necessariis causis bellum intulit
tantumque afuit a cupiditate quoquo modo imperium uel belli-
cam gloriam augendi ut quorundam barbarorum principes in

---

southwest of Gaul; Pannonia, -ae (f.): region b/w Dalmatia and the Danube; Delmatia, -ae (f.): Dalmatia, country on the east coast of the Adriatic Sea; Illyricum, -i (n.): territory of the Illyrians, east of the Adriatic Sea; Raetia, -ae (f.): region in the Alps, including the Tyrol and parts of Bavaria and Switzerland; Vindelici, -orum (m. pl.): a people situated b/w Raetia and the Danube; Salassi, -orum (m. pl.): a sub-Alpine tribe in northwest Italy; Inalpinus, -a, -um: living in the Alps

coerceo, coercere, coercui, coercitum restrain within bounds, confine, restrict (<con- + arceo)
Daci, -orum (m. pl.) the Dacians, a people north of the Danube
incursio, -onis (f.) attack, raid; Dacian incursions occurred in 11–10 BCE, 6 CE, and perhaps also 13–14 CE
tribus ... ducibus ... caesis abl. abs. (AG #419); tres, tria (pl. adj.): three (for decl., s. AG #134b); copia, -ae (f.): body of men; caedo, caedere, cecidi, caesum: kill
ultra (prep. + acc.) beyond, to the farther side of
Albis, -is (m.) the river Elbe in Germany; the area b/w the Rhine and Elbe was conquered during 12–8 BCE, but was not securely held (s. ch. 23)
fluuius, -(i)i (m.) river, stream
summoueo, summouere, summoui, summotum move away, drive off, expel (<sub- + moueo)
quibus (relat. pron.) anteced. *Germanos*
Suebos ... dedentis se ptc. phr., acc. obj. of *traduxit*; Suebi, -orum (m. pl.): the Suebi, German tribes centered east of the Elbe; Sugambri, -orum (m. pl.): the Sugambri, a German tribe situated east of the Rhine; dedo, dedere, dedidi, deditum: (reflex.) give oneself up, surrender; *dedentis*: acc. pl.
traduco, traducere, traduxi, traductum move, transfer (<trans- + duco)
Gallia, -ae (f.) Gaul
Rhenus, -i (m.) the Rhine river; *Rheno*: dat. w/ *proximis* (AG #384)
conloco (1) put in a particular place, settle (<con- + loco)
natio, -onis (f.) people, nation
male quietas "restless" (LITOTES, AG #641); quietus, -a, -um: at rest, free from war, peaceful
obsequium, -(i)i (n.) compliance, servility, allegiance

21.2
ulli genti dat. indir. obj. w/ *intulit*
sine iustis ... causis iustus, -a, -um: lawful, just, having good cause; necessarius, -a, -um: essential, necessary; Augustus is reported to have maintained the longstanding Roman principle that wars were undertaken for self-defense or the defense of allies
infero, inferre, intuli, illatum carry into (<in- + fero); bellum inferre (+ dat.): make war on (*OLD* 9c)
tantumque afuit "and he was so far removed"
a cupiditate ... augendi "from a desire for increasing"; cupiditas, -atis (f.): desire, ambition (w/ obj. gen. *augendi*); *quoquo modo*: "by any means"; bellicus, -a, -um: military; gloria, -ae (f.): honor, glory; *augendi*: gen. of ger. w/ dir. obj. (AG #504a); Suet. here stresses the idea that Augustus' military campaigns were justified, not motived by bold ambition
ut ... coegerit result cl. (AG #537); barbarus, -i (m.): a foreigner; *in aede Martis Vltoris*: "in the temple of Mars Ultor," the temple which was the focal point of Augustus' new forum and became a

aede Martis Vltoris iurare coegerit mansuros se in fide ac pace
quam peterent, a quibusdam uero—nouum genus obsidum—
feminas exigere temptauerit quod neglegere marum pignera
sentiebat, et tamen potestatem semper omnibus fecit quotiens
uellent obsides recipiendi. neque aut crebrius aut perfidiosius
rebellantis grauiore umquam ultus est poena quam ut captiuos
sub lege uenundaret ne in uicina regione seruirent neue intra
tricensimum annum liberarentur. 3. qua uirtutis moderationisque fama Indos etiam ac Scythas auditu modo cognitos

---

    center for foreign affairs (s. ch. 29.1–2); *iuro* (1): swear, affirm by oath; *iurare*: inf. w/ vb. of comm. (AG #563a)

mansuros [esse] **se in ... pace** indir. disc. (AG #580) ff. *iurare*; *fides, -ei* (f.): trust, loyalty; *pax, pacis* (f.): pact, peace

quam peterent relat. cl. w/ subjv. in indir. disc. (AG #580); *quam* (relat. pron.): anteced. *pace*

a quibusdam ... temptauerit a second result cl. (AG #537); *obses, -idis* (m./f.): hostage; *femina, -ae* (f.): woman; *feminas* in appos. w/ *genus* (AG #282); *exigere*: compl. inf. w/ *temptauerit* (AG #456); *tempto* (1): try

quod ... sentiebat causal cl. (AG #540) containing indir. disc.; [*eos*] *neglegere marum pignera*: indir. disc. ff. *sentiebat* (AG #580); *neglego, neglegere, neglexi, neglectum*: disregard, fail to respect (<nec- + lego); *mas, maris* (m.): male; *marum*: appos. gen. (AG #343d); *pignus, -eris* (n.): pledge, hostage; *sentio, sentire, sensi, sensum*: perceive, sense

potestatem ... recipiendi "the opportunity to recover"; *potestas, -tatis* (f.): opportunity (w/ gen. of ger.); *fecit*: pf. w/ *semper* where impf. is expected; *quotiens uellent*: "whenever they wished," iterative subjv. w/ *quotiens* (BG #567n)

neque (conj. adv.) and not, nor

aut crebrius ... rebellantis ptc. phr., dir. obj. of *ultus est*; *crebro* (adv.): frequently, often (compar. = -brius); *perfidiose* (adv.): treacherously (compar. = -ius); *rebello* (1): revolt, rebel (<re- + bello); *rebellantis*: acc. pl. subst, "those rebelling"; the use of two compar. adv. here adds emphasis to Augustus' restrained response

grauiore ... poena abl. of means introd. compar. w/ *quam*

ulciscor, ulcisci, ultus sum take vengeance on

quam ut ... uenundaret "than that he put up for sale," subst. cl. of result ff. *quam* after compar. (AG #571a); *captiuus, -a, -um*: captured in war, (subst.) a captive; *sub lege*: "under the provision"; *uenundo, uenundare*: put up for sale

ne seruirent neue ... liberarentur "that they not serve ... or be freed"; proviso cl. (AG #528); *seruio, seruire, seruiui (-ii), seruitum*: serve as a slave; *uicinus, -a, -um*: neighboring; *regio, -onis* (f.): district, region; *intra tricensimum annum*: "for thirty years"; *libero* (1): free, manumit, release

21.3

qua ... fama "by this reputation"; *qua*: relat. pron. as connective (AG #308f); *uirtus, -utis* (f.): valor, virtue, excellence; *moderatio, -onis* (f.): restraint, moderation; *uirtutis moderationisque*: objv. gen. (AG #348); *fama, -ae* (f.): reputation, renown

Indos ... cognitos ptc. phr., obj. of *pellexit*; *Indus, -i* (m.): Indian, an inhabitant of India; *Scythes, -ae* (m.): Scythian, belonging to a people from north of the Black Sea; *auditus, -us* (m.): hearing, hearsay

pellexit ad amicitiam suam populique Rom. ultro per legatos petendam. Parthi quoque et Armeniam uindicanti facile cesserunt et signa militaria quae M. Crasso et M. Antonio ademerant reposcenti reddiderunt obsidesque insuper optulerunt, denique pluribus quondam de regno concertantibus non nisi ab ipso
22 electum probauerunt. Ianum Quirinum semel atque iterum a condita urbe ante memoriam suam clausum in multo breuiore temporis spatio terra marique pace parta ter clusit. bis ouans ingressus est urbem, post Philippense et rursus post Siculum

---

pellicio, pellicere, pellexi, pellectum induce (w/ *ad*) (<per- + lacio)
ad amicitiam ... petendam ad + gerv. to denote purp. (AG #506); amicitia, -ae (f.): friendship; *populi Rom[ani]*; ultro (adv.): of one's own accord (*OLD* 5)
Parthi, -orum (m. pl.) Parthians, people of Parthia to the south of the Caspian Sea; *Parthi*: nom. pl. subj.
Armenia, -ae (f.) Armenia
uindico (1) assert one's title to, lay claim to; *uindicanti* [*Augusto*]: indir. obj. w/ *cesserunt*
cedo, cedere, cessi, cessum yield, give up
signum, -i (n.) military standard; the Parthians had captured Roman legionary standards after defeating M. Licinius Crassus in 53 BCE (*OCD* s.v. Licinius Crassus (1), Marcus, 833) and M. Antony in 36 BCE; the standards were recovered in 20 BCE
quae (relat. pron.) anteced. *signa*, obj. of *ademerant*
reposco, reposcere demand back (<re- + posco); *reposcenti* [*Augusto*]: indir. obj. w/ *reddiderunt*
insuper (adv.) in addition, as well
pluribus ... concertantibus abl. abs. (AG #419); regnum, -i (n.): the office of king, kingship; concerto (1): contend, dispute (<con- + certo)
non nisi ab ipso electum probauerunt "they did not approve [a new king] unless he had been chosen by Augustus"; nisi: unless, describing a unique condition (AG #525a.1); eligo, eligere, elegi, electum: select, choose (<ex- + lego); probo (1): give approval to, approve of; Suet. overstates Augustus' role here; although Vonones was returned to Parthia from Rome to take up the kingship in 8 CE, others had taken the throne without Augustus being consulted

22.

Ianum Quirinum ... clausum ptc. phr., dir. obj. of *clusit*; Ianus Quirinus: the shrine of Janus Quirinus located in the Roman Forum; *semel atque iterum*: once and again, twice only; claudo, claudere, clausi, clausum: close, shut; the gates of the shrine stood open whenever the Roman state was at war and were only closed on the rare occasions when peace was secured
multo abl. of deg. of diff. (AG #414)
brevis, -e short (compar. = -ior)
spatium, -ii (n.) period, stretch of time
terra ... pace parta abl. abs. (AG #419); *terra marique*: "on land and sea," abl. of place where w/out prep. (AG #429); mare, -is (n.): sea; pax, pacis (f.): peace; pario, parere, peperi, partum: produce, create
ter (adv.) three times; closure of the gates of Janus Quirinus are attested for 29 and 25 BCE; the date of the third closure is contested
bis (adv.) twice, on two occasions; Augustus celebrated ovations in 40 and 36 BCE
ouo (1) celebrate a minor triumph or ovation

bellum. curulis triumphos tris egit, Delmaticum, Actiacum, Alexandrinum, continuo triduo omnes.

23 Graues ignominias cladesque duas omnino nec alibi quam in Germania accepit, Lollianam et Varianam, sed Lollianam maioris infamiae quam detrimenti, Varianam paene exitiabilem tribus legionibus cum duce legatisque et auxiliis omnibus caesis. hac nuntiata excubias per urbem indixit ne quis tumultus existeret et praesidibus prouinciarum propagauit imperium ut a peritis et assuetis socii continerentur.   2. uouit et magnos

---

curulis triumphos "curule triumphs," victory parades celebrated by driving a chariot through the city of Rome; curulis, -e: belonging to a chariot; the only other use of this unusual phr. is found in *RG* 22; Suet.'s use of this phr. here is the strongest evidence that he consulted Augustus' tomb inscription as a source; Augustus celebrated his triple triumph on August 13–15, 29 BCE
tres, tria (pl. adj.) three (for decl., s. AG #134b)
continuo triduo abl. of time within which (*AG* #423.1); triduum, -i (n.): space of three days

Military disgraces and defeats (*graves ignominias cladesque*). The next chapter explores military setbacks and disasters. The decision to include this topic demonstrates that Suetonius is not writing a simple panegyric, but rather is striving to present a balanced and comprehensive biography. As with his discussion of the wars, the focus here is on the response and actions of Augustus himself.

23.1
ignominia, -ae (f.) military disgrace
clades, -is (f.) disaster, military defeat
alibi (adv.) in another place, elsewhere; introd. compar. w/ *quam*
Lollianam et Varianam "Lollius' disaster and that of Varius"; acc. in appos. w/ *ignominias cladesque duas* (AG #282); M. Lollius (*OCD* 857) was defeated as legate in Gaul, probably in 16 BCE; P. Quinctilius Varus (*OCD* 1250) was legate on the Rhine when he was defeated in 9 CE
maioris ... detrimenti "of greater dishonor than actual loss," gen. of quality (AG #345); infamia, -ae (f.): dishonor; *maioris* introd. compar. w/ *quam* (AG #407); detrimentum, -i (n.): harm, loss
exitiabilis, -e fatal, deadly
tribus legionibus ... et auxiliis omnibus caesis abl. abs. (AG #419); auxilia, -orum (n. pl.): auxiliary forces; caedo, caedere, cecidi, caesum: kill
hac nuntiata tmp. abl. abs. (AG #420.1); nuntio (1): announce
excubiae, -arum (f. pl.) the keeping of a watch, guard
indico, indicere, indixi, indictum proclaim, impose (<in- + dico)
ne ... existeret negat. purp. cl. (AG #531); *quis* = aliquis: some (AG #310); existo, existere, extiti: arise (<ex- + sisto)
praeses, -idis (m.) a governor (of a province); *praesidibus*: dat. indir. obj. w/ *propagauit*
propagauit imperium "prolonged their command"; propago (1): prolong, continue
ut ... socii continerentur purp. cl. (AG #531); peritus, -a, -um: experienced; assuetus, -a, -um: familiar; *a peritis et assuetis*: subst., abl. of agent (AG #405); socius, -(i)i (m.): an ally, a provincial; contineo, continere, continui, contentum: hold together, contain (<con- + teneo)

23.2
uoueo, uouere, uoui, uotum vow, promise to a god
magnos ludos "great games"; ludi magni were extraordinary games established by a vow

ludos Ioui Optimo Maximo si res p. in meliorem statum
uertisset, quod factum Cimbrico Marsicoque bello erat. adeo
denique consternatum ferunt ut per continuos menses barba
capilloque summisso caput interdum foribus illideret uocife-
rans, 'Quintili Vare, legiones redde!', diemque cladis quotannis
maestum habuerit ac lugubrem.

24 In re militari et commutauit multa et instituit atque etiam ad
antiquum morem nonnulla reuocauit. disciplinam seuerissime
rexit: ne legatorum quidem cuiquam, nisi grauate hibernisque

Iupiter Optimus Maximus Jupiter "Best and Greatest," whose temple was on the Capitoline Hill in Rome
si res p[ublica] . . . uertisset "if the state should change"; plupf. subjv. for fut. pf. in prot. of FMV condit.
   in indir. disc. ff. *uouit* (AG #589a.3); melior, -ius: better, more favorable (compar. of bonus); status, -us
   (m.): condition, state; uerto, uertere, uerti, uersum: turn, change; the games vowed by Augustus were
   never held, as the territory in Germany was not recovered
quod factum . . . erat "a thing which had been done"; *Cimbrico Marsicoque bello*: abl. of time when
   (AG #424d); the Cimbric war dates to 105–101 BCE; the Marsic, to 90–88 BCE.
denique (adv.) finally, indeed
consternatum [esse] indir. disc. (AG #580) ff. *ferunt*, "they say"; Augustus is the implied acc. subj.; consterno
   (1): shock, mentally disturb (<con- + sterno)
ut . . . illideret result cl. (AG #537); *barba capilloque summisso*: abl. abs. (AG #419); barba, -ae (f.): beard;
   capillus, -i (m.): hair; summitto, summittere, summisi, summissum: allow to grow long (<sub- + mitto);
   summisso: sg. ptc. in place of pl. (AG #286a); caput, -itis (n.): head; foris, -is (f.): door, doorway; illido,
   illidere, illisi, illisum: to beat, strike against (w/ acc. *caput* and dat. *foribus*) (<in- + laedo)
uociferor (1) shout, cry out
redde sg. impv.
diemque . . . habuerit a second result cl. (AG #537); quotannis (adv.): every year; maestus, -a, -um:
   mournful; *habuerit*: pf. subjv. to denote past action (AG #485b), "he considered"; lugubris, -e:
   inducing sorrow, grievous; *maestum . . . ac lugubrem*: pred. acc. (AG #393)

Other military matters (*re militari*). Chapters 24–25 consider other matters related to military affairs.
This section provides a bridge between the preceding treatment of wars and the upcoming discussion of
magistracies and civil administration.

24.1
re militari "military affairs"; Suet. often uses res w/ adj. in place of a noun (cf. ch. 1.1: *rem diuinam*)
commuto (1) change, alter (<con- + muto)
antiquus, -a, -um ancient, old
nonnulla n. acc. pl. subst. (AG #288)
reuoco (1) recall, restore (<re- + uoco)
disciplina, -ae (f.) orderly conduct, military discipline; *disciplinam*: cognate acc. (BG #333.2); strict
   military discipline was a traditional Roman virtue
seuere (adv.) rigorously, with strictness (superl. = -issime); Suet. frequently uses superl. adv.
rego, regere, rexi, rectum direct, exercise
legatus, -i (m.) lieutenant, deputy, legate; Augustus ruled the provinces assigned to him through legates
cuiquam dat. indir. obj. w/ *permisit*
grauate (adv.) grudgingly, reluctantly

demum mensibus, permisit uxorem interuisere; equitem
R., quod duobus filiis adulescentibus causa detrectandi sacra-
menti pollices amputasset, ipsum bonaque subiecit hastae,
quem tamen, quod inminere emptioni publicanos uidebat,
liberto suo addixit, ut relegatum in agros pro libero esse sineret;
2. decimam legionem contumacius parentem cum ignominia
totam dimisit, item alias immodeste missionem postulantes

---

hibernisque demum mensibus abl. of time within which (AG #424b); hibernus, -a, -um: of or belonging to winter
uxorem ... interuisere subst. cl. of purp w/ inf. (AG #563c) ff. *permisit*; *uxorem*: acc. obj. of *interuisere*; interuiso, interuisere, interuisi, interuisum: go and see, pay a visit (<inter- + uiso)
equitem R[omanum] a Roman knight (*OCD* s.v. equites, 530–532)
quod ... amputasset causal cl. w/ subjv. indicating authority of another (AG #540); *filiis*: dat. of separ. (AG #381); adulescens, -ntis: young, youthful; *causa* (abl.): "for the sake of," w/ gen. of gerv. to express purp. (AG #504b); note unusual placement of causa before gerv.; detrecto (1): evade, refuse to undertake (<de- + tracto); sacramentum, -i (n.): oath, the military oath of allegiance; by METONYMY, "military service" (AG #641); pollex, -icis (m.): thumb; amputo (1): cut off; *amputasset* = contr. form of amputauisset (AG #181)
ipsum bonaque "the man himself and his possessions"; bonum, -i (n.): property (*OLD* 8)
subiecit hastae "he put up for auction"; hasta, -ae (f.): spear; a spear was set up at public auctions as though the sale were of military plunder
quem (relat. pron.) anteced. *ipsum* (the eques), obj. of *addixit*
quod inminere emptioni publicanos uidebat causal cl. w/ indic. (AG #540) w/ indir. disc. (AG #580) ff. *uidebat*; inmineo, inminere: be intent on (w/ dat. *emptioni*; emptio, -onis (f.): purchasing; publicanus, -i (m.): tax collector
liberto suo addixit "he (= Augustus) awarded him to one of his own freedmen"; addico, addicere, addixi, addictum: assign legally, adjudge (w/ dat.) (<ad- + dico); by this action the eques came indirectly under Augustus' authority
ut ... sineret purp. cl. (AG #531) introd. subst. cl. of purp. (= indir. comm.) w/ inf. *relegatum ... esse* (AG #563c); relego (1): banish to a specified place (<re- + lego); *pro libero*: "as a free man"; sino, sinere, siui (sii), situm: allow; relegatio in agros was a relatively mild form of banishment where the individual could remain in Italy under watch

24.2

decimam legionem ... parentem ... totam ptc. phr., obj. of *dimisit*; decimus, -a, -um: tenth; contumaciter (adv.): stubbornly, defiantly (compar. = -ius); pareo, parere, parui, paritum: obey commands; *contumacius parentem*: OXYMORON (AG #641); ignominia, -ae (f.): disgrace, military disgrace with loss of status; totus, -a, -um: whole, entire; the tenth Legion was given a dishonorable discharge for insubordination
alias ... postulantes ptc. phr., obj. of *exauctorauit*; immodeste (adv.): immoderately, impudently; missio, -onis (f.): discharge from service; postulo (1): ask for, demand

citra commoda emeritorum praemiorum exauctorauit;
cohortes, si quae cessissent loco, decimatas hordeo pauit; centuriones statione deserta itidem ut manipulares capitali animaduersione puniit, pro cetero delictorum genere uariis ignominis
adfecit, ut stare per totum diem iuberet ante praetorium, interdum tunicatos discinctosque, nonnumquam cum decempedis,
uel etiam caespitem portantes.

25 Neque post bella ciuilia aut in contione aut per edictum ullos
militum 'commilitones' appellabat, sed 'milites', ac ne a filiis

---

citra (prep. + acc.) without the use of, without regard to

commoda emeritorum praemiorum "the benefits of the rewards that they had earned" (BRACHYLOGY, AG #640); emereo, emerere, emerui, emeritum: obtain by merit, earn (<ex- + mereo); Suet. refers to the benefits paid to soldiers upon completion of their service

exauctoro (1) release from military service, dismiss dishonorably (<ex- + auctoro)

cohortes...decimatas tmp. ptc. phr. (AG #496), obj. of *pauit*, "after the forces had been decimated"; cohors, -rtis (f.): armed force, cohort; *si quae cessissent loco*: mixed gener. condit. w/ plupf. subjv. indicating repeated action in the past (AG #518c), "if any [cohorts] yielded ground"; *quae* = aliquae; cedo, cedere, cessi, cessum: yield, give ground (w/ *loco*) (*OLD* 3b); decimo (1): decimate, punish with death every tenth man

hordeum, -i (n.) barley, the regular feed for pack animals who travelled with the legions; wheat was the normal ration for soldiers, but barley might be substituted as a punishment

pasco, pascere, paui, pastum feed, supply (troops) with

centurio, -onis (m.) centurion, an officer commanding a military century

statione deserta condit. abl. abs. (AG #420.4); statio, -onis (f.): military post; desero, deserere, deserui, desertum: leave, desert (<de- + sero)

itidem (adv.) in the same way, similarly (w/ *ut*)

manipularis, -is (m.) common soldier

capitali animaduersione "with capital punishment"; capitalis, -e: capital, involving death; animaduersio, -onis (f.): punishment; capital punishment was an extreme penalty for an officer

punio, punire, puniui (-ii), punitum punish

pro...genere prep. phr.; delictum, -i (n): misdeed, offence

ignominis contr. form of ignominiis (AG #43e, n2); ignominia, -ae (f.): a disgrace, loss of status

adficio, adficere, adfeci, adfectum affect, cause to suffer (+ abl.) (<ad- + facio)

ut...iuberet...portantes "such as when he ordered"; explanatory consecutive cl. (= result cl.) (AG #537, BG #557) introd. subst. cl. of purp. (= indir. comm.) ff. *iuberet* w/ inf. and implied subj. acc. eos (AG #563a); Suet. here provides an example of a punishment that combines public shaming with physical ordeal; sto, stare, steti, statum: stand, stand up; totus, -a, -um: the whole, entire; praetorium, -(i)i (n.): general's headquarters; tunicatus, -a, -um: wearing a tunic; discinctus, -a, -um: not wearing a belt; decempeda, -ae (f.): a measuring pole ten feet long; caespes, -itis (m.): sod, turf cut from the ground; porto (1): carry

25.1

ciuilis, -e civil, suited to a citizen

contio, -onis (f.) public meeting, assembly

militum partit. gen. (AG #346a.2)

commilito, -onis (m.) fellow soldier, comrade; commilito was a casual term, regularly used by Julius Caesar

appello (1) refer to, address as (w/ dir. obj. + pred. acc., AG #393)

ne...quidem "not even" (AG #322f)

quidem aut priuignis suis imperio praeditis aliter appellari passus est, ambitiosius id existimans quam aut ratio militaris aut temporum quies aut sua domusque suae maiestas postularet. **2.** libertino milite, praeterquam Romae incendiorum causa et si tumultus in grauiore annona metueretur, bis usus est, semel ad praesidium coloniarum Illyricum contingentium, iterum ad tutelam ripae Rheni fluminis, eosque seruos adhuc

---

a filiis ... priuignis ... praeditis abl. of agent (AG #405); *priuignus, -i* (m.): stepson; *praeditus, -a, -um*: endowed with, provided with (adj. w/ abl.); *filiis* = Gaius and Lucius Caesar; *priuignis* = Tiberius and Drusus; s. introduction for family tree

aliter appellari passus est "he allowed them [the soldiers] to be addressed otherwise [than as 'soldiers']"; subst. cl. of purp. w/ inf. (AG #563c) ff. *passus est*

ambitiosius id pred. acc. and dir. obj. ff. *existimans* (AG #393); *ambitiosus, -a, -um*: ingratiating, self-serving (*OLD* 2b) (compar. = -ior)

quam ... ratio ... postularet subst. cl. of result ff. *quam* after compar. (AG #571a), "than military discipline ... requires"; *ratio militaris*: "military discipline"; *quies, -ietis* (f.): peaceful conditions, calm; *maiestas, -atis* (f.): dignity, majesty; *postulo* (1): demand, require

25.2

libertino milite collective sg., abl. w/ *usus est*, "he used freedmen as soldiers"; *libertinus, -i* (m.): freedman, former slave (alt. form of libertus)

praeterquam (conj.) except, apart from

Romae locat. (AG #427.3)

incendiorum causa "for the sake of [fighting] fires"; *incendium, -(i)i* (n.): conflagration, destructive fire; *causa* (abl.): "for the sake of" (w/ gen.)

si ... metueretur prot. of mixed gener. condit. w/ impf. subjv. indicating repeated action in present (AG #518c); *in grauiore annona*: "in times of severe food shortages"; *annona, -ae* (f.): grain supply (of Rome); *metuo, metuere, metui, metutum*: fear; especially severe shortages occurred in 6–8 CE

bis (adv.) twice, on two occasions; Suet. expands on the two occasions: *semel ... iterum*

semel (adv.) once

ad praesidium "for a garrison"; *praesidium, -(i)i* (n.): defence, garrison; *ad* + acc., indicating the end or purp. (BG #340r.2); the special garrisons were instituted during the Pannonian revolt in 6 CE

coloniarum Illyricum contingentium "for the colonies bordering Illyricum," objv. gen. (AG #348); *colonia, -ae* (f.): settlement, colony; *Illyricum, -i* (n.): territory of the Illyrians, east of the Adriatic Sea; *contingo, contingere, contigi, contactum*: be in contact with, be connected with (+ acc.) (<con- + tango)

tutela, -ae (f.) protection, defence

ripa, -ae (f.) bank (of a river)

Rhenus, -i (m.) the Rhine river; the Rhine was reinforced following the defeat of Varus in 9 CE (s. ch. 23.1)

flumen, -inis (n.) river

eosque seruos ... indictos ... manumissos ptc. phr., dir. obj. of *habuit*, "slaves provided by wealthy men and women and freed without delay"; *pecuniosus, -a, -um*: well provided with money, moneyed (compar. = -ior); *indico, indicere, indixi, indictum*: impose the obligation of providing (w/ dat.) (<in- + dico); *mora, -ae* (f.): delay; *manumitto, manumittere, manumisi, manumissum*: emancipate, free

uiris feminisque pecuniosioribus indictos ac sine mora manumissos sub priore uexillo habuit neque aut commixtos cum ingenuis aut eodem modo armatos. **3.** Dona militaria aliquanto facilius phaleras et torques, quicquid auro argentoque constaret quam uallares ac murales coronas, quae honore praecellerent, dabat. has quam parcissime et sine ambitione ac saepe etiam caligatis tribuit. M. Agrippam in Sicilia post naualem uictoriam caeruleo uexillo donauit. solos triumphales,

---

sub priore uexillo "under a separate standard"; prior, prius: former (compar. adj.); uexillum, -i (n.): military standard; the meaning here is unclear as these new recruits would not have had a "former" standard under which to fight
commisceo, commiscere, commiscui, commixtum mix together, combine (<con- + misceo)
ingenuus, -a, -um freeborn
eodem modo "in the same manner"
armo (1) arm, furnish with weapons

25.3
dona militaria "military decorations," awards to soldiers for distinguished service; donum, -i (n.): gift, award
facilius compar. adv. w/ *quam*
phaleras et torques acc. in appos. w/ *dona*; phalerae, -arum (f. pl.): metal discs (worn as an ornament); torques, -is (m.): collar or neckband of twisted metal
quicquid ... constaret relat. cl. of char. (AG #535); quisquid, quicquid: anyone who, anything that, whatever; aurum, -i (n.): gold; argentum, -i (n.): silver; consto, constare, constiti: be composed of (w/ abl.) (<con- + sto)
uallares ac muralles coronas "crowns for scaling ramparts and city walls," crowns (coronae) awarded to the soldier who first storms the defences of an enemy camp (uallum) or city wall (murus)
quae ... praecellerent relat. cl. of char. (AG #535); *honore*: abl. of specif. (AG #418); praecello, praecellere: be superior to others, excel
has = coronas
quam parcissime "as seldom as possible," *quam* w/ superl. (AG #291c); parce (adv.): sparingly
ambitio, -onis (f.) partiality (*OLD* 5)
caligatus, -a, -um wearing military boots; (m. subst.): a common soldier
tribuo, tribuere, tribui, tributum grant, award
M. Vipsanius Agrippa (*OCD* 1554–1555) lifelong friend and later son-in-law of Augustus (s. ch. 63.1); for Agrippa's role in the Sicilian war, s. ch. 16.2
naualis, -e naval, of or belonging to a ship
caeruleus, -a, -um blue, colored blue
uexillum, -i (n.) military standard; the awarding of a blue standard to Agrippa for his naval victory was an innovation
solos triumphales ... impertiendos [esse] "that only triumphant generals should never be given a share," indir. disc. (AG #580) ff. *putauit*; triumphalis, -e: (subst.) "triumphant generals"; socius, -(i)i (m.): companion, partner; expeditio, -onis (f.): military operation; particeps, -cipis: participating in, having a share of; impertio, impertire, impertiui (-ii), impertitum: give a share of (w/ dat.); *impertiendos* [*esse*]: pass. periphr. (AG #196, 500)

quamquam et socios expeditionum et participes uictoriarum
suarum, numquam donis impertiendos putauit, quod ipsi
quoque ius habuissent tribuendi ea quibus uellent.

    4. Nihil autem minus perfecto duci quam festinationem
temeritatemque conuenire arbitrabatur. crebro itaque illa
iactabat, σπεῦδε βραδέως,

        ἀσφαλὴς γὰρ ἐστ' ἀμείνων ἢ θρασὺς στρατηλάτης,
et 'sat celeriter fieri quidquid fiat satis bene'. proelium quidem
aut bellum suscipiendum omnino negabat nisi cum maior
emolumenti spes quam damni metus ostenderetur. nam minima commoda non minimo sectantis discrimine similes aiebat
esse aureo hamo piscantibus, cuius abrupti damnum nulla
captura pensari posset.

---

quod ... habuissent causal cl. (AG #540); *tribuendi*: gen. of ger. w/ *ius*: "the right of awarding"; *ea*: "these things"; *quibus uellent*: "to whomever they wished"; *uellent*: subjv. by attraction (AG #593)

25.4

nihil ... conuenire indir. disc. (AG #580) ff. *arbitrabatur*; minus (compar. adv.): less, introd. compar. w/ *quam*; perfectus, -a, -um: mature, experienced; festinatio, -onis (f.): undue haste; temeritas, -atis (f.): recklessness, impetuosity; conuenio, conuenire, conueni, conuentum: be consistent with, befit (w/ dat. *perfecto duci*) (<con- + uenio)

arbitror (1) judge, consider

crebro (adv.) frequently, often

itaque postpos., as often in Suet.

illa "these things," obj. of *iactabat*; the following quotes in Greek and Latin are in appos.

iacto (1) toss out, utter with force

σπεῦδε βραδέως "make haste slowly," a Gk. aphorism

ἀσφαλὴς γὰρ ἐστ' ἀμείνων ἢ θρασὺς στρατηλάτης "a safe commander is better than a bold one," a quote from Euripides' tragedy *Phoenissae*

sat celeriter fieri quidquid fiat satis bene "whatever is done well enough is done quickly enough"; sat (adv.): enough, sufficiently; celeriter (adv.): quickly; probably an adaptation of a well-known saying of Cato the Elder

proelium ... suscipiendum [esse] indir. disc. (AG #580) ff. *negabat*; *suscipiendum* [*esse*]: pass. periphr. (AG #196, 500)

cum ... spes ... ostenderetur circumst. cum cl. (AG #546); *maior*: introd. compar. w/ *quam*; emolumentum, -i (n.): advantage, benefit; damnum, -i (n.): loss

minima ... sectantis ... similes ... esse ... piscantibus indir. disc. (AG #580) ff. *aiebat*: "he used to say"; minimus, -a, -um: smallest, least important; *commoda*: acc. pl. obj. of *sectantis*; sector (1): follow, pursue; *sectantis*: acc. pl. subst. subj. of indir. disc., "men pursuing"; discrimen, -inis (n.): risk, dangerous situation; *similes*: pred. acc. (w/ dat. *piscantibus*); hamus, -i (m.): a fish-hook; piscor (1): fish; *piscantibus*: pres. act. ptc. dat. pl. subst., "to men fishing"

cuius ... damnum ... posset relat. cl. w/ subjv. in indir. disc. (AG #580), "the loss of which was able"; *cuius*: anteced. *hamo*; abrumpo, abrumpere, abrupi, abruptum: break, break off (<ab- + rumpo); captura, -ae (f.): gain, act of catching (fish), here = the amount of fish caught; penso (1): compensate, make up for with (w/ abl. *nulla captura*)

26 Magistratus atque honores et ante tempus et quosdam noui
generis perpetuosque cepit. consulatum uicesimo aetatis anno
inuasit admotis hostiliter ad urbem legionibus missisque qui
sibi nomine exercitus deposcerent, cum quidem cunctante
senatu Cornelius centurio, princeps legationis, reiecto sagulo
ostendens gladii capulum non dubitasset in curia dicere, 'hic
faciet, si uos non feceritis'. 2. secundum consulatum post
nouem annos, tertium anno interiecto gessit, sequentis usque

Magistracies and public offices (*magistratus atque honores*). Suetonius treats all of Augustus' political posts collectively as a distinct category within the biography, counter to the practice of writers of annalistic history, who focus on the actions of magistrates during each year in office.

26.1
magistratus atque honores "magistracies and formal positions"; honor, -oris (m.): elective political office (*OLD* 5); the distinction b/w the two terms may refer here to the consulship, which is treated in ch. 26, and other special powers and positions that Augustus was voted, which are taken up in ch. 27

ante tempus "before the established time"; Augustus did not follow the traditional minimum age requirements and mandated intervals b/w magistracies

noui generis gen. of quality (AG #345); the "new type" refers to the triumvirate (s. ch. 27.1–4)

perpetuos a reference to tribunician power and supervision of morals (s. ch. 27.5)

uicesimo aetatis anno "in his twentieth year" (age nineteen, in Roman reckoning), abl. of time when (AG #423.1); Augustus entered his first consulship on August 19, 43 BCE, just a month shy of his twentieth birthday

inuado, inuadere, inuasi, inuasum seize possession of, usurp, push one's way into (<in- + uado); *inuasit* is a strong vb. that emphasizes the unusual circumstances

admotis ... legionibus missisque abl. abs. w/ two cl.; admoueo, admouere, admoui, admotum: move, bring up (<ad- + moueo); hostiliter (adv.): in a hostile way, in the manner of an enemy; the relat. cl. that follows defines those who were sent

qui ... deposcerent relat. cl. of purp. (AG #531.2); *qui*: relat. pron. w/out anteced. (AG #307c); *nomine* + gen.: "in the name of"; deposco, deposcere, deposci: demand (<de- + posco)

cum ... non dubitasset ... dicere circumst. cum cl. (AG #546); *cunctante senatu*: causal abl. abs. (AG #420.2); cunctor (1): be slow in taking action, hesitate; centurio, -onis (m.): centurion; legatio, -onis (f.): embassy; *reiecto sagulo*: abl. abs.; reicio, reicere, reieci, reiectum: push back (<re- + iacio); sagulum, -i (n.): woolen cloak, military cloak; gladius, -(i)i (m.): sword; capulus, -i (m.): sword-handle, hilt; dubito (1): hesitate; *dubitasset* = contr. form of dubitauisset (AG #181); curia, -ae (f.): the meeting-place of the senate, a meeting of the senate; *dicere*: compl. inf. (AG #456)

hic faciet, si uos non feceritis FMV condit. w/ fut. pf. in apod. (AG #516c); *hic* = gladius; Suet. presents as a dir. quote the threat of the centurion; Augustum consulem is understood as dir. obj. and pred. acc.

26.2
nouem (indecl. adj.) nine

anno interiecto abl. abs. (AG #419); intericio, intericere, interieci, interiectum: insert, place between (<inter- + iacio); Augustus held his second consulship in 33 BCE, his third in 31 BCE.

sequentis [consulatus] **... continuauit** "he held the following consulships up to the eleventh without break"; *sequentis*: acc. pl.; undecimus, -a, -um: eleventh; continuo (1): make continuous, renew (an office) without break; Augustus was consul each year from 30 to 23 BCE

ad undecimum continuauit multisque mox cum deferrentur
recusatis duodecimum magno—id est septemdecim annorum—
interuallo et rursus tertium decimum biennio post ultro petit
ut C. et Lucium filios amplissimo praeditus magistratu suo
quemque tirocinio deduceret in forum. 3. quinque medios
consulatus a sexto ad decimum annuos gessit, ceteros aut
nouem aut sex aut quattuor aut tribus mensibus, secundum
uero paucissimis horis. nam die Kal. Ian., cum mane pro aede
Capitolini Iouis paululum curuli sella praesedisset, honore abiit

---

multisque [consulatibus] ... **recusatis** abl. abs. (AG #419) interrupted by circumst. cum cl. (AG #546); defero, deferre, detuli, delatum: offer (<de- + fero); recuso (1): decline
duodecimus, -a, -um twelfth; Augustus' twelfth consulship dates to 5 BCE
magno ... interuallo abl. abs. w/out ptc. (AG #419a) or abl. of deg. of diff. w/ *post* (AG #414); septemdecim (indecl. adj.): seventeen; interuallum, -i (n.): an interval, an intervening period of time
tertium decimum [consulatum] Augustus' thirteenth consulship dates to 2 BCE
biennio post ultro "after another two year period"; *biennio*: abl. of deg. of diff. (AG #414)
ut ... deduceret purp. cl. (AG #531); praeditus, -a, -um: endowed with, provided with (adj. w/ abl. *magistratu*); *quemque*: acc. obj. of *deduceret* in appos. w/ *C. et Lucium*; *suo tirocinio deduceret in forum*: "introduce in the forum at the start of his public career," a rite of passage that marks the introduction to adulthood and public life; tirocinium, -(i)i (n.): the state of being new to public life (having just assumed the toga uirilis); deduco, deducere, deduxi, deductum: lead down, escort (<de- + duco); for Gaius and Lucius, s. ch. 64.1

26.3
quinque medios consulatus "his five middle consulships," held in the years 28–24 BCE; quinque (indecl. adj.): five
decimus, -a, -um tenth
annuus, -a, -um lasting a year, year-long
ceteros Suet. is probably wrong as it is likely that Augustus also held his fifth consulship, in 29 BCE, for the full year
aut nouem ... aut tribus mensibus abl. instead of acc. for duration of time (AG #424b); sex (indecl. adj.): six; quattuor (indecl. adj.): four; tres, tria (pl. adj.): three; Suet's neat categorization of the length of Augustus' consulships is disputed by scholars; when a consul resigned his position, a suffect consul took office in his place
paucus, -a, -um few, a small number (superl. = -issimus)
die Kal[endarum] **Ian**[uariarum] "on the first of January" (for dates on the Roman calendar, s. AG #631)
cum ... praesedisset circumst. cum cl. (AG #546); mane (adv.): in the morning; *pro aede Capitolini Iouis*: "in front of the temple of Jupiter Capitolinus"; paululum (adv.): for a short while; *curuli sella*: "on the magistrate's chair"; sella, -ae (f.): stool, chair; praesideo, praesidere, praesedi: preside (<prae- + sedeo)
abeo, abire, abii (-iui), abitum go away, resign (from an office) (w/ abl. *honore*) (<ab- + eo)

suffecto alio in locum suum. nec omnes Romae, sed quartum
consulatum in Asia, quintum in insula Samo, octauum et
nonum Tarracone init.

27 Triumuiratum rei p. constituendae per decem annos administrauit, in quo restitit quidem aliquamdiu collegis ne qua fieret
proscriptio sed inceptam utroque acerbius exercuit. namque
illis in multorum saepe personam per gratiam et preces exorabilibus solus magno opere contendit ne cui parceretur
proscripsitque etiam C. Toranium tutorem suum, eundem col-

---

suffecto alio in locum suum abl. abs. (AG #419); sufficio, sufficere, suffeci, suffectum: appoint to a
magistracy in place of another (*OLD* 2) (<sub- + facio)
Romae locat. (AG #427.3); for religious reasons the consulship was entered into in Rome, but military
necessity justified Augustus' breaking tradition
Samos, -i (f.) the island of Samos, in the eastern Aegean
Tarraco, -onis (f.) Tarraco, modern Tarragona on the northeastern coast of Spain; *Tarracone*: locat. (AG #427.3)
ineo, inire, inii (-iui), initum go into, enter into (<in- + eo)

Continuing the discussion of magistracies, Suetonius devotes a chapter to the ten years Augustus served as
triumvir, which he considers a "new kind" of position (s. *noui generis*, ch. 26.1). The discussion here focuses on
Augustus' personal actions and, in contrast to other sections of the biography, is strongly critical of Augustus.

27.1
triumuiratus, -us (m.) the triumvirate, the office of triumvir (s. ch. 8.3); the triumvirate was established
by the Lex Titia in 43 BCE
rei p[ublicae] constituendae "for setting in order the state"; *constituendae*: dat. gerv. to indicate function of
office (AG #505b)
administro (1) perform duties of (an office) (*OLD* 3) (<ad- + ministro)
quo (relat. pron.) anteced. *triumuiratum*
resto, restare, restiti stand firm in opposition (w/ dat. *collegis*) (<re- + sto)
aliquamdiu (adv.) for some time, for a considerable time
collegis Antony and Lepidus were fellow triumviri
ne qua fieret proscriptio negat. purp. cl. (AG #531.1); *qua* = aliqua (AG #310); fio, fieri: be instituted;
proscriptio, -onis (f.): proscription, publication of names of citizens declared outlaws (*OCD* 1223)
incipio, incipere, incepi, inceptum start, begin (<in- + capio); *inceptam* [*proscriptionem*]
utroque abl. of compar. (AG #406)
acerbe (adv.) harshly, cruelly (compar. = -ius)
exerceo, exercere, exercui, exercitum carry on, enforce (<ex- + arceo)
illis ... exorabilibus conces. abl. abs. w/out ptc. (AG #419a, 420.3); *in multorum personam*: "in the case of many"
(*OLD* persona 5c); prex, -ecis (f.): entreaty, prayer; exorabilis, -e: capable of being moved by entreaty
magno opere (adv.) greatly, strongly, especially
contendo, contendere, contendi, contentum assert, demand, press (<con- + tendo)
ne cui parceretur "that no one be spared," negat. subst. cl. of purp. (= indir. comm.) (AG #563); *cui* = alicui;
parco, parcere, peperci: spare; *parceretur*: impers. pass. (w/ dat.) (AG #208d)
proscribo, proscribere, proscripsi, proscriptum proscribe, publish the name in a list of outlaws (<pro- + scribo)
C. Toranium Gaius Toranius, praetor in 44 BCE
tutor, -oris (m.) guardian; after the death of Augustus' father (s. ch. 8.1), Gaius Toranius was appointed as
Augustus' guardian until he came of age

legam patris sui Octaui in aedilitate. **2.** Iulius Saturninus hoc amplius tradit, cum peracta proscriptione M. Lepidus in senatu excusasset praeterita et spem clementiae in posterum fecisset quoniam satis poenarum exactum esset, hunc e diuerso professum ita modum se proscribendi statuisse ut omnia sibi reliquerit libera. in cuius tamen pertinaciae paenitentiam postea T. Vinium Philopoemenem, quod patronum suum proscriptum celasse olim diceretur, equestri dignitate honorauit. **3.** in eadem hac potestate multiplici flagrauit inuidia. nam et Pinarium equitem R., cum contionante se admissa turba

---

aedilitas, -atis (f.) the aedileship; *in aedilitate*: prep. phr. as attrib. modifier of *collegam*

27.2
Iulius Saturninus Julius Saturninus, an otherwise unknown author
hoc amplius this besides, more
cum ... M. Lepidus ... excusasset ... fecisset circumst. cum cl. (AG #546); *peracta proscriptione*: abl. abs. (AG #419); perago, peragere, peregi, peractum: carry out, finish (<per- + ago); excuso (1): excuse, justify; *excusasset* = contr. form of excusauisset (AG #181); praeteritus, -a, -um: past, former; (n. subst.): past events; clementia, -ae (f.): clemency, leniency; *in posterum*: "in the future"
quoniam satis poenarum exactum esset causal cl. (BG #541); *poenarum*: partit. gen. w/ *satis* (AG #346a.4)
hunc (= Augustum) **... professum** [esse] indir. disc. (AG #580) ff. *tradit*; Suet. is here paraphrasing what Julius Saturninus reported; diuersus, -a, -um: differing; *e diuerso*: "from an opposing viewpoint"
ita modum se ... statuisse indir. disc. (AG #580) ff. *professum*, here presenting Augustus' declaration; statuo, statuere, statui, statutum: establish
ut omnia sibi reliquerit libera result cl. (AG #537.1), "that he left all options open for himself"; liber, -era, -erum: free, open; at the time, Augustus wanted to retain the right to pursue Caesar's assassins
in cuius tamen pertinaciae paenitentiam "nevertheless, in regret for this stubbornness"; *cuius*: relat. as connective (AG #308f); pertinacia, -ae (f.): stubborness, obstinancy; paenitentia, -ae (f.): regret for one's action; Augustus' change of heart likely dates to 39 BCE
T. Vinius Philopoemen freedman of the senator Titus Vinius
quod ... diceretur causal cl. w/ subjv. vb. indicating authority of another (AG #540); patronus, -i (m.): a patron; celo (1): conceal, hide; *celasse* = contr. form of celauisse
dignitas, -atis (f.) rank, status
honoro (1) confer an honor on, honor

27.3
potestas, -tatis (f.) command (here = as a member of the triumvirate)
multiplex, -icis multitudinous, varied; *multiplici*: sg. subst. as dat. of ref., "of numerous people" (AG #377)
flagro (1) burn, be intensely subject to (w/ abl. *inuidia*)
inuidia, -ae (f.) spite, envy, hatred
Pinarius a Roman eques, otherwise unknown; *Pinarium*: acc. obj. of *ratus*
cum ... animaduertisset circumst. cum cl. (AG #546) w/ two abl. abs.; *contionante se*: abl. abs. (AG #419); contionor (1): deliver a public speech; *admissa turba paganorum*: abl. abs.; paganus, -i (m.): peasant,

paganorum apud milites subscribere quaedam animaduertisset, curiosum ac speculatorem ratus coram confodi imperauit,
et Tedium Afrum consulem designatum, quia factum quoddam
suum maligno sermone carpsisset, tantis conterruit minis ut is
se praecipitauerit,   4. et Quintum Gallium praetorem, in officio
salutationis tabellas duplices ueste tectas tenentem suspicatus
gladium occulere nec quicquam statim, ne aliud inueniretur,
ausus inquirere, paulo post per centuriones et milites raptum e

---

civilian (as opposed to a soldier); subscribo, subscribere, subscripsi, subscriptum: write down, record (<sub- + scribo); *subscribere*: inf. in indir. disc. (AG #580) ff. *animaduertisset* w/ Pinarius as implied acc. subj.; *quaedam*: (n. pl.) "certain things"; note the extraordinary number of ptc. used by Suet. here and ff.

curiosum ac speculatorem ratus causal ptc. phr. (AG #496); curiosus, -a, -um: eager for knowledge; speculator, -oris (m.): spy (vb. subst. <speculo); reor, reri, ratus sum: think, suppose, believe

[Pinarium] **coram confodi** subst. cl. of purp. (= indir. comm.) w/ acc. subj. + inf. ff. *imperauit* (AG #563a); coram (adv.): openly, publicly; confodio, confodere, confodi, confossum: run through, stab (<con- + fodio); Augustus violated Roman law by summarily executing a citizen

impero (1) order

Tedius Afer consul elect during the period of the triumvirate, his exact identity is disputed; Suet. here notes that he was driven to suicide before he took office

designatus, -a, -um designated, appointed (but not yet installed) (ppp. <designo)

quia ... carpsisset causal cl. w/ subjv. vb. indicates authority of another (AG #540); *factum quoddam suum*: "some act of his"; the vague language emphasizes the harsh actions of Augustus; malignus, -a, -um: spiteful, unkind; carpo, carpere, carpsi, carptum: criticize (*OLD* 9b)

conterreo, conterrere, conterrui, conterritum fill with terror, frighten thoroughly (<con- + terreo)

minae, -arum (f. pl.) threats

ut is se praecipitauerit "that he threw himself to his death," pf. subjv. in cl. of result (AG #485c, 537); praecipito (1): hurl down

27.4

Quintum Gallium ... tenentem ptc. phr.; *Quintum Gallium* is acc. subj. of indir. disc.; Quintus Gallius was praetor perhaps in 43 BCE; salutatio, -onis (f.): a formal morning call paid by a client on his patron; tabella, -ae (f.): tablet, writing tablet; duplex, -icis: double, having two parts; tego, tegere, texi, tectum: cover, conceal

suspicor (1) imagine, suspect; *suspicatus*: pf. act. ptc., Augustus is subj.

[Quintum Gallium] **... gladium occulere** indir. disc. (AG #580) ff. *suspicatus*; gladius, -(i)i (m.): sword; occulo, occulere, occului, occultum: hide, conceal (<ob- + celo)

ne aliud inueniretur "lest something different be found," negat. cl. of purp. (AG #531); inuenio, inuenire, inueni, inuentum: find, discover

audeo, audere, ausus sum intend, dare (w/ inf.)

inquiro, inquirere, inquisiui (-sii), inquisitus search out, investigate (<in- + quaero)

paulo post "a short while later"

centurio, -onis (m.) centurion, an officer commanding a military century

tribunali seruilem in modum torsit ac fatentem nihil iussit
occidi, prius oculis eius sua manu effossis. quem tamen scribit
conloquio petito insidiatum sibi coniectumque a se in custodiam, deinde urbe interdicta dimissum naufragio uel latronum
insidiis perisse.

5. Tribuniciam potestatem perpetuam recepit, in qua semel
atque iterum per singula lustra collegam sibi cooptauit, recepit
et morum legumque regimen aeque perpetuum, quo iure, quamquam sine censurae honore, censum tamen populi ter egit,
primum ac tertium cum collega, medium solus.

---

tribunal, -alis (n.) platform (used for judicial purposes)
seruilem in modum "in a way befitting a slave" (*OLD* modus 11c); seruilis, -e: servile, ignoble
torqueo, torquere, torsi, tortum torture, torment
fateor, fateri, fassus sum concede, admit, confess
[Gallium] occidi subst. cl. of purp. (= indir. comm.) w/ acc. subj. + inf. ff. *iussit* (AG #563a)
prius oculis ... effossis abl. abs. (AG #419); prius (adv.): beforehand, first; manus, -us (f.): hand; effodio, effodere, effodi, effossum: gouge out (<ex- + fodio); note the reflex. poss. adj. *sua*, which indicates that Augustus did the deed himself
quem ... perisse indir. disc. (AG #580) ff. *scribit*; Suet. here reports Augustus' own version of the events; *quem* (relat. pron.): anteced. *Quintum Gallium*, subj. acc. w/ three ptc.: *insidiatum ... coniectum ... dimissum*; *conloquio petito*: abl. abs. (AG #419); conloquium, -ii (n.): meeting; insidior (1): plot against (w/ dat. *sibi*); conicio, conicere, conieci, coniectum: throw, put (in prison) (<con- + iacio); custodia, -ae (f.): prison, confinement; *urbe interdicta*: abl. abs. (AG #419), "with the city declared off-limits to him"; interdico, interdicere, interdixi, interdictum: forbid, debar (<inter- + dico); naufragium, -(i)i (n.): shipwreck; latro, -onis (m.): bandit, robber; insidiae, -arum (f. pl.): ambush; pereo, perire, perii (-iui), peritum: die, perish (<per- + eo)

27.5
tribunicia potestas tribunician power, the rights and powers of a tribune of the plebs; tribunicius, -a, -um: tribunician, of a tribune; potestas, -atis (f.): power; Augustus was awarded the full power of a tribune in 23 BCE by vote of the people and senate; the power was renewed each year throughout his life
qua (relat. pron.) anteced. *tribuniciam potestam*
semel atque iterum once and again, twice, repeatedly
lustrum, -i (n.) period of five years (< the lustrum, a purification ceremony performed at the conclusion of the census)
collegam M. Agrippa and Tiberius were granted tribunician powers at different times
coopto (1) choose as one's colleague in office, co-opt (<con- + opto)
regimen, -inis (n.) management, supervision; the nature and extent of Augustus' authority is disputed
quo iure "with this power"; *quo*: relat. pron. as connective (AG #308f)
censura, -ae (f.) the censorship, the office of censor
census, -us (m.) the census, the registration of Roman citizens (*OCD* 296–297)
ter (adv.) three times, on three occasions; Augustus conducted the census in 28 BCE, 8 BCE, and 14 CE (cf. *RG* 8.2)

28 De reddenda re p. bis cogitauit, primo post oppressum statim
Antonium, memor obiectum sibi ab eo saepius quasi per ipsum
staret ne redderetur, ac rursus taedio diuturnae ualitudinis,
cum etiam magistratibus ac senatu domum accitis rationarium
imperii tradidit. sed reputans et se priuatum non sine periculo
fore et illam plurium arbitrio temere committi in retinenda
perseuerauit, dubium euentu meliore an uoluntate. **2.** quam
uoluntatem cum prae se identidem ferret quodam etiam edicto

Following his discussion of the positions Augustus held, Suetonius reports that Augustus twice thought about relinquishing his control over the state, but ultimately never did so. Suetonius views the entire period from 31 BCE to 14 CE as being dominated by Augustus (s. ch. 8.3 and introduction for discussion).

28.1
de reddenda re p[ublica] "about restoring the state"; *reddenda*: abl. gerv. (AG #503, 507)
cogito (1) think, consider
opprimo, opprimere, oppressi, oppressum crush, overwhelm (<ob- + premo)
memor, -oris mindful, having in memory (w/ acc. + inf.)
obiectum [esse] ... **saepius** impers. acc. + inf. constr. ff. *memor*, "that it was very often laid out as a charge"; *sibi* = Augusto; *eo* = Antonio
quasi per ipsum staret ne redderetur "that it was due to him [Augustus] that it was not restored"; *quasi ... staret*: *quasi* w/ subjv. to express a belief or rumor (AG #524, BG #602n4); sto, stare, steti, statum: (impers.) be due to (w/ per + acc.) (*OLD* 22); *ne redderetur*: subst. cl. of purp. (AG #563d)
taedium, -(i)i (n.) weariness; *taedio*: abl. of cause (AG #404)
diuturnus, -a, -um long-lasting
cum ... tradidit tmp. cl. (AG #545); *magistratibus ac senatu domum accitis*: abl. abs. (AG #419);
domum: acc. place to which w/out prep. (AG #427.2); accio, accire, acciui (-ii), accitum: summon (<ad- + ci(e)o); rationarium, -(i)i (n.): financial survey, account (an unusual wd. <ratio); imperium, -(i)i (n.): empire; the event dates to 23 BCE
reputo (1) take into consideration, consider (<re- + puto)
se priuatum ... fore indir. disc. (AG #580) ff. *reputans*, "that he, as a private citizen, would not be without danger"; priuatus, -a, -um: not holding public office; *fore* = futurum esse; *non sine periculo*: LITOTES (AG #641)
illam ... committi indir. disc. (AG #580) ff. *reputans*, "that the state (*illam*) is placed in the control of more (than one person) recklessly"; plus, -uris: more; *plurium*: gen. pl. (for decl., AG #120); arbitrium, -(i)i: control (*OLD* 5); committo, committere, commisi, commissum: place (w/ dat. *arbitrio*) (*OLD* 12) (<con- + mitto)
in retinenda [re publica] gerv. agreeing w/ implied noun
perseuero (1) persist, continue resolutely (w/ in + abl.) (<per- + seuero)
dubium euentu meliore an uoluntate "it is uncertain whether the outcome or the intention was better," disjunctive quest. ff. adj. (cf. ch. 19.2); dubius, -a, -um: uncertain; euentus, -us (m.): outcome; uoluntas, -atis (f.): intention; *euentu* and *uoluntate*: abl. of quality (AG #415); Suet. here seems to be praising both the result of Augustus' continued rule and his plan for the principate as a whole

28.2
quam uoluntatem cum ... ferret conces. cum cl. (AG #549); *quam uoluntatem*: relat. pron. as connective (AG #308f); Suet. places special emphasis on Augustus' intention; prae se ferre: display, make no secret of (*OLD* prae 3); identidem (adv.): again and again

his uerbis testatus est,
> ita mihi saluam ac sospitem rem p. sistere in sua sede liceat atque
> eius rei fructum percipere quem peto, ut optimi status auctor dicar et
> moriens ut feram mecum spem mansura in uestigio suo fundamenta
> rei p. quae iecero,

fecitque ipse se compotem uoti, nisus omni modo ne quem noui status paeniteret.

3. Vrbem neque pro maiestate imperii ornatam et inundationibus incendiisque obnoxiam excoluit adeo ut iure sit gloriatus

---

testor (1) affirm, declare; Suet. follows with dir. quotation of the edict that uses the language of a traditional Roman vow; the precise date and context of the edict are unknown

ita mihi ... sistere ... liceat ... percipere "may I be permitted to..."; *liceat*: impers. opt. subjv (AG #441) w/ two inf. cl.; saluus, -a, -um: safe, secure; sospes, -itis: safe and sound, unscathed; sisto, sistere, steti (stiti), statum: set up, stabilize; *sistere*: inf. as subj. of impers. vb. (AG #454); sedes, -is (f.): seat, foundation; licet, licere, licuit: be permitted (w/ dat. *mihi* + inf.); fructus, -us (m.): fruit, benefit, reward; percipio, percipere, percepi, perceptum: reap, earn (<per- + capio); *percipere*: inf. as subj. of impers. vb. (AG #454)

quem (relat. pron.) anteced. *fructum*, obj. of *peto*

ut ... dicar result cl. (AG #537); optimus, -a, -um: best; status, -us (m.): state of affairs, political situation; *auctor*: pred. nom. (AG #284)

morior, mori, mortuus sum die, perish

ut feram mecum spem result cl. (AG #537)

mansura [esse] ... **fundamenta** indir. disc. ff. *spem* (AG #580a); uestigium, -(i)i (n.): track, path, position; fundamentum, -i (n.): foundation

quae (relat. pron.) anteced. *fundamenta*, obj. of *iecero*

iacio, iacere, ieci, iactum throw, lay (foundations) (*OLD* 6b)

compotem uoti pred. acc. (AG #393); compos, -otis: in possession of; uotum, -i (n.): desire, wish

nitor, niti, nixus sum strive, direct one's efforts toward (w/ ut/ne + subjv.)

ne ... paeniteret negat. purp. cl. (AG #531), "lest anyone regret the new state of affairs"; *quem* = aliquem: anyone (AG #310); paeniteo, paenitere, paenitui: (impers.) be a reason for complaint (w/ acc. of pers. *quem* and gen. of cause *noui status*, AG #354b)

Rome: buildings and religion (*urbem*). The focus of the biography shifts to the city of Rome. Suetonius begins with the physical structure of the city, discussing in the following chapters the major buildings constructed or repaired by Augustus and the building projects of other leading men that spanned a period of many decades.

28.3

urbem ... ornatam ... obnoxiam acc. obj. of *excoluit*; *pro maiestate*: "in accordance with the majesty"; maiestas, -atis (f.): dignity, majesty; imperium, -(i)i (n.): empire; orno (1): arrange, adorn, decorate; inundatio, -onis (f.): flooding, inundation; incendium, -(i)i (n.): fire, conflagration; obnoxius, -a, -um: exposed to (w/ dat.)

excolo, excolere, excolui, excultum improve, develop, adorn (<ex- + colo)

adeo to such a degree

ut ... sit gloriatus result cl. (AG #537); iure (adv.): rightfully; glorior (1): boast

marmoream se relinquere quam latericiam accepisset, tutam
uero, quantum prouideri humana ratione potuit, etiam in
29 posterum praestitit. publica opera plurima extruxit, e quibus
uel praecipua forum cum aede Martis Vltoris, templum
Apollinis in Palatio, aedem Tonantis Iouis in Capitolio. fori extruendi causa fuit hominum et iudiciorum multitudo, quae
uidebatur non sufficientibus duobus etiam tertio indigere,
itaque festinatius necdum perfecta Martis aede publicatum

---

marmoream [urbem] **se reliquere** indir. disc. (AG #580) ff. *gloriatus sit*; marmoreus, -a, -um: made of marble

quam ... accepisset relat. cl. w/ subjv. in indir. disc. (AG #580); *quam* (relat. pron.): anteced. *urbem*; latericius, -a, -um: made of brick

tutus, -a, -um safe, protected from danger

quantum ... potuit (impers.) "to what degree it was able to be foreseen"; quantum (relat. adv.): to what degree, how much; prouideo, prouidere, prouidi, prouisum: see in advance, foresee (<pro- + uideo); *prouideri*: pres. pass. compl. inf. (AG #456); humanus, -a, -um: human

in posterum "for the future"

praesto, praestare, praestiti, praestatum furnish, render (<prae- + sto)

29.1

ex quibus uel praecipua ... in Capitolio relat. cl. listing three prominent works built by Augustus; grammatically *extruxit* should be understood as governing *praecipua* (acc. pl.), with *forum, templum*, and *aedem* in appos.; note lack of conj. (ASYNDETON, AG #640); *quibus* (relat. pron.): anteced. *publica opera*; *uel praecipua*: "the most outstanding [works]" (AG #291c); Mars Ultor: "Mars the Avenger"; Mars, Martis (m.): the god Mars; ultor, -oris (m.): avenger; the Temple of Mars Ultor was dedicated in 2 BCE; the Temple of Apollo Palatinus was dedicated in 28 BCE; Palatium, -(i)i (n.): the Palatine Hill; Iuppiter Tonans: "Jupiter the Thunderer"; tono (1): thunder; the Temple of Jupiter Tonans was dedicated in 22 BCE

fori extruendi causa "the reason for building the forum"; *extruendi*: gerv., objv. gen. (AG #348); *causa*: nom. sg. subj.

iudicium, -(i)i (n.) legal proceedings, trial

multitudo, -inis (f.) multitude, large number; *multitudo*: pred. nom. (AG #284)

quae uidebatur ... indigere "which seemed to require," relat. cl. w/ pers. indir. disc. ff. *uidebatur* (AG #582); *quae* (relat. pron.): anteced. *multitudo*; *non sufficientibus duobus* [*foris*]: causal abl. abs. (AG #420.2); sufficio, sufficere, suffeci, suffectum: be sufficient (<sub- + facio); duo, duae, duo (pl. adj.): two; the Forum Romanum and Forum Iulium were both in use; indigeo, indigere, indigui: stand in need, require (w/ dat.) (<indu- + egeo)

itaque (adv.) and so, then

festinanter (adv.) speedily, hurriedly (compar. = festinantius)

necdum perfecta ... aede abl. abs. (AG #419); necdum: not yet; perficio, perficere, perfeci, perfectum: complete, finish (<per- + facio)

publico (1) make public property; Augustus had purchased the land privately to undertake construction (s. ch. 56.2); formal transfer to the state marked the opening of the forum

est cautumque ut separatim in eo publica iudicia et sortitiones iudicum fierent.   **2.** aedem Martis bello Philippensi pro ultione paterna suscepto uouerat: sanxit ergo ut de bellis triumphisque hic consuleretur senatus, prouincias cum imperio petituri hinc deducerentur quique uictores redissent huc insignia triumphorum conferrent.   **3.** templum Apollinis in ea parte Palatinae domus excitauit quam fulmine ictam desiderari a deo haruspices pronuntiarunt, addidit porticus cum bibliotheca Latina

---

caueo, cauere, caui, cautum make legal provision, decree; *cautum* [*est*]: impers.
ut ... publica iudicia et sortitiones ... fierent subst. cl. of purp. (= indir. comm.) (AG #563); separatim (adv.): separately, apart from the rest; sortitio, -onis (f.): drawing of lots, lottery; iudex, -icis (m.): juror, member of a panel appointed to hear a case; fio, fieri: take place, occur

29.2
bello Philippensi ... suscepto tmp. abl. abs. (AG #420.1); Philippensis, -e: of or belonging to Philippi, a town in N. Greece; ultio, -onis (f.): act of taking vengeance, revenge; paternus, -a, -um: paternal; on the war at Philippi, s. ch. 13
uoueo, uouere, uoui, uotum vow, promise to a god
sancio, sancire, sanxi, sanctum ratify solemnly, prescribe by law
ergo (adv.) therefore, accordingly
ut ... consuleretur senatus ... petituri hinc deducerentur ... quique uictores ... conferrent subst. cl. of purp. (= indir. comm.) (AG #563) w/ three cl.; Suet. here sets out official uses that were established for the new temple; hic (adv.): in this place, here; *petituri*: "those about to seek," fut. act. ptc. as subst.; hinc (adv.): from here; deduco, deducere, deduxi, deductum: lead away, escort (<de- + duco); *quique ... redissent*: "and those who returned as victors"; uictor, -oris (m.): victor, *uictores*: pred. appos. (AG #282); *redissent*: subjv. by attraction (AG #593); huc (adv.): to this place; insigne, -is (n.): emblem or symbol, visible token (a laurel wreath, palm branch, or enemy spoils might serve as tokens of victory)

29.3
Palatinae domus "of his Palatine home," gen. sg.; Palatinus, -a, -um: of the Palatine Hill, Palatine; to expand his residence Augustus had bought up property on the Palatine, a portion of which was used for the new temple of Apollo
excito (1) raise, build, erect (*OLD* 8) (<ex- + cito)
quam ... desiderari a deo "[the part] which was desired by the god," relat. cl. and indir. disc. (AG #580) ff. *pronuntiarunt*; quam (relat. pron.): anteced. *parte*; quam [*partem*]: acc. subj.; fulmen, -inis (n.): lightning, thunderbolt; icio, icere, ici, ictum: strike; desidero (1): desire, request; *desiderari*: pres. pass. inf.,
haruspex, -icis (m.) diviner, Etruscan soothsayer
pronuntiarant = contr. form of pronuntiauerunt (AG #181)
porticus, -us (f.) a covered walkway, portico, colonnade
bibliotheca, -ae (f.) a library
Latinus, -a, -um Latin

Graecaque, quo loco iam senior saepe etiam senatum habuit decuriasque iudicum recognouit. Tonanti Ioui aedem consecrauit liberatus periculo cum expeditione Cantabrica per nocturnum iter lecticam eius fulgur praestrinxisset seruumque praelucentem exanimasset. **4.** quaedam etiam opera sub nomine alieno—nepotum scilicet et uxoris sororisque—fecit, ut porticum basilicamque Gai et Luci, item porticus Liuiae et Octauiae theatrumque Marcelli. sed et ceteros principes uiros saepe hortatus est ut pro facultate quisque monimentis uel nouis uel refectis et excultis urbem adornarent. **5.** multaque a

---

quo loco ... habuit ... recognouit relat. cl. w/ anteced. in cl. (AG #307b); *quo loco*: "in which place," abl. of place where w/out prep. (AG #429.1); senex, -is: old, aged (compar. = senior); decuria, -ae (f.): panel of men (from which jurors were selected); iudex, -icis (m.): juror, member of a panel appointed to hear a case; recognosco, recognoscere, recognoui, recognitum: review, inspect (<re- + cognosco); on the jury panels, s. ch. 32.3

consecro (1) dedicate, consecrate (to a god)

libero (1) free, release, deliver

periculo abl. of separ. (AG #401) w/ *liberatus*

cum ... fulgur praestrinxisset ... exanimasset circumst. cum cl. (AG #546); *expeditione Cantabrica*: abl. of time when (AG #424d) (s. ch. 20); expeditio, -onis (f.): military operation; Cantabricus, -a, -um: of the Cantabri, a people of the north coast of Spain; nocturnus, -a, -um: occurring at night; fulgur, -uris (n.): flash of lightning; praestringo, praestringere, praestrinxi, praestrictum: graze, touch lightly (<prae- + stringo); praeluceo, praelucere, praeluxi: shine a light in front, light the way (<prae- + luceo); exanimo (1): kill; *exanimasset* = contr. form of exanimauisset (AG #181)

29.4

sub nomine alieno "in the name of others"; alienus, -a, -um: of others, belonging to others

nepotum ... sororisque gen., w/ sub nomine understood; scilicet (adv.): that is to say, for example; s. introduction for family tree

ut "such as"; Suet. provides examples of buildings Augustus completed in the name of his family members over the course of more than four decades: the Portico of Gaius and Lucius, the Basilica of Gaius and Lucius, the Portico of Livia, the Portico of Octavia, and the Theater of Marcellus

basilica, -ae (f.) colonnaded hall, basilica

Liuia Augustus' wife, Livia Drusilla (*OCD* 851) (s. ch. 62.2)

Octauia Augustus' sister (*OCD* s.v. Octavia (2), 1031) (s. ch. 4.1)

Marcellus Marcus Claudius Marcellus (*OCD* s.v. Claudius Marcellus (5), Marcus, 327), the son of Augustus' sister Octavia

princeps, -cipis leading, most distinguished

hortor (1) urge to action, incite

ut ... adornarent subst. cl. of purp (AG #563) (= indir. comm.) ff. *hotatus est*; facultas, -atis (f.): ability; *quisque*: partit. appos. w/ pl. subj. (AG #317e); monimentum, -i (n.): monument, commemorative building; reficio, reficere, refeci, refectum: restore, repair (<re- + facio); excolo, excolere, excolui, excultum: improve, adorn (<ex- + colo); adorno (1): decorate, adorn

29.5

multa nom. pl. subj., "many works"

multis tunc extructa sunt, sicut a Marcio Philippo aedes Herculis
Musarum, a L. Cornificio aedes Dianae, ab Asinio Pollione
atrium Libertatis, a Munatio Planco aedes Saturni, a Cornelio
Balbo theatrum, a Statilio Tauro amphitheatrum, a M. uero
Agrippa complura et egregia.

30   Spatium urbis in regiones uicosque diuisit instituitque ut illas
annui magistratus sortito tuerentur, hos magistri e plebe cuiusque uiciniae lecti. aduersus incendia excubias nocturnas uigi-
lesque commentus est. ad coercendas inundationes alueum

---

sicut (conj.) just as, as indeed, for instance
aedes Herculis Musarum the Temple of Hercules and the Muses; L. Marcius Philippus
  (*OCD* 897), Augustus' stepfather, undertook a restoration of the temple following his triumph
  in 33 BCE
aedes Dianae the Temple of Diana; L. Cornificius (*OCD* 385) restored the temple of Diana on the
  Aventine Hill following his triumph (probably in 32 BCE)
atrium Libertatis the Hall of Liberty; C. Asinius Pollio (*OCD* 184) restored the Atrium Libertatis and
  opened Rome's first public library in the years following his triumph in 39 BCE
aedes Saturni the Temple of Saturn; L. Munatius Plancus (*OCD* 972) restored the temple following his
  triumph in 43 BCE
theatrum the Theater of Balbus; L. Cornelius Balbus (*OCD* 376–377) built his theater following his triumph
  in 19 BCE. His was the last triumph and major building project to celebrate someone outside the family of
  Augustus
amphitheatrum the amphitheater of T. Statilius Taurus (*OCD* 1396–1397), begun after his triumph in 34
  BCE, was the first permanent amphitheater in Rome
complures, -a (pl. adj.) numerous, many; the building projects of M. Vipsanius Agrippa (*OCD* 1554–1555)
  included the Aqua Julia, Aqua Virgo, Pantheon, and other sites in Rome
egregius, -a, -um outstanding, splendid

30.1
spatium, -ii (n.) space, area
regio, -onis (f.) district, region; in 7 BCE Augustus divided Rome into fourteen administrative regions
uicus, -i (m.) neighborhood, ward
ut illas [regiones] **annui magistratus ... tuerentur ... hos** [vicos] **magistri ... lecti** subst. cl. of
  purp. (AG #563) ff. *instituit* w/ two cl. w/ *tuerentur* as vb. in both cl.; annuus, -a, -um: lasting
  a year, year-long; sortito: "selected by lot," adv. abl. abs., impers. ppp. < sortio (AG #419c);
  tueor, tueri, tuitus sum: watch over, protect; magister, -tri (m.): chief officer, master; uicinia, -ae
  (f.): neighborhood, locality
incendium, -(i)i (n.) fire, conflagration
excubiae, -arum (f. pl.) keeping of a watch, watch-station
nocturnus, -a, -um occurring at night
uigil, -ilis (m.) watchman, one who keeps guard
comminiscor, comminisci, commentus sum think up, devise
ad coercendas inundationes ad w/ gerv. for purp. (AG #506); coerceo, coercere, coercui, coercitum: control
  (<con- + arceo); inundatio, -onis (f.): flood
alueus, -i (m.) channel, bed (of a river)

Tiberis laxauit ac repurgauit completum olim ruderibus et aedificiorum prolationibus coartatum. quo autem facilius undique urbs adiretur, desumpta sibi Flaminia uia Arimino tenus munienda reliquas triumphalibus uiris ex manubiali pecunia sternendas distribuit. **2.** aedes sacras uetustate conlapsas aut incendio absumptas refecit easque et ceteras opulentissimis donis adornauit, ut qui in cellam Capitolini Iouis sedecim milia pondo auri gemmasque ac margaritas quingenties sestertium una donatione contulerit.

Tiberis, -is (m.) the river Tiber
laxo (1) make larger, widen
repurgo (1) clean, free from obstructions (<re- + purgo)
completum ... coartatum ptc. phr., acc. obj. of *repurgauit*; compleo, complere, compleui, completum: fill (<con- + pleo); *completum* w/ *alueum*; rudus, -eris (n.): rubble, broken stones; aedificium, -(i)i (n.): building, edifice; prolatio, -onis (f.): enlargement, extension; coarto (1): make narrower, constrict
quo ... urbs adiretur relat. cl. of purp. w/ compar. (AG #531.2a); undique (adv.): from all sides
desumpta ... Flaminia uia ... munienda abl. abs. (AG #419); desumo, desumere, desumpsi, desumptum: choose, pick out (<de- + sumo); Flaminia uia (f.): the Flaminian Way; Ariminum, -i (m.): Rimini, a town in Umbria; tenus (prep. w/ preceding abl.): as far as; munio, munire, muniui (-ii), munitum: repair; *munienda*: abl. sg. gerv. w/ *Flaminia via*, "repairing the Flaminian Way"
reliquas [uias] **... sternendas** ptc. phr., obj. of *distribuit*; triumphalis, -e: having triumphal status, associated with a triumph; manubialis, -e: obtained from the sale of booty, a very unusual adj. (<manubiae); the triumphant general used the funds from spoils for public works (s. ch. 29.5); sterno, sternere, straui, stratum: lay (stones), pave (*OLD* 3b); *sternendas*: gerv.
distribuo, distribuere, distribui, distributum divide up, distribute (<dis- + tribuo)

30.2
aedes ... conlapsas aut ... absumptas ptc. phr., obj. of *refecit*; sacer, -cra, -crum: sacred, holy; uetustas, -atis (f.): age, old age; conlabor, conlabi, conlapsus sum: fall down, collapse (<con- + labor)
reficio, reficere, refeci, refectum restore, repair (<re- + facio); cf. *RG* 20.4, where Augustus notes that he restored eighty-two temples
opulentus, -a, -um opulent, rich, sumptuous (superl. = -issmus)
donum, -i (n.) gift
adorno (1) adorn, decorate (<ad- + orno)
ut qui ... contulerit "as he conveyed," relat. cl. of char. expressing cause (AG #535e); cella, -ae (f.): chamber, cella (in the Temple of Jupiter on the Capitoline Hill); *sedecim milia*: sixteen thousand; pondo (adv.): by weight; aurum, -i (n.): gold; *auri*: partit. gen. (AG #346a.2); gemma, -ae (f.): gem; margarita, -ae (f.): pearl; *quingenties sestertium*: "worth fifty million sesterces", gen. of quality (AG #345b); donatio, -onis (f.): gift, donation; the gift was made from the spoils following Augustus' triumph in 29 BCE

31 Postquam uero pontificatum maximum, quem numquam uiuo Lepido auferre sustinuerat, mortuo demum suscepit, quidquid fatidicorum librorum Graeci Latinique generis nullis uel parum idoneis auctoribus uulgo ferebatur, supra duo milia contracta undique cremauit ac solos retinuit Sibyllinos—hos quoque dilectu habito—condiditque duobus forulis auratis sub Palatini Apollinis basi. **2.** annum a Diuo Iulio ordinatum sed postea neglegentia conturbatum atque confusum rursus ad pristinam

---

Following naturally from the discussion of restoration of temples in Rome, Suetonius takes up religious reforms undertaken by Augustus.

31.1

postquam ... suscepit tmp. cl. (AG #543); postquam: after; pontificatus, -us (m.): office of pontiff; *pontificatum maximum*: the position of pontifex maximus; *uiuo Lepido*: dat. of separ. ff. *auferre* (AG #381), note parallel structure w/ *[Lepido] mortuo*; uiuus, -a, -um: living; aufero, auferre, abstuli, ablatum: take away (<ab- + fero); sustineo, sustinere, sustinui: have the courage, be able (to do something) w/ inf. (*OLD* 6) (<sub- + teneo); mortuus, -a, -um: dead; M. Aemilius Lepidus (*OCD* s.v. Aemilius Lepidus (3), Marcus, 20) became pontifex maximus after Caesar's assassination and retained the position until his death in 13 BCE; Augustus was elected Pontifex Maximus in 12 BCE

quidquid fatidicorum librorum "whatever books of prophecy," indef. pron. w/ partit. gen.; quisquis, quidquid: whoever, whatever; fatidicus, -a, -um: prophetic, oracular; liber, -bri (m.): book

nullis uel parum idoneis auctoribus "with anonymous or unsuitable authors," abl. of quality (description) (AG #415); *parum idoneis*: LITOTES (AG #641); idoneus, -a, -um: suitable

uulgo ferebatur "were circulating publicly"; uulgo (adv.): publicly

supra duo milia "more than two thousand"

contracta w/ *milia*, but referring to libri

undique (adv.) from all sides, from every source

cremo (1) destroy by fire, burn

Sibyllinus, -a, -um Sibylline; *Sibyllini libri*: Sibylline books, prophetic works written by the Sibyl

dilectu habito abl. abs. (AG #419); dilectus, -us (m.): process of choosing

condo, condere, condidi, conditum put away, preserve, keep safe (<con- + do)

duobus forulis auratis abl. of place where (AG #429.2); forulus, -i (m.): a bookcase, small cabinet (dim. <forus, a form favored by Suet.); auratus, -a, -um: gilded, adorned with gold

Apollo Palatinus Palatine Apollo (the cult and temple of Apollo on the Palatine Hill)

basis, -is (f.) foundation, base, pedestal

31.2

annum ... ordinatum sed ... conturbatum atque confusum ptc. phr., obj. of *redegit*; ordino (1): organize, manage; as pontifex maximus, Julius Caesar had reformed the calendar in 46 BCE; neglegentia, -ae (f.): carelessness, neglect; conturbo (1): mix up, upset, put out of order (<con- + turbo); confundo, confundere, confudi, confusum: jumble, confuse (<con- + fundo)

pristinus, -a, -um former, previous

rationem redegit. in cuius ordinatione Sextilem mensem e suo
cognomine nuncupauit, magis quam Septembrem quo erat
natus, quod hoc sibi et primus consulatus et insignes uictoriae
optigissent.   **3.** sacerdotum et numerum et dignitatem sed et
commoda auxit, praecipue Vestalium uirginum, cumque in
demortuae locum aliam capi oporteret ambirentque multi ne
filias in sortem darent, adiurauit si cuiusquam neptium suarum
competeret aetas, oblaturum se fuisse eam.   **4.** nonnulla etiam

---

redigo, redigere, redegi, redactum return, restore (<re- + ago); Augustus corrected the practice of inserting an extra day, which had been done every three years, not the correct four
cuius (relat. pron.) anteced. *annum*
ordinatio, -onis (f.) arrangement, organization, act of ordering
Sextilis, -is (m.) the eighth month of the Roman calendar (originally the sixth month)
cognomen, -inis (n.) the surname of an individual, here = "Augustus"
nuncupo (1) declare, appoint; Suet. abbreviates the process by which a decree of the senate and a plebiscite conferred this honor in 8 BCE
magis quam "rather than"
Septembrem [*mensem*] "the month of September"; September, -bris, -bre: of the month of September
quo [*mense*] relat. pron., abl. of time when (AG #423)
quod ... optigissent causal cl. w/ subjv. relying on the authority of another pers. (AG #540); *hoc* [*mense*]: abl. of time when; insignis, -e: notable, significant; optingo, optingere, optigi: fall to one's lot, occur (w/ dat. *sibi*) (<ob- + tango); on Augustus' first consulship, s. ch. 26.1; Augustus had captured Alexandria on August 1, 30 BCE and celebrated his triple triumph in August of 29 BCE

31.3
sacerdos, -otis (m./f.) priest, priestess; *sacerdotum*: gen. pl., note placement to mark new sub-topic
dignitas, -atis (f.) rank, status
uirgo Vestalis a Vestal Virgin (a priestess of Vesta); uirgo, -inis (f.): virgin
cum ... oporteret ambirentque multi circumst. cum cl. (AG #546); demorior, demori, demortuus sum: die; *demortuae*: (subst.) "of a deceased Vestal"; capio, capere, cepi, captum: select (*OLD* 9); oportet, oportere, oportuit: (impers.) it is fitting, it is right (w/ acc. *aliam* + inf. *capi*, AG #565); ambio, ambire, ambiui (-ii), ambitum: solicit, seek to obtain (<ambi- + eo); Suet. reports here the Captio, the technical process of selecting a Vestal by lot
ne ... darent negat. purp. cl. (AG #531); sors, -rtis (f.): lot, lottery
adiuro (1) swear, affirm with an oath (<ad- + iuro)
si ... competeret ... oblaturum fuisse pres. C-to-F condit. in indir. disc. (AG #589b) ff. *adiurauit*; competo, competere, competiui (-ii), competitum: be sufficient (<con- + peto); *oblaturum fuisse*: inf. in apod.; *se*: acc. subj.

31.4
nonnulla ... abolita ptc. phr., obj. of *restituit*; antiquus, -a, -um: ancient, old; caerimonia, -ae (f.): religious rites, ceremonies (usu. pl.); paulatim (adv.): little by little, gradually; aboleo, abolere, aboleui, abolitum: lapse, drop

ex antiquis caerimonis paulatim abolita restituit, ut Salutis augurium, Diale flamonium, sacrum Lupercale, ludos Saeculares et Compitalicios. Lupercalibus uetuit currere inberbes, item Saecularibus ludis iuuenes utriusque sexus prohibuit ullum nocturnum spectaculum frequentare nisi cum aliquo maiore natu propinquorum. Compitales Lares ornari bis anno instituit uernis floribus et aestiuis.

5. Proximum a dis immortalibus honorem memoriae ducum praestitit qui imperium p. R. ex minimo maximum reddidis-

---

restituo, restituere, restitui, restitutum restore, reinstate (<re- + statuo)
ut such as (*OLD* 6)
augurium Salutis "the augury of Safety," an augury to ascertain whether to offer prayers for the safety of the state
flamonium Diale "the office of flamen Dialis," the priest of Jupiter
sacrum Lupercale "the sacred rite of the Lupercal," the Lupercalia festival held on February 15
ludi Saeculares "the Saecular Games," a religious celebration marking the start of a new century (saeculum), held by Augustus in 17 BCE
ludi Compitalicii "the games of the Compitalia," an annual festival in association with neighborhood wards in Rome
Lupercalibus "at the Lupercalia," abl. of time when (AG #424d)
ueto, uetare, uetui, uetitum forbid (someone to do something)
curro, currere, cucurri, cursum run; the ritual of the Lupercalia required the Luperci to run around the Palatine Hill
inberbis, -e beardless
Saecularibus ludis "at the Saecular Games," abl. of time when (AG #424d)
iuuenes ... frequentare subst. cl. of purp. (= indir. comm.) w/ acc. subj. + inf. ff. *prohibuit* (AG #563a); sexus, -us (m.): sex; prohibeo, prohibere, prohibui, prohibitum: prevent (<pro- + habeo); nocturnus, -a, -um: occurring at night
maior natu "older"; *natu*: abl. sg. (<supine of nascor)
propinquus, -i (m.) relative, kinsman
Compitales Lares ornari ... aestiuis subst. cl. of purp. (= indir. comm.) w/ acc. subj. + inf. ff. *instituit* (AG #563d); Compitales Lares: "the Lares of the Crossroads"; Lar, Laris (m.): a protective spirit, tutelary deity; orno (1): adorn, decorate; *anno*: abl. of time when or within which (AG #423); uernus, -a, -um: of spring, vernal; flos, -oris (m.): flower, blossom; aestiuus, -a, -um: of summer

31.5

proximum a dis immortalibus "next to the honor he paid the immortal gods"; immortalis, -e: immortal, eternal
praesto, praestare, praestiti, praestatum offer, render (<prae- + sto)
qui ... reddidissent relat. cl. of char. (AG #535); *qui* (relat. pron.): m. nom. pl., anteced. *ducum*; *imperium p[opuli] R[omani]*: "the empire of the Roman people," very formal language; *ex minimo maximum*: "very great from the smallest [beginning]", a rhetorically powerful juxtaposition

sent. itaque et opera cuiusque manentibus titulis restituit et
statuas omnium triumphali effigie in utraque fori sui porticu
dedicauit, professus et edicto commentum id se ut ad illorum
uelut exemplar et ipse dum uiueret et insequentium aetatium
principes exigerentur a ciuibus. Pompei quoque statuam contra
theatri eius regiam marmoreo iano superposuit translatam e
curia in qua C. Caesar fuerat occisus.

32 Pleraque pessimi exempli in perniciem publicam aut ex
consuetudine licentiaque bellorum ciuilium durauerant aut per
pacem etiam extiterant. nam et grassatorum plurimi palam

---

titulus, -i (m.) inscription; Augustus left the names of the original benefactors on the buildings he restored (cf. *RG* 20.1)
triumphali effigie "with triumphal regalia"; effigies, -ei (f.): outward appearance, guise
in utraque fori sui porticu "in each portico of his forum"; porticus, -us (f.): portico, colonnade; the Forum of Augustus included a pair of porticoes that flanked the Temple of Mars Ultor
commentum [esse] ... **se** Suet. presents the wd. of the edict in indir. disc. (AG #580) ff. *professus*; comminiscor, comminisci, commentus sum: think up, devise
ut ... ipse ... principes ... exigerentur subst. cl. of purp. (= indir. comm.) ff. *commentum* (AG #563); *ad illorum uelut exemplar*: "against the model, so to speak, of those men"; uelut (adv.): so to speak; exemplar, -aris (n.): example, model; *dum uiueret*: "while he lived" (AG #556); exigo, exigere, exegi, exactum: judge (w/ ad) (*OLD* 11) (<ex- + ago); ciuis, -is (m.): citizen
Pompei statuam the statue of Pompey the Great
contra (prep. w/ acc.) opposite, facing
regia, -ae (f.) main door of a theater stage
marmoreus, -a, -um made of marble
ianus, -i (m.) archway, arch
superpono, superponere, superposui, superpositum place on top (<super- + pono)
occisus fuerat = occisus erat, a form common in Suet.; Caesar had been assassinated in the Curia of Pompey, falling at the feet of the statue of Pompey the Great

Administration in Rome. In place of a concise rubric heading, Suetonius opens this section with a highly alliterative sentence. Here Suetonius presents a wide variety of problems that Augustus addressed.

32.1
pleraque n. pl. subst. as subj., "very many things"
pessimus, -a, -um worst (superl. of malus)
exemplum, -i (n.) example, model, kind
in perniciem publicam "for public ruin"; pernicies, -ei (f.): physical destruction, ruin; note the ALLITERATION (AG #641) in the first line of this new section exploring matters of law and order
ex consuetudine licentiaque a rare example in Suet. of HENDIADYS (AG #640); consuetudo, -inis (f.): a habitual practice, custom; licentia, -ae (f.): unruly behavior, licence
duro (1) endure, continue on
pax, pacis (f.) peace
existo, existere, extiti arise (<ex- + sisto)
grassator, -oris (m.) a highway robber (vb. subst. <grassor); *grassatorum*: partit. gen. (AG #346b)
palam (adv.) openly, without concealment

se ferebant succincti ferro quasi tuendi sui causa, et rapti per
agros uiatores sine discrimine liberi seruique ergastulis possessorum supprimebantur, et plurimae factiones titulo collegi noui
ad nullius non facinoris societatem coibant. igitur grassaturas
dispositis per oportuna loca stationibus inhibuit, ergastula
recognouit, collegia praeter antiqua et legitima dissoluit.
2. tabulas ueterum aerari debitorum—uel praecipuam calumniandi materiam—exussit, loca in urbe publica iuris ambigui

---

succinctus, -a, -um equipped (w/ abl.)

ferrum, -i (n.) sword

quasi tuendi sui causa "as if for the sake of protecting themselves"; *causa* (abl.): "for the sake of," w/ gen. of gerv. to express purp. (AG #504b); tueor, tueri, tuitus sum: watch over, protect

rapti ... uiatores ... liberi seruique ptc. phr., nom. subj.; uiator, -oris (m.): traveler; discrimen, -inis (n.): distinction, difference; liber, -era, -erum: free, *liberi*: m. nom. pl. subst.

ergastulum, -i (n.) prison or workhouse for slaves; *ergastulis*: abl. w/ *supprimebantur*

possessor, -oris (m.) owner, landowner

supprimo, supprimere, suppressi, suppressum weigh down, suppress, detain (<sub- + premo)

factio, -onis (f.) band, faction; *factiones*: nom. pl. subj.

titulo collegi noui "with the title of a 'new association'"; titulus, -i (m.): title; collegium, -(i)i (n.): guild, board, association

ad ... societatem "to form a partnership to commit some crimes"; *nullius non*: LITOTES (AG #326a, 641); facinus, -oris (n.): crime; societas, -atis (f.): partnership

coeo, coire, coii, coitum come together, band together (<con- + eo)

igitur note placement at start of sentence, not usu. postpos. (AG #324j); here Suet shifts the subj. back to Augustus to present his solutions to the problems

grassatura, -ae (f.) highway robbery (an unusual wd. <grassor)

dispositis ... stationibus abl. abs. (AG #419); dispono, disponere, disposui, dispositum: distribute, set out (<dis- + pono); oportunus, -a, -um: advantageous; statio, -onis (f.): armed post, garrison

inhibeo, inhibere, inhibui, inhibitum restrain, check, prevent (<in- + habeo)

recognosco, recognoscere, recognoui, recognitum examine, review, inspect (<re- + cognosco)

antiquus, -a, -um ancient, old

legitimus, -a, -um legal, lawful

dissoluo, dissoluere, dissolui, dissolutum break up, dissolve, do away with (<dis- + soluo)

32.2

tabula, -ae (f.) tablet, (pl.) account-books (*OLD* 7)

debitum, -i (n.) debt

uel ... materiam phr. in appos. to *tabulas*; uel (adv.): perhaps, possibly; calumnior (1): bring false accusations; *calumniandi*: gen. of ger. (AG #504); materia, -ae (f.): material, means

exuro, exurere, exussi, exustum destroy by fire, burn (<ex- + uro)

iuris ambigui "of uncertain legal standing," gen. of quality (AG #345); ambiguous, -a, -um: doubtful, uncertain; Suet. here is likely referring to land seizures that had taken place during the civil wars

possessoribus adiudicauit, diuturnorum reorum et ex quorum
sordibus nihil aliud quam uoluptas inimicis quaereretur
nomina aboleuit, condicione proposita ut si quem quis repetere
uellet par periculum poenae subiret. ne quod autem maleficium negotiumue inpunitate uel mora elaberetur, triginta
amplius dies, qui honoraris ludis occupabantur, actui rerum
accommodauit.   3. ad tris iudicum decurias quartam addidit ex
inferiore censu, quae ducenariorum uocaretur iudicaretque de

---

adiudico (1) award as judge (to), assign (to) (<ad- + iudico)
diuturnus, -a, -um long-lasting, longstanding
reus, -i (m.) defendant
ex quorum sordibus nihil ... quaereretur relat. cl. of char. (AG #535); *quorum* (relat. pron.): anteced. *reorum*; sordes, -is (f.): (pl.) the dark clothes worn by defendants in court (*OLD* 2b); uoluptas, -atis (f.): delight; inimicus, -a, -um: unfriendly, (subst.) enemy; *inimicis*: dat. of ref. (AG #377); quaero, quaerere, quaes(i)i (-siui), quaesitum: seek, gain, obtain
nomina aboleuit "he dropped the prosecution"; aboleo, abolere, aboleui, abolitum: put an end to, drop (the prosecution of); Augustus put an end to the frivolous prosecutions
condicione proposita abl. abs. (AG #419); condicio, -onis (f.): agreement
ut ... subiret proviso cl. (AG #528b) w/ condit., "that if anyone wished to call someone back for a trial, he would submit to a similar risk of penalty"; repeto, repetere, repetiui (-ii), repetitum: call for retrial (*OLD* 11) (<re- + peto); subeo, subire, subii (-iui), subitum: undergo, submit to (<sub- + eo)
ne ... elaberetur negat. purp. cl. (AG #531); *quod* = aliquod; maleficium, -(i)i (n.): offense, crime; negotium, -(i)i (n.): lawsuit (*OLD* 9); Suet. here uses technical language to refer to criminal (*maleficium*) and civil (*negotium*) legal matters; *inpunitate uel mora*: abl. of cause (AG #404); inpunitas, -atis (f.): impunity, freedom from punishment; mora, -ae (f.): delay; elabor, elabi, elapsus sum: slip by, escape (<ex- + labor)
triginta amplius dies "thirty more days," acc. dir. obj. of *accommodauit*; triginta (indecl. adj.): thirty
qui (relat. pron.) anteced. *dies*
ludi honorarii games paid for by magistrates from their own resources (in contrast to public games)
occupo (1) take up, fill
actus, -us (m.) transaction, carrying out; *actui rerum*: "for the carrying out of legal business"
accommodo (1) make available for (w/ dat. and acc.) (<ad- + commodo); Augustus is reported to have made thirty more days available for conducting business by allowing courts to meet on days when discretionary games were held

32.3
tres, tria three (decl., AG #134b)
iudex, -icis (m.) juror, member of a panel appointed to hear a case
decuria, -ae (f.) panel of men (from which jurors were selected); jurors had traditionally been selected from senators, equites, and a third group called tribuni aerarii
inferior, -ius lower
census, -us (m.) census, the members of a particular census class (*OLD* 2c)
quae [decuria] ... uocaretur iudicaretque relat. cl. of char. (AG #535), "which was called the panel of ducenarii and would judge cases"; ducenarius, -a, -um: owning 200,000 sesterces; iudico (1): judge, try (a case)

leuioribus summis. iudices a tricensimo aetatis anno adlegit, id est quinquennio maturius quam solebant, ac plerisque iudicandi munus detractantibus uix concessit ut singulis decuriis per uices annua uacatio esset et ut solitae agi Nouembri ac Decembri mense res omitterentur.

33   Ipse ius dixit assidue et in noctem nonnumquam, si parum corpore ualeret lectica pro tribunali collocata uel etiam domi cubans. dixit autem ius non diligentia modo summa sed et lenitate, siquidem manifestum parricidii reum, ne culleo insueretur (quod non nisi confessi adficiuntur hac poena), ita fertur

---

tricensimus, -a, -um thirtieth; Suet. is in error here as Augustus must have lowered the age for service to twenty-five from the traditional age of thirty
adlego, adlegere, adlegi, adlectum elect, recruit, appoint (for a duty/office) (<ad- + lego)
quinquennium, -(i)i (n.) a period of five years; *quinquennio*: abl. of degr. of diff. (AG #414)
mature (adv.) early (compar. = -ius)
plerisque ... detractantibus abl. abs. (AG #419); iudico (1): judge; *iudicandi*: gen. of ger. (AG #504); detracto (1): refuse to undertake (<de- + tracto)
ut ... uacatio esset subst. cl. of purp. (= indir. comm.) ff. *concessit* (AG #563); *singulis decuriis*: dat. of poss. (AG #373); *per uices*: "by turn"; annuus, -a, -um: lasting a year, year-long; uacatio, -onis (f.): exemption from service
ut ... res omitterentur a second subst. cl. of purp. (= indir. comm.) (AG #563); *solitae ... res*: nom. pl.; solitus, -a, -um: accustomed (w/ inf.); *Nouembri ac Decembri mense*: abl. of time when (AG #423)

33.1

ius dicere administer justice, give legal decisions; Augustus' role as presiding judge in legal matters is much debated, but his tenure of the consulship and consular power, as well as his proconsular command, provided multiple opportunities to administer justice
si ... ualeret impf. subjv. in prot. of condit. to show repeated action (AG #518c); *corpore*: abl. of specif. (AG #418); ualeo, ualere, ualui, ualitum: be well
lectica ... collocata abl. abs. (AG #419).; tribunal, -alis (n.): dais or platform (used for judicial purposes); colloco (1): put in place (<con- + loco)
domi "at home," locat. (AG #427.3)
non ... modo ... sed et not only ... but even
diligentia ... summa ... et lenitate abl. of manner (AG #412); diligentia, -ae (f.): carefulness, attentiveness; summus, -a, -um: highest, utmost; lenitas, -atis (f.): mildness, clemency, leniency
siquidem seeing that, since, in that (giving the reason for or illustrating a stmt.)
manifestum ... reum acc. obj. of *interrogasse*; manifestus, -a, -um: detected in the act (*OLD* 2); parricidium, -(i)i (n.): parricide, murder of one's own father; reus, -i (m.): defendant
ne ... insueretur negat. purp. cl. (AG #531); culleus, -i (m.): leather sack; insuo, insuere, insui, insutum: sew up (in) (w/ dat.) (<in- + suo)
quod ... adficiuntur hac poena causal cl. (AG #540); non nisi: not unless, only (on specified terms); confiteor, confiteri, confessus sum: admit, confess (<con- + fateor); *confessi*: subst. subj., "men who confessed"; adficio, adficere, adfeci, adfectum: affect, visit with (punishment) (w/ abl.) (<ad- + facio)
fertur "he [Augustus] is said" (pass. <fero) (w/ inf.)

interrogasse, 'certe patrem tuum non occidisti?' **2.** et cum de falso testamento ageretur omnesque signatores lege Cornelia tenerentur, non tantum duas tabellas, damnatoriam et absolutoriam, simul cognoscentibus dedit sed tertiam quoque, qua ignosceretur iis quos fraude ad signandum uel errore inductos constitisset. **3.** appellationes quotannis urbanorum quidem litigatorum praetori delegabat urbano, at prouincialium consularibus uiris quos singulos cuiusque prouinciae negotiis praeposuisset.

---

interrogasse contr. form of interrogauisse (AG #181)
certe . . . occidisti Suet. reports Augustus' wd. in dir. speech; note that Augustus' question was carefully worded to elicit a negative response; certe (adv.): certainly

33.2
cum . . . ageretur omnesque . . . tenerentur circumst. cum cl. (AG #546); falsus, -a, -um: counterfeited; *ageretur*: (impers.) "it was being pled"; signator, -oris (m.): witness to a document; teneo, tenere, tenui, tentum: hold liable; the lex Cornelia de falsis, put forward by L. Cornelius Sulla Felix (*OCD* 384–385), established a court and penalty for cases of forgery
non tantum . . . sed not only . . . but
tabella, -ae (f.) tablet (used for voting)
damnatorius, -a, -um indicating condemnation
absolutorius, -a, -um favoring acquittal
cognoscens, -ntis (m.) juror, one taking part in a judicial case
qua ignosceretur iis "by which they might be forgiven," relat. cl. of purp. (AG #531.2); ignosco, ignoscere, ignoui, ignotum: forgive (impers. w/ dat. of offender) (<in- + (g)nosco)
quos . . . inductos [esse] **constitisset** "those whom it had been established had been induced," relat. cl., of char. (AG #535) introd. indir. disc. ff. impers. *constitisset*; fraus, -dis (f.) deceit, fraud; signo (1): sign; *ad signandum*: ger. indicating purp. (AG #506); error, -oris (m.): error, mistake; induco, inducere, induxi, inductum: induce, lead (<in- + duco); consisto, consistere, constiti: be established (<con- + sisto)

33.3
appellatio, -onis (f.) appeal
quotannis (adv.) every year
urbanus, -a, -um urban, connected with the city (Rome)
litigator, -oris (m.) litigant, one engaged in a lawsuit (vb. subst. <litigo)
praetori urbano the praetor urbanus was the magistrate responsible for administration of justice in Rome
delego (1) assign, delegate, refer (w/ dat. and acc.) (<de- + lego)
prouincialis, -e provincial, belonging to a province; *prouincialium* [*litigatorum*]
consularis, -e of a consul, of consular rank
quos . . . praeposuisset subord. cl. w/ subjv. in informal indir. disc. (AG #592.1); negotium, -(i)i (n.): lawsuit (*OLD* 9); praepono, praeponere, praeposui, praepositum: put in charge of (w/ acc. and dat.) (<prae- + pono)

34 Leges retractauit et quasdam ex integro sanxit, ut sumptuariam
et de adulteriis et de pudicitia, de ambitu, de maritandis ordinibus. hanc cum aliquanto seuerius quam ceteras emendasset,
prae tumultu recusantium perferre non potuit nisi adempta
demum lenitaue parte poenarum et uacatione trienni data auc-
tisque praemiis. 2. sic quoque abolitionem eius publico spectaculo pertinaciter postulante equite, accitos Germanici liberos
receptosque partim ad se partim in patris gremium ostentauit,

---

Laws (*leges*). A prominent rubric header introduces a chapter devoted to the laws proposed by Augustus, the *leges Iuliae*.

34.1
retracto (1) revise, reconsider (<re- + tracto)
integer, -gra, -grum fresh, not touched; *ex integro*: afresh, anew (*OLD* 3a)
sancio, sancire, sanxi, sanctum ratify, enact
ut sumptuariam [legem] et ... de maritandis ordinibus Suet. lists selected examples of Augustus' legislation, focusing on measures from 18–17 BCE that maintained status distinctions and addressed moral and social issues; sumptuarius, -a, -um: concerning expenditure; adulterium, -(i)i (n.): adultery; pudicitia, -ae (f.): chastity, sexual purity; ambitus, -us (m.): electoral bribery (*OLD* 6); *de maritandis ordinibus*: "concerning social classes marrying"; marito (1): marry; *maritandis*: gerv.
hanc = Lex Iulia de maritandis ordinibus, passed in 18 BCE; the law was modified by the Lex Papia Poppaea of 9 CE
cum ... emendasset causal cum cl. (AG #549); seuere (adv.): severely, extensively (compar. = -ius); emendo (1): revise; *emendasset* = contr. form of emendauisset (AG #181); the earliest law on the topic dated back to the fifth century BCE; Augustus' legislation added new restrictions and requirements, including penalties for those who remained unmarried
prae (prep. w/ abl.) in the face of, in view of
recuso (1) make an objection, protest; *recusantium*: gen. pl. of pres. act. ptc. used subst., "of people protesting"
perfero, perferre, pertuli, perlatum carry, get passed (a law) (<per- + fero); *perferre*: compl. inf. (AG #456)
adempta ... parte poenarum abl. abs. (AG #419); lenio, lenire, leniui (-ii), lenitum: moderate
uacatione ... data abl. abs. (AG #419); uacatio, -onis (f.): exemption; triennis, -e: three-year; the three-year delay in implementing the measure gave people the opportunity to comply with the measure in order to avoid penalities
auctis ... praemiis abl. abs. (AG #419); among the rewards were priority in office for the candidate with the most children

34.2
sic ... postulante equite abl. abs. (AG #419); abolitio, -onis (f.): annulment; *publico spectaculo*: abl. of time when (AG #424d); pertinaciter (adv.): determinedly; postulo (1): demand; eques, -itis (m.): equestrian; (collective sg.) the equestrian order
accitos ... liberos receptosque ... in patris gremium ptc. phr., obj. of *ostentauit*; accio, accire, acciui (-ii), accitum: summon, send for (<ad- + ci(e)o); Germanicus, Augustus' grandson by adoption (*OCD* s.v. Iulius Caesar, Germanicus, 760–761); partim (adv.): in part, partly; gremium, -ii (n.): a person's lap; the event described likely dates to 9 CE when Germanicus had two young sons, Nero and Drusus
ostento (1) exhibit, display

manu uultuque significans ne grauarentur imitari iuuenis exemplum, cumque etiam inmaturitate sponsarum et matrimoniorum crebra mutatione uim legis eludi sentiret, tempus sponsas habendi coartauit, diuortiis modum imposuit.

35   Senatorum affluentem numerum deformi et incondita turba— erant enim super mille, et quidam indignissimi ut post necem Caesaris per gratiam et praemium adlecti, quos orciuos uulgus uocabat—ad modum pristinum et splendorem redegit duabus

---

uultus, -us (m.) facial expression, face
significo (1) indicate, demonstrate, convey
ne grauarentur... exemplum negat. subst. cl. of purp. (= indir. comm.) (AG #563); grauo (1): (pass.) show reluctance, refuse (w/ inf.); imitor (1): copy, follow; *imitari*: compl. inf. (AG #456); *iuuenis* = Germanici; exemplum, -i (n.): example
cum... uim legis eludi sentiret circumst. cum cl. (AG #546) with indir. disc. (AG #580) ff. *sentiret*; immaturitas, -atis (f.): immaturity; sponsa, -ae (f.): fiancée; matrimonium, -(i)i (n.): marriage; creber, -bra, -brum: frequent; mutatio, -onis (f.) change; uis, uis (f.): force; *uim*: acc. sg. subj. of indir. disc. (AG #79 for irreg. decl.); eludo, eludere, elusi, elusum: evade (<ex- + ludo); *eludi*: pres. pass. inf.; sentio, sentire, sensi, sensum: perceive, sense
tempus sponsas habendi "the duration of engagements"; *habendi*: gen. of ger. w/ dir. obj. (AG #504a)
coarto (1) shorten, restrict (<con- + arto)
diuortium, -(i)i (n.) divorce; the details concerning the restrictions that Augustus placed on divorce are unknown
impono, imponere, imposui, impositum place, impose (<in- + pono)

Senators (*senatorum*). The Senatorial Order is the topic of the next four chapters. Augustus took steps to reduce the size of the senate, engage more senators in government administration, and enhance the prestige of the order.

35.1
affluo, affluere, affluxi be present in overflowing number, be superabundant (<ad- + fluo)
numerum dir. obj. of *redegit*
deformi et incondita turba abl. of means ff. *affluentem* (AG #409a); deformis, -e: discreditable, unseemly; inconditus, -a, -um: crude, disordered
erant enim... uocabat Suet. interrupts the sentence with a comment about the number of new senators who had gained their positions by disreputable means; indignus, -a, -um: unworthy, shameful (superl. = -issimus); ut: "such as"; nex, necis (f.): killing, death; adlego, adlegere, adlegi, adlectum: elect, appoint (for a duty/office) (<ad- + lego); *quos* (relat. pron.): anteced. *adlecti*; *orciuos*: "Orcus-men," slaves granted freedom under the terms of a will, here a derogatory term applied to those enrolled in the senate allegedly at the request of the late Caesar; uulgus, -i (n.): the common people
ad modum pristinum et splendorem pristinus, -a, -um: former, previous; splendor, -oris (m.): splendor, glory; Augustus eventually succeeded in reducing the size of the senate to 600 members, far more than the traditional size of 300; the senate continued to enroll 600 members in Suet.'s day, and afterward
duo, duae, duo (pl. adj.) two

lectionibus, prima ipsorum arbitratu, quo uir uirum legit,
secunda suo et Agrippae, quo tempore existimatur lorica sub
ueste munitus ferroque cinctus praesedisse decem ualentissimis senatorii ordinis amicis sellam suam circumstantibus.
2. Cordus Cremutius scribit ne admissum quidem tunc quemquam senatorum nisi solum et praetemptato sinu. quosdam ad
excusandi se uerecundiam compulit seruauitque etiam excusatis
insigne uestis et spectandi in orchestra epulandique publice
ius.   3. quo autem lecti probatique et religiosius et minore

---

lectio, -onis (f.) review, selection; a lectio senatus was a revision of the senate roster usually undertaken by the censors
prima [lectione] "in the first review," abl. of time within which (AG #424c); Suet. confuses the order of the two reviews
arbitratus, -us (m.) choice; (abl.) according to the decision of (w/ gen. *ipsorum* = senatorum)
quo uir uirum legit "by which one man chose another man," a form of cooptation as senators were to nominate others to continue to serve; Dio (54.13.2–4) provides further details of this review in 18 BCE
suo et Agrippae [arbitratu] Augustus and Agrippa, with the power of censors, conducted a review in 29 BCE
quo tempore "at which time," abl. of time when (AG #423)
existimatur "he is thought," pers. constr. w/ inf. (AG #582)
lorica sub ueste munitus ferroque cinctus ptc. phr.; lorica, -ae (f.): cuirass, defensive breastplate and backplate; *lorica*: abl. of means; munio, munire, muniui (-ii), munitum: guard, defend; ferrum, -i (n.): sword; cingo, cingere, cinxi, cinctum: gird, equip (w/ abl.)
praesideo, praesidere, praesedi preside (<prae- + sedeo); *praesedisse*: pf. inf. w/ *existimatur*
decem ualentissimis ... amicis ... circumstantibus abl. abs. as cl. of accompanying circumst. (AG #420.5); decem (indecl. adj.): ten; ualens, -ntis: sturdy, strong (superl. = -ntissimus); senatorius, -a, -um: senatorial; sella, -ae (f.): chair; circumsto, circumstare, circumsteti (-iti): stand around (<circum- + sto)

35.2

Cremutius Cordus Aulus Cremutius Cordus (*OCD* 392), a historian writing at the time of Augustus and Tiberius
admissum [esse] ... **quemquam** ... **sinu** indir. disc. (AG #580) ff. *scribit*; admitto, admittere, admisi, admissum: let in (to the senate house) (<ad- + mitto); *praetemptato sinu*: tmp. abl. abs. (AG #420.1); praetempto (1): test (<prae- + tempto); sinus, -us (m.): a fold (of a toga) used as a pocket
ad excusandi se uerecundiam "to resign" (lit: "to the modest act of excusing themselves"); uerecundia, -ae (f.): modesty, attitude of restraint; excuso (1): (reflex.) excuse oneself; *excusandi se*: ger. w/ obj. (AG #503, 504)
compello, compellere, compuli, compulsum compel, force (<con- + pello)
seruo (1) preserve, save; Augustus allowed for the men expelled from the senate (*excusatis*) to retain certain privileges
insigne uestis "the distinction of dress" (the broad purple stripe of a senator's toga); insigne, -is (n.): emblem or symbol
spectandi ... epulandique ... ius "the right of watching ... and dining"; *spectandi*: obj. gen. of ger. (AG #504); orchestra, -ae (f.): area in front of the stage, orchestra; epulor (1): dine, banquet

35.3

quo ... lecti probatique ... fungerentur relat. cl. of purp. w/ compar. (AG #531.2a); probo (1): approve;

molestia senatoria munera fungerentur, sanxit ut prius quam
consideret quisque ture ac mero supplicaret apud aram eius dei
in cuius templo coiretur, et ne plus quam bis {in} mense legitimus senatus ageretur, Kalendis et Idibus, neue Septembri
Octobriue mense ullos adesse alios necesse esset quam sorte
ductos per quorum numerum decreta confici possent, sibique
instituit consilia sortiri semestria cum quibus de negotiis ad
frequentem senatum referendis ante tractaret.   4. sententias
de maiore negotio non more atque ordine sed prout libuisset

---

religiose (adv.): in accordance with religious law (compar. = -ius); molestia, -ae (f.): trouble; senatorius, -a, -um: senatorial; *munera*: acc. dir. obj. of *fungerentur*

sancio, sancire, sanxi, sanctum prescribe by law, enact

ut ... quisque ... supplicaret subst. cl. of purp. (= indir. comm.) (AG #563) ff. *sanxit*; *prius quam consideret*: anticipatory cl. implying expectancy in past time (AG #551b); consido, considere, consedi: sit down (<con- + sido); tus, turis (n.): incense; merum, -i (n.): unmixed wine; supplico (1): make an offering, do worship; *in cuius templo coiretur*: relat. cl., "in whose temple they were meeting"; *cuius* (relat. pron.): anteced. *dei*; coeo, coire, coii, coitum: come together, meet (<con- + eo); *coiretur*: impers. pass. (AG #208d), subjv. by attraction (AG #593); the senate was required to meet in a templum, either a temple or another building that had been ritually inaugurated

ne ... ageretur negat. subst. cl. of purp. (= indir. comm.) (AG #563) ff. *sanxit*; plus (compar. adv.): more; legitimus, -a, -um: regular; ago, agere, egi, actum: conduct, hold; *Kalendis et Idibus*: abl. of time when (AG #423), "on the Kalends and the Ides" (for the Roman calendar, AG #631)

neue ... necesse esset negat. subst. cl. of purp. (= indir. comm.) (AG #563) ff. *sanxit*; *Septembri Octobriue mense*: "in September or October," abl. of time when (AG #423); adsum, adesse, adfui: be present (<ad- + sum); necesse est: be necessary for (w/ acc. + inf.); *sorte ductos*: "those selected by lot"; sors, -rtis (f.): lot, lottery

per quorum numerum decreta ... possent relat. cl. w/ subjv. by attraction (AG #593); *quorum* (relat. pron.): anteced. *ductos* [*senatores*]; decretum, -i (n.): decree; conficio, conficere, confeci, confectum: complete, finish (<con- + facio); *confici*: pres. pass., compl. inf. (AG #456)

consilia sortiri semestria subst. cl. of purp. (= indir. comm.) w/ acc. subj. + inf. ff. *instituit* (AG #563a); consilium, -(i)i (n.): advisory council (*OLD* 3); sortior, sortiri, sortitus sum: appoint by lot; semestris, -e: of six months' duration, six-monthly

cum quibus ... tractaret relat. cl. of purp. (AG #531.2), "with whom he might deliberate"; frequens, -ntis: full; *referendis*: abl. pl. gerv. w/ *negotiis*; ante (adv.): in advance; tracto (1): deliberate

35.4

sententia, -ae (f.) opinion, sentiment

non more atque ordine "not according to custom and proper order"; normally senators were called upon in order of rank and seniority

prout libuisset "just as he wished"; prout (conj.): according as (<pro + ut); libet, libere, libuit: (impers.) be pleasing; *libuisset*: plpf. subjv. in generalizing stmt. (AG #518c)

LIFE OF AUGUSTUS WITH COMMENTARY

perrogabat, ut perinde quisque animum intenderet ac si censendum magis quam adsentiendum esset.

36   Auctor et aliarum rerum fuit, in quis ne acta senatus publicarentur, ne magistratus deposito honore statim in prouincias mitterentur, ut proconsulibus ad mulos et tabernacula quae publice locari solebant certa pecunia constitueretur, ut cura aerari a quaestoribus urbanis ad praetorios praetoresue transiret, ut centumuiralem hastam, quam quaestura functi

---

perrogo (1) ask for or solicit in turn (<per- + rogo)
ut ... intenderet purp. cl. (AG 531.1); *perinde* (adv.; correl. w/ *prout*): correspondingly; intendo, intendere, intendi, intentum: exert, concentrate (<in- + tendo)
ac si "as if"
censendum ... adsentiendem esset "an opinion must be given rather than be agreed upon," impers. pass. periphr. (AG #500.3); censeo, censere, censui, censum: give as one's considered opinion, recommend (a course of action); *magis quam*: rather than; adsentio, adsentire, adsensi, adsensum: agree, approve (<ad- + sentio)

36
auctor pred. nom. (AG #284)
in quis = in quibus (AG #150c), "among which"; Suet. follows with a list of examples, each taking the form of a subst. cl. of purp. (= indir. comm.) (AG #563)
ne acta ... publicarentur negat. subst. cl. of purp. (AG #563); *acta senatus*: the official minutes of meetings of the Roman senate; actum, -i (n.): act, deed (usu. pl.); publico (1): make public, publish; Augustus reversed a measure of Julius Caesar that had made these records public
ne magistratus ... mitterentur negat. subst. cl. of purp. (AG #563); *deposito honore*: tmp. abl. abs. (AG #420.1); depono, deponere, deposui, depositum: lay down, resign (<de- + pono); a period of five years was now required b/w magistracies and provincial governorships
ut ... certa pecunia constitueretur subst. cl. of purp. (AG #563); proconsul, -lis (m.): proconsul, governor of a province; mulus, -i (m.): mule; tabernaculum, -i (n.): tent; *quae ... solebant*: relat. cl.; loco (1): contract for (having a thing done), lease; *certa pecunia*: nom., "a fixed sum of money"; proconsuls did not receive a salary, but Augustus established a fixed allowance to cover expenses
ut cura ... transiret subst. cl. of purp. (AG #563); cura, -ae (f.): care, administration; quaestor, -oris (m.): quaestor (the lowest magistrate in the senatorial cursus honorum); urbanus, -a, -um: urban, connected with the city (Rome); praetorius, -a, -um: (m. subst.) ex-praetor; transeo, transire, transiui (-ii), transitum: pass (from one to another), transfer (<trans- + eo)
ut ... decemuiri cogerent subst. cl. of purp. (AG #563); *centumuiralem hastam*: "the centumviral court," a standing court that heard civil cases related to inheritances and other matters; hasta, -ae (f.): spear (the symbol of the centumviral court); *quaestura functi*: "former quaestors" (those who had held the quaestorship); quaestura, -ae (f.): quaestorship; consuesco, consuescere, consueui, consuetum: become accustomed to (w/ inf.) (<con- + suesco); *consuerant* = contr. form of consueuerant (AG #181); decemuir, -uiri (m.): member of the board of ten

103

37 consuerant cogere, decemuiri cogerent, quoque plures partem
administrandae rei p. caperent noua officia excogitauit: curam
operum publicorum, uiarum, aquarum, aluei Tiberis, frumenti
populo diuidundi, praefecturam urbis, triumuiratum legendi
senatus et alterum recognoscendi turmas equitum quotiensque
opus esset. censores creari desitos longo interuallo creauit,
numerum praetorum auxit, exegit etiam ut quotiens consulatus
sibi daretur binos pro singulis collegas haberet, nec optinuit,
reclamantibus cunctis satis maiestatem eius imminui quod
honorem eum non solus sed cum altero gereret.

37

quoque plures ... caperent relat. cl. of purp. w/ compar. (AG #531.2a); plures, -a: (m. pl. as subst.) more men (senators are understood as the subj.); *administrandae rei p*[*ublicae*]: "in managing the state," objv. gen. of ger. (AG #504); once Augustus' plan was fully realized, more than one hundred senators each year would take up new administrative duties

officium, -(i)i (n.) post, position

excogito (1) devise, invent (<ex- + cogito); Augustus devised new positions that would evolve into the civil bureaucracy of Suet.'s day

curam ... frumenti populo diuidundi Suet. lists a number of curatorships, which oversaw specific administrative functions in Rome and Italy; cura, -ae (f.): care, administration; uia, -ae (f.): road; aqua, -ae (f.): supply of water, aqueduct; alueus, -i (m.): channel, bed (of a river); Tiberis, -is (m.): the river Tiber; *frumenti populo diuidundi*: "of distributing grain to the people"; frumentum, -i (n.): grain; *diuidundi*: objv. gen. of gerv. w/ *frumenti* (AG #504)

praefectura, -ae (f.) administrative appointment, prefecture

triumuiratus, -us (m.) three-man board

legendi objv. gen. of gerv. w/ *senatus* (AG #504)

alterum [triumuiratum]

recognosco, recognoscere, recognoui, recognitum examine, review, inspect; *recognoscendi*: objv. gen. of ger. w/ obj. (AG #504a)

turma, -ae (f.) squadron, unit, company

quotiens opus esset "as often as was needed"; opus est: it is necessary; *esset*: iterative subjv. w/ *quotiens* (BG #567n)

censor, -oris (m.) censor

creo (1) create, institute (an office), appoint (a magistrate); *creari*: pr. pass. inf. w/ *desitos*

desino, desinere, des(i)i (-iui), desitum cease (w/ inf.) (<de- + sino)

longo interuallo "for a long time"; longus, -a, -um: long, lengthy; interuallum, -i (n.): intervening period of time; after a gap of two decades, censors were elected in 22 BCE

numerum praetorum the number of praetors was raised from eight to ten

ut ... haberet subst. cl. of purp. (indir. comm.) ff. *exegit* (AG #563); *quotiens ... daretur*: iterative subjv. w/ *quotiens* (BG #567n); bini, -ae, -a (pl. adj.): two, a set of two

optineo, optinere, optinui, optentum achieve (an aim), prevail (<ob- + teneo)

reclamantibus cunctis causal abl. abs. (AG #419.2); reclamo (1): object loudly, protest (<re- + clamo); cunctus, -a, -um: all

satis maiestatem ... imminui indir. disc. (AG #580) ff. *reclamantibus* (AG #580); maiestas, -atis (f.): dignity, majesty; imminuo, imminuere, imminui, imminutum: diminish (<in- + minuo); *imminui*: pr. pass. inf.

quod ... gereret causal cl. w/ subjv. indicating authority of another (AG #540)

38 Nec parcior in bellica uirtute honoranda super triginta ducibus iustos triumphos et aliquanto pluribus triumphalia ornamenta decernenda curauit. 2. liberis senatorum, quo celerius rei p. assuescerent, protinus <sumpta> uirili toga latum clauum induere et curiae interesse permisit militiamque auspicantibus non tribunatum modo legionum sed et praefecturas alarum dedit. ac ne qui expers castrorum esset, binos plerumque lati-

---

38.1
parcus, -a, -um thrifty, restrained (compar. = -ior)
in bellica uirtute honoranda gerv. phr. (AG #507.3); bellicus, -a, -um: warlike, military; uirtus, -utis (f.): valor, virtue, excellence; honoro (1): honor, celebrate
super triginta ducibus "to more than thirty leaders," dat. indir. obj. w/ *decernenda*; Suet. seems to be counting all triumphs voted by the senate from 43 BCE to 14 CE
iustos triumphos ... triumphalia ornamenta decernenda [esse] subst. cl. of purp. w/ acc. subj. + inf. ff. *curauit* (AG #563a) w/ ELLIPSIS of esse; iustus, -a, -um: lawful, having good cause; *aliquanto pluribus*: "to somewhat more [than thirty]", dat. indir. obj. w/ *decernenda*; triumphalia ornamenta: "triumphal insignia" (a lesser honor celebrated without the triumphal procession); ornamentum, -i (n.): (usu. pl.) ornament, insignia; decerno, decernere, decreui, decretum: decree (<de- + cerno); *decernenda* w/ both *triumphos* and *ornamenta* (AG #317b); triumphal honors, bestowed by the senate, were the highest mark of distinction (*OCD* s.v. triumph, 1509–1510)

38.2
quo ... assuescerent relat. cl. of purp. w/ compar. (AG #531.2a); celeriter (adv.): quickly (compar. = -ius); *rei p[ublicae]*: "public service"; assuesco, assuescere, assueui, assuetum: become accustomed to (w/ dat.) (<ad- + suesco)
protinus (adv.) immediately, straight away
sumpta uirili toga tmp. abl. abs. (AG #420.1); toga uirilis: the adult toga; the assumption of the toga uirilis formally marked a young man's coming of age
latus clauus the broad purple stripe of the tunic, a mark of senatorial rank; latus, -a, -um: broad; clauus, -i (m.): purple stripe
induo, induere, indui, indutum put on, don; *induere*: inf. w/ *permisit* (AG #563c)
intersum, interesse, interfui attend, take part in (w/ dat.) (<inter- + sum); *interesse*: inf. w/ *permisit* (AG #563c); sons of senators probably observed meetings of the senate from outside the doors
militiamque auspicantibus "and to those starting military service," indir. obj. w/ *dedit*; militia, -ae (f.): military service; auspicor, auspicari, auspicatus sum: begin, enter upon; *auspicantibus*: dat. pl. pres. act. ptc. as subst.
tribunatus, -us (m.) office of (military) tribune
praefectura, -ae (f.) prefecture, command
ala, -ae (f.) unit of cavalry
ne qui ... esset negat. purp. cl. (AG #531); *qui* = aliqui: someone, anyone; expers, -rtis: lacking experience (w/ gen.)
bini, -ae, -a (pl. adj.) two, a set of two
plerumque (adv.) on most occasions, mostly, often
laticlauius, -a, -um wearing the broad purple stripe (indicating senatorial rank); *laticlauios*: subst.

clauios praeposuit singulis alis. **3.** equitum turmas frequenter
recognouit, post longam intercapedinem reducto more trauectionis, sed neque detrahi quemquam in trauehendo ab accusatore passus est, quod fieri solebat, et senio uel aliqua corporis
labe insignibus permisit praemisso in ordine equo ad respondendum quotiens citarentur pedibus uenire. mox reddendi
equi gratiam fecit eis qui maiores annorum quinque et triginta
39 retinere eum nollent. impetratisque a senatu decem adiutoribus unum quemque equitum rationem uitae reddere coegit

---

praepono, praeponere, praeposui, praepositum put in charge of (w/ acc. and dat.) (<prae- + pono)

Equites (*equitum turmas*). Suetonius turns next to Augustus' actions toward men of the equestrian class, progressing in his categories down the social ladder.

38.3
turma, -ae (f.) squadron, unit, company
recognosco, recognoscere, recognoui, recognitum examine, review, inspect (<re- + cognosco)
post ... reducto more trauectionis abl. abs. (AG #419) w/ prep. phr.; longus, -a, -um: long, lengthy; intercapedo, -inis (f.): intermission, interval; reduco, reducere, reduxi, reductum: bring back (<re- + duco); trauectio, -onis (f.): action of riding past, procession; the transuectio equitum was the traditional review of the equites by the censor, revived by Augustus in modified form in 18 BCE
detrahi quemquam ... ab accusatore subst. cl. of purp. w/ inf. + subj. acc. ff. *passus est* (AG #563c); detraho, detrahere, detraxi, detractum: pull down, remove (<de- + traho); *detrahi*: pres. pass. inf.; traueho, trauehere, trauexi, trauectum: pass by, ride past (in a procession) (<trans- + ueho); *trahendo*: abl. of ger. (AG #507); accusator, -oris (m.): accuser, prosecutor, informer
quod fieri solebat "a thing which used to be done," indef. relat. cl. lacking anteced. (AG #307c,d)
senium, -ii (n.) condition of old age, dotage
labes, -is (f.) physical defect
insignis, -e notable for, distinguished by (w/ abl.); *insignibus*: dat. w/ *permisit*
praemisso ... equo abl. abs. (AG #419); praemitto, praemittere, praemisi, praemissum: send in advance, send ahead (<prae- + mitto); equus, -i (m.): horse
ad respondendum quotiens citarentur "whenever they were summoned to respond"; *respondendum*: ger. w/ ad (AG #506); cito (1): call, summon; *citarentur*: iterative subjv. w/ *quotiens* (BG #567n)
pedibus "on foot" (*OLD* 6)
uenio, uenire, ueni, uentum come, approach; *uenire*: inf. ff. *permisit* (AG #563c)
reddendi equi gratiam fecit "he granted permission to return the horse"; *reddendi*: objv. gen. gerv.; gratiam facere: grant leave (to do something) (w/ gen.) (*OLD* 1b)
qui maiores ... nollent relat. cl. of char. (AG #535); *annorum quinque et triginta*: "thirty-five years old," gen. of quality (AG #345b); *retinere*: compl. inf. (AG #456) ff. *nollent*; *eum* = equum; nolo, nolle, nolui: be unwilling, not want (<ne- + uolo); the turmae equitum were military in origin and thus forty-five was the normal age to move from active duty as iuniores to the status of seniores; Augustus lowered the age for some

39
impetratis ... adiutoribus abl. abs. (AG #419); impetro (1): obtain by request; decem (indecl. adj.): ten; adiutor, -oris (m.): helper (vb. subst. <adiuuo)
unum quemque equitum ... reddere subst. cl. of purp. (= indir. comm.) w/ acc. subj. + inf. ff. *coegit* (AG #563a); *unum quemque equitum*: "every single one of the equestrians" (unus quisque, AG #313); ratio, -onis (f.): account

atque ex improbatis alios poena, alios ignominia notauit, plures admonitione, sed uaria. lenissimum genus admonitionis fuit traditio coram pugillarium quos taciti et ibidem statim legerent, notauitque aliquos quod pecunias leuioribus usuris mutuati
40 grauiore faenore collocassent. ac comitiis tribuniciis si deessent candidati senatores, ex equitibus R. creauit ita ut potestate transacta in utro uellent ordine manerent. cum autem plerique equitum attrito bellis ciuilibus patrimonio spectare ludos e quattuordecim non auderent metu poenae theatralis, pronun-

---

ex improbatis "of those rejected"; improbo (1): reject; Suet. divides this group into three subsets: *alios ... alios ... plures*
ignominia, -ae (f.) disgrace, loss of status
admonitio, -onis (f.) warning, admonishment
lenis, -e gentle, mild (superl. = -issimus); *lenissimum genus*: nom.
traditio, -onis (f.) handing over, delivering
coram (adv.) openly, publicly
pugillares, -ium (m. pl.) set of small writing tablets
quos taciti ... legerent "for the men to read silently," relat. cl. of purp. (AG #531.2); tacitus, -a, -um: silent; *taciti*: adj. w/ adv. force (AG #290); ibidem (adv.): in that very place
quod ... mutuati ... collocassent causal cl. w/ subjv. (AG #540); *pecunias ... mutuati*: tmp. ptc. phr. (AG #496), "after the men had borrowed money"; usura, -ae (f.): (pl.) monthly payment of interest; mutuor (1): borrow; *mutuati*: nom. pl. pf. act. ptc.; faenus, -oris (n.): interest (on capital); colloco (1): invest (money) (<con- + loco); *collocassent* = contr. form of collocauissent (AG #181)

40.1
comitiis tribuniciis "at the tribunician elections", abl. of time when (AG #424d); tribunicius, -a, -um: tribunician, of a tribune
si deessent impf. subjv. for repeated action in prot. of mixed condit. (AG #518c); desum, deesse, defui: be lacking (<de- + sum)
candidatus, -i (m.) candidate for office; *candidati*: appos. (AG #282)
equitibus R [omanis] the Roman knights (*OCD* s.v. equites, 530–532)
creo (1) create, appoint (a magistrate); [*eos*] *creauit*: ELLIPSIS of pron.
ita ut ... manerent proviso cl. (AG #528b); *potestate transacta*: tmp. abl. abs. (AG #420.1), "after they had carried out the position"; potestas, -tatis (f.): office, position; transigo, transigere, transegi, transactum: carry through to the end (<trans- + ago); *in utro uellent ordine*: "in whichever order they wished"; uter, utra, utrum: whichever of two; *uellent*: subjv. by attraction (AG #593)
cum ... auderent circumst. cum cl. (AG #546); *attrito ... patrimonio*: abl. abs. (AG #419); attero, atterere, attriui, attritum: wear away, diminish (<ad- + tero); ciuilis, -e: civil; patrimonium, -(i)i (n.): private or personal possessions, estate; *spectare*: compl. inf. (AG #456); *e quattuordecim*: "from the fourteen [rows]" (reserved for equites); audeo, audere, ausus sum: dare
metu abl. of cause (AG #404)
theatralis, -e relating to the theater; the poena theatralis relates to the provisions of the lex Roscia of 67 BCE that had reserved the front fourteen rows in the theater for use by the equites

tiauit non teneri ea quibus ipsis parentibusue equester census umquam fuisset.

2. Populi recensum uicatim egit ac ne plebs frumentationum causa frequentius ab negotiis auocaretur ter in annum quaternum mensium tesseras dare destinauit, sed desideranti consuetudinem ueterem concessit rursus ut sui cuiusque mensis acciperet. comitiorum quoque pristinum ius reduxit ac multiplici poena coercito ambitu Fabianis et Scaptiensibus tribulibus suis die comitiorum, ne quid a quoquam candidato

---

non [eos] **teneri ea** [poena] "that they were not bound by that penalty"; indir. disc. (AG #580) ff. *pronuntiauit*; ELLIPSIS of *eos* as acc. subj. and anteced. of *quibus*

quibus ... fuisset relat. cl. in indir. disc. (AG #580); *ipsis parentibusue*: dat. of poss. (AG #373); parens, -ntis (m.): parent, father; *equester census*: nom., "the property qualification to be an eques (knight)"; census, -us (m.): census class; as with senators (cf. ch. 35.2), Augustus preserved some of the privileges of those who lost their status

The common people (*populi*). Augustus' actions related to the Roman people (40.2: *populi*) and slaves (40.4: *seruos*) completes the discussion of different social classes that started with the senate in chapter 35.

40.2
recensus, -us (m.) review, census, count

uicatim (adv.) by district, street by street; Suet. regularly uses adv. in -tim

ne plebs ... auocaretur negat. purp. cl. (AG #531); frumentatio, -onis (f.): distribution of grain; *causa* (abl.): "for the sake of," preceded by gen. (AG #359); auoco (1): call away (<ab- + uoco)

ter in annum ... tesseras dare subst. cl. of purp. w/ inf. (AG #563d) ff. *destinauit*; *ter in annum*: "three times in a year"; ter (adv.): three times, on three occasions; quaterni, -ae, -a (pl. adj.): four each, four at a time; *quaternum mensium*: gen. of quality (AG #345b) w/ *tesseras*; tessera, -ae (f.): ticket or voucher (for a supply of grain); Augustus' proposed innovation was to distribute four vouchers for grain distributions three times a year instead of distributing vouchers monthly; the plebs would exchange a voucher each month to receive an allotment of free grain

desidero (1) desire, request; *desideranti*: dat. sg. pres. act. ptc., "to the plebs requesting"

consuetudo, -inis (f.) habitual practice, custom

ut ... acciperet "that each man receive his own voucher each month," subst. cl. of purp. (AG #563); *cuiusque mensis*: gen. of quality (AG #345); supply *tesseras* as dir. obj.

comitiorum ... pristinum ius "the old right of elections"; pristinus, -a, -um: former, previous; contested elections were restored in 28–27 BCE after many years in which candidates had been selected by the triumvirs

reduco, reducere, reduxi, reductum bring back (<re- + duco)

multiplici poena coercito ambitu abl. abs. (AG #419); multiplex, -icis: multitudinous, varied; *multiplici poena*: abl. of means; coerceo, coercere, coercui, coercitum: control (<con- + arceo); ambitus, -us (m.): electoral bribery (*OLD* 6)

Fabianis et Scaptiensibus tribulibus suis "to his fellow Fabian and Scaptian tribesmen," indir. obj. w/ *diuidebat*; tribulis, -is (m.): fellow tribesman; Roman citizens were divided into voting tribes; Augustus was born into the Fabian tribe, but gained an association with the Scaptian through his adoption by Julius Caesar

die comitiorum "on election day"; *die*: abl. of time when (AG #423)

ne ... desiderarent negat. purp. cl. (AG #531); *quid* = aliquid; candidatus, -i (m.): candidate; desidero (1): look for, desire

desiderarent, singula milia nummum a se diuidebat. **3.** magni praeterea existimans sincerum atque ab omni colluuione peregrini ac seruilis sanguinis incorruptum seruare populum et ciuitates Romanas parcissime dedit et manumittendi modum terminauit. Tiberio pro cliente Graeco petenti rescripsit non aliter se daturum quam si praesens sibi persuasisset quasi iustas petendi causas haberet, et Liuiae pro quodam tributario Gallo roganti ciuitatem negauit, immunitatem optulit affirmans facilius se passurum fisco detrahi aliquid quam ciuitatis Romanae

---

singula milia nummum "individual payments of a thousand coins"; milia, -ium (n. pl.): thousands; *nummum*: gen. pl.; gifts to fellow tribesmen were not considered bribes
a se = de sua pecunia

40.3
magni ... existimans "thinking it of great importance"; *magni*: gen. of indef. value (AG #417)
praeterea (adv.) in addition, furthermore
sincerum ... incorruptum seruare populum "to keep the populace pure and untainted"; sincerus, -a, -um: sound, unblemished, pure; colluuio, -onis (f.): contamination, impure mixture; peregrinus, -a, -um: foreign, alien; seruilis, -e: servile, belonging to a slave; sanguis, -inis (m.): blood; incorruptus, -a, -um: unspoilt, untainted; seruo (1): preserve, save
ciuitas, -atis (f.) state, citizenship, (pl.) the gift of citizenship to single persons
parce (adv.) sparingly (superl. = -issime); Suet. commonly uses superl. adv.
manumittendi modum terminauit "he restricted the practice of freeing slaves"; manumitto, manumittere, manumisi, manumissum: emancipate, free; *manumittendi*: gen. of ger. (AG #504); modus, -i (m.): quantity, way, manner; termino (1): restrict, limit in scope; emancipation of slaves was common in the Roman world (*OCD* s.v. freedmen, 589); Augustus introduced new restrictions on the number of slaves who might be freed and on the ways in which manumission might take place
Tiberio ... petenti ptc. phr., indir. obj. w/ *rescripsit*; cliens, -ntis (m.): client; citizenship is understood as the obj. of *petenti*
rescribo, rescribere, rescripsi, rescriptum write in reply, write back to (<re- + scribo)
non aliter se daturum [esse] indir. disc. (AG #580) ff. *rescripsit*; aliter (adv.): otherwise (introd. compar. w/ *quam*)
quam si praesens sibi persuasisset plupf. subjv. in mixed condit. in indir. disc. (AG #589); praesens, -ntis: present, face to face; *sibi* = Augusto; persuadeo, persuadere, persuasi, persuasum: persuade (<per- + suadeo); Augustus required the Greek man to make his petition in person
quasi ... haberet "that he had just causes for seeking it"; *quasi* w/ subjv. to express belief (AG #524, BG #602n4); iustus, -a, -um: just; *petendi*: objv. gen. of ger. (AG #504)
Liuiae ... roganti ptc. phr. indir. obj. w/ *negauit*; Livia Drusilla, Augustus' wife (*OCD* 851); tributarius, -a, -um: liable to tax, tribute-paying; Gallus, -i (m.): a Gaul; rogo (1): ask
immunitas, -atis (f.) exemption from taxation or tribute
affirmo (1) assert positively, affirm, confirm (<ad- + firmo)
facilius se passurum [esse] **... quam** "that he would more readily allow", indir. disc. (AG #580) ff. *affirmans* w/ cl. of compar. w/ *quam* (AG #407); *fisco detrahi aliquid*: subst. cl. of purp. w/ acc. subj. + inf. ff. *passurum* (AG #563c); fiscus, -i (m.): the imperial treasury; *fisco*: dat. of separ. w/ compd.

uulgari honorem.   **4.** seruos non contentus multis difficultatibus a libertate et multo pluribus a libertate iusta remouisse, cum et de numero et de condicione ac differentia eorum qui manumitterentur curiose cauisset, hoc quoque adiecit, ne uinctus umquam tortusue quis ullo libertatis genere ciuitatem adipisceretur.   **5.** etiam habitum uestitumque pristinum reducere studuit, ac uisa quondam pro contione pullatorum turba indignabundus et clamitans, 'en Romanos, rerum dominos gentemque togatam!', negotium aedilibus dedit ne quem posthac paterentur in foro circaue nisi positis lacernis togatum consistere.

---

vb. *detrahi* (AG #381); detraho, detrahere, detraxi, detractum: to pull down, remove (<de- + traho); *detrahi*: pres. pass. inf.; *aliquid*: subj. acc.; *uulgari honorem*: a second subj. acc. + pass. inf.; uulgo (1): make available to the mass of people, cheapen

40.4

seruos non contentus ... remouisse "not satisfied to have blocked slaves from," Augustus is subj.; contentus, -a, -um: content, satisfied (w/ inf.); difficultas, -atis (f.): difficulty; *multis difficultatibus*: abl. of means (AG #409); *a libertate et ... a libertate iusta*: "from freedom and ... from full citizenship"; iusta libertas: full rights of citizenship; *multo pluribus [difficultatibus]*; remoueo, remouere, remoui, remotum: debar, block (a person) from (w/ ab) (<re- + moueo); note the placement of *seruos* at the start of the sentence to mark the transition to a new topic

cum ... cauisset circumst. cum cl. (AG #546); *et ... et*: both ... and; condicio, -onis (f.): situation, status; differentia, -ae (f.): distinction; *qui manumitterentur*: relat. cl. of char. (AG #535); curiose (adv.): carefully

ne ... quis ... adipisceretur negat. subst. cl. of purp. (= indir. comm.) ff. adiecit (AG #563); *uinctus ... tortusue*: tmp. ptc. phr. (AG #496), "after he had been bound or tortured"; uincio, uincire, uinxi, uinctus: fetter, bind; torqueo, torquere, torsi, tortum: torture; *quis* = aliquis (nom. sg.); adipiscor, adipisci, adeptus sum: obtain (<ad- + apiscor)

40.5

habitum uestitumque a rare example of HENDIADYS in Suet. (AG #640); habitus, -us (m.): style of dress; uestitus, -us (m.): apparel, clothes

pristinus, -a, -um former, previous

studeo, studere, studui devote oneself, concentrate (w/ inf. *reducere*)

uisa ... turba abl. abs. (AG #419); *pro contione*: "in front of an assembly"; pullatus, -a, -um: dressed in dark or dingy clothes; *pullatorum*: m. gen. pl. subst.

indignabundus, -a, -um furious (an unusual adj. <indignor + -bundus)

clamito (1) shout repeatedly (frequent. vb. <clamo, a vb. form favored by Suet.)

en (interj.) behold! see!; Suet. quotes directly the wd. of Augustus, who himself quotes Vergil

Romanos, rerum dominos gentemque togatam a dir. quote from Verg. *Aen.* 1.282; togatus, -a, -um: wearing a toga

aedilis, -is (m.) aedile, a magistrate charged with supervising buildings, games, markets, etc.

ne quem paterentur ... consistere negat. subst. cl. of purp. (= indir. comm.) (AG #563) introd. a second subst. cl. of purp. w/ subj. acc. + inf. ff. *paterentur* (AG #563c); *quem* = aliquem; circa (adv.): in the vicinity; *nisi ... togatum*: "unless dressed in a toga"; *positis lacernis*: abl. abs. (AG #419); lacerna, -ae (f.): cloak usually worn over the toga; consisto, consistere, constiti: stand (<con- + sisto)

41 Liberalitatem omnibus ordinibus per occasiones frequenter exhibuit. nam et inuecta urbi Alexandrino triumpho regia gaza tantam copiam nummariae rei effecit ut faenore deminuto plurimum agrorum pretiis accesserit, et postea quotiens ex damnatorum bonis pecunia superflueret usum eius gratuitum iis qui cauere in duplum possent ad certum tempus indulsit. senatorum censum ampliauit ac pro octingentorum milium summa duodecies sestertium taxauit suppleuitque non haben-

---

Acts of generosity (*liberalitatem*). Augustus is shown to exhibit unselfish liberality, not self-serving ambition. His sponsorship of public entertainments and his own attendance at events receive special attention (ch. 43–45).

41.1
liberalitas, -atis (f.) generosity, liberality
occasio, -onis (f.) opportunity; *per occasiones*: at favorable opportunities, as occasions arose
exhibeo, exhibere, exhibui, exhibitum display, exhibit, practice (<ex- + habeo)
nam et ... effecit ... et ... indulsit note the developed parallel structure as Suet. gives two examples w/ Augustus as subj. of *effecit* and *indulsit*
inuecta ... regia gaza abl. abs. (AG #419); inueho, inuehere, inuexi, inuectum: carry in (w/ dat.) (<in- + ueho); *Alexandrino triumpho*: abl. of time when (AG #424d); Alexandrinus, -a, -um: Alexandrian; regius, -a, -um: royal; gaza, -ae (f.): treasure; the triumph was celebrated in 29 BCE
nummarius, -a, -um relating to coins; *res nummaria*: currency, money; Suet. often uses res w/ adj. in place of a noun (cf. ch. 1: *rem divinam*, ch. 24.1: *re militari*)
efficio, efficere, effeci, effectum cause to occur, bring about (<ex- + facio)
ut ... accesserit result cl. (AG #537); *faenore deminuto*: abl. abs. (AG #419); faenus, -oris (n.): interest (on capital); deminuo, deminuere, deminui, deminutum: lessen, reduce (<de- + minuo); plurimum (adv): to the greatest extent; pretium, -(i)i (n.): value, price; accedo, accedere, accessi, accessum: add to (w/ dat.) (<ad- + cedo); *accesserit*: pf. subjv. in secondary seq. (AG #485c)
quotiens ... pecunia superflueret iterative subjv. w/ *quotiens* (BG #567n); damno (1): condemn, pass judgment against; *damnatorum*: m. gen. pl. of ppp as subst.; bonum, -i (n.): a good thing, (pl.) possessions, property; superfluo, superfluere, superfluxi: overflow, be superabundant (<super- + fluo)
usum eius "the use of this [money]"
gratuitus, -a, -um free of charge, costing nothing
qui ... possent relat. cl. of char. (AG #535); caueo, cauere, caui, cautum: give surety, provide guarantees; *in duplum*: for twice as much
ad certum tempus "for a fixed period of time," *ad* (OLD 10) expressing limit of time
indulgeo, indulgere, indulsi, indultum grant as a favor, bestow
census, -us (m.) census, property qualification (for a particular class)
amplio (1) increase the size of, make greater
pro octingentorum milium summa "in place of the sum of 800,000"
duodecies sestertium 1,200,000 sesterces (centena milia omitted, AG #634)
taxo (1) assess the worth, value
suppleo, supplere, suppleui, suppletum make full, make good a deficiency (<sub- + pleo)
non habentibus dat. pl. pres. act. ptc., "for those not having [the sum]"

tibus. **2.** congiaria populo frequenter dedit, sed diuersae fere summae—modo quadringenos, modo trecenos, nonnumquam ducenos quinquagenosque nummos—ac ne minores quidem pueros praeteriit, quamuis non nisi ab undecimo aetatis anno accipere consuessent. frumentum quoque in annonae difficultatibus saepe leuissimo, interdum nullo pretio uiritim admensus est tesserasque nummarias duplicauit.

42 Sed ut salubrem magis quam ambitiosum principem scires,

41.2
congiarium, -(i)i (n.) quantity of goods distributed to the people, gift, donation; Suet. here summarizes information given in full by Augustus (*RG* 15)

diuersae fere summae gen. of quality (AG #345) w/ *congiaria*; diuersus, -a, -um: differing

modo ... modo ... nonnumquam ... nummos "first ... then ... sometimes" (coordinate conj., AG #224); quadringeni, -ae, -a (pl. adj.): four hundred each; treceni, -ae, -a (pl. adj.): three hundred each, three hundred at a time; duceni, -ae, -a (pl. adj.): two hundred each, two hundred at a time; quinquageni, -ae, -a (pl. adj.): fifty each, fifty at a time; nummus, -i (m.): coin

ne ... quidem not even (AG #322f)

praetereo, praeterire, praeterii (-iui), praeteritum pass by, omit, pass over (<praeter- + eo)

quamuis ... consuessent conces. cl. w/ subjv (AG #527a), "although they had not been accustomed to receive it, except from age ten"; undecimus, -a, -um: eleventh; "in the eleventh year" in Roman reckoning = age ten; consuesco, consuescere, consueui, consuetum: become accustomed to (w/ inf.) (<con- + suesco); *consuessent* = contr. form of consueuissent (AG #181); pueri is understood as subj.

frumentum, -i (n.) grain

annona, -ae (f.) the supply of grain

difficultas, -atis (f.) difficulty

pretium, -(i)i (n.) value, price; *leuissimo* w/ *pretio*

uiritim (adv.) man by man, per man, individually; Suet. regularly uses adv. in -tim

admetior, admetiri, admensus sum measure out, distribute (<ad- + metior)

tessera, -ae (f.) ticket or voucher

nummarius, -a, -um relating to coins, financial; the tessera nummaria entitled the holder to a distribution of coins or a share of grain (s. ch. 40.2)

duplico (1) double, double in amount

42.1
ut ... scires purp. cl. (AG #531), "so that you might know [that Augustus was] a leader concerned about well-being, rather than being self-serving"; saluber, -bris, -bre: concerned about health or well-being; *magis quam*: "rather than," introd. compar. b/w *salubrem* and *ambitiosum*; ambitiosus, -a, -um: eager to please, self-seeking; *principem* = Augustum, dir. obj.; scio, scire, scii (-iui), scitum: know; Suet. directly addresses his reader (note 2nd pers. sg. form of *scires*) and begins a detailed refutation of the charge that Augustus pandered to the populace

querentem de inopia et caritate uini populum seuerissima coercuit uoce, satis prouisum a genero suo Agrippa perductis pluribus aquis ne homines sitirent. **2.** eidem populo promissum quidem congiarium reposcenti bonae se fidei esse respondit, non promissum autem flagitanti turpitudinem et impudentiam edicto exprobrauit affirmauitque non daturum se quamuis dare destinaret. nec minore grauitate atque constantia, cum proposito congiario multos manumissos insertosque ciuium numero comperisset, negauit accepturos quibus promissum non esset

---

querentem ... populum ptc. phr., obj. of *coercuit*; inopia, -ae (f.): lack of provisions, dearth; caritas, -atis (f.): high price; uinum, -i (n.): wine

seuerus, -a, -um stern, strict, severe (superl. = -issimus)

coerceo, coercere, coercui, coercitum restrain, keep under control, check (<con- + arceo)

satis prouisum [esse] **a ... Agrippa** impers. indir. disc. (AG #582) ff. *uoce*, "it had been foreseen well enough"; prouideo, prouidere, prouidi, prouisum: foresee, consider in advance (<pro- + uideo); gener, -eri (m.): son-in-law

perductis pluribus aquis abl. abs. (AG #419); perduco, perducere, perduxi, perductum: extend, carry (<per- + duco); aqua, -ae (f.): supply of water, aqueduct; Agrippa's construction of the Aqua Julia (33 BCE) and the Aqua Virgo (19 BCE) had almost doubled the water supply of Rome

ne homines sitirent negat. purp. cl. (AG #531); sitio, sitire: be thirsty

42.2

eidem populo ... reposcenti ptc. phr., dat. indir. obj. w/ *respondit*; promitto, promittere, promisi, promissum: promise, guarantee (<pro- + mitto); congiarium, -(i)i (n.): gift, donation; reposco, reposcere: demand (<re- + posco)

bonae se fidei esse indir. disc. (AG #580) ff. *respondit*; *bonae fidei*: gen. of quality (AG #345); fides, -ei (f.): trust, good faith

non promissum [congiarium] **autem flagitanti** ptc. phr., "to the people pressing for a distribution that had not been promised"; flagito (1): press with demands, clamor for; *flagitanti*: dat. indir. obj. w/ *exprobrauit*

turpitudo, -inis (f.) shameful quality, disgrace

impudentia, -ae (f.) shamelessness, impudence

edicto abl. of means, "in an edict"

exprobro (1) bring up as a reproach

affirmo (1) assert positively, affirm, confirm (<ad- + firmo)

daturum [esse] **se** indir. disc. (AG #580) ff. *affirmauit*

quamuis ... destinaret conces. cl. w/ subjv (AG #527a); destino (1): intend (w/ inf.)

grauitas, -atis (f.) weight, seriousness

constantia, -ae (f.) steadfastness, resolution

cum ... comperisset circumst. cum cl. (AG #546); *proposito congiario*: abl. abs. (AG #419); *multos manumissos insertosque* [esse]: indir. disc. (AG #580) ff. *comperisset*; manumitto, manumittere, manumisi, manumissum: emancipate, free; insero, insere, inserui, insertum: insert, include (w/ dat.) (<in- + sero); ciuis, -is (m.): citizen; comperio, comperire, comperi, compertum: find out, learn

accepturos [esse] indir. disc. (AG #580) ff. *negauit*

quibus promissum non esset "those to whom it had not been promised," relat. cl. in indir. disc. w/ subjv. (AG #580); Augustus refused the gift to those newly enrolled as citizens

ceterisque minus quam promiserat dedit ut destinata summa
sufficeret.   3. magna uero quondam sterilitate ac difficili
remedio cum uenalicias et lanistarum familias peregrinosque
omnes exceptis medicis et praeceptoribus partimque seruitio-
rum urbe expulisset, ut tandem annona conualuit, impetum se
cepisse scribit frumentationes publicas in perpetuum abolendi
quod earum fiducia cultura agrorum cessaret, neque tamen
perseuerasse quia certum haberet posse per ambitionem quandoque restitui. atque ita posthac rem temperauit ut non minorem
aratorum ac negotiantium quam populi rationem duceret.

---

ceteris "to the others"
quam promiserat compar. cl. ff. *minus* (AG #407)
ut...sufficeret purp. cl. (AG #531); sufficio, sufficere, suffeci, suffectum: be sufficient (<sub- + facio)

42.3
magna...sterilitate ac...remedio abl. of time when (AG #423); sterilitas, -atis (f.): failure of crops; difficilis, -e: hard to carry out, difficult; remedium, -(i)i (n.): remedy
cum...expulisset circumst. cum cl. (AG #546); uenalicius, -a, -um: purchasable, offered for sale; *uenalicias* w/ *familias*: "the slaves up for sale"; lanista, -ae (m.): manager or trainer of gladiators; familia, -ae (f.): group of slaves; peregrinus, -a, -um: foreign; *exceptis...praeceptoribus*: abl. abs. (AG #419); medicus, -i (m.): doctor; praeceptor, -oris (m.): teacher; seruitium, -(i)i (n.): the slave class; expello, expellere, expuli, expulsum: drive out, expel (w/ acc. dir. obj. + abl. of place from which) (<ex- + pello)
ut...conualuit tmp. cl. w/ indic. (AG #543); annona, -ae (f.): the supply of grain; conualesco, conualescere, conualescui: recover (<con- + ualesco)
impetum se cepisse...perseuerasse indir. disc. (AG #580) ff. *scribit*; impetus, -us (m.): an impulse, impetus (w/ gen.); *impetum...abolendi*: "the impetus to abolish," obj. of *cepisse*; frumentatio, -onis (f.): distribution of grain; *in perpetuum*: permanently; aboleo, abolere, aboleui, abolitum: put an end to, abolish; *abolendi*: gen. of ger.
quod...cultura...cessaret causal cl. in indir. disc. (AG #540.2b); *earum fiducia*: "trusting in them [the grain distributions]"; fiducia, -ae (f.): (abl. w/ gen.) trusting in; cultura, -ae (f.): cultivation; cesso (1): be neglected
[se] perseuerasse continuation of indir. disc. ff. *scribit*; perseuero (1): persist, continue resolutely (in a course of action); *perseuerasse* = contr. form of perseuerauisse
quia...haberet causal cl. in indir. disc. (AG #540.2b); certum habeo: know for certain
posse...restitui "that it [the distribution of grain] would at some time be able to be restored," indir. disc. (AG #580) ff. *certum haberet;* ambitio, -onis (f.): courting, currying favor; quandoque (adv.): at some time, some day; restituo, restituere, restitui, restitutum: restore, reinstate (<re- + statuo), *restitui*: compl. inf. (AG #456) w/ *posse*; Augustus recognized the political importance of the grain supply, and feared its use by a rival seeking the favor of the people
tempero (1) moderate, temper
ut...rationem duceret result cl. (AG #537); arator, -oris (m.): farmer (vb. subst. <aro); negotior (1): do business; *negotiantium*: pres. ptc. as subst: "of traders"; rationem ducere: take account of

43   Spectaculorum et assiduitate et uarietate et magnificentia
omnes antecessit. fecisse se ludos ait suo nomine quater, pro
aliis magistratibus qui aut abessent aut non sufficerent ter et
uicies, fecitque nonnumquam etiam uicatim ac pluribus scaenis
per omnium linguarum histriones, <et circenses et munera
gladiatoria interiecta Africanarum uenatione> non in foro
modo nec in amphitheatro sed et in circo et in Saeptis et aliquando nihil praeter uenationem edidit, athletas quoque extructis in campo Martio sedilibus ligneis, item nauale proelium
circa Tiberim cauato solo in quo nunc Caesarum nemus est.

Augustus' sponsorship of public entertainment, in his own name and in the name of others, receives special attention.

43.1
assiduitate ... magnificentia   abl. of specif. (AG #418); assiduitas, -atis (f.): frequency, recurrence; uarietas, -atis (f.): variety, diversity; magnificentia, -ae (f.): splendor, magnificence

antecedo, antecedere, antecessi, antecessum   outstrip, surpass, excel (<ante- + cedo); *antecessit*: Augustus is understood as subj.

fecisse se ... ter et uicies   indir. disc. (AG #580) ff. *ait*, "he says" (for forms, AG #206a); Suet. is following *RG* 22.2; facio, facere, feci, factum: hold (games); quater (adv.): four times, on four occasions; *qui ... abessent ... sufficerent*: relat. cl. in indir. disc. w/ subjv. (AG #580); sufficio, sufficere, suffeci, suffectum: have sufficient wealth (<sub- + facio); *ter et uicies*: twenty-three times

fecitque nonnumquam   "and he sometimes held them [the games]"

uicatim   (adv.) by district, street by street; Suet. regularly uses adv. in -tim

scaena, -ae   (f.) stage, performance platform; *pluribus scaenis*: abl. of quality (AG #415)

lingua, -ae   (f.) tongue, language; *omnium linguarum*: gen. of quality (AG #345)

histrio, -onis   (f.) actor, performer

<et circenses ... uenatione>   the phr. here is supplied from *RG* 22.3 to fill a lacuna; circenses, -ium (m. pl.): circus games; munus, -eris (n.): (gladiatorial) games (*OLD* 4b); *interiecta Africanarum uenatione*: abl. abs. (AG #419); intericio, intericere, interieci, interiectum: insert, place between (<inter- + iacio); Africanae [bestiae]: "wild [African] beasts"; uenatio, -onis (f.): an animal-hunt in the arena (as a spectacle)

non ... modo ... sed et ... et   "not only ... but even ... and"; Suet. emphasizes not only the variety of the shows, but also the diversity of venues; the forum in Rome was used for shows as well as for civic business; amphitheatrum, -i (m.): amphitheater, the Amphitheater of Statilius Taurus (s. ch. 29.5); circus, -i (m.): circus, the Circus Maximus in Rome; saeptum, -i (n.): enclosure, (pl.) the Saepta Julia, the voting enclosure in the Campus Martius

aliquando   (adv.) sometimes, at some time or other

athleta, -ae   (m.) athlete, (pl.) an athletic contest

extructis ... sedilibus ligneis   abl. abs. (AG #419); Campus Martius: the "Field of Mars" in Rome; sedile, -is (m.): seat, bench; ligneus, -a, -um: wooden

naualis, -e   naval, of or belonging to a ship; Augustus restaged the clash b/w Greeks and Persians at the battle of Salamis in 480 BCE

Tiberis, -is   (m.) the river Tiber

cauato solo   abl. abs. (AG #419); cauo (1): hollow out; solum, -i (n.): earth, ground

in quo   (relat. pron.) anteced. *solo*

nemus, -oris   (n.) forest, grove; the "Grove of the Caesars" was located across the Tiber, in the area called Trastevere in modern Rome

quibus diebus custodes in urbe disposuit, ne raritate remanentium grassatoribus obnoxia esset. **2.** in circo aurigas
cursoresque et confectores ferarum {et} nonnumquam ex
nobilissima iuuentute produxit sed et Troiae lusum edidit fre-
quentissime maiorum minorumque puerorum, prisci decorique moris existimans clarae stirpis indolem sic notescere. in
hoc ludicro Nonium Asprenatem lapsu debilitatum aureo
torque donauit passusque est ipsum posterosque Torquati

---

quibus diebus "on such days," abl. of time when (AG #423); *quibus*: relat. pron. as connective
(AG #308f)
custos, -odis (m.) guard, watchman, sentry
dispono, disponere, disposui, dispositum distribute, set out, station (<dis- + pono)
ne ... esset negat. purp. cl. (AG #531); the city of Rome (urbs) is the implied subj.; *raritate
remanentium*: "by the lack of people remaining"; raritas, -atis (f.): sparceness; remaneo, remanere,
remansi: remain (<re- + maneo); *remanentium*: gen. pl. pres. ptc. as subst.; grassator, -oris
(m.): robber; obnoxius, -a, -um: exposed to (w/ dat.); some 250,000 spectators could attend
races at the Circus Maximus; Augustus' new Naumachia (the artificial lake for naval fights) might
accommodate even more

43.2
auriga, -ae (m.) charioteer
cursor, -oris (m.) runner (in a race) (vb. subst. <curro)
confector, -oris (m.) slayer, destroyer (vb. subst. <conficio)
fera, -ae (f.) wild animal, beast
nobilis, -e noble, well-born (superl. = -issimus); members of the senatorial and equestrian orders were
given an enhanced public role by such appearances
iuuentus, -utis (f.) youth, young men
produco, producere, produxi, productum bring forth, produce (<pro- + duco)
Troiae lusum "the Troy Game"; Troia, -ae (f.): the city of Troy; lusus, -us (m.): sport, game
maiorum minorumque puerorum "of senior and junior boys"; the distinction may be one of age or
social class
prisci decorique moris gen. of quality (AG #345) w/ *existimans*; priscus, -a, -um: ancient; decorus, -a, -
um: glorious, noble
clarae stirpis indolem sic notescere indir. disc. (AG #580) ff. *existimans*; clarus, -a, -um: well-known,
celebrated; stirps, stirpis (f.): stem (of a plant), family stock; indoles, -is (f.): choicest part, flower (of a
class); notesco, notescere, notui: become known, become famous
ludicrum, -i (n.) public entertainment, show
Nonium Asprenatem ... debilitatum ptc. phr.; Nonius Asprenas, perhaps the son of L. Nonius Asprenas,
cos. 6 CE; lapsus, -us (m.): act of slipping, falling; debilito (1): weaken, disable, impair
torques, -is (m.) decorative collar of twisted metal, neck-ring, torque
ipsum posterosque ... ferre subst. cl. of purp. w/ acc. subj. + inf. ff. *passus est* (AG #563c); posteri, -
orum (m. pl.): descendants; cognomen, -inis (n.): surname of a family or individual, the third part
of the Roman tria nomina; the young Nonius Asprenas and his descendants took up the cognomen
Torquatus

ferre cognomen. mox finem fecit talia edendi Asinio Pollione
oratore grauiter inuidioseque in curia questo Aesernini nepotis
sui casum, qui et ipse crus fregerat.   **3.** ad scaenicas quoque et
gladiatorias operas et equitibus Romanis aliquando usus est,
uerum priusquam senatus consulto interdiceretur. postea nihil
sane praeterquam adulescentulum Lycium honeste natum
exhibuit, tantum ut ostenderet, quod erat bipedali minor,
librarum septemdecim ac uocis immensae.   **4.** quodam autem
muneris die Parthorum obsides tunc primum missos per

---

finem fecit talia edendi "he stopped producing such games"; finis, -is (m.): end, stop; *edendi*: objv. gen. (AG #348) of ger. w/ *talia* as obj.

Asinio ... questo ... casum abl. abs. (AG #420.2) taking the place of a causal. cl. explaining why the Troy Games were stopped; Asinius Pollio (*OCD* 184); orator, -oris (m.): orator; grauiter (adv.): passionately; inuidiose (adv.): bitterly; *Aesernini*: M. Claudius Marcellus Aeserninus; casus, -us (m.): fall, accident; the event likely dates to 2 BCE

qui (relat. pron.) anteced. *Aesernini nepotis*

crus, -uris (n.) leg

frango, frangere, fregi, fractum break, shatter, crush

43.3

scaenicus, -a, -um theatrical, connected to the theater

gladiatorius, -a, -um gladiatorial

aliquando (adv.) sometimes, at some time or other

priusquam ... interdiceretur anticipatory cl. implying expectancy in past time (AG #551b), "before it was forbidden"; *senatus consulto*: "by resolution of the senate"; consultum, -i (n.): resolution; interdico, interdicere, interdixi, interdictum: forbid (<inter- + dico); the restrictions likely date to 22 BCE

nihil sane absolutely nothing

praeterquam (conj.) except, apart from

adulescentulus, -i (m.) young man; this youth named Lycius is otherwise unknown

honeste natum "well-born," indicating either equestrian or senatorial status; honeste (adv.): honorably

exhibeo, exhibere, exhibui, exhibitum display, exhibit (<ex- + habeo)

tantum ut ostenderet proviso cl. (AG #528), "he only displayed him"

quod erat bipedali minor causal cl. w/ indic. (AG #540); bipedalis, -e: two feet high; *bipedali*: abl. of compar. ff. *minor* (AG #406)

librarum septemdecim gen. of quality (AG #345b); libra, -ae (f.): pound, measure of weight of twelve Roman ounces; septemdecim (indecl. adj.): seventeen

uocis immensae gen. of quality (AG #345); immensus, -a, -um: great, immense

43.4

quodam ... die abl. of time when (AG #423)

Parthorum obsides ... missos ptc. phr., obj. of *induxit*; Parthi, -orum (m. pl.): Parthians; obses, -sides (m./f.): hostage; s. ch. 21.3

mediam harenam ad spectaculum induxit superque se subsel-
lio secundo collocauit. solebat etiam citra spectaculorum dies,
si quando quid inuisitatum dignumque cognitu aduectum
esset, id extra ordinem quolibet loco publicare, ut rhinocero-
tem apud Saepta, tigrim in scaena, anguem quinquaginta cubitorum pro comitio.   5.   accidit uotiuis circensibus ut correptus
ualitudine lectica cubans tensas deduceret, rursus commissione
ludorum quibus theatrum Marcelli dedicabat euenit ut laxatis
sellae curulis compagibus caderet supinus. nepotum quoque

---

harena, -ae (f.) sand, the arena of an amphitheater
ad spectaculum "for a show," w/ dbl. meaning—both to see the spectacle, and to be seen as a spectacle
induco, inducere, induxi, inductum lead in, bring in (<in- + duco)
subsellium, -(i)i (n.) bench, low seat
colloco (1) put in a particular place, settle (<con- + loco)
citra (prep. + acc.) before, sooner than
si quando quid ... aduectum esset tmp. cl. in prot. of past gener. condit. showing repeated action in past time (AG #518c, 542); *quando* = aliquando: ever; *quid* = aliquid, nom. sg.; inuisitatus, -a, -um: not previously seen, unfamiliar; dignus, -a, -um: deserving (w/ abl.); cognitus, -us (m.): getting to know; aduebo, aduebere, aduexi, aduectum: bring in (from abroad) (<ad- + ueho)
extra ordinem "as a special event" (*OLD* ordo 15b)
quolibet loco "in any place"; quilibet, quaelibet, quodlibet: whatever you please, any
publico (1) exhibit publicly; *publicare*: compl. inf. (AG #456) w/ *solebat*
ut ... pro comitio Suet. lists a number of examples of special displays; ut (conj.): such as; rhinoceros, -otis (m.): a rhinoceros; saeptum, -i (n.): enclosure, (pl.) the Saepta Julia, the voting enclosure in the Campus Martius; tigris, -is (m.): tiger; scaena, -ae (f.): stage (of a theater), performance platform; anguis, -is (m./f.): snake; *quinquaginta cubitorum*: gen. of quality (AG #345b), quinquaginta (indecl. adj.): fifty; cubitum, -i (n.): cubit, the distance from the elbow to the tip of the finger; comitium, -(i)i (n.): ancient place of assembly in the Forum Romanum, the Comitium; here and elsewhere in this section Suet. displays detailed knowledge that is fitting for someone who also penned a book about Roman spectacles (s. introduction)

43.5
accidit ... ut ... deduceret "it happened that he led," subst. cl. of result ff. impers. vb. (AG #569.2); accido, accidere, accidi: happen (<ad- + cado); *uotiuis circensibus*: abl. of time (AG #424d); uotiuus, -a, -um: votive, performed to fulfil a vow; circenses, -ium (m. pl.): circus games; *correptus ualitudine*: causal. ptc. phr. (AG #496), "because he had been seized by an illness"; corripio, corripere, corripui, correptum: seize (<con- + rapio); tensa, -ae (f.): wagon used for transporting images of gods for a procession; deduco, deducere, deduxi, deductum: lead (<de- + duco); the event probably dates to 28 BCE
commissio, -onis (f.) commencement, holding (of games); *commissione*: abl. of time when (AG #423)
quibus ... dedicabat explanatory relat. cl.; *theatrum Marcelli*: Theater of Marcellus; the games marked the opening of the theater in 13 BCE (s. ch. 29.4)
euenit ut ... caderet supinus "it happened that he fell," subst. cl. of result ff. impers. vb. (AG #569.2); euenio, euenire, eueni, euentum: come out, happen (<ex- + uenio); *laxatis ... compagibus*: causal abl. abs. (AG #420.2); laxo (1): loose; sella, -ae (f.): chair; sella curulis: magistrate's chair; compages, -is (f.): joint, framework; *caderet*: impf. subjv. used by Suet. in place of pf. to express single act; supinus, -a, -um: lying flat on one's back
nepotum ... suorum munere abl. of time (AG #424d); these were likely the funeral games for Agrippa held by Gaius and Lucius in 7 BCE

suorum munere, cum consternatum ruinae metu populum
retinere et confirmare nullo modo posset, transiit e loco suo
atque in ea parte consedit quae suspecta maxime erat.

44   Spectandi confusissimum ac solutissimum morem correxit
ordinauitque, motus iniuria senatoris quem Puteolis per cele-
berrimos ludos consessu frequenti nemo receperat. facto igitur
decreto patrum ut quotiens quid spectaculi usquam publice
ederetur primus subselliorum ordo uacaret senatoribus, Romae
legatos liberarum sociarumque gentium uetuit in orchestra

---

cum ... posset circumst. cum cl. (AG #546); *consternatum ... populum*: ptc. phr., dir. obj.; consterno
  (1): shock (<con- + sterno); ruina, -ae (f.): collapse; *retinere et confirmare*: compl. inf. (AG #456) w/
  posset; confirmo (1): reassure (<con- + firmo)
transeo, transire, transiui (-ii), transitum go across (<trans- + eo)
consido, considere, consedi sit down (<con- + sido)
quae suspecta maxime erat "which was most unstable"; *quae* (relat. pron.): anteced. *parte*; suspicio,
  suspicere, suspexi, suspectum: regard with mistrust (<sub- + specio)

Suetonius marks a transition of topic to Augustus' organization of the audience at shows (*spectandi*), including
the provisions of the *lex Iulia theatralis*, which was sponsored by Augustus in 18 or 17 BCE.

44.1
spectandi gen. of ger.; note the emphatic placement to mark the shift in topic
confusus, -a, -um disordered, jumbled (superl. = -issimus)
solutus, -a, -um loose, loosely organized (superl. = -issimus)
corrigo, corrigere, correxi, correctum straighten out, reform (<con- + rego)
ordino (1) organize, manage
motus iniuria senatoris causal ptc. phr. (AG #496); moueo, mouere, moui, motum: move, stir up, disturb;
  iniuria, -ae (f.): insult, injury
quem (relat. pron.) anteced. *senatoris*, obj. of *receperat*
Puteoli, -orum (m. pl.) Puteoli (a town on the bay of Naples); *Puteolis*: locat. (AG #427)
celeber, -bris, -bre busy, frequented, crowded (superl.: -berrimus)
consessu frequenti abl. of place where w/out prep. (AG #429.2); consessus, -us (m.): gathering, audience;
  frequens, -ntis: crowded, full
nemo, neminis (m.) nobody, no one; *nemo receperat*: no one had received the senator as a distinguished
  guest at the games
facto ... decreto patrum abl. abs. (AG #419); decretum, -i (n.): decree (of the senate)
ut ... ordo uacaret subst. cl. of purp. (AG #563) ff. *facto ... decreto*, interrupted by tmp. cl. w/ iterative
  subjv. *quotiens quid ... ederetur* (BG #567n); *quid spectaculi*: "any show," partit. gen. (AG #346.3);
  usquam (adv.): anywhere; subsellium, -(i)i (n.): bench, low seat; uaco (1): be available to (w/ dat.
  senatoribus); the decree of the senate in 26 BCE extended throughout Italy the privilege of front row
  seats that senators had long enjoyed in Rome
Romae locat. (AG #427.3)
legatos ... sedere subst. cl. of purp. w/ inf. and subj. acc. ff. *vetuit* (AG #563a); *legatos ... gentium*: "ambassadors
  from free or allied peoples"; liber, -era, -erum: free; socius, -a, -um: allied; ueto, uetare, uetui, uetitum: forbid
  (someone to do something); orchestra, -ae (f.): area in front of the stage, the orchestra; the lex Iulia theatralis,
  put forward by Augustus in 18 or 17 BCE, is likely the source of this restriction and the measures that follow

sedere, cum quosdam etiam libertini generis mitti deprendisset.
2. militem secreuit a populo, maritis e plebe proprios ordines assignauit, praetextatis cuneum suum et proximum paedagogis, sanxitque ne quis pullatorum media cauea sederet. feminis ne gladiatores quidem, quos promiscue spectari sollemne olim erat, nisi ex superiore loco spectare concessit.
3. solis uirginibus Vestalibus locum in theatro separatim et

---

cum ... deprendisset causal cl. w/ subjv. (AG #549), "since he had discovered"; *quosdam ... mitti*: indir. disc. (AG #580) ff. *deprendisset*; libertinus, -a, -um: of a freedman; deprendo, deprendere, deprendi, deprensum: discover, recognize (<de- + pre(he)ndo); the envoys of some states were former slaves and thus were restricted from mixing with the highest orders; s. ch. 74 for similar practices in private dining

44.2
miles, militis (m.) the soldiery (collective sg.)
secerno, secernere, secreui, secretum separate, detach (<se- + cerno)
maritus, -a, -um having a wife or husband, (m. subst.) a married man
proprius, -a, -um one's own, belonging to one person
assigno (1) assign, allocate (w/ acc. and dat.) (<ad- + signo); *assignauit* has three dir. obj.: *proprios ordines, cuneum suum, proximum* [*cuneum*]
praetextatus, -a, -um wearing the toga praetexta (the toga worn by boys before manhood), (m. subst.) a boy
cuneus, -i (m.) wedge, wedge-shaped block of seats in a theater
paedagogus, -i (m.) paedagogus, a slave who supervised children
sanxitque ne quis ... sederet subst. cl. of purp. (= indir. comm.) (AG #563) ff. *sanxit*; sancio, sancire, sanxi, sanctum: prescribe by law, enact; *quis* = aliquis: some (AG #310); pullatus, -a, -um: dressed in dingy or dark clothes; *pullatorum* (m. subst.): "men wearing dark cloaks," such people included the urban poor and foreigners; *media cauea*: abl. of place where w/out prep. (AG #429.2); cauea, -ae (f.): auditorium of a theater
femina, -ae (f.) woman; *feminis*: dat. w/ *concessit*
ne ... quidem "not even" (AG #322f)
gladiator, -oris (m.) gladiator
quos ... spectari solemne olim erat explanatory relat. cl., "gladiators whom it once was the practice for men and women to watch together"; *spectari*: inf. in appos. w/ *solemne* (AG #452.2); promiscue (adv.): as a single group (men and women together); sollemne, -is (n.): customary practice; gladiatorial shows had been privately sponsored events; Augustus sought to regulate them after they became public entertainments in 22 BCE
superus, -a, -um situated above, upper (compar. = -ior); women were restricted to the upper tier of seats
spectare inf. w. vb. of permitting ff. *concessit* (AG #563c)

44.3
uirgo Vestalis Vestal Virgin, a priestess of Vesta; uirgo, -inis (f.): virgin
separatim (adv.) separately, apart from the rest

contra praetoris tribunal dedit, athletarum uero spectaculo
muliebre secus omne adeo summouit ut pontificalibus
ludis pugilum par postulatum distulerit in insequentis diei
matutinum tempus edixeritque mulieres ante horam quintam
uenire in theatrum non placere.

45   Ipse circenses ex amicorum fere libertorumque cenaculis spec-
tabat, interdum ex puluinari et quidem cum coniuge ac liberis
sedens. spectaculo plurimas horas, aliquando totos dies aberat,
petita uenia commendatisque qui suam uicem praesidendo

---

contra praetoris tribunal contra (prep. w/ acc.): opposite, facing; tribunal, -alis (n.): platform, tribunal; the praetor presided over games and maintained order

athletarum...spectaculo "from athletic competitions"; abl. of separ. (AG #401) ff. *summouit*; athleta, -ae (m.): athlete; these Greek-style competitions featured nude competitors

muliebre secus omne "the whole female sex," acc. sg.; muliebris, -e: of a woman, female; secus (n.): a sex, members of a sex (defect. noun, found only in nom. and acc., AG #103a)

summoueo, summouere, summoui, summotum drive off, expel (<sub- + moueo)

ut...distulerit...edixeritque result cl. (AG #537) w/ pf. subjv. in secondary seq. (AG #485c); *pontificalibus ludis*: "at the pontifical games," abl. of time when (AG #424d); games were sponsored in Rome every four years by a priestly college; *pugilum par postulatum*: ptc. phr., "the promised pair of boxers"; pugil, -ilis (m.): boxer; par, paris (n.): pair; postulo (1): ask for; differo, differre, distuli, dilatum: postpone (<dis- + fero); *in...matutinum tempus*: prep. phr.; matutinus, -a, -um: of the early morning; edico, edicere, edixi, edictum: decree (<ex- + dico)

mulieres...uenire...non placere "that women not be allowed to come," the decree is presented in indir. disc. (AG #580) ff. *edixerit* w/ impers. vb. *placere* w/ *mulieres uenire* as apparent subj. (AG #454, 455); mulier, -eris (f.): woman; quintus, -a, -um: fifth; placeo, placere, placui, placitum: be pleasing, be resolved

45.1

ipse "Augustus himself"; Suet. now focuses on Augustus' attendance at games

circenses, -ium (m. pl.) circus games, games held in the Circus Maximus

ex...cenaculis prep. phr.; cenaculum, -i (n.): top-story room or apartment; the cenacula were located on the Palatine Hill, which overlooked the Circus Maximus

puluinar, -aris (n.) the pulvinar, a viewing platform in the Circus Maximus (cf. *RG* 19.1)

coniunx, -ugis (f.) wife

sedens note emphatic placement, as Augustus sat rather than reclining like a god (cf. Suet. *Nero*, ch. 12)

spectaculo abl. of separ. (AG #401) w/ *aberat*

plurimas horas...totos dies acc. of extent of time (AG #423); aliquando (adv.): sometimes; totus, -a, -um: whole, entire

petita uenia abl. abs. (AG #419); uenia, -ae (f.): forgiveness, pardon

commendatisque a second abl. abs. w/ the relat. cl. used subst. w/ the ptc. (AG #419b), "with men entrusted with the task"; commendo (1): entrust with a task (<con- + mando)

qui...fungerentur relat. cl. of purp. (AG #531.2); uicis (gen. (f.) (nom. sg. not found): function; *uicem*: acc. dir. obj. w/ *fungerentur*; praesideo, praesidere, praesedi: preside (<prae- + sedeo); *praesidendo*: "by presiding," abl. of ger. (AG #507)

fungerentur. uerum quotiens adesset nihil praeterea agebat seu
uitandi rumoris causa quo patrem Caesarem uulgo reprehensum commemorabat, quod inter spectandum epistulis libellisque legendis aut rescribendis uacaret, seu studio spectandi ac
uoluptate qua teneri se neque dissimulauit umquam et saepe
ingenue professus est.   **2.**   itaque corollaria et praemia in alienis
quoque muneribus ac ludis et crebra et grandia de suo offerebat
nullique Graeco certamini interfuit quo non pro merito
quemque certantium honorarit. spectauit autem studiosissime

---

quotiens adesset   iterative subjv. w/ *quotiens* (BG #567n); adsum, adesse, adfui: be present (<ad- + sum)
praeterea   (adv.) in addition, moreover
seu uitandi rumoris causa   gen. of gerv. w/ causa to express purp. (AG #504b); seu ... seu: disjunctive conj. used to introduce alternatives, "either ... or" (AG #324f); uito (1): avoid, steer clear of; rumor, -oris (m.): rumor, ill repute
quo ... commemorabat   relat. cl., "with which, he remembered, his father had been censured publicly"; *quo* (relat. pron.): anteced. *rumoris*, abl. of means w/ *reprehensum*; uulgo (adv.): publicly; reprehendo, reprehendere, reprehendi, reprehensum: censure (<re- + prehendo); commemoro (1): recall (to oneself), remember (<con- + memoro)
quod ... uacaret   causal cl. w/ subjv. (AG #540); *inter* w/ ger. *spectandum*: "while occupied with"; *epistulis ... rescribendis*: dat. gerv. phr. ff. *uacaret* (AG #505); rescribo, rescribere, rescripsi, rescriptum: write in reply, write back (<re- + scribo); uaco (1): give one's time to (+ dat.)
seu studio spectandi ac uoluptate   an alternative explanation is provided, note parallel structure w/ *causa* (above) and *studio* and *uoluptate* as abl. of cause (AG #404); studium, -(i)i (n.): enthusiasm, eagerness for (w/ gen.); *spectandi*: ger.; uoluptas, -atis (f.): delight, pleasure
qua   (relat. pron.) antec. *uoluptate*, "by which [pleasure]"
teneri se   indir. disc. (AG #580) ff. *dissimulauit*
dissimulo   (1) conceal (<dis- + simulo)
ingenue   (adv.) candidly, in a manner befitting a freeborn person

45.2
itaque   (adv.) and so, then
corollarium, -(i)i   (n.) wreath (dim. <corona)
alienus, -a, -um   of others, belonging to others
creber, -ra, -rum   frequent
grandis, -e   ample, large
de suo   "from his own funds" (*OLD* de 7)
nullique Graeco certamini ... quo non ... honorarit   two negat. used to express a universal affirmative (AG #326b), "he attended no Greek competition where he did not honor"; *nulli Graeco certamini*: dat. w/ *interfuit*; certamen, -inis (n.): a contest, competition; "Greek contests" involved athletics; intersum, interesse, interfui: attend, take part in (w/ dat.) (<inter- + sum); quo (relat. adv.): where; meritum, -i (n.): meritorious action; certo (1): compete; *certantium*: gen. pl. pres. act. ptc. as subst., "of the competitors"; honoro (1): confer an honor, celebrate; *honorarit* = contr. form of honorauerit (AG #181)
studiose   (adv.) ardently, attentively (superl. = -issime); Suet. commonly uses superl. adv.

pugiles et maxime Latinos, non legitimos atque ordinarios
modo, quos etiam committere cum Graecis solebat, sed et
cateruarios oppidanos inter angustias uicorum pugnantis
temere ac sine arte.   3. uniuersum denique genus operas
aliquas publico spectaculo praebentium etiam cura sua digna-
tus est: athletis et conseruauit priuilegia et ampliauit, gladiatores sine missione edi prohibuit, coercitionem in histriones
magistratibus omni tempore et loco lege uetere permissam
ademit praeterquam ludis et scaena.   4. nec tamen eo minus

---

pugil, -ilis (m.) boxer
Latinus, -a, -um Latin
non ... modo ... sed et not only ... but even
legitimus, -a, -um regular, lawful, professional
ordinarius, -a, -um of the usual kind, regular
committo, committere, commisi, commissum join, engage (w/ cum) (<con- + mitto); *committere*:
    compl. inf. w/ *solebat* (AG #456)
Graecis subst. adj. (AG #288)
cateruarios oppidanos ... pugnantis temere ac sine arte ptc. phr.; cateruarius, -a, -um: belonging to
    a troop or band (an unusual adj. <caterua); oppidanus, -i (m.): townsman; angustia, -ae (f.): narrow
    passage, alleyway; uicus, -i (m.): neighborhood; pugno (1): fight, engage in boxing; *pugnantis*: acc. pl.
    pres. act. ptc.; ars, artis (f.): skill, art

45.3
uniuersum ... genus ... praebentium "the whole class of people offering any activities for public shows,"
    a summarizing conclusion to the section on shows; *uniuersum genus*: dir. obj. of *dignatus est*; denique
    (adv.): finally, indeed; *praebentium*: partit. gen. w/ *genus*, pres. act. ptc. as subst. w/ *operas aliquas* as obj.
cura, -ae (f.) attention
dignor (1) consider worthy of, honor with (w/ acc. and abl.)
athleta, -ae (m.) athlete
conseruo (1) preserve, keep unchanged
priuilegium, -(i)i (n.) special right, privilege; athletes enjoyed special privileges, including exemption
    from military service
amplio (1) increase, make greater
gladiatores ... edi subst. cl. of purp. w/ inf. + subj. acc. ff. *prohibuit* (AG #563a); gladiator, -oris
    (m.): gladiator; missio, -onis (f.): discharge from service, the release of a wounded gladiator from a
    contest; edo, edere, edidi, editum: exhibit publicly (<ex- + do); *edi*: pres. pass. inf.
prohibeo, prohibere, prohibui, prohibitum prevent, forbid, ban (<pro- + habeo)
coercitionem ... permissam ptc. phr. as dir. obj. of *ademit*; coercitio, -onis (f.): right to inflict summary
    punishment; histrio, -onis (m.): actor, performer; *magistratibus*: dat. of separ. (AG #381); *lege uetere*: "by
    ancient law"; before Augustus' reforms actors had been subject to summary punishment
praeterquam (conj.) except, apart from
ludis et scaena abl. of time when (AG #424d); scaena, -ae (f.): stage, performance

45.4
nec tamen eo minus "nonetheless"; Suet. concludes the section on Augustus' generosity (liberalitatem,
    ch. 41.1) by noting that despite his leniency and fondness for games, Augustus enforced the rules

aut xysticorum certationes aut gladiatorum pugnas seuerissime
semper exegit. nam histrionum licentiam adeo compescuit ut
Stephanionem togatarium, cui in puerilem habitum circumton-
sam matronam ministrasse compererat, per trina theatra uirgis
caesum relegauerit, Hylan pantomimum querente praetore
in atrio domus suae nemine excluso flagellis uerberarit, et
Pyladen urbe atque Italia summouerit quod spectatorem a quo
exibilabatur demonstrasset digito conspicuumque fecisset.

---

xysticus, -i (m.) wrestler, athlete (a Gk. wd. w/ Latinized spelling)
certatio, -onis (f.) competition, contest
pugna, -ae (f.) fight, battle
seuerissime ... exegit "he enforced most strictly"; seuere (adv.): rigorously, with strictness (superl. = -issime); Suet. commonly uses superl. adv.
licentia, -ae (f.) unruly behavior, licence
compesco, compescere, compescui check, restrain
ut Stephanionem ... Hylan ... et Pyladen result cl. ff. *adeo compescuit* (AG #537); in three parallel cl., Suet. offers three examples of actors censured by Augustus: Stephanio, Hylas, and Pylades
togatarius, -i (m.): actor in Roman plays (an unusual wd. <togatus, found only here in Latin literature)
cui ... matronam ministrasse compererat relat. cl. in indir. disc. (AG #580) ff. *compererat*; "whom he [Augustus] had learned a matron had served"; *cui* (relat. pron.): anteced. *Stephanionem*; *in puerilem habitum*: "in a boyish style"; puerilis, -e: of a boy; habitus, -us (m.): style; circumtonsus, -a, -um: having the hair cut all around; matrona, -ae (f.): matron, married woman; ministro (1): act as servant to, wait on (w/ dat. *cui*); *ministrasse* = contr. form. of ministrauisse (AG #181); comperio, comperire, comperi, compertum: find out, learn
per trina theatra uirgis caesum "after he had been beaten ...," tmp. ptc. phr. (AG #496) w/ *Stephanionem*, obj. of *relegauerit*; trini, -ae, -a: three; uirga, -ae (f.): rod or stick (used for punishment); caedo, caedere, cecidi, caesum: strike, beat; the three permanent theaters in Rome were those of Pompey, Marcellus, and Balbus
relego (1): banish to a specified place (<re- + lego); *relegauerit*: pf. subjv. in result cl. in secondary seq. (AG #485c)
Hylan ... uerberarit result cl. (AG #537); Hylas, -ae (m.): a Gk. name (for decl., AG #44); pantomimus, -i (m.): performer in pantomime; *querente praetore*: causal abl. abs. (AG #420.2); atrium, -(i)i (n.): atrium, the front main room of a house; *nemine excluso*: abl. abs.; nemo, neminis (m.): nobody, no one; Suet. uses *nemine* in place of the more common nullo (AG #314a); excludo, excludere, exclusi, exclusum: exclude, shut out (<ex- + claudo); flagellum, -i (n.): whip, lash; uerbero (1): flog; *uerberarit* = contr. form of uerberauerit (AG #181), pf. subjv. in result cl. in secondary seq. (AG #485c)
Pyladen ... summouerit result cl. (AG #537); Pylades, -ae (m.): a Gk. name (for decl., AG #44); summoueo, summouere, summoui, summotum: drive off, expel (w/ acc. and abl.) (<sub- + moueo); *summouerit*: pf. subjv. in result cl. in secondary seq. (AG #485c)
quod ... demonstrasset ... fecisset causal cl. w/ subjv. relying on the authority of another pers. (AG #540); spectator, -oris (m.): spectator, observer (vb. subst. <specto); *a quo exibilabatur*: relat. cl.; exibilo (1): to hiss (an actor) off the stage (<ex- + sibilo); demonstro (1): point to (<de- + monstro); *demonstrasset* = contr. form of demonstrauisset (AG #181); digitus, -i (m.): finger; conspicuus, -a, -um: clearly seen, conspicuous; Pylades had "given the finger" to an audience member, an obscene gesture then as now

46 Ad hunc modum urbe urbanisque rebus administratis Italiam
duodetriginta coloniarum numero deductarum a se frequentauit operibusque ac uectigalibus publicis plurifariam instruxit,
etiam iure ac dignatione urbi quodam modo pro parte aliqua
adaequauit, excogitato genere suffragiorum quae de magistratibus urbicis decuriones colonici in sua quisque colonia ferrent
et sub die comitiorum obsignata Romam mitterent. ac necubi
aut honestorum deficeret copia aut multitudinis suboles, equestrem militiam petentis etiam ex commendatione publica

---

Italy (*Italiam*). The focus of the biography moves outwards from Rome to explore Augustus' actions in Italy (ch. 46), followed by the provinces (ch. 47), and client kingdoms (ch. 48).

46

ad hunc modum urbe urbanisque rebus administratis abl. abs.; *ad hunc modum*: "in this manner," *ad* (OLD 36) expressing in a manner or way; urbanus, -a, -um: of the city (Rome); in this concise phr. Suet. summarizes the previous chapters (28.3–45)

Italiam acc. dir. obj. of three vb.: *frequentauit, instruxit,* and *adaequauit*; the emphatic position marks the shift in topic from Rome to Italy

duodetriginta coloniarum numero deductarum a se ptc. phr., gen. w/ *frequentauit* (AG #356, 409a, n), "with twenty eight colonies"; duodetriginta (indecl. adj.): twenty-eight; colonia, -ae (f.): settlement, colony; *numero*: "in number," abl. sg.; deduco, deducere, deduxi, deductum: found, settle (a colony) (<de- + duco); Suet. draws upon Augustus' own statement at *RG* 28.2

frequento (1) fill with inhabitants, populate

uectigalibus publicis "indirect public taxes"; uectigal, -alis (n.): revenue from public property

plurifariam (adv.) in many places, extensively (an unusual numeral adv. in -fariam)

instruo, instruere, instruxi, instructum build, furnish with (w/ abl.) (<in- + struo)

iure et dignatione abl. of specif. (respect) (AG #418); dignatio, -onis (f.): esteem, respect

urbi = Romae, dat. w/ *adaequauit*

quodam modo pro parte aliqua "in a certain way in some part," PLEONASM (AG #640), an emphatic qualifying phr. explained by the abl. abs. that follows

adaequo (1) make equal to, put on equal footing with (w/ dat.) (<ad- + aequo)

excogitato genere suffragiorum abl. abs. (AG #419); excogito (1): devise, invent (<ex- + cogito); suffragium, -(i)i (n.): vote, voting

quae ... decuriones colonici ... ferrent ... mitterent relat. cl. of char. (AG #535); *quae* (relat. pron.): acc. pl., anteced. *suffragiorum*; urbicus, -a, -um: of the city (of Rome), urban; decurio, -onis (m.): member of the municipal senate, town councilor; colonicus, -a, -um: colonial, of a colony; *quisque*: appos. w/ *decuriones*, nom. sg. w/ pl. vb. (AG #317e); suffragium ferre: cast a vote; *sub die*: "before the day"; obsigno (1): affix a seal to, seal up (<ob- + signo); *obsignata*: ppp. w/ *quae* [*suffragia*]; Augustus devised a sort of absentee ballot for elections in Rome that could be cast by members of Italian town councils

necubi ... deficeret copia aut ... suboles negat. purp. cl. (AG #531); necubi (adv.): lest at any place, lest on any occasion; honestus, -a, -um: well-born, of high rank; *honestorum*: (subst.) "of high-ranked men," a term in use in Suet.'s day; deficio, deficere, defeci, defectum: be lacking (<de- + facio); multitudo, -inis (f.): the common people; suboles, -is (f.): offspring

equestrem militiam "equestrian military service"; militia, -ae (f.): military service; the men appointed were termed tribuni militum a populo

petentis acc. pl. pres. act. ptc. as subst., "men seeking"

commendatio, -onis (f.) recommendation, approval

cuiusque oppidi ordinabat, at iis qui e plebe regiones sibi reuisenti filios filiasue approbarent singula nummorum milia pro
singulis diuidebat.

47 Prouincias ualidiores et quas annuis magistratuum imperiis
regi nec facile nec tutum erat ipse suscepit, ceteras proconsulibus sortito permisit, et tamen nonnullas commutauit interdum
atque ex utroque genere plerasque saepius adiit. urbium
quasdam foederatas sed ad exitium licentia praecipites libertate priuauit, alias aut aere alieno laborantis leuauit aut terrae

---

ordino (1) appoint (to a position)
qui ... approbarent "who would show," relat. cl. of char. (AG #535); *regiones sibi reuisenti*: tmp. ptc.
  phr. (AG #496), indir. obj. of *approbarent*, "to him [Augustus] when he was revisiting the districts";
  regio, -onis (f.): district; reuiso, reuisere: revisit (<re- + uiso); approbo (1): show, demonstrate the
  existence of (<ad- + probo)
nummus, -i (m.) coin; *nummorum*: partit. gen. w/ *milia* (thousands); Augustus' gifts of 1,000 sesterces for
  each child anticipates the later imperial alimentary endowments

47
prouincias ualidiores note emphatic placement to indicate a shift in topic; ualidus, -a, -um: strong,
  powerful (compar. = -ior)
quas ... regi nec facile nec tutum erat relat. cl., "provinces which it was neither easy nor safe to be
  governed"; annuus, -a, -um: lasting a year, year-long; rego, regere, rexi, rectum: govern, control;
  regi: pres. pass. inf. w/ *erat* (AG #452); facilis, -e: easy, straightforward; tutus, -a, -um: safe, free from risk
ipse suscepit by a measure passed in 27 BCE, Augustus himself was empowered to govern the majority of
  the empire through legates (s. *OCD* s.v. province (4), 1230)
proconsul, -lis (m.) proconsul, governor of a province
sortito (adv.) by lot, after drawing lots
permisit as usual, Augustus is the subj.; Suet.'s concision here masks the role of the senate in appointing
  governors
commuto (1) change, alter (<con- + muto); over the years there were changes made to the list of
  provinces Augustus governed
urbium quasdam foederatas ... praecipites dir. obj. of *priuauit*; foederatus, -a, -um: bound by treaty to
  Rome; exitium, -(i)i (n.): destruction, disaster; licentia, -ae (f.): unruly behavior, licence; *licentia*: abl.
  of cause (AG #404); praeceps, -ipitis: rushing headlong, plunging (w/ ad + acc.); the city of Cyzicus
  in Asia Minor, for example, had put to death Roman citizens and was punished with a loss of
  independence in 20 BCE
priuo (1) deprive of (w/ acc. and abl.)
alias [urbes] ... **laborantis** ptc. phr., obj. of *leuauit*; aes, aeris (n.): money; aes alienum: debt, money
  borrowed from another; laboro (1): labor, be distressed, suffer from (w/ abl.); *laborantis*: acc. pl. pres.
  act. ptc.
leuo (1) lift up, support, relieve
terrae motu subuersas ptc. phr., obj. of *condidit*; motus, -us (m.): movement; terrae motus: an earthquake;
  subuerto, subuertere, subuerti, subuersum: overturn, ruin, destroy (<sub- + uerto); numerous
  earthquakes are recorded, particularly in the east, and Augustus' benefactions were many (cf. *RG*
  appendix 4)

motu subuersas denuo condidit aut merita erga populum
R. adlegantes Latinitate uel ciuitate donauit. nec est ut opinor
prouincia, excepta dum taxat Africa et Sardinia, quam non
adierit. in has fugato Sex. Pompeio traicere ex Sicilia apparantem continuae et immodicae tempestates inhibuerunt nec mox
occasio aut causa traiciendi fuit.

48   Regnorum quibus belli iure potitus est praeter pauca aut isdem
quibus ademerat reddidit aut alienigenis contribuit. reges

---

denuo (adv.) anew, from a fresh beginning; Augustus was celebrated as a new "founder" of the city of Tralles, for example, after seeing to the restoration of the city following an earthquake in 26 or 25 BCE
merita ... adlegantes [alias urbes] ptc. phr., obj. of *donauit*; meritum, -i (n.): meritorious action; erga (prep. w/ acc.): toward, for; adlego (1): plead, cite in support of a request
Latinitas, -atis (f.) the privilege of Latin rights
ciuitas, -atis (f.) citizenship (full Roman citizenship)
opinor (1) think, believe; *ut opinor*: "if I am not mistaken"
excepta ... Sardinia abl. abs. (AG #419); *dum taxat*: provided that, as long as
quam ... adierit relat. cl. of char. (AG #535a); *quam* (relat. pron.): anteced. *prouincia*
in has [prouincias] **... apparantem** ptc. phr., obj. of *inhibuerunt*; *fugato Sex. Pompeio*: tmp. abl. abs. (AG #420.1); fugo (1): cause to flee, frighten off; for the struggle with Sextus Pompey, s. ch. 16; traicio, traicere, traieci, traiectum: traverse, cross over (<trans- + iacio); *traicere*: compl. inf. (AG #456) w/ *apparantem* [*Augustum*]; apparo (1): prepare, get ready, plan (<ad- + paro)
continuus, -a, -um uninterrupted, incessant
immodicus, -a, -um immoderately severe, very great
tempestas, -atis (f.) storm; *tempestates*: nom. pl. subj.
inhibeo, inhibere, inhibui, inhibitum restrain, check, prevent (<in- + habeo)
nec ... fuit subst. vb. (AG #286b), "nor was there"; mox (adv.): in the future, afterward; occasio, -onis (f.): opportunity; *traiciendi*: "for crossing," objv. gen. of ger. (AG #348)

48

regnorum ... praeter pauca prep. phr. interrupted by relat. cl.; note the wd. order with the introduction of a new rubric topic of "kingdoms"; regnum, -i (n.): kingdom, realm; *regnorum*: partit. gen. w/ *pauca* (AG #346b); *quibus* (relat. pron.): anteced. *regnorum*; *belli iure*: "by the laws of warfare"; potior, potiri, potitus sum: take possession of, control, possess (w/ abl.); paucus, -a, -um: few, a small number
aut ... aut "either ... or"
isdem dat. pl. subst. w/ *reddidit*
reddidit supply regna as dir. obj.; many of the kings ruling kingdoms on the eastern borders of the empire had sided with Antony in the Actium campaign; Augustus reconfirmed the positions of many of them
alienigena, -ae (m.) foreigner; for example, King Herod of Judaea was assigned some of the territories that Cleopatra had controlled
contribuo, contribuere, contribui, contributum allot, assign, attach (to a ruler for political purposes) (<con- + tribuo)
rex, regis (m.) king

socios etiam inter semet ipsos necessitudinibus mutuis iunxit,
promptissimus affinitatis cuiusque atque amicitiae conciliator
et fautor, nec aliter uniuersos quam membra partisque imperii
curae habuit, rectorem quoque solitus apponere aetate paruis
aut mente lapsis donec adolescerent aut resipiscerent, ac
plurimorum liberos et educauit simul cum suis et instituit.

49   Ex militaribus copiis legiones et auxilia prouinciatim distribuit,
classem Miseni et alteram Rauennae ad tutelam Superi et Inferi

---

socius, -a, -um allied, associated
inter semet ipsos "even with each other"; *semet*: emphatic reflex. pron. (<se + -met (enclitic pcl.))
necessitudo, -inis (f.) a bond or tie; here Suet. is referencing political marriages which united dynasties in the east
mutuus, -a, -um mutual, reciprocal, done in return
iungo, iungere, iunxi, iunctum join
promptissimus ... conciliator et fautor phr. in appos. (AG #282) w/ Augustus as unexpressed subj.
  of *iunxit*; promptus, -a, -um: keen, active (superl: -issimus); affinitas, -atis (f.): marriage connection;
  amicitia, -ae (f.): friendship; conciliator, -oris (m.): mediator, agent (vb. subst. <concilio); fautor, -oris
  (m.): supporter, promoter (vb. subst. <faueo)
nec aliter ... curae habuit "nor did he value them all in another way than as members and parts of the
  empire"; membrum, -i (n.): member, limb; *partis*: acc. pl.; *curae habuit*: "he valued"; the allied kings
  were treated as part of the body politic of the empire
rectorem ... solitus apponere ... lapsis causal ptc. phr. (AG #496), "since he was accustomed to appoint
  a guardian ..."; rector, -oris (m.): a tutor, guardian (vb. subst. <rego); appono, apponere, apposui,
  appositum: assign, appoint (w/ acc. and dat.) (<ad- + pono); *apponere*: compl. inf. (AG #456) w/ *solitus*;
  paruus, -a, -um: small; *aetate paruis*: "to the young"; *aetate*: abl. of specif. (AG #418); labor, labi, lapsus
  sum: slip; *mente labi*: go out of one's mind (*OLD* 9c)
donec ... resipiscerent impf. subj. in tmp. cl. implying expectancy (AG #553); *donec*: until; adolesco, adolescere,
  adoleui (adolui), adultum: grow up, mature; resipisco, resipiscere, resipui (-ii): recover one's reason
educo (1) bring up, rear, raise; eight of Herod's sons had been sent to Rome to be brought up in Augustus'
  household
cum suis "with his [Augustus'] own children"

Military arrangements (*militaribus copiis*). Augustus' efforts to regularize the military and to ensure the loyalty of his soldiers are summarized here. The chapter flows naturally from the earlier discussion of his administration of the provinces and client kingdoms as the troops were stationed along the frontiers.

49.1
auxilia, -orum (n. pl.) auxiliary military forces; auxilia refers to non-citizen infantry and cavalry units that
  were recruited from, and stationed in, the provinces
prouinciatim (adv.) province by province; Suet. regularly uses adv. in -tim
distribuo, distribuere, distribui, distributum divide up, distribute (<dis- + tribuo)
classem ... conlocauit note CHIASMUS (AG #641) in arrangement of ports and seas; Misenum, -i (n.):
  Misenum, town and port in the Bay of Naples; *Miseni*: locat. (AG #427); Rauenna, -ae (f.): Ravenna,
  a port town on the Adriatic Sea; *Rauennae*: locat. (AG #427); tutela, -ae (f.): protection, defence; *ad
  tutelam*: "for the protection," Suet. regularly uses ad or in w/ acc. to show purp. (cf. *in ... custodiam*
  below); Superum Mare: the upper sea, the Adriatic Sea; mare, -is (n.): sea; superus, -a, -um: upper;
  Inferum Mare: the lower sea, the Tuscan (Tyrrhenian) Sea; inferus, -a, -um: lower; conloco (1): put in a
  particular place, set up, settle (<con- + loco)

maris conlocauit, ceterum numerum partim in urbis partim in
sui custodiam adlegit, dimissa Calagurritanorum manu quam
usque ad deuictum Antonium, item Germanorum quam usque
ad cladem Varianam inter armigeros circa se habuerat. neque
tamen umquam plures quam tres cohortes in urbe esse passus
est easque sine castris, reliquas in hiberna et aestiua circa fini-
tima oppida dimittere assuerat. 2. quidquid autem ubique
militum esset ad certam stipendiorum praemiorumque formulam adstrinxit, definitis pro gradu cuiusque et temporibus
militiae et commodis missionum, ne aut aetate aut inopia post

---

ceterum numerum "the remaining troops," the urban cohorts and praetorian guard
in ... custodiam "for the protection"; partim (adv.): in part, partly; *urbis ... sui*: objv. gen. w/ *custodiam* (AG #347, 348); custodia, -ae (f.): protection, defence
adlego, adlegere, adlegi, adlectum recruit, appoint (for a duty or office) (<ad- +lego)
dimissa Calagurritanorum manu ... quam ... habuerat an extended tmp. abl. abs. in two cl. (AG #420.1), w/ two relat. cl.; note the parallel structure; Calagurritani, -orum (m. pl.): people of Calagurris (a city in Spain); *quam ... Antonium*: relat. cl., supply habuerat; *quam* (relat. pron.): anteced. *manu*; deuinco, deuincere, deuici, deuictum: defeat decisively, subdue (<de- + uinco); Germani, -orum (m. pl.): Germans; *quam ... habuerat*: relat. cl., supply *manu* as anteced.; clades, -is (f.): disaster, military defeat (s. ch. 23); armigerus, -eri (m.): armed man, bodyguard
plures quam tres cohortes in urbe esse ... easque sine castris subst. cl. of purp. w/ acc. subj. + inf. ff. *passus est* (AG #563c); plus, -ris: more (for decl., AG #120), introd. compar. w/ *quam* (AG #407); cohors, -rtis (f.): armed force, cohort, a unit of approximately 500 men
hiberna, -orum (n. pl.) winter quarters
aestiua, -orum (n. pl.) summer quarters
finitimus, -a, -um neighboring
dimittere compl. inf. (AG #456)
assuesco, assuescere, assueui, assuetum become accustomed (w/ inf.) (<ad- + suesco); *assuerat* = contr. form of assueuerat (AG #181)

49.2
quidquid ... esset "whatever soldiers there might be in any place," relat. cl. serves as dir. obj. of *adstrinxit*; quisquis, quidquid (indef. relat. pron.): whoever, whatever; ubique (adv.): in any place, anywhere; *militum*: partit. gen. w/ *quidquid* (AG #346a.3); *esset*: impf. subjv. in condit. relat. cl. (AG #520.3)
stipendium, -(i)i (n.) salary
formula, -ae (f.) rule, procedure, standard pattern
adstringo, adstringere, adstrinxi, adstrictum restrict (to specified limits) (<ad- + stringo)
definitis ... et temporibus ... et commodis missionum abl. abs. (AG #419); definio, definire, definiui (-ii), definitum: limit, define (<de- + finio); gradus, -us (m): rank, position; militia, -ae (f.): military service; missio, -onis (f.): discharge from service
ne ... possent negat. purp. cl. (AG #531); inopia, -ae (f.): poverty; sollicito (1): tempt or encourage (to a course of action) (w/ ad); *sollicitari*: pres. pass. compl. inf. ff. *possent* (AG #456); res novae: revolution

missionem sollicitari ad res nouas possent, utque perpetuo ac
sine difficultate sumptus ad tuendos eos prosequendosque
suppeteret aerarium militare cum uectigalibus nouis constituit.
3. et quo celerius ac sub manum adnuntiari cognoscique
posset quid in prouincia quaque gereretur, iuuenes primo
modicis interuallis per militaris uias, dehinc uehicula disposuit.
commodius id uisum est ut idem qui aliquo perferunt litteras
interrogari quoque, si quid res exigant, possint.

50   In diplomatibus libellisque et epistulis signandis initio sphinge
usus est, mox imagine Magni Alexandri, nouissime sua

---

utque ... sumptus ... suppeteret purp. cl. (AG #531); **perpetuo** (adv.): continuously, permanently; **difficultas, -atis** (f.): difficulty; **sumptus, -us** (m.): expenditure, outlay; *sumptus*: nom. sg. subj. of cl.; **tueor, tueri, tuitus sum**: maintain; *ad tuendos ... prosequendosque*: ad + gerv. for purp. (AG #506); **prosequor, prosequi, prosecutus sum**: reward (<pro- + sequor); **suppeto, suppetere, suppetiui (-ii)**: be available (<sub- + peto)
uectigal, -alis (n.) tax revenue; taxes on public sales and inheritances were established to support the military on an ongoing basis

49.3
quo celerius ... posset "so that it [what was being done] might be more quickly able"; relat. cl. of purp. w/ compar. (AG #531.2a); **celeriter** (adv.): quickly (compar. = -ius); *sub manum*: immediately, simultaneously with the act (*OLD* manus 6d); **adnuntio** (1): report (<ad- + nuntio); *adnuntiari cognoscique*: pres. pass. compl. inf. (AG #456) w/ *posset*
quid ... gereretur "what was being done"; indir. quest. w/ impf. subjv. (AG #574)
modicis interuallis "at short distances"; **interuallum, -i** (n.): interval, distance
uia, -ae (f.) road
dehinc (adv.) after this, then
uehiculum, -i (n.) vehicle, wagon, carriage
dispono, disponere, disposui, dispositum distribute, set out, station (<dis- + pono)
commodius id uisum est impers. constr., "it seemed more advantageous"; **commodus, -a, -um**: advantageous (compar. = -ior)
ut idem ... possint "that the same men be able," subst. cl. of result used as subj. of impers. *id uisum est* (AG #569.2); *qui ... perferunt litteras*: relat. cl., anteced. *idem*; **aliquo** (adv.): somewhere; **perfero, perferre, pertuli, perlatum**: carry (<per- + fero); *interrogari*: pres. pass. compl. inf. (AG #456) w/ *possint*; *si ... res exigant*: prot. of FLV condit. (AG #516b), "if the matters should demand anything"; *quid* = aliquid

50
in ... signandis abl. of gerv. w/ in (AG #507.3); **diploma, -atis** (n.): diploma, an official personal document granting privileges; **signo** (1): sign; Suet.'s position as director of the emperor's correspondence (s. introduction) may explain the special interest and details included in this ch.
initio (adv.) in the beginning, at first
sphinx, -ngis (f.) sphinx; Augustus' first signet ring bore the image of a sphinx
imago, -inis (f.) image, likeness
Alexander, -dri (m.) Alexander the Great of Macedon (*OCD* s.v. Alexander (3) III, 56–58)
nouissime (superl. adv.) most recently, last (in time)
sua [imagine] **Dioscuridis manu sculpta** *sua sculpta*: abl. w/ *usus est*; **Dioscurides, -is** (m.): Dioscurides; *manu*: abl. of means (AG #409); **sculpo, sculpere, sculpsi, sculptum**: carve, engrave

Dioscuridis manu sculpta, qua signare insecuti quoque principes
perseuerarunt. ad epistulas omnis horarum quoque momenta—
nec diei modo sed et noctis—quibus datae significarentur
addebat.

51 Clementiae ciuilitatisque eius multa et magna documenta sunt.
ne enumerem quot et quos diuersarum partium uenia et inco-
lumitate donatos principem etiam in ciuitate locum tenere
passus sit, Iunium Nouatum et Cassium Patauinum e plebe
homines alterum pecunia, alterum leui exilio punire satis
habuit, cum ille Agrippae iuuenis nomine asperrimam de se

---

qua (relat. pron.) anteced. *sua imagine*
insecuti quoque principes "also the principes who followed"; *insecuti*: pf. act. ptc.; Trajan and Hadrian are known to have used Augustus' image on a seal
perseuero (1) persist, continue resolutely (w/ inf.) (<per- + seuero); *perseuerarunt* = contr. form of perseuerauerunt (AG #181)
momenta horarum "records of the precise hours"; momentum, -i (n.): minute measure
nec...modo sed et not only...but even
quibus datae significarentur "by which their time of production might be indicated"; relat. cl. of purp. (AG #531.2); *datae* [*epistulae*]: ppp. < do; significo (1): indicate

Acts of clemency and citizen-like behavior (*clementiae ciuilitatisque*). Suetonius devotes six chapters (51–56) to recounting Augustus' acts of mercy, refusal of divine and special political honors, support of free speech, and performance of civic duties.

51.1
clementia, -ae (f.) clemency, leniency, mercy
ciuilitas, -atis (f.) behavior as a private citizen, citizen-like behavior (an unusual wd. <ciuilis)
documentum, -i (n.) example, evidence, proof
ne enumerem "not to mention," negat. purp. cl. (AG #531); enumero (1): enumerate, list; Suet. uses 1st per. to insert himself modestly into the text, emphasizing the extraordinary number of acts of clemency
quot et quos...passus sit indir. quest. ff. *enumerem* (AG #574); *quot et quos...donatos*: ptc. phr. as acc. subj. of subst. cl. of purp. (AG #563c) ff. *passus sit*; quot: how many; *diuersarum partium*: opposing factions; diuersus, -a, -um: different; uenia, -ae (f.): forgiveness, pardon; incolumitas, -atis (f.): immunity; *principem...locum*: obj. of *tenere*; princeps, -ipis: leading, most distinguished; *tenere*: inf. in subst. cl. of purp. (AG #563c)
Iunius Nouatus and Cassius Patauinus two plebeians, otherwise unknown
alterum...alterum Iunius and Cassius; Suet. discusses the punishment of each man separately
levis, -e light, mild
exilium, -(i)i (n.) banishment, exile
punio, punire, puniui (-ii), punitum punish; *punire*: compl. inf. (AG #456) ff. *satis habuit*
satis habuit "he considered it sufficient"
cum ille...edidisset conces. cum cl. w/ subjv. (AG #549); *ille* = Iunius Nouatus; Agrippa iuuenis: Agrippa Postumus (s. ch. 64–65); *nomine*: "in the name of"; asper, -era, -erum: harsh (superl. = -errimus); *de se*: prep. phr. as attrib. modifier of *epistulam*; *se* = Augusto; uulgus, -i (n.): the common people; *in uulgus*: publicly; the episode likely dates to 6–7 CE

epistulam in uulgus edidisset, hic conuiuio pleno proclamasset
neque uotum sibi neque animum deesse confodiendi eum.
2. quadam uero cognitione, cum Aemilio Aeliano Cordubensi
inter cetera crimina uel maxime obiceretur quod male opinari
de Caesare soleret, conuersus ad accusatorem commotoque
similis, 'uelim', inquit, 'hoc mihi probes: faciam sciat Aelianus
et me linguam habere. plura enim de eo loquar', nec quicquam
ultra aut statim aut postea inquisiit. **3.** Tiberio quoque de
eadem re sed uiolentius apud se per epistulam conquerenti

---

hic ... proclamasset a second conces. cum cl. w/ subjv. (AG #549) setting out Cassius' transgression; *hic* = Cassius Patauinus; *conuiuio pleno*: abl. of time when (AG #424d); plenus, -a, -um: full, crowded; proclamo (1): shout out, exclaim (<pro- + clamo); *proclamasset* = contr. form of proclamauisset (AG #181)

neque uotum ... neque animum deesse indir. disc. (AG #580) ff. *proclamasset*; uotum, -i (n.): desire; *sibi* = Cassio; animus, -i (m.): courage; desum, deesse, defui: be lacking (<de- + sum); confodio, confodere, confodi, confossum: fatally wound, stab (<con- + fodio); *confodiendi*: gen. of ger. w/ dir. obj. *eum* (= Augustum) (AG #504a)

51.2

quadam ... cognitione abl. of time when (AG #424d); cognitio, -onis (f.): judicial inquiry

cum ... obiceretur circumst. cum cl. (AG #546); Aemilius Aelianus Cordubensis: an otherwise unknown man, his identity as being from Corduba suggests that the incident took place when Augustus was in Spain from 15-13 BCE; crimen, -inis (n.): accusation; *obiceretur*: (impers.) lay as a charge against (w/ dat.) (<ob- + iacio)

quod ... soleret causal cl. w/ subjv. relying on the authority of another pers. (AG #540); opinor (1): express as an opinion; *male opinari*: to express a bad opinion

conuerto, conuertere, conuerti, conuersum turn, turn toward (w/ ad) (<con- + uerto)

accusator, -oris (m.) accuser, prosecutor, informer (vb. subst. <accuso)

commotoque similis "like someone who was irritated"; commotus, -a, -um: angry, irritated; *commoto*: m. dat. sg. subst.

uelim "I should wish," pres. subjv. equivalent to opt. subjv. (AG #442b)

probes "you would prove," pres. subjv. in subst. cl. w/out ut used as obj. of *uelim* (AG #565); probo (1): prove

faciam "I'll make," fut. indic. or pres. subjv.

sciat Aelianus subst. cl. of result ff. *faciam* (AG #568) w/ ut omitted; scio, scire, scii (-iui), scitum: know

et me linguam habere "I too have a tongue," indir. disc. (AG #580) ff. *sciat*; *et*: introd. similar sentiment (*OLD* 4); lingua, -ae (f.): tongue

plus, pluris more; *plura*: n. acc. pl. (for decl., AG #120)

loquar "I could say," potent. subjv. (AG #445)

quicquam ultra "anything further," indef. pron. quisquam; ultra (adv.): further

inquiro, inquirere, inquisiui (-sii), inquisitus look into, investigate (w/ acc.) (<in- + quaero)

51.3

Tiberio ... conquerenti ptc. phr., indir. obj. of *rescripsit*; uiolenter (adv.): forcefully (compar. = -ius); *apud se*: "to him [Augustus]"; conqueror, conqueri, conquestus sum: complain of (<con- + queror)

ita rescripsit, 'aetati tuae, mi Tiberi, noli in hac re indulgere
et nimium indignari quemquam esse qui de me male loquatur.
satis est enim si hoc habemus, ne quis nobis male facere possit'.

52 Templa quamuis sciret etiam proconsulibus decerni solere
in nulla tamen prouincia nisi communi suo Romaeque
nomine recepit. nam in urbe quidem pertinacissime abstinuit
hoc honore atque etiam argenteas statuas olim sibi positas
conflauit omnis exque iis aureas cortinas Apollini Palatino dedicauit. dictaturam magna ui offerente populo genu nixus deiecta

---

rescribo, rescribere, rescripsi, rescriptum write in reply, write back (<re- + scribo)
aetati tuae dat. w/ *indulgere*; Suet. here begins to quote directly from Augustus' letter
mi Tiberi voc. (AG #49c)
noli ... indulgere ... indignari prohibition (negat. comm.) w/ impv. of nolo + inf. (AG #450); indulgeo, indulgere, indulsi, indultum: give in to, get carried away by (w/ dat.); nimium (adv.): too much; indignor (1): take offence, be aggrieved
quemquam esse "that there is someone," indir. disc. (AG #580) ff. *indignari*; *esse*: subst. vb. (AG #284b)
qui ... loquatur relat. cl. w/ subjv. in indir. disc. (AG #580); male loqui: speak ill of
ne quis ... possit negat. subst. cl. of result in appos. w/ *hoc* (AG #570, 537a, n), "that no one is able"; *quis* = aliquis; male facere: do harm to (w/ dat.)

52
templa ... solere indir. disc. (AG #580) ff. *sciret*; *quamuis sciret*: conces. cl. (AG #527a); proconsul, -lis (m.): proconsul, governor of a province; decerno, decernere, decreui, decretum: decree (<de- + cerno); *decerni*: pres. pass. inf., compl. w/ *solere* (AG #456); cults to Roman officials in the east date back to the second century BCE
communi suo Romaeque nomine "in his own name jointly with the name of Rome"; communis, -e: shared, joint; cult was directed toward Roma and Augustus jointly
pertinaciter (adv.) determinedly (superl. = -issime); Suet. commonly uses superl. adv.
abstineo, abstinere, abstinui, abstentum abstain, keep away from (w/ abl.) (<ab- + teneo); Augustus' refusal of divine honors in the city of Rome set the standard for future principes; only the tyrannical "bad" emperors accepted such honors (cf. Suet. *Cal.* 22.3)
argenteas statuas ... positas ... omnis ptc. phr., dir. obj. of *conflauit*; argenteus, -a, -um: made of silver; *omnis*: acc. pl. w/ *statuas*
conflo (1) melt down (<con- + flo)
exque = et ex, unusual use of enclitic w/ prep.
cortina, -ae (f.) a tripod with cauldron
Apollo Palatinus the god Apollo whose temple on the Palatine Hill was completed by Augustus in 28 BCE; the dedications to Apollo are also recorded by Augustus (*RG* 24.2)
dictaturam ... offerente populo abl. abs. (AG #419); dictatura, -ae (f.): office of dictator, the dictatorship; uis, uis (f.): force; *ui*: abl. sg. (for irreg. decl., AG #79); the refusal of extraordinary powers is a key example of Augustus' citizen-like behavior (*ciuilitas*) (cf. *RG* 5–6)
genu nixus "kneeling"; genu, -us (n.): knee; nitor, niti, nexus sum: lean on
deiecta ... toga abl. abs. (AG #419); deicio, deicere, deieci, deiectum: throw down (<de- + iacio); umerus, -i (m.): shoulder

53   ab umeris toga nudo pectore deprecatus est. domini appellationem ut maledictum et obprobrium semper exhorruit. cum
spectante eo ludos pronuntiatum esset in mimo,

   o dominum aequum et bonum!,

et uniuersi quasi de ipso dictum exultantes comprobassent, et
statim manu uultuque indecoras adulationes repressit et insequenti die grauissimo corripuit edicto dominumque se posthac
appellari ne a liberis quidem aut nepotibus suis uel serio uel
ioco passus est atque eius modi blanditias etiam inter ipsos
prohibuit.   2. non temere urbe oppidoue ullo egressus aut

---

nudo pectore abl. of quality (AG #415); nudus, -a, -um: bare, unclothed; pectus, -oris (n.): chest
deprecor (1) beg to be excused, decline (<de- + precor)

53.1
domini appos. gen. (AG #343d); the term was freely applied to the master of a household, but in public discourse the meaning was charged and suggested a tyrant
appellatio, -onis (f.) name, title
ut maledictum et obprobrium "as an insult and reproach"; maledictum, -i (n.): insult, reproach; obprobrium, -i (n.): shame, insult
exhorresco, exhorrescere, exhorrui shudder at (<ex- + horresco)
cum ... pronuntiatum esset in mimo circumst. cum cl. (AG #546); *spectante eo* (= Augusto) *ludos*: tmp. abl. abs. (AG #420.1); *pronuntiatum esset*: impers.; mimus, -i (m.): mime (performance)
O dominum aequum et bonum! acc. of exclamation (AG #397d); aequus, -a, -um: fair, just; bonus, -a, -um: good; here Suet. quotes directly the line from the performance
et universi ... exultantes comprobassent a second circumst. cum cl. (AG #546); *quasi de ipse dictum*: "as if it had been said about him [Augustus]"; exulto (1): leap up (<ex- + salto); comprobo (1): express approval (<con- + probo); *comprobassent* = contr. form of comprobauissent (AG #181)
uultus, -us (m.) facial expression, face
indecorus, -a, -um unbecoming, improper
adulatio, -onis (f.) fawning, obsequious flattery, adulation
reprimo, reprimere, repressi, repressum hold in check, subdue, repress (<re- + premo)
insequenti die abl. of time when (AG #423)
corripio, corripere, corripui, correptum censure, rebuke (<con- + rapio)
dominumque se posthac appellari subst. cl. of purp. w/ inf. + subj. acc. ff. *passus est* (AG #563c); appello (1): refer to, address as
ne ... quidem "not even" (AG #322f)
serio (adv.) seriously
ioco "in jest," abl. of manner w/out cum (AG #412)
blanditia, -ae (f.) flattery, ingratiating behavior
prohibeo, prohibere, prohibui, prohibitum prevent, forbid (<pro- + habeo)

53.2
nec temere (adv.) "and scarcely"
urbe oppidoue ullo omission of ex (AG #428g); *urbe* = Roma
egredior, egredi, egressus sum come out from, leave (<ex- + gradior); *egressus [est]*

quoquam ingressus est nisi uespera aut noctu, ne quem officii
causa inquietaret. in consulatu pedibus fere, extra consulatum
saepe adaperta sella per publicum incessit. promiscuis salutationibus admittebat et plebem, tanta comitate adeuntium
desideria excipiens ut quendam ioco corripuerit quod sic sibi
libellum porrigere dubitaret, 'quasi elephanto stipem'. 3. die
senatus numquam patres nisi in curia salutauit et quidem
sedentis ac nominatim singulos nullo submonente, etiam

---

quoquam (adv.) to any place, anywhere
uespera, -ae (f.) evening; *uespera* (abl.): "in the evening"
noctu (adv.) at night
ne ... inquietaret negat. purp. cl. (AG #531); *quem* = aliquem; *officii causa*: "for the sake of performing their duty"; *causa* (abl.): "for the sake of" (w/ gen.) (AG #359b); inquieto (1): trouble, disturb; by traveling in the evening or at night Augustus avoided the ceremonies that traditionally marked a departure or entrance into a city by a Roman official
in consulatu abl. of time within which, usu. w/out prep. (AG #424a)
pedibus "on foot" (*OLD* 6)
extra (prep. + acc.) outside of, out of
adaperta sella abl. of means; adapertus, -a, -um: open, uncovered; sella, -ae (f.): chair; use of an open litter demonstrated that Augustus was available to the people even when traveling
publicum, -i (n.) public
incedo, incedere, incessi advance, proceed (<in- + cedo)
promiscuis salutationibus "at his open audiences"; promiscuus, -a, -um: open to all, general, indiscriminate; salutatio, -onis (f.): formal morning call paid by a client on his patron
et plebem "even the common people"; Suet. emphasizes the accessibility of Augustus, in contrast to later emperors such as Domitian
tanta comitate abl. of manner (AG #412); comitas, -atis (f.): friendliness, courtesy
adeuntium gen. pl. subst., pres. act. ptc., "of those approaching him"
desiderium, -(i)i (n.) expressed request
ut ... corripuerit result cl. (AG #537); *ioco*: "in jest"; corripio, corripere, corripui, correptum: censure, rebuke (<con- + rapio)
quod ... dubitaret causal cl. w/ subjv. (AG #540); libellus, -i (m.): petition; porrigo, porrigere, porrexi, porrectum: offer, present (<por- + rego); *porrigere*: compl. inf. ff. *dubitaret* (AG #456); dubito (1): hesitate
sic ... quasi elephanto stipem "in the same way as one offers a coin to an elephant"; elephantus, -i (m.): elephant; stips, stipis (f.): small coin; Augustus' jest is also reported by Quintillian (*Inst.* 6.3.59) and Macrobius (*Sat.* 2.4.3)

53.3
die senatus abl. of time when (AG #423), "on the day of a senate meeting"
saluto (1) greet, call on; Suet. notes that senators were not obliged to appear at Augustus' home for the salutatio
et quidem sedentis "and what is more, with them seated"; *sedentis*: pres. act. ptc., acc. pl. w/ *patres*; senators were not expected to rise before Augustus as they had for Julius Caesar
nominatim (adv.) by name; Suet. regularly uses adv. in -tim
singulos [patres] a second dir. obj. of *salutauit*
nullo submonente abl. abs. (AG #419); submoneo, submonere, submonui, submonitum: advise privately, prompt (<sub- + moneo); Augustus did not use a nomenclator to prompt him with the names of senators

discedens eodem modo sedentibus ualere dicebat. officia cum
multis mutuo exercuit nec prius dies cuiusque sollemnes frequentare desiit quam grandior iam natu et in turba quondam
sponsaliorum die uexatus. Gallum Cerrinium senatorem minus
sibi familiarem sed captum repente oculis et ob <id> inedia
mori destinantem praesens consolando reuocauit ad uitam.

54   In senatu uerba facienti dictum est 'non intellexi', et ab alio
'contra dicerem tibi, si locum haberem'. interdum ob immodi-
cas disceptantium altercationes e curia per iram se proripienti
quidam ingesserunt licere oportere senatoribus de re p. loqui.

---

discedo, discedere, discessi, discessum depart, go away (<dis- + cedo)
ualeo, ualere, ualui, ualitum be well, farewell; ualere dicere (w/ dat.): "say goodbye"
officia "social calls"
mutuo (adv.) reciprocally, in return
nec prius ... desiit quam ... uexatus [est] "nor did he cease ... before he was injured," tmp. cl. w/ pf.
    indic. stating fact in past time (AG #551a); sollemnis, -e: celebrated; *dies sollemnes*: "family holidays"
    (such as birthdays, weddings, and anniversaries); desino, desinere, des(i)i, desitum: cease (w/ inf.)
    (<de- + sino); *grandior natu*: "quite elderly"; sponsalia, -iorum (n. pl.): betrothal party; *die*: abl. of time
    when (AG #423.1); uexo (1): injure; *uexatus* [*est*]
Gallum Cerrinium ... captum ... destinantem ptc. phr., dir. obj. of *reuocauit*; Cerrinius Gallus: an
    otherwise unknown senator; minus (compar. adv.): to a smaller degree, much less; familiaris, -e: closely
    associated by friendship, intimate; *minus familiarem*: LITOTES (AG #641); *captum repente oculis*: "suddenly
    blind"; *captum*: ppp. w/ abl. "afflicted in"; inedia, -ae (f.): starvation; *inedia*: abl. of means; morior, mori,
    mortuus sum: die, perish; *mori*: compl. inf. w/ *destinantem* (AG #457)
praesens, -ntis present, face to face
consolor (1) offer consolation, comfort (<con- + solor); *consolando*: abl. of ger., "by comforting"
reuoco (1) recall, restore (<re- + uoco)

54
uerba facienti [Augusto] tmp. ptc. phr. (AG #496), indir. obj., "to Augustus, when he was explaining a
    motion in the senate"; *uerba facere*: talk, speak, give an explanation of a motion in the senate
dictum est (impers.) "it was said"
intellego, intellegere, intellexi, intellectum understand (<inter- + lego)
contra dicerem tibi si locum haberem pres. C-to-F condit. (AG #517), "I would speak against you, if I had
    the opportunity"; contra (adv.): in opposition, in reply
ob ... altercationes ... proripienti [Augusto] tmp. ptc. phr. (AG #496), indir. obj., "to Augustus,
    as he was rushing"; immodicus, -a, -um: immoderately severe, very great; discepto (1): dispute,
    debate (<dis- + capto); *disceptantium*: subst. pres. act. ptc., "of the men debating"; altercatio, -onis
    (f.): altercation, argument; ira, -ae (f.): anger, rage, indignation; *per iram*: advl. phr.; *se proripienti*: indir.
    obj. of *ingesserunt*; proripio, proripere, proripui, proreptum: (reflex.) rush (<pro- + rapio)
ingero, ingerere, ingessi, ingestum say repeatedly (<in- + gero)
licere oportere ... loqui indir. disc. ff. *ingesserunt*; "it ought to be permitted for senators to speak"; licet,
    licere, licuit: (impers.) be permitted (w/ inf.); oportet, oportere, oportuit: (impers.) be proper; *de re
    p*[*ublica*]: "about public affairs"

Antistius Labeo senatus lectione cum uir uirum legeret M. Lepidum hostem olim eius et tunc exulantem legit interrogatusque ab eo an essent alii digniores, suum quemque iudicium habere respondit. nec ideo libertas aut contumacia fraudi
55 cuiquam fuit. etiam sparsos de se in curia famosos libellos nec expauit et magna cura redarguit ac ne requisitis quidem auctoribus id modo censuit, cognoscendum posthac de iis qui libellos aut carmina ad infamiam cuiuspiam sub alieno nomine edant.

Antistius Labeo a leading jurist and senator (*OCD* 109)
senatus lectione "at the review of the senate," abl. of time when (AG #424d); lectio, -onis (f.): review, selection; the lectio senatus was the revision of the senate roster, here dating to 18 BCE (s. ch. 35.1)
cum uir uirum legeret circumst. cum cl. (AG #546); each senator could nominate a peer
M. Lepidum ... exultantem ptc. phr., dir. obj. of *legit*; Marcus Aemilius Lepidus (*OCD* s.v. Aemilius Lepidus (3), Marcus, 20), s. ch. 8.3, 16.4; exulo (1): live in exile, be banished
interrogatus ab eo (= Augusto) tmp. ptc. phr. (AG #496)
an essent alii digniores indir. quest. (AG #574) ff. *interrogatus*; *an* = annon; dignus, -a, -um: deserving (compar. = -ior)
suum quemque iudicium habere indir. disc. (AG #580) ff. *respondit*, "each man has his own judgment"; iudicium, -(i)i (n.): judgment, decision
nec ideo ... fuit "therefore neither independence or obstinancy was a harm to anyone"; ideo (adv.): for the reason, therefore; contumacia, -ae (f.): obstinancy, defiant behavior; *fraudi cuiquam*: dbl. dat. (purp. and ref.) w/ *fuit* (AG #382.1n1), fraus, fraudis (f.): detriment, harm; this final sentence serves as a rubric summary for this ch.

55
sparsos ... libellos ptc. phr., dir. obj. of *expauit*; spargo, spargere, sparsi, sparsum: scatter, spread about; famosus, -a, -um: notorious, defamatory; libellus, -i (m.): pamphlet
expauesco, expauescere, expaui take fright at (<ex- + pauesco)
redarguo, redarguere, redargui prove wrong, refute (<re- + arguo)
ne requisitis quidem auctoribus abl. abs. (AG #419); requiro, requirere, requisiui (-sii), requisitum: look for, seek (<re- + quaero)
censeo, censere, censui, censum recommend, decide (in a formal proposal)
cognoscendum [esse] posthac de iis subst. cl. of purp. (indir. comm.) w/ acc. + inf. (AG #563d) expanding on *id* as obj. of *censuit*, "they must be investigated" (lit., "it must be investigated about these men"); cognosco, cognoscere, cognoui, cognitum: investigate judicially, try (a case) (<con- + nosco)
qui ... edant relat. cl. of char. (AG #535), anteced. *iis*; carmen, -inis (n.): poem, song; *ad infamiam cuiuspiam*: "to discredit someone"; infamia, -ae (f.): discredit, disgrace; quispiam, quaepiam, quippiam: someone, anybody; alienus, -a, -um: of others; *edant*: pres. subjv. where impf. is expected; Suet. may be quoting here from a decree of the senate that curbed libel by prohibiting publication under a pseudonym

56   iocis quoque quorundam inuidiosis aut petulantibus lacessitus contra dixit edicto et tamen ne de inhibenda testamentorum licentia quicquam constitueretur intercessit.

Quotiens magistratuum comitiis interesset, tribus cum candidatis suis circuibat supplicabatque more sollemni, ferebat et ipse suffragium in tribu ut unus e populo. testem se in iudiciis et interrogari et refelli aequissimo animo patiebatur.   2.   forum angustius fecit non ausus extorquere possessoribus proximas domos. numquam filios suos populo commendauit ut non adice-

---

56.1
iocis ... inuidiosis aut petulantibus abl. of means w/ *lacessitus*; *quorundam*: (subst.) "of certain men"; inuidiosus, -a, -um: odious; petulans, -ntis: insolent, aggressive

lacesso, lacessere, lacessiui (-ii), lacessitum challenge, provoke, assail

contra (adv.) in opposition, in reply

ne ... quicquam constitueretur negat. purp. cl. (AG #531); *de inhibenda testamentorum licentia*: "concerning checking freedom of speech in wills"; inhibeo, inhibere, inhibui, inhibitum: restrain, check (<in- + habeo); *inhibenda*: abl. gerv. w/ *licentia* (AG #503, 507); licentia, -ae (f.): freedom to act as one pleases, freedom of speech

intercedo, intercedere, intercessi, intercessum intervene, impose a veto (<inter- + cedo); Augustus might have used his tribunician power to block the proposed measure, allowing free speech to continue

quotiens ... interesset iterative subjv. w/ *quotiens* (BG #567n), "whenever he was present"; *magistratuum comitiis*: "at electoral assemblies"; intersum, interesse, interfui: be present, attend (w/ dat.) (<inter- + sum)

tribus, -us (f.) tribe; *tribus*: acc. pl. obj. of *circuibat*; Roman citizens were divided among thirty-five voting tribes

candidatus, -i (m.) candidate for office

circueo, circuire, circuii (-iui), circuitum go around, make the circuit of (<circum- + eo)

supplico (1) make an appeal, petition

more sollemni abl. of manner (w/out cum) (AG #412), "in the traditional way"; sollemnis, -e: solemn, customary; in traditional Roman practice members of the elite would accompany candidates in public and solicit votes for them

suffragium ferre cast a vote; suffragium, -(i)i (n.): vote

ut unus e populo "as one of the people"; *e* instead of partit. gen. w/ *unus* (AG #346c)

testem se ... et interrogari et refelli subst. cl. of purp. w/ acc. + inf. ff. *patiebatur* (AG #563c); testis, -is (m.): one who gives evidence in court, witness; *testem*: appos. w/ *se* (AG #282); iudicium, -(i)i (n.): legal proceedings, court; refello, refellere, refelli: refute, rebut (<re- + fallo)

aequissimo animo "with the greatest patience," abl. of manner (AG #412); aequus, -a, -um: level (superl. = -issimus)

56.2
angustus, -a, -um narrow, small (compar. = -ior); the Forum of Augustus, bordered by the densely inhabitated Subura region of Rome, was built with an irregular northern wall

non ausus ... domos causal ptc. phr. (AG #496); audeo, audere, ausus sum: have the courage, dare (w/ inf.); extorqueo, extorquere, extorsi, extortum: obtain by force (<ex- + torqueo); *extorquere*: compl. inf. w/ *ausus* (AG #456); possessor, -oris (m.): owner; *possessoribus*: dat. of separ. (AG #381)

commendo (1) recommend (as a candidate for office) (<con- + mando)

ut non adiceret "when he did not add," condit. relat. tmp. cl. w/ ut + subjv. (AG #542)

ret 'si merebuntur'; eisdem praetextatis adhuc assurrectum ab
uniuersis in theatro et a stantibus plausum grauissime questus
est. amicos ita magnos et potentes in ciuitate esse uoluit ut
tamen pari iure essent quo ceteri legibusque iudiciariis aeque
tenerentur.   **3.** cum Asprenas Nonius artius ei iunctus causam
ueneficii accusante Cassio Seuero diceret, consuluit senatum
quid officii sui putaret—cunctari enim se ne si superesset
eripere legibus reum, sin deesset destituere ac praedamnare
amicum existimaretur—et consentientibus uniuersis sedit in

'si merebuntur' prot. of FMV condit. (AG #516); mereor, mereri, meritus sum: deserve; Augustus' phr. is quoted directly

eisdem praetextatis adhuc assurrectum ... plausum ptc. phr., obj. of *questus est*, "the applause raised for these same two while still boys"; praetextatus, -a, -um: wearing the toga praetexta (the toga worn by boys before manhood); assurgo, assurgere, assurrexi, assurrectum: rise, rise up (<ad- + surgo); *ab uniuersis*: abl. of agent; sto, stare, steti, statum: stand; *a stantibus*: a second abl. of agent emphasizing that the boys received a standing ovation; plausus, -us (m.): applause; note the CHIASMUS (AG #641) in the intricate arrangement of ptc. and nouns

grauiter (adv.) sternly, vehemently (superl. = -issime); Suet. commonly uses superl. adv.

amicos ... esse subst. cl. of purp. w/ acc. + inf. ff. *uoluit* (AG #563b.2); potens, -ntis: powerful, influential

ut ... essent ... tenerentur "that they nevertheless possess the same rights as others and be equally bound by the judicial laws," result cl. describing proviso (AG #537b); *pari iure*: abl. of specif. (AG #418); *quo ceteri*: "by which others are held" (a greatly abbrev. relat. cl.); iudiciarius, -a, -um: of the law courts

56.3

cum Asprenas Nonius ... diceret circumst. cum cl. (AG #546); L. Nonius Asprenas: a senator and close friend of Augustus; arte (adv.): closely, tightly (compar. = -ius); *ei* = Augusto; iungo, iungere, iunxi, iunctum: join; ueneficium, -(i)i (n.): poisoning; *accusante Cassio Seuero*: abl. abs. (AG #419); accuso (1): charge with a crime; Cassius Seuerus: a noted orator of the time (*OCD* 289); causam dicere: plead a case; Nonius had been charged with poisoning guests at a dinner party

consuluit Augustus is subj.

quid ... putaret "what it thought his duty was," indir. quest. ff. *consuluit* (AG #574); puto (1): think

cunctari enim se Suet. shifts to indir. disc. (AG #580) to report Augustus' wd.; cunctor (1): hesitate

ne ... existimaretur "lest he be thought," negat. purp. cl. (AG #532) interrupted by the prot. of two pres. C-to-F condit., each followed by indir. disc. w/ pers. constr. (AG #582); *si superesset*: "if he [Augustus] were at his service"; supersum, superesse, superfui: be at service (of a client) (*OLD* 8) (<super- + sum); *eripere legibus reum*: pers. indir. disc. ff. *existimaretur*, "to be rescuing the defendant from the laws"; eripio, eripere, eripui, ereptum: snatch away, rescue (<ex- + rapio); *legibus*: dat. of separ. (AG #381); reus, -i (m.): defendant; *sin deesset*: prot. of second pres. C-to-F condit.; sin (conj.): if however, but if; desum, deesse, defui: fail to support (<de- + sum); *destituere ac praedamnare amicum*: pers. indir. disc. ff. *existimaretur*; destituo, destituere, destitui, destitutum: abandon, desert (<de- + statuo); praedamno (1): prejudge as guilty (<prae- + damno)

consentientibus uniuersis abl. abs. (AG #419); consentio, consentire, consensi, consensum: be in harmony, agree (<con- + sentio)

subselliis per aliquot horas, uerum tacitus et ne laudatione
quidem iudiciali data.   4. affuit et clientibus, sicut Scutario
cuidam euocato quondam suo, qui postulabatur iniuriarum.
unum omnino e reorum numero ac ne eum quidem nisi preci-
bus eripuit exorato coram iudicibus accusatore, Castricium per
quem de coniuratione Murenae cognouerat.

---

subsellium, -(i)i (n.) bench, low seat
aliquot (indecl. adj.) a number of, several
tacitus, -a, -um silent
ne laudatione quidem iudiciali data "without even giving a formal speech in praise (of Nonius),"
    abl. abs. (AG #419); laudatio, -onis (f.): laudatory speech, testimonial of character; iudicialis, -e: judicial

56.4
adsum, adesse, adfui be present, appear as an advocate for (w/ dat.) (<ad- + sum); Suet. employs technical legal terminology in this example
cliens, -ntis (m.) client
sicut (conj.) just as, for instance
Scutarius a veteran soldier and client of Augustus; *Scutario*: dat. in appos. w/ *clientibus*
euocatus, -i (m.) soldier called to special service, senior soldier
qui (relat. pron.) anteced. *Scutario*, subj. of *postulabatur*
postulo (1) prosecute, arraign
iniuria, -ae (f.) an insult, legal slander (*OLD* 4); *iniuriarum*: gen. of charge (AG #352)
unum omnino e reorum numero "just one out of the whole number of defendants"; Suet. emphasizes Augustus' reluctance to request special treatment
eum appos. w/ *unum* (AG #282)
prex, precis (f.) entreaty, prayer
exorato coram iudicibus accusatore abl. abs. (AG #419); exoro (1): beseech, prevail upon, persuade (<ex- + oro); coram (as prep. w/ abl.): in the presence of; iudex, -icis (m.): juror; accusator, -oris (m.): prosecutor (vb. subst. <accuso)
Castricius Castricius' role as informant of the plot of Murena was a uniquely important service that warranted Augustus' direct intervention; *Castricium*: appos. w/ *eum* (AG #282)
quem (relat. pron.) anteced. *Castricium*
coniuratio, -onis (f.) conspiracy, plot
Murena A. Terentius Varro Murena (*OCD* 1443), whose conspiracy probably dates to 22 BCE (s. ch. 19.1)

57 Pro quibus meritis quanto opere dilectus sit facile est aestimare. omitto senatus consulta, quia possunt uideri uel necessitate expressa uel uerecundia. equites R. natalem eius sponte atque consensu biduo semper celebrarunt. omnes ordines in lacum Curti quotannis ex uoto pro salute eius stipem iaciebant, item Kal. Ian. strenam in Capitolio etiam absenti, ex qua summa pretiosissima deorum simulacra mercatus uicatim dedicabat,

---

Love for Augustus (*quanto opere dilectus sit*). The discussion of Augustus' public life concludes with four chapters (57–60) devoted to the people's esteem for Augustus and the honors presented to him.

57.1

pro quibus meritis "for these meritorious actions"; *quibus* (relat. pron.) serves as a connective, relating back to all of the material thus far discussed in the biography (AG #308f); meritum, -i (n.): meritorious action, praiseworthy conduct

quanto opere dilectus sit indir. quest. (AG #574); *quanto opere* (interr. adv.): how greatly; diligo, diligere, dilexi, dilectum: love, hold dear (<dis- + lego)

facilis, -e easy, straightforward

aestimo (1) estimate, assess, judge; *aestimare*: pres. act. inf. as subj. (AG #452.1)

omitto a rare use of the 1st pers. sg. by Suet.

consultum, -i (n.) a resolution; *senatus consulta*: decrees of the senate; numerous decrees of the senate honoring Augustus are known from other sources

quia possunt ... uerecundia causal cl. w/ indic. (AG #540); *uel necessitate expressa [esse] uel uerecundia*: indir. disc. w/ pers. constr. (AG #582) ff. *uideri*; necessitas, -atis (f.): need, necessity, constraint; exprimo, exprimere, expressi, expressum: extract, express (<ex- + premo); uerecundia, -ae (f.): deference, respect

equites R[omani] the Roman equites, the social class below the senate; Suet.'s discussion is arranged hierarchically, descending through the ranks of society

natalis, -is (m.) birthday; *eius* = Augusti

sponte atque consensa abl. of manner w/out cum (AG #412); (spons) -ntis (f.): will, volition (only gen. and abl.); *sponte*: "without prompting"; consensus, -us (m.): agreement, unanimity; *consensu*: "by general assent"

biduum, -i (n.) period of two days; *biduo*: abl. of time when or within which (AG #423)

celebro (1) honor with ceremonies, celebrate; *celebrarunt* = contr. form of celebrauerunt (AG #181)

lacus Curti the Lacus Curtius (a pond in the Forum Romanum); lacus, -us (m.): lake, pool

quotannis (adv.) every year

uotum, -i (n.) vow, a votive offering; *ex uoto*: "in fulfillment of a vow"

salus, -utis (f.) well-being, health

stips, stipis (f.) small coin

iacio, iacere, ieci, iactum throw, toss

Kal[endis] **Ian**[uariis] abl. of time when, "on the first of January" (for dates on the Roman calendar, AG #631)

strena, -ae (f.) gift, lucky coin, a traditional offering at the start of the new year; *strenam*: dir. obj., supply *dabant*

etiam absenti [Augusto] "even to him when absent"

ex qua summa ... dedicabat relat. cl.; *qua* (relat. pron.): anteced. *summa* in relat. cl. (AG #307b), "from which sum"; the new year's gifts provided the funds with which Augustus purchased new statues to dedicate; pretiosus, -a, -um: expensive, precious (superl. = -issimus); simulacrum, -i (n.): image, statue; mercor (1): purchase, buy; *mercatus*: pf. act. ptc. w/ Augustus as subj.; uicatim (adv.): by district, note Suet.'s use of adv. in -tim here and below (*singillatim*)

ut Apollinem Sandaliarium et Iouem Tragoedum aliaque. 2. in
restitutionem Palatinae domus incendio absumptae ueterani,
decuriae, tribus atque etiam singillatim e cetero genere
hominum libentes ac pro facultate quisque pecunias contule-
runt, delibante tantum modo eo summarum aceruos neque ex
quoquam plus denario auferente. reuertentem ex prouincia
non solum faustis ominibus sed et modulatis carminibus prose-
quebantur. obseruatum etiam est ne quotiens introiret urbem
supplicium de quoquam sumeretur.

---

ut (relat. adv.) such as, as for example
Apollo Sandalarius "Apollo of the Sandal-makers," whose shrine was in a district near the forum
Iupiter Tragoedus "Jupiter the Tragedian," whose shrine was in the northern Campus Martius

57.2
in restitutionem "for the rebuilding"; restitutio, -onis (f.): rebuilding; Suet. regularly uses ad or in w/ acc. to show purp.
Palatinae domus incendio absumptae ptc. phr.; Palatinus, -a, -um: of the Palatine Hill, Palatine; *incendio absumptae*: "which had been destroyed by fire"; incendium, -(i)i (n.): fire, conflagration; the fire on the Palatine dates to 3 CE
ueteranus, -a, -um mature, experienced; *ueterani*: m. nom. pl. subst., "veteran soldiers"
decuria, -ae (f.) panel of men (from which jurors were selected)
tribus, -us (f.) tribe
singillatim (adv.) one by one, singly
libens, -ntis willing, glad
pro facultate quisque "each according to his own ability"; facultas, -atis (f.): ability; by cataloging all who gave funds, Suet. emphasizes Augustus' popularity with all members of society
delibante ... eo (= Augusto) **... neque ... auferente** conces. abl. abs. (AG #420.3) w/ two ptc.; delibo (1): take a little from (<de- + libo); *tantum modo*: only; aceruus, -i (m.): heap, pile; *plus denario*: "more than a silver denarius"; plus, pluris: more; denarius, -(i)i (m.): silver coin; *denario*: abl. of compar. ff. *plus* (AG #406); aufero, auferre, abstuli, ablatum: take away (<ab- + fero); Augustus took care to present himself as a generous benefactor, even when he was the recipient of monetary gifts
reuertor, reuerti, reuersus sum return, come back (<re- + uertor); *reuertentem* [*Augustum*]: pres. act. ptc.; the cheering crowds that accompanied Augustus upon his return from the provinces developed into the imperial ritual of the aduentus (formal arrival)
non solum ... sed et not only ... but even
faustis ominibus "shouts of blessings"; faustus, -a, -um: fortunate, bringing good fortune
modulatus, -a, -um musical, harmonius; *modulata carmina*: rhythmic chants
prosequor, prosequi, prosecutus sum accompany (a person with greetings) (<pro- + sequor)
obseruo (1) observe, carry out in practice (<ob- + seruo); *obseruatum est*: (impers.) "it was observed"
ne ... supplicium de quoquam sumeretur negat. purp. cl. (AG #531) interrupted by iterative cl.; *quotiens introiret urbem*: "whenever he entered the city," iterative subjv. w/ *quotiens* (BG #567n); introeo, introire, introiui (-ii), introitum: enter (<intro- + eo); supplicium, -(i)i (n.): punishment; *de quoquam*: "concerning anyone"; sumo, sumere, sumpsi, sumptum: take up, undertake

58 Patris patriae cognomen uniuersi repentino maximoque consensu detulerunt ei, prima plebs legatione Antium missa, dein quia non recipiebat ineunti Romae spectacula frequens et laureata, mox in curia senatus, neque decreto neque adclamatione sed per Valerium Messalam is mandantibus cunctis: **2.** 'quod bonum', inquit, 'faustumque sit tibi domuique tuae, Caesar

---

Suetonius offers a particularly detailed account of Augustus receiving the honorific name Pater Patriae (Father of the Country) in 2 BCE, an honor that Augustus himself emphasizes at the end of the *Res Gestae* (35). The direct quotation of the words of both Valerius Messala and Augustus emphasize the importance of the honor.

58.1

pater patriae "Father of the Country"; patria, -ae (f.): one's native land, fatherland; *patris patriae*: appos. gen. (AG #343d)

cognomen, -inis (n.) surname of a family or individual, an additional proper name

uniuersi nom. pl. subst., "everyone"

repentinus, -a, -um sudden, unrehearsed

maximus, -a, -um greatest (superl. to magnus)

consensus, -us (m.) agreement, unanimity

defero, deferre, detuli, delatum confer, offer (<de- + fero)

ei (= Augusto) dat. indir. obj. w/ *detulerunt*

prima first (in order of time); w/ *plebs*

legatione Antium missa abl. abs. (AG #419); legatio, -onis (f.): embassy; Antium, -(i)i (n.): Antium, a town in Latium; *Antium*: acc. place to which (AG #427.2)

quia non recipiebat causal cl. w/ indic. (AG #540)

ineunti Romae spectacula "to him [Augustus] going to the games in Rome"; ineo, inire, inii (-iui), initum: go into, enter into (<in- + eo); *ineunti*: dat. sg. pres. act. ptc., indir. obj. w/ *detulerunt*; *Romae*: locat. (AG #427.3)

frequens et laureata w/ *plebs*; frequens, -ntis: crowded, in full force; laureatus, -a, -um: adorned with laurel

neque decreto neque adclamatione abl. of means (AG #409); decretum, -i (n.): decree; adclamatio, -onis (f.): acclamation, shout of approval; Suet. emphasizes that the award was not a formal resolution of the senate, but rather was based on universal consent

Marcus Valerius Messala Corvinus consul in 31 BCE and a leading public figure (*OCD* 1534–1535)

is mandantibus cunctis abl. abs. (AG #419); *is* = eis; mando (1): give instructions, order, command; cunctus, -a, -um: all

58.2

quod bonum ... faustumque sit tibi domuique tuae, Caesar Auguste! "May it be a good and fortunate thing for you and your house, Caesar Augustus!"; Suet. quotes dir. the wd. of Valerius Messala which adapted the traditional prelude to a senate motion to include here Augustus and his family; *quod*: relat. pron. referring to an idea (AG #307d, n); faustus, -a, -um: fortunate, bringing good fortune; *sit*: pres. act. opt. subjv. (AG #441); *Caesar Auguste*: voc.

Auguste! sic enim nos perpetuam felicitatem rei p. et †laeta
huic† precari existimamus:senatus te consentiens cum populo
R. consalutat patriae patrem'. cui lacrimans respondit Augustus
his uerbis—ipsa enim, sicut Messalae, posui—'compos factus
uotorum meorum, p. c., quid habeo aliud deos immortales
precari quam ut hunc consensum uestrum ad ultimum finem
uitae mihi perferre liceat?'

59   Medico Antonio Musae, cuius opera ex ancipiti morbo conualuerat, statuam aere conlato iuxta signum Aesculapi statuerunt.
nonnulli patrum familiarum testamento cauerunt ut ab here-

---

nos ... precari indir. disc. (AG #580) ff. *existimamus*; felicitas, -atis (f.): good fortune; *rei p*[*ublicae*]: dat.;
laetus, -a, -um: happy; *laeta*: n. pl. subst., "blessings"; *huic*: dat. sg., "for this [city, empire]"; precor
(1): pray for; the text here is corrupted, but the meaning is clear
consentio, consentire, consensi, consensum be in harmony, agree with (<con- + sentio)
consaluto (1) greet as, hail as (w/ dir. obj. *te* + pred. acc. *patrem*, AG #393) (<con- + saluto)
cui (relat. pron.) anteced. Valerius Messala, dat. w/ *respondit*
lacrimo (1) shed tears, weep
his uerbis abl. of means; Suet. presents the actual words
ipsa enim, sicut Messalae, posui a rare 1st pers. interj. by Suet. to note that he has set down the exact wd.
of Augustus just as he had of Messala; *ipsa* [*uerba*]; sicut: just as
compos factus uotorum meorum "having achieved my hopes"; compos, -otis: in possession of; *compos
uotorum*: having obtained one's prayers; uotum, -i (n.): vow, desire, hope
p[**atres**] **c**[**onscripti**] voc.; senators (lit., those enrolled as members of the senate)
quid habeo aliud deos immortales precari "what else do I have to pray to the immortal gods for";
immortalis, -e: immortal
quam ut ... mihi perferre liceat "than that it be permitted for me to retain," subst. result. cl. after compar.
aliud ... quam (AG #571a); consensus, -us (m.): agreement, unanimity; uester, -tra, -trum: your;
ultimus, -a, -um: final; finis, -is (m.): end, limit; perfero, perferre, pertuli, perlatum: maintain, retain
(<per- + fero); licet, licere, licuit: be permitted (impers.).

59

medico Antonio Musae dat. indir. obj. w/ *statuerunt*; medicus, -i (m.): physician, doctor; for Antonius
Musa, s. *OCD* 113
cuius opera ... [Augustus] **conualuerat** relat. cl.; *cuius* (relat. pron.): anteced. *Antonio Musae*, gen. w/ *opera*
(abl.), "by whose effort"; anceps, -ipitis: critical, life-or-death (*OLD* 7); morbus, -i (m.): illness, sickness;
conualesco, conualescere, conualui: grow strong, recover (<con- + ualesco); Augustus is subj. of relat. cl.
aere conlato abl. abs. (AG #419); aes, aeris (n.): money
iuxta (prep. w/ acc.) next to, beside
signum, -i (n.) statue (of a god) (*OLD* 12)
Aesculapius, -(i)i (m.) Aesculapius (Asclepius), the god of healing
statuo, statuere, statui, statutum put up, erect; the subj. of the 3rd pers. pl. vb. is not provided, but is likely
"everyone" (uniuersi), meaning the senate and people of Rome, following ch. 58.1 above
nonnulli patrum familiarum "some heads of families"; pater familias: head of the family, householder
testamento "in their wills"
ut ... uictumae ... ducerentur uotumque ... solueretur subst. cl. of purp. ff. *cauerunt* (AG #563d); heres,
-edis (m./f.): heir; *praelato titulo*: abl. abs. (AG #419); praefero, praeferre, praetuli, praelatum: carry in

dibus suis praelato titulo uictumae in Capitolium ducerentur
uotumque pro se solueretur quod superstitem Augustum
reliquissent. quaedam Italiae ciuitates diem quo primum ad
se uenisset initium anni fecerunt. prouinciarum pleraeque
super templa et aras ludos quoque quinquennales paene oppi-
60 datim constituerunt. reges amici atque socii et singuli in suo
quisque regno Caesareas urbes condiderunt et cuncti simul
aedem Iouis Olympii Athenis antiquitus incohatam perficere
communi sumptu destinauerunt Genioque eius dedicare,

---

    front (<prae- + fero); titulus, -i (m.): placard, sign; uictuma, -ae (f.): animal offered in sacrifice; uotum, -i (n.): votive offering; *pro se*: "on their behalf"; soluo, soluere, solui, solutum: pay
quod . . . reliquissent causal cl. w/ subjv. vb. relying on authority of another (AG #540); superstes, -itis: remaining alive; the heads of the families were grateful that Augustus had outlived them
quaedam Italiae ciuitates "certain cities in Italy"; cities managed their own domestic affairs and thus could act independently to honor Augustus
quo . . . uenisset relat. cl. of char. (AG #535); *quo* (relat. pron.): anteced. *diem*, abl. of time when, "the day on which"; uenio, uenire, ueni, uentum: come; different calendars were in use by cities throughout Italy
plerus, -a, -um (pl.) most of; *plerae [ciuitates]*
super templa et aras prep. phr.; on temples to Augustus, s. ch. 52
quinquennalis, -e occurring every five years (four years, when accounting for Roman inclusive reckoning)
oppidatim (adv.) city by city, in every town; Suet. regularly uses adv. in -tim

60
reges amici atque socii Suet. presents an abbrev. form of the official designation of "client" kings (s. ch. 48); rex, regis (m.): king; amicus, -a, -um: friendly, having friendly relations with one's state; socius, -a, -um: allied, associated by treaty
et singuli . . . et cuncti the kings' actions are set out in two cl. as individual initiatives and joint plans
in suo quisque regno "each in his own kingdom"; regnum, -i (n.): kingdom, realm
Caesareas urbes "cities called 'Caesarea' "; Caesareas were established in Palestine and Mauretania, and throughout the client kingdoms
cunctus, -a, -um all
aedem . . . incohatam ptc. phr., dir. obj. of *perficere*; the temple of Olympian Zeus (Jupiter Olympius) in Athens was begun in the sixth century BCE and although work was undertaken at the time of Augustus, the temple was not finally completed until 132 CE under Hadrian; Athenae, -arum (f.): Athens; *Athenis*: locat. (AG #427.3); antiquitus (adv.): long ago; incoho (1): start, initiate
perficio, perficere, perfeci, perfectum complete, finish (<per- + facio); *perficere*: compl. inf. (AG #456) ff. *destinauerunt*
communis, -e shared, joint
sumptus, -us (m.) expenditure, outlay
Genius, -ii (m.) the divine spirit of an individual; s. ch. 52 for the establishment of cults to Rome and Augustus, which was acceptable outside of the city of Rome
dedicare compl. inf. (AG #456) ff. *destinauerunt*

ac saepe regnis relictis non Romae modo sed et prouincias peragranti cotidiana officia togati ac sine regio insigni more clientium praestiterunt.

61 Quoniam qualis in imperis ac magistratibus regendaque per terrarum orbem pace belloque re p. fuerit exposui, referam nunc interiorem ac familiarem eius uitam quibusque moribus atque fortuna domi et inter suos egerit a iuuenta usque ad supremum uitae diem.

---

regnis relictis abl. abs. (AG #419)
Romae locat. (AG #427.3)
prouincias peragranti "to Augustus as he was travelling around the provinces"; peragro (1) traverse, travel around; *peragranti* [*Augusto*]: dat. sg. pres. act. ptc.
cotidianus, -a, -um daily; *cotidiana officia*: "their daily duty," daily attendance at the salutatio (s. ch. 53.2–3), dir. obj. of *praestiterunt*
togatus, -a, -um wearing a toga; *togati*: nom. pl. w/ *reges*
sine regio insigni "without a sign of royal status"; regius, -a, -um: royal; insigne, -is (n.): emblem, mark of status; a diadem was the usual signifier of royal status in the east
more clientium "in the manner of clients"; cliens, -ntis (m.): client
praesto, praestare, praestiti, praestatum offer, render (<prae- + sto)

Transition to Augustus' personal life (*referam nunc interiorem ac familiarem eius uitam*). Suetonius marks the transition from the discussion of Augustus' civic life and his conduct of public affairs (ch. 9–60) to a focus on Augustus' personal life and his conduct of matters related to his household (ch. 61–93).

61.1
quoniam (conj.) since, seeing that
qualis . . . fuerit "what sort of man he was," indir. quest. w/ pf. subjv. (AG #574) ff. *exposui*; qualis, -e: what kind of; *regendaque . . . re p*[*ublica*]: "and in governing the state"; rego, regere, rexi, rectum: guide, direct; *regenda*: f. abl. sg. gerv.; orbis, -is (m.): orb, disk; *orbis terrarum*: "the world"; *pace belloque*: "in peace and war"; Suet. here summarizes the topics covered in ch. 9–60
exposui, referam note CHIASMUS (AG #641) and use of 1st pers. vb. here and ff. as Suet. marks the change in topics; expono, exponere, exposui, expositum: set out, relate, describe (<ex- + pono); refero, referre, rettuli, relatum: record, report (<re- + fero); *referam*: 1st pers. sg. fut.
interior, -us private, intimate (compar. <inter)
familiaris, -e personal, associated with one's household
quibusque moribus atque fortuna . . . egerit "with what customs and fortunes he lived his life"; indir. quest. (AG #574) ff. *referam*; fortuna, -ae (f.): fortune, circumstance; *domi*: "at home," locat.; *egerit*: "he lived," pf. subjv. (<ago)
iuuenta, -ae (f.) youth, the period of youth
supremus, -a, -um last, final

2. Matrem amisit in primo consulatu, sororem Octauiam quinquagensimum et quartum agens aetatis annum. utrique cum praecipua officia uiuae praestitisset, etiam defunctae honores maximos tribuit.

62 Sponsam habuerat adulescens P. Seruili Isaurici filiam, sed reconciliatus post primam discordiam Antonio, expostulantibus utriusque militibus ut et necessitudine aliqua iungerentur, priuignam eius Claudiam, Fuluiae ex P. Clodio filiam, duxit uxorem uixdum nubilem ac simultate cum Fuluia socru orta

---

Mother (*matrem*) **and sister** (*sororem*). Starting with Augustus' mother, Suetonius discusses family members by category. Augustus' mother, sister, wives, children, and grandchildren form subcategories of this section. Here women in the family are highlighted, as the male ancestors had been discussed at the beginning of the biography (ch. 1–4). See introduction for family tree.

61.2
mater, -tris (f.) mother
amitto, amittere, amisi, amissum lose (<ab- + mitto); Augustus' mother Atia (*OCD* s.v. Atia (1), 199) died in 42 BCE
sororem Octauiam Octavia, Augustus' full sister (*OCD* s.v. Octavia (2), 1032)
quinquagensimum et quartum fifty-fourth; Augustus was fifty-three (living his fifty-fourth year) when Octavia died in 11 BCE
cum ... praestitisset conces. cum cl. w/ plupf. subjv. (AG #549); uiuus, -a, -um: living, alive; *uiuae*: dat. sg. w/ *utrique*; praesto, praestare, praestiti, praestatum: present (<prae- + sto)
defunctae dat. sg. w/ *utrique*
tribuo, tribuere, tribui, tributum grant, bestow; both Atia and Octavia were granted public funerals

Fiancée and wives (*sponsam*). Augustus' betrothals and marriages are explored in the next chapter. Like other members of the Roman elite, Augustus had a series of marriages that linked him to other leading families.

62.1
sponsa, -ae (f.) fiancée, woman promised in marriage
adulescens, -ntis (m.) young man; *adulescens*: "as a young man," pred. appos. (AG #282)
Publius Seruilius Isauricus co-consul with Caesar in 48 BCE (*OCD* 1355)
reconciliatus ... Antonio ptc. phr.; reconcilio (1): bring back into friendship, reconcile (<re- + concilio); discordia, -ae (f.): discord, disagreement; the reconciliation refers to the creation of the triumvirate in 43 BCE (s. ch. 12–13)
expostulantibus ... militibus abl. abs. (AG #419); expostulo (1): demand (<ex- + postulo)
ut ... iungerentur subst. cl. of purp. (AG #563) ff. *expostulantibus*; necessitudo, -inis (f.): bond or tie; iungo, iungere, iunxi, iunctum: join
priuignam eius Claudiam ... filiam priuigna, -ae (f.): stepdaughter; *eius* = Antoni; Claudia: daughter of Antony's wife, Fulvia (*OCD* 593), by her first husband P. Clodius Pulcher (*OCD* 336); Clodius is the popular spelling of Claudius, taken on after Clodius was transferred to plebeian status in order to run for the tribunate
uxorem ducere marry
uixdum (adv.) scarcely yet, only just
nubilis, -e of an age suitable for marriage, nubile; Claudia was at most 13 in 43 BCE
simultate ... orta tmp. abl. abs. (AG #420.1); simultas, -atis (f.): quarrel; socrus, -us (f.): mother-in-law; orior, oriri, ortus sum: rise

dimisit intactam adhuc et uirginem. **2.** mox Scriboniam in matrimonium accepit nuptam ante duobus consularibus, ex altero etiam matrem. cum hac quoque diuortium fecit 'pertaesus', ut scribit, 'morum peruersitatem eius', ac statim Liuiam Drusillam matrimonio Tiberi Neronis et quidem praegnantem abduxit dilexitque et probauit unice ac perseueranter.

63 Ex Scribonia Iuliam, ex Liuia nihil liberorum tulit, cum maxime cuperet; infans qui conceptus erat immaturus est editus. Iuliam

---

dimitto, dimittere, dimisi, dimissum send away, divorce (<dis- + mitto); the divorce dates to 41 BCE; divorce was a private matter and involved no public authority (s. *OCD* s.v. marriage law, Roman, 902–903)
intactus, -a, -um untouched
uirgo, -inis (f.) virgin

62.2
Scribonia (*OCD* 1331), married Augustus in 40 BCE
matrimonium, -(i)i (n.) marriage
nuptam ... etiam matrem *nuptam* (ppp.) w/ *Scriboniam*; nubo, nubere, nupsi, nuptum: get married, marry (w/ dat.); *ex altero*: "from one of them"; the precise identities of the two consular husbands of Scribonia remain disputed, although a connection to the noble Cornelius Scipio family is known
diuortium, -(i)i (n.) divorce; diuortium facere cum + abl.: to divorce
pertaesus ... morum peruersitatem eius pertaedeo, pertaedere, pertaesus sum: fill with disgust (<per- + taedet); *pertaesus*: pf. act. ptc. w/ acc.: disgusted at (an unusual semi-deponent vb. found in Suet., AG #192); peruersitas, -atis (f.): unreasonableness, perversity; *eius* = Scriboniae; the quote likely comes from Augustus' autobiography or a personal letter
Liuia Drusilla (*OCD* 851), Augustus married Livia in January of 38 BCE and remained married to her for the rest of his life; Livia died in 29 CE
Tiberius Claudius Nero (*OCD* 328) first husband of Livia, with whom she had two sons, Tiberius (born 42 BCE) and Drusus (born early in 38 BCE, after Livia's marriage to Augustus)
praegnans, -ntis pregnant, with child
abduco, abducere, abduxi, abductum lead off, carry away from (<ab- + duco); Suet. may be drawing upon Antony's account (s. ch. 69.1)
diligo, diligere, dilexi, dilectum love, hold dear (<dis- + lego)
probo (1) approve of, esteem
unice (adv.) to a singular degree, especially
perseueranter (adv.) steadfastly, persistently

Augustus' daughter (*Iuliam*). Following the discussion of Augustus' wives, Suetonius turns to his descendants.

63.1
Iulia Julia (*OCD* s.v. Iulia (3), 753–754), Augustus' only child
liberorum partit. gen. (AG #346)
fero, ferre, tuli, latum bear, father
cum ... cuperet conces. cum cl. (AG #549); cupio, cupere, cupiui (-ii), cupitum: wish for, desire
infans, -ntis (m./f.) infant, small child
concipio, concipere, concepi, conceptum conceive (<con- + capio)
immaturus, -a, -um immature, premature
edo, edere, edidi, editum produce, give birth to (<ex- + do)

primum Marcello Octauiae sororis suae filio tantum quod
pueritiam egresso, deinde ut is obiit M. Agrippae nuptum
dedit exorata sorore ut sibi genero cederet; nam tunc Agrippa
alteram Marcellarum habebat et ex ea liberos. **2.** hoc quoque
defuncto multis ac diu etiam ex equestri ordine circumspectis
condicionibus Tiberium priuignum suum elegit coegitque
praegnantem uxorem et ex qua iam pater erat dimittere.
M. Antonius scribit primum eum Antonio filio suo despondisse
Iuliam, dein Cotisoni Getarum regi, quo tempore sibi quoque in
uicem filiam regis in matrimonium petisset.

Marcello ... egresso ptc. phr., dat. indir. obj. w/ *dedit*; Marcus Claudius Marcellus (*OCD* s.v. Claudius Marcellus (5), Marcus, 327), born in 42 BCE, was the son of C. Claudius Marcellus and Octavia; *tantum quod*: only just; pueritia, -ae (f.): boyhood; egredior, egredi, egressus sum: (tr.) leave (<ex- + gradior); *egresso*: dat. sg. w/ *Marcello*; Marcellus married Julia in 25 BCE; s. introduction for family tree

ut is obiit tmp. cl. w/ indic. (AG #543); obeo, obire, obii, obitum: die (<ob- + eo); Marcellus died in 23 BCE

M. Vipsanius Agrippa (*OCD* 1554–1555) lifelong friend of Augustus

nuptum "to marry," supine (<nubo) w/ vb. of motion to express purp. (AG #509)

exorata sorore abl. abs. (AG #419); exoro (1): persuade (<ex- + oro)

ut sibi genero cederet subst. cl. of purp. (AG #563) ff. *exorata*; gener, -eri (m.): son-in-law; cedo, cedere, cessi, cessum: yield (w/ dat. indir. obj. *sibi* + abl. of the thing yielded *genero*; AG #366n2)

alteram Marcellarum "one of the Marcellas"; Octavia had two daughters named Marcella, the eldest of whom was married to Agrippa

63.2

hoc quoque defuncto abl. abs. (AG #419); Agrippa died in 12 BCE

multis ... circumspectis condicionibus abl. abs. (AG #419); equester ordo: "the equestrian order"; circumspicio, circumspicere, circumspexi, circumspectum: search for (<circum- + specio); condicio, -onis (f.): marriage contract

Tiberius son of Livia (s. 62.2), the future emperor (*OCD* 1478–1479)

priuignus, -i (m.) stepson

eligo, eligere, elegi, electum select, choose (<ex- + lego)

[eum] ... dimittere subst. cl. of purp. ff. *coegit* w/ inf. + subj. acc. (AG #563a); praegnans, -ntis: pregnant, with child; dimitto, dimittere, dimisi, dimissum: divorce (<dis- + mitto); Tiberius had been married to Vipsania Agrippina, daughter of M. Agrippa and Pomponia Attica, with whom he had a son Drusus

M. Antonius scribit Suet.'s source, whether a letter or political pamphlet written by Antony, is unknown, but must date to the period of hostilities before Actium

eum (= Augustum) **... despondisse** indir. disc. (AG #580) ff. *scribit*; Marcus Antonius Antyllus (*OCD* 112), was the son of Antony and Fulvia; despondeo, despondere, despondi, desponsum: betroth (<de- + spondeo); Cotiso (or perhaps Coson), was king of a Dacian tribe; Getae, -arum (m. pl.): the Getae, a Thracian tribe; rex, regis (m.): king

quo tempore ... petisset subord. cl. in indir. disc. w/ subjv. (AG #580); *in uicem*: in return; matrimonium, -(i)i (n.): marriage; *petisset* = contr. form of petiuisset (AG #181); Antony's accusations against Augustus here were likely made in response to attacks against his own relations with Cleopatra

64 Nepotes ex Agrippa et Iulia tres habuit, C. et L. et Agrippam, neptes duas, Iuliam et Agrippinam. Iuliam L. Paulo censoris filio, Agrippinam Germanico sororis suae nepoti collocauit. Gaium et L. adoptauit domi per assem et libram emptos a patre Agrippa tenerosque adhuc ad curam rei p. admouit et consules designatos circum prouincias exercitusque dimisit. **2.** filiam et neptes ita instituit ut etiam lanificio assuefaceret uetaretque loqui aut agere quicquam nisi propalam et quod in diurnos

---

Grandchildren (*nepotes*).

64.1

C[aium] et L[ucium] et Agrippam acc. in appos. w/ *nepotes*; Gaius (*OCD* s.v. Iulius Caesar (3), Gaius, 760) was born in 20 BCE; Lucius (*OCD* s.v. Iulius Caesar (4), Lucius, 761) in 17 BCE; Agrippa (*OCD* s.v. Iulius Caesar, Agrippa, 756-7) in 12 BCE (after the death of his father M. Agrippa); Suet. uses the names they assumed after their adoption by Augustus

Iuliam et Agrippinam acc. in appos. w/ *neptes*; Julia (s. Iulia 4, *OCD* 753–754) was born in 19 BCE, Agrippina (*OCD* s.v. Vipsania Agrippina (2), 1554) probably in 14 BCE

L. Paulus (*OCD* s.v. Aemilius Paullus (4), Lucius, 21) was the grandson of Scribonia

censor, -oris (m.) censor; Lucius' father was censor in 22 BCE

Germanicus s. *OCD* s.v. Iulius Caesar, Germanicus, 760–761; Augustus' sister Octavia's daughter (by Marc Antony), Antonia the younger, married Augustus' stepson, Drusus; Germanicus was their son

colloco (1) place, give in marriage to (w/ acc. and dat.) (<con- + loco)

Gaium et L[ucium] ... emptos ptc. phr., obj. of *adoptauit*; adopto (1): adopt legally (<ad- + opto); the adoption took place in 17 BCE; *domi*: "at home," locat. (AG #427.3); *per assem et libram*: "by coin and scale" (the formal ritual for transferal by adoption bet/ households); as, assis (m.): copper coin; libra, -ae (f.): pair of scales; emo, emere, emi, emptum: buy, purchase

tener, -era, -erum of tender age, young; among the early honors they received, at age fourteen, both boys were designated to fill the consulship in five years' time; Gaius served as consul in 1 CE; Lucius died before he reached office

ad curam rei p[ublicae] admouit "he raised them to public service"; admoueo, admouere, admoui, admotum: lead towards, raise (<ad- + moueo)

consules designatos acc. in appos. w/ *Gaium et L[ucium]*; designatus, -a, -um: designated, appointed (but not yet installed)

circum (prep. w/ acc.) round about, to (several places); by dispatching Gaius and Lucius on assignments around the empire, Augustus was training them while also introducing them to the troops as his sons

64.2

ut ... assuefaceret uetaretque result cl. (AG #537); lanificium, -(i)i (n.): wool-working, spinning, weaving; assuefacio, assuefacere, assuefeci, assuefactum: make accustomed or used to (<assue- (assuesco) + facio); ueto, uetare, uetui, uetitum: forbid; Augustus raised the women in his household in strict, traditional fashion

loqui aut agere quicquam subst. cl. of purp. (AG #563a) w/ inf. ff. *uetaret*; *loqui*: pres. act. inf.; propalam (adv.): openly, in full view

quod ... referretur relat. cl. of char. (AG #535), "and the sort of thing which could be recorded"; diurnus, -a, -um: daily, giving a day-by-day account; commentarius, -(i)i (m.): notebook, journal

commentarios referretur. extraneorum quidem coetu adeo prohibuit ut L. Vinicio, claro decoroque iuueni, scripserit quondam parum modeste fecisse eum quod filiam suam Baias salutatum uenisset.   3. nepotes et litteras et natare aliaque rudimenta per se plerumque docuit ac nihil aeque elaborauit quam ut imitarentur chirographum suum. neque cenauit una nisi ut in imo lecto assiderent, neque iter fecit nisi ut uehiculo anteirent aut circa adequitarent.

---

extraneus, -a, -um not belonging to one's family, (subst.) a person from outside the household
coetus, -us (m.) meeting, encounter; *coetu*: abl. of separ. (AG #401)
prohibeo, prohibere, prohibui, prohibitum prevent, keep from (<pro- + habeo)
ut ... scripserit result cl. (AG #537) w/ pf. subjv. in secondary seq. (AG #485c); for Lucius Vinicius, s. *OCD* 1553; clarus, -a, -um: well-known, celebrated; decorus, -a, -um: handsome, noble
quondam parum modeste fecisse eum indir. disc. (AG #580) ff. *scripserit*; *parum modeste*: "inappropriately," LITOTES (AG #641), lit., "not modestly enough"; modeste (adv.): modestly; *fecisse eum*: "he had acted"
quod ... uenisset causal cl. w/ subjv. indicating authority of another (AG #540); Baiae, -arum (f. pl.): Baiae, a resort on the bay of Naples with a reputation as a playground for wealthy Romans; *Baias*: acc. place to which w/out prep. (AG #426.2); saluto (1): call on, greet; *salutatum*: acc. supine (vb. noun) used to express purp. after vb. of motion (AG #508–509)

64.3

litteras ... aliaque rudimenta acc. of secondary obj. ff. *docuit* (AG #396); nato (1): swim; rudimentum, -i (n.): first lesson, basic skill
per se by his own efforts, by himself (*OLD* per 15b); Augustus directed the upbringing of his sons Gaius and Lucius himself, in traditional Roman fashion
plerumque (adv.) on most occasions, mostly, often
doceo, docere, docui, doctum instruct, teach (w/ acc. of pers. and acc. of thing, AG #396)
aeque (adv.) as much as (w/ *quam*)
elaboro (1) take pains, bestow care and effort on (<ex- + laboro)
ut imitarentur chirographum suum purp. cl. (AG #531); imitor (1): copy, follow; chirographum, -i (n.): handwriting (a Gk. wd. w/ Latinized spelling)
una (adv.) together, in one company
nisi ut ... assiderent subjv. explanatory cl. (BG #557n2, 591b, r3); *nisi ut*: unless, except on condition that; *in imo lecto*: "on the lowest couch"; imus, -a, -um: lowest, bottommost; lectus, -i (m.): couch; assideo, assidere, assedi, assessum: sit near (<ad- + sedeo); the lowest couch in a triclinium was occupied by the host who reclined; Augustus had his sons sit (upright) at the end of the same couch
nisi ut ... anteirent ... adequitarent a second subjv. explanatory cl. (BG #557n2, 591b, r3); uehiculum, -i (n.): vehicle, carriage; anteeo, anteire, anteiui (-ii), anteitum: walk in front of, go before (w/ dat.) (<ante- + eo); circa (adv.): on either side; adequito (1): ride (nearby) (<ad- + equito); Augustus made sure that Gaius and Lucius were honored, but were not presented as his equals

65 Sed laetum eum atque fidentem et subole et disciplina domus
Fortuna destituit. Iulias filiam et neptem omnibus probris contaminatas relegauit, C. et L. in duodeuiginti mensium spatio
amisit ambos, Gaio in Lycia, Lucio Massiliae defunctis. tertium
nepotem Agrippam simulque priuignum Tiberium adoptauit in
foro lege curiata, ex quibus Agrippam breui ob ingenium sor-
didum ac ferox abdicauit seposuitque Surrentum. 2. aliquanto
autem patientius mortem quam dedecora suorum tulit. nam

A discussion of the family misfortunes that beset Augustus follows next. Suetonius explores Augustus' reaction to these misfortunes, rather than focusing on the events themselves.

65.1
laetum eum atque fidentem ... domus here Augustus unusually appears as the acc. dir. obj. w/ a ptc. phr. building suspense as Suet. reveals his change in fortune; laetus, -a, -um: cheerful, happy; fido, fidere, fisus sum: trust in, have confidence in (w/ abl.); suboles, -is (f.): offspring, progeny; disciplina, -ae (f.): teaching, instruction, training; domus, -us (f.): household, family; *domus*: gen. (for decl., AG #93)
fortuna, -ae (f.) fortune; *Fortuna*: the goddess Fortune
destituo, destituere, destitui, destitutum abandon, desert (w/ acc. obj.) (<de- + statuo)
Iulias ... contaminatas ptc. phr.; probrum, -i (n.): disgrace, fault; contamino (1): pollute, stain
relego (1) banish to a specified place (<re- + lego); the elder Julia was banished in 2 BCE, the younger in 8 CE
C[aium] et L[ucium] dir. obj. of *amisit*
in duodeuiginti mensium spatio "in the space of eighteen months"; Lucius died in August of 2 CE, Gaius in February of 4 CE
ambo, -ae, -o (pl.) two of a pair, both (decl., AG #134b)
Gaio ... Lucio ... defunctis abl. abs. (AG #419), an unusual use as Gaius and Lucius also appear as dir. obj. of sentence; Lycia, -ae (f.): Lycia, a region in southern Asia Minor; Massilia, -ae (f.): city at the mouth of the Rhône (modern Marseilles); *Massiliae*: locat. (AG #427.3)
priuignus, -i (m.) stepson; for Tiberius, s. ch. 63.2
adopto (1) adopt legally (<ad- + opto); the adoptions took place in June of 4 CE
lege curiata "by a law passed by the curiate assembly"; lex curiata: a law passed by the Comitia Curiata, the formal mechanism for adopting independent individuals; the Comitia Curiata met in the forum
ex quibus Agrippam ... abdicauit seposuitque in Surrentum relat. cl.; *ex quibus* (relat. pron.): "of these [two]"; breuis, -e: short, small; *breui* (n. subst.) "after a short space of time" (*OLD* 6); ingenium, -(i)i (n.): temperament, disposition, character; sordidus, -a, um: foul, disreputable, base; ferox, -ocis: savage, ferocious; *ferox*: n. acc. sg. w/ *ingenium*; abdico (1): disown, renounce (<ab- + dico); sepono, seponere, seposui, sepositum: banish, exile (<se- + pono); Surrentum, -i (n.): coastal town in Campania, modern Sorrento; *Surrentum*: acc. place to which w/out prep. (AG #427); Agrippa was probably banished to Sorrento in 6 CE, then later transferred to the island of Planasia (s. below, ch. 65.4)

65.2
patienter (adv.) patiently (compar. = -ius)
mortem quam dedora compar. (AG #407) ff. *patientius*; dedecus, -oris (n.): dishonor, disgraceful action
suorum (subst.) "of his own family members"
nam C[aii] Lucique casu non adeo fractus ptc. phr.; casus, -us (m.): misfortune, fall, fate; frango, frangere, fregi, fractum: break, shatter, crush

C. Lucique casu non adeo fractus, de filia absens ac libello
per quaestorem recitato notum senatui fecit abstinuitque
congressu hominum diu prae pudore, etiam de necanda deli-
berauit. certe cum sub idem tempus una ex consciis, liberta
Phoebe, suspendio uitam finisset, maluisse se ait Phoebes
patrem fuisse.   3. relegatae usum uini omnemque delicatiorem
cultum ademit neque adiri a quoquam libero seruoue nisi se
consulto permisit et ita ut certior fieret qua is aetate, qua
statura, quo colore esset, etiam quibus corporis notis uel cica-

---

absens, -ntis absent, not present in person (pres. ptc. <absum)
libello ... recitato ptc. phr., abl. of means; quaestor, -oris (m.): quaestor, a magistrate; Augustus' report to the senate is likely Suet.'s source here; the details of Julia's adultery, and perhaps also political plotting, are omitted
notum facere make it known (w/ de + abl.); notus, -a, -um: known
abstineo, abstinere, abstinui, abstentum keep distant, keep away from (w/ abl.) (<ab- + teneo)
congressus, -us (m.) meeting, encounter
prae (prep. w/ abl.) in the face of, in view of
pudor, -oris (m.) feeling of shame, dishonor
neco (1) put to death, kill; *de [ea] necanda*: "about killing her," gerv. phr. (AG #507)
delibero (1) engage in careful thought, deliberate
certe (adv.) certainly, at all events
cum ... una ... uitam finisset circumst. cum cl. (AG #546); *sub idem tempus*: "at almost the same time" (*OLD* sub 23); *una ex consciis*: "one of her (= Julia's) accomplices," conscius, -a, -um: sharing knowledge, privy, (subst.) an accomplice; *liberta Phoebe*: nom. sg., appos. w/ *una*; liberta, -ae (f.): freedwoman (former slave); Phoebe, Phoebes (f.): Phoebe (Gk. noun of 1st decl., AG #44); suspendium, -(i)i (n.): act of hanging oneself; finio, finire, finii (-iui), finitum: end
maluisse se ... Phoebes patrem fuisse indir. disc. (AG #580) ff. *ait*: "he said" (for forms, AG #206a); malo, malle, malui: wish, prefer (w/ compl. inf. *fuisse*); *maluisse*: "would have preferred"

65.3

relegatae [Iuliae] dat. indir. obj. w/ *ademit* and *permisit*; Augustus is subj.; in 2 BCE Julia was relegated to the small island of Pandateria off the coast of Italy
uinum, -i (n.) wine
delicatus, -a, -um luxurious, elegant (compar. = -ior)
cultus, -us (m.) adornment, finery
adimo, adimere, ademi, ademptum deny (w/ dat. and acc.) (<ad- + emo)
adiri ... nisi se consulto subst. cl. of purp. w/ inf. ff. *permisit* (AG #563c); *adiri*: pres. pass. inf.; liber, -era, -erum: free, (subst.) a free man (as opposed to a slave); *nisi se consulto*: "unless he was consulted," condit. abl. abs. (AG #420.4)
ita ut certior fieret "in such a way that he be informed," condensed result cl. (AG #537); certiorem facere: to inform; *fieret*: impf. pass. subjv.
qua is aetate ... esset ... quibus ... cicatricibus four indir. quest. (AG #574) ff. *certior fieret* w/ abl. of description, "what age he was"; statura, -ae (f.): height, stature; color, -oris (m.): complexion, color of the skin; nota, -ae (f.): mark; cicatrix, -icis (f.): scar

tricibus. post quinquennium demum ex insula in continentem
lenioribusque paulo condicionibus transtulit eam. nam ut
omnino reuocaret exorari nullo modo potuit, deprecanti saepe
p. R. et pertinacius instanti tales filias talesque coniuges pro
contione imprecatus.   **4.** ex nepte Iulia post damnationem
editum infantem adgnosci alique uetuit. Agrippam nihilo trac-
tabiliorem, immo in dies amentiorem in insulam transportauit
saepsitque insuper custodia militum, cauit etiam s. c. ut eodem
loci in perpetuum contineretur. atque ad omnem et eius et

---

quinquennium, -(i)i (n.) period of five years
continens, -ntis (f.) mainland; Julia was transferred to Rhegium at the toe of Italy
lenis, -e gentle, mild (compar. = -ior)
ut ... reuocaret "that he restore her entirely," subst. cl. of purp. ff. *exorari* (AG #563); reuoco (1): recall,
    restore (<re- + uoco)
exoro (1) win over, persuade (<ex- + oro); *exorari*: pres. pass. compl. inf. (AG #456) ff. *potuit*
nullo modo in no way, not at all
deprecanti saepe p[opulo] R[omano] et pertinacius instanti ptc. phr., dat. sg. indir. obj. of *imprecatus*;
    deprecor (1): ask for pardon (<de- + precor); pertinaciter (adv.): persistently (compar. = -ius); insto,
    instare, institi: press, insist (<in- + sto)
talis, -e of such a character, of such a kind
coniunx, -ugis (f.) wife
contio, -onis (f.) public meeting, assembly; *pro contione*: "in front of an assembly"
imprecor (1) pray for (w/ acc. and dat.); *imprecatus*: pf. act. ptc., Augustus is subj.

65.4
damnatio, -onis (f.) condemnation; Julia (s. Iulia 4, *OCD* 753–754) was relegated to the island of
    Trimerus in 8 CE
editum infantem adgnosci alique subst. cl. of purp. w/ acc. + inf. ff. *vetuit* (AG #563a); adgnosco,
    adgnoscere, adgnoui, adgnitum: recognize, acknowledge (a child) as one's own (<ad- + nosco); alo,
    alere, alui, altum: feed, raise
ueto, uetare, uetui, uetitum forbid (someone to do something)
nihilum, -i (n.) not anything; *nihilo*: abl. w/ compar., "by no degree"
tractabilis, -e easy to handle, manageable (compar. = -ior)
immo (adv.) rather, more correctly
in dies each day, as the days proceed
amens, -ntis demented, insane (compar. = -ntior)
transporto (1) carry across, transport (<trans- + porto); Augustus confined his grandson Agrippa to the
    island of Planasia (modern Pianosa, south of Elba)
saepio, saepire, saepsi, saeptum surround, confine
insuper (adv.) in addition, as well
custodia, -ae (f.) protective guard
s[enatus] c[onsulto] "by a decree of the senate"; the decree ensured that Agippa's punishment would
    endure, even after Augustus' own death
ut ... contineretur subst. cl. of purp. (AG #563) ff. *cauit*; *eodem loci*: "in that same place"; *in perpetuum*: permanently,
    for an indefinite period; contineo, continere, continui, contentum: confine, detain (<con- + teneo)

Iuliarum mentionem ingemiscens proclamare etiam solebat,
   αἴθ' ὄφελον ἄγαμός τ' ἔμεναι ἄγονος τ' ἀπολέσθαι,
nec aliter eos appellare quam tris uomicas ac tria carcinomata sua.

66 Amicitias neque facile admisit et constantissime retinuit, non tantum uirtutes ac merita cuiusque digne prosecutus sed uitia quoque et delicta dumtaxat modica perpessus. neque enim temere ex omni numero in amicitia eius afflicti reperientur praeter Saluidienum Rufum, quem ad consulatum usque, et Cornelium Gallum, quem ad praefecturam Aegypti ex infima

---

mentio, -onis (f.) reference to a subject, mention of (w/ gen.)
ingemisco, ingemiscere, ingemui groan, moan
proclamo (1) shout out, exclaim (<pro- + clamo); *proclamare*: compl. inf. ff. *solebat* (AG #456)
αἴθ' ὄφελον ἄγαμός τ' ἔμεναι ἄγονος τ' ἀπολέσθαι "If only I had never married and had died childless"; Augustus adapted a line of Homer's *Iliad* (3.40) to his situation, modifying the original wd. of Hector to Paris: "If only you had never been born and had died unmarried"
appello (1) address, call (by name); *appellare*: compl. inf. ff. *solebat* (AG #456)
uomica, -ae (f.) abscess, boil, gathering of pus; *uomicas*: pred. acc. ff. *appellare* (AG #393)
carcinoma, -atis (n.) ulcer, tumor (a Gk. wd. w/ Latinized spelling); *carcinomata*: pred. acc. ff. *appellare* (AG #393)

Friendships (*amicitias*). Following family relations, Suetonius explores Augustus' friendships in the next chapter.

66.1
amicitia, -ae (f.) friendship
constanter (adv.) firmly, steadfastly (superl. = -tissime); Suet. commonly uses superl. adv.
non tantum ... prosecutus ptc. phr.; uirtus, -utis (f.): valor, virtue, excellence; meritum, -i (n.): meritorious action, good service; digne (adv.): in a fitting manner, appropriately, worthily; prosequor, prosequi, prosecutus sum: honor, reward (<pro- + sequor); *prosecutus*: pf. act. ptc.
sed ... perpessus ptc. phr.; uitium, -(i)i (n.): fault, defect of character, vice; delictum, -i (n.): misdeed, offence; *dumtaxat*: provided that, as long as; perpetior, perpeti, perpessus sum: put up with, tolerate to the end (<per- + patior); *perpessus*: pf. act. ptc.
neque temere (adv.) "and scarcely"
affligo, affligere, afflixi, afflictum strike down, reduce the power of (<ad- + fligo); *afflicti*: ppp. as subst. nom. pl. subj., "men struck down"
reperio, reperire, repperi, reppertum find, discover (<re- + pario)
praeter (prep. + acc.) besides; w/ *Saluidienum* and *Cornelium* as obj.
Saluidienus Rufus (*OCD* 1312), an early supporter of the young Augustus who conspired to join with Antony in 40 BCE
quem ad consulatum usque relat. cl., supply vb. *prouexerat* from second relat. cl. in parallel structure; *quem* (relat. pron.): anteced. *Saluidienum Rufum*
Cornelius Gallus (*OCD* 378–379), a commander during Augustus' Egyptian campaign whose fall dates to 27 or 26 BCE
quem ... prouexerat a second relat. cl.; *quem* (relat. pron.): anteced. *Cornelium Gallum*; praefectura, -ae (f.): administrative appointment, prefecture; Egypt (Aegyptus) was overseen by a prefect appointed

utrumque fortuna prouexerat. **2.** quorum alterum res nouas molientem damnandum senatui tradidit, alteri ob ingratum et maliuolum animum domo et prouinciis suis interdixit. sed Gallo quoque et accusatorum denuntiationibus et senatus consultis ad necem conpulso laudauit quidem pietatem tanto opere pro se indignantium, ceterum et inlacrimauit et uicem suam conquestus est, quod sibi soli non liceret amicis quatenus uellet irasci. **3.** reliqui potentia atque opibus ad finem uitae sui

---

by Augustus; infimus, -a, -um: lowest, most undistinguished; fortuna, -ae (f.): fortune, circumstance; proueho, prouehere, prouexi, prouectum: advance, promote (<pro- + ueho)

66.2

quorum (relat. pron.) anteced. Saluidienus Rufus and Cornelius Gallus; relat. pron. as connective (AG #308f)

alterum ... molientem ptc. phr., obj. of *tradidit*; *alterum* = Salvidienus Rufus; res nouae: revolution (*OLD* nouus 10); molior, moliri, molitus sum: set in motion, stir

damno (1) pass judgment against, condemn; *damnandum*: gerv. indicating purp. (AG #500.4) ff. *tradidit*; Salvidienus was condemned to death for conspiring against the state

alteri = Cornelius Gallus

ob ... animum prep. phr.; ingratus, -a, -um: ungrateful, unappreciative; maliuolus, -a, -um: spiteful, malevolent; animus, -i (m.): mind, attitude; in contrast to Salvidienus, Gallus' initial offenses were directed at Augustus rather than the state and were punished by Augustus himself

interdico, interdicere, interdixi, interdictum prohibit, debar (w/ dat. of pers. and abl.); Augustus banned Gallus from his home and the provinces under his command

Gallo ... conpulso tmp. abl. abs. (AG #420.1); accusator, -oris (m.): accuser, prosecutor, informer (vb. subst. <accuso); denuntiatio, -onis (f.): denunciation, allegation of wrongdoing; nex, necis (f.): death; conpello, conpellere, conpuli, conpulsum: force (<con- + pello); a second phase of Gallus' punishment involved action by the senate

laudo (1) praise, commend

pietas, -atis (f.) dutiful respect

tanto opere (adv.) to such a great degree, so very

indignor (1) take offence, be aggrieved (w/ pro); *pro se indignantium*: pres. act. ptc. gen. pl. subst., "of those taking offence on his behalf"

ceterum (adv.) moreover, however that may be

inlacrimo (1) weep over, shed tears (<in- + lacrimo)

uicem suam "his own lot"; uicis, gen. (f.) (nom. sg. not found): lot, turn

conqueror, conqueri, conquestus sum complain of, bewail (<con- + queror)

quod sibi soli ... liceret ... irasci causal cl. w/ subjv. indicating authority of another (AG #540); *soli*: dat. (for decl., AG #113); licet, licere, licuit: be permitted (impers.) w/ dat. + inf.; *quatenus uellet*: indir. quest. (AG #574); quatenus (interr. adv.): to what point, how far; irascor, irasci: feel resentment, be angry (w/ dat.)

66.3

reliqui m. nom. pl. subst., "the remaining [friends]"

potentia, -ae (f.) power, influence

(ops), opis (f.) aid, support, (pl.) wealth, financial resources (defect. noun, AG #103)

finis, -is (m.) end, last part

sui quisque ordinis principes "each one as leaders of their own order"; *quisque*: partit. appos. (AG #282a, 317e)

quisque ordinis principes floruerunt, quamquam et offensis
interuenientibus. desiderauit enim nonnumquam—ne de
pluribus referam—et M. Agrippae patientiam et Maecenatis
taciturnitatem, cum ille ex leui frigoris suspicione et quod
Marcellus sibi anteferretur Mytilenas se relictis omnibus contulisset, {et} hic secretum de comperta Murenae coniuratione
uxori Terentiae prodidisset.

    4. Exegit et ipse in uicem ab amicis beniuolentiam mutuam,
tam a defunctis quam a uiuis. nam quamuis minime appeteret
hereditates, ut qui numquam ex ignoti testamento capere

---

floreo, florere, florui prosper, flourish
quamquam et offensis interuenientibus conces. abl. abs. (AG #420.3); offensa, -ae (f.): an offence;
    interuenio, interuenire, interueni, interuentum: occur (<inter- + uenio)
desidero (1) long for, find lacking, miss
ne de pluribus referam "I will not mention more"; Suet. here inserts an authorial aside with a negat. hort.
    subjv. (AG #439)
patientia, -ae (f.) tolerance, patience
Gaius Maecenas (*OCD* 883) an eques and close friend of Augustus
taciturnitas, -atis (f.) discretion, maintaining silence
cum ille ... contulisset causal cum cl. (AG #549); *ille* = Agrippa; frigus, -oris (m.): lack of affection,
    coldness; suspicio, -onis (f.): suspicion, inkling; *quod Marcellus sibi anteferretur*: causal cl. w/ subjv.
    indicating authority of another (AG #540); antefero, anteferre, antetuli, antelatum: prefer, esteem
    more highly (<ante- + fero); Mytilenae, -arum (f. pl.): Mytilene, city on the Aegean island of Lesbos;
    Mytilenas: acc. place to which (AG #427.2); *relictis omnibus*: abl. abs. (AG #419); Marcellus had
    married Augustus' daughter Julia in 25 BCE (s. ch. 63.1); Agrippa withdrew to Mytilene in 23 BCE,
    returning to Rome two years later
hic ... prodidisset continuation of the causal cum cl. (AG #549); *hic* = Maecenas; secretum, -i
    (n.): secret; *de comperta Murenae coniuratione*: tmp. ptc. phr. (AG #496), "about the conspiracy of
    Murena which had been uncovered"; comperio, comperire, comperi, compertum: find out, learn (a
    fact); coniuratio, -onis (f.): conspiracy, plot; prodo, prodere, prodidi, proditum: reveal (<pro- + do);
    Maecenas revealed to his wife Terentia that Murena's conspiracy (s. ch. 19.1) had been uncovered; in
    turn Terentia, who was the sister of the conspirator Murena, alerted her brother

66.4

in uicem "in return"
beniuolentia, -ae (f.) good will, benevolence, friendliness
mutuus, -a, -um mutual, reciprocal
tam ... quam as much ... as
uiuus, -a, -um living, alive
quamuis ... appeteret hereditates conces. cl. (AG #527a); minime (superl. adv.): by no means, not
    at all; appeto, appetere, appetivi (-ii), appetitum: seek, strive after (<ad- + peto); hereditas, -atis
    (f.): inheritance
ut qui ... sustinuerit causal. relat. cl. of char. (AG #535e); *ut qui*: "as one who," "since he"; ignotus,
    -a, -um: unfamiliar, (subst.) a stranger; sustineo, sustinere, sustinui: tolerate, accept (w/ inf.)
    (<sub- + teneo)

quicquam sustinuerit, amicorum tamen suprema iudicia
morosissime pensitauit, neque dolore dissimulato, si parcius
aut citra honorem uerborum, neque gaudio, si grate pieque
quis se prosecutus fuisset. legata uel partes hereditatium a qui-
buscumque parentibus relicta sibi aut statim liberis eorum
concedere aut, si pupillari aetate essent, die uirilis togae uel
nuptiarum cum incremento restituere consueuerat.

67   Patronus dominusque non minus seuerus quam facilis et
clemens multos libertorum in honore et usu maximo habuit, ut

---

suprema iudicia final judgments, wills; iudicium, -(i)i (n.): legal judgment, decision; Romans enjoyed freedom in expressing their true opinions in their wills; Augustus was eager to be thought of positively

morose (adv.) exactingly, critically (superl. = -issime); Suet. commonly uses superl. adv.

pensito (1) weigh in one's mind, consider (frequent. <penso, a vb. form favored by Suet.)

neque ... neque ... si ... prosecutus fuisset neither ... nor; parallel structure, with an abl. abs. followed by the prot. of a past gener. condit. (AG #518c), is used to set out two different reactions of Augustus to receiving legacies; *dolore dissimulato*: abl. abs. (AG #419); dolor, -oris (m.): pain, distress; dissimulo (1): conceal, disguise (<dis- + simulo); parce (adv.): sparingly (compar. = -ius); citra (prep. + acc.): falling short of, without reference to; honor uerborum: "words of praise"; *gaudio [dissimulato]*: abl. abs. (AG #419); gaudium, -(i)i (n.): joy, delight; *si ... quis se prosecutus fuisset*: "if anyone had honored him"; grate (adv.): gratefully; pie (adv.): dutifully, with all the proper observances; *quis* = aliquis; prosequor, prosequi, prosecutus sum: honor (<pro- + sequor); *prosecutus fuisset* = prosecutus esset, plupf. act. subjv., a form common in Suet.

legata uel partes ... relicta sibi ptc. phr., dir. obj. of *concedere* and *restituere*; legatum, -i (n.): legacy, bequest; quicumque, quaecumque, quodcumque (adj.): any; parens, -ntis (m.): parent, father; although Augustus wished to be remembered through bequests, his refusal of legacies reflects his desire to maintain wealth within family units

concedere compl. inf. (AG #456) w/ *consueuerat*

si pupillari aetate essent "if they were of an age to require a guardian"; gen. condit. w/ impf. subjv. (AG #518c); pupillaris, -e: of a minor

die abl. of time when (AG #423.1)

toga uirilis the adult toga; the assumption of the *toga uirilis* formally marked a young man's coming of age

nuptiae, -arum (f. pl.) wedding, marriage ceremony

incrementum, -i (n.) increase (i.e., interest on the money)

restituo, restituere, restitui, restitutum restore, give back (<re- + statuo); *restituere*: compl. inf. (AG #456) w/ *consueuerat*

consuesco, consuescere, consueui, consuetum be accustomed, be in the habit of (<con- + suesco)

Augustus' role as patron and master (*patronus dominusque*). Augustus is shown to be appropriately strict in his relations with his freedmen and slaves, and capable of good humor.

67.1

patronus dominusque ... clemens "as patron and master ...", pred. appos. (AG #282); patronus, -i (m.): patron; dominus, -i (m.): master, owner of slaves; *non minus ... quam*: "no less ... than"; minus introd. compar. w/ *quam* (AG #407); seuerus, -a, -um: stern, strict; facilis, -e: accommodating, indulgent; clemens, -ntis: merciful, lenient; by combining strictness with mercy and leniency, Augustus is held up as a model of behavior; note the differences in appropriate treatment for people of different status

in honore et usu maximo habuit "he held in honor and the greatest intimacy"; maximus, -a, -um: greatest (superl. to magnus)

ut (relat. adv.) such as, as for example

Licinum et Celadum aliosque. Cosmum seruum grauissime de se opinantem non ultra quam compedibus coercuit. Diomeden dispensatorem, a quo simul ambulante incurrenti repente fero apro per metum obiectus est, maluit timiditatis arguere quam noxae remque non minimi periculi, quia tamen fraus aberat, in iocum uertit.   2.   idem Polum ex acceptissimis libertis mori coegit compertum adulterare matronas, Thallo a manu, quod

---

Lucinus   C. Iulius Lucinus, freedman of Augustus, who served as procurator in Gaul
Celadus   C. Iulius Celadus, a freedman of Gk. origin
Cosmum ... opinantem   ptc. phr., obj. of *coercuit*; Cosmus: an otherwise unknown Gk. slave of Augustus; grauiter (adv.): harshly, vehemently (superl. = -issime); Suet. commonly uses superl. adv.; opinor (1): express an opinion
non ultra quam   "no more than"
compes, -edis   (f.) shackles for the feet, fetters; being bound by shackles was a lenient punishment for a slave
coerceo, coercere, coercui, coercitum   restrain, check (<con- + arceo)
Diomedes   probably another freedman of Augustus; that the steward was named after the great Greek hero Diomedes makes the story particularly humorous
dispensator, -oris   (m.) steward, financial administrator
a quo ... obiectus est   relat. cl.; *quo* (relat. pron.): anteced. *Diomeden*, abl. of agent w/ *obiectus est*, "by whom he was thrown in front of"; *simul ambulante*: tmp. ptc. phr. (AG #496), "when they were walking together"; ambulo (1): walk; *ambulante*: abl. pres. act. ptc. w/ *quo*; *incurrenti repente fero apro*: dat. indir. obj.; incurro, incurrere, incurri, incursum: rush at, charge (<in- + curro); ferus, -a, -um: wild; aper, apri (m.): boar
maluit timiditatis arguere quam noxae   compar. w/ *quam* ff. *maluit* (AG #407); malo, malle, malui: prefer (w/ compl. inf.); timiditas, -atis (f.): timidity, cowardice; arguo, arguere, argui, argutum: accuse, charge (w/ gen. of charge, AG #352); noxa, -ae (f.): wrongdoing, injury
remque non minimi periculi   "a matter of no small danger," LITOTES (AG #326c, 641); minimus, -a, -um: smallest, least
quia tamen fraus aberat   causal cl. w/ indic. (AG #540); fraus, fraudis (f.): deceit, harmful intent
uerto, uertere, uerti, uersum   turn

67.2
idem   "yet the same man" (Augustus); *idem* used to emphasize inconsistency of action (AG #298b, *OLD* 10); following the examples of mercy set out above, Suet. presents three examples of Augustus inflicting (appropriately) harsh punishments
Polum ... mori   subst. cl. of purp. (AG #563) w/ subj. acc. + inf. ff. *coegit*; Polus (a Gk. pers. name); acceptus, -a, -um: well-liked, esteemed (superl. = -issimus); morior, mori, mortuus sum: die, perish
compertum adulterare matronas   causal ptc. phr. (AG #496); comperio, comperire, comperi, compertum: find (to have committed an offence) w/ inf.; *compertum*: acc. ppp. w/ *Polum*; adultero (1): commit adultery with (w/ acc.); matrona, -ae (f.): a matron, married woman
Thallus   a Gk. name; *Thallo*: dat. of disadvantage (AG #376)
a manu   "a secretary"; an amanuensis was a private secretary who took down letters dictated by the master
quod ... accepisset   causal cl. w/ subjv. relying on the authority of another pers. (AG #540); prodo, prodere, prodidi, proditum: reveal (<pro- + do); denarius, -ii (m.): silver coin; quingenti, -ae, -a: five hundred

pro epistula prodita denarios quingentos accepisset, crura {ei} fregit, paedagogum ministrosque C. fili per occasionem ualitudinis mortisque eius superbe auareque in prouincia grassatos oneratis graui pondere ceruicibus praecipitauit in flumen.

68 Prima iuuenta uariorum dedecorum infamiam subiit. Sextus Pompeius ut effeminatum insectatus est, M. Antonius <ut> adoptionem auunculi stupro meritum, item L. Marci frater quasi pudicitiam delibatam a Caesare Aulo etiam Hirtio in

---

crus, -uris (n.) leg
frango, frangere, fregi, fractum break, shatter, crush
paedagogum ministrosque ... grassatos causal ptc. phr. (AG #496), obj. of *praecipitauit*; paedagogus, -i (m.): paedagogus, a slave who supervised children; minister, -tri (m.): servant, attendant; C[*aii*]; occasio, -onis (f.): opportunity; superbe (adv.): proudly, haughtily; auare (adv.): greedily, avariciously; grassor (1): behave (in a certain manner); the transgressions must date to 4 CE, the year of Gaius' death
oneratis ... ceruicibus abl. abs. (AG #419); onero (1): load, weigh down; pondus, -eris (n.): weight; ceruix, -icis (f.): neck
praecipito (1) hurl down, throw headlong
flumen, -inis (n.) river

Disgraceful acts (*uariorum dedecorum infamiam*). Suetonius devotes four chapters to cataloging Augustus' vices and disgraceful personal habits. Evidence is cited to support charges of effeminacy and homosexual acts (ch. 68), adultery (ch. 69), and extravagance and fondness for gambling (ch. 70). Balancing the account, Suetonius catalogues Augustus' refutations of some of these charges (ch. 71).

68
prima iuuenta abl. of time when (AG #423.1); iuuenta, -ae (f.): youth
uariorum dedecorum objv. gen. (AG #348); dedecus, -oris (n.): dishonor, disgraceful action; Suet. sets out below three examples in ascending order of severity
infamia, -ae (f.) discredit, disgrace, bad reputation
subeo, subire, subii (-iui), subitum endure, sustain (<sub- + eo)
Sextus Pompeius (*OCD* 1180–1181) the son of Pompey the Great and Augustus' rival from 45–36 BCE; note that the sources of the charges against Augustus are his political rivals
ut effeminatum "as effeminate"; effeminatus, -a, -um: effeminate, unmanly
insector (1) pursue with hostile words, harry, taunt (<in- + sector); supply *eum* (= Augustum) as obj.
ut adoptionem ... meritum ptc. phr. used to report Antonius' taunt; adoptio, -onis (f.): adoption; auunculus, -i (m.): uncle; stuprum, -i (n.): illicit sex; the implication is that Augustus was sexually violated by his great-uncle Julius Caesar; mereor, mereri, meritus sum: earn, procure
L[ucius] Marci frater Lucius Antonius (*OCD* 113), brother of Marcus Antonius; frater, -tris (m.): brother
quasi ... substrauerit *quasi* w/ subjv. to express a belief or rumor (AG #524, BG #602n4); *pudicitiam delibatam a Caesare*: tmp. ptc. phr. (AG #496), "after his chastity had been deflowered by Caesar"; pudicitia, -ae (f.): chastity, sexual purity; delibo (1): take away, deflower (<de- + libo); *Hirtio*: Aulus Hirtius; Hispania, -ae (f.): Spain; *trecentis milibus nummum*: "for three hundred thousand coins," abl. of price (AG #416); substerno, substernere, substraui, substratum: spread out under (w/ dat.) (<sub- + sterno), here with sexual connotations: "he offered himself to Aulus Hirtius"

Hispania trecentis milibus nummum substrauerit solitusque sit
crura suburere nuce ardenti quo mollior pilus surgeret. sed et
populus quondam uniuersus ludorum die et accepit in contu-
meliam eius et adsensu maximo conprobauit uersum in scaena
pronuntiatum de gallo Matris deum tympanizante,

    uidesne ut cinaedus orbem digito temperat?

69   Adulteria quidem exercuisse ne amici quidem negant, excusantes sane non libidine sed ratione commissa quo facilius
consilia aduersariorum per cuiusque mulieres exquireret.
M. Antonius super festinatas Liuiae nuptias obicit et feminam
consularem e triclinio uiri coram in cubiculum abductam,

---

solitusque sit crura suburere nuce ardenti *quasi* cl. continues (AG #524, BG #602n4); crus, -uris (n.): leg; suburo, suburere: singe, burn slightly (<sub- + uro); *suburere*: compl. inf. (AG #456); nux, nucis (f.): nut; ardeo, ardere, arsi: burn, be fiercely hot

quo mollior pilus surgeret relat. cl. of purp. w/ compar. (AG #531.2a); mollis, -e: soft (compar. = -ior); pilus, -i (m.): a hair; surgo, surgere, surrexi, surrectum: grow

contumelia, -ae (f.) insult, affront; *in contumelia eius*: "as an insult against him"

adsensus, -us (m.) applause

conprobo (1) approve, express approval of (<con- + probo)

uersum ... pronuntiatum ptc. phr., obj. of both *accepit* and *conprobauit*; scaena, -ae (f.): stage

de gallo Matris deum tympanizante "about a priest of the Mother of the Gods playing his drum"; gallus, -i (m.): a eunuch priest of Cybele (Magna Mater, the great mother of the gods); *deum* = deorum (AG #49g); tympanizo (1): play the tympanum (a small drum or tambourine) (a Gk. wd. w/ Latinized spelling)

uidesne ut cinaedus ... temperat? a dir. quotation of the verse; ut: how; cinaedus, -i (m.): a deviant, a sexually passive man; orbis, -is (m.): circular object, disk, the world; digitus, -i (m.): finger; tempero (1): moderate, control; based on the dbl. meaning of *orbem* as a drum or the world, the crowd interpreted the line as referring to Augustus; in turn Suet. sees in this anecdote the ultimate example of Augustus' reputation for effeminacy

69.1

adulteria ... exercuisse indir. disc. (AG #580) ff. *negant*; adulterium, -(i)i (n.): adultery; Augustus is the unexpressed acc. subj.; Augustus' many adulteries are presented in detail in this ch.; Suet.'s audience would be aware that both engaging in adultery and procuring women for others were later made public crimes under Augustus' Lex Iulia de adulteriis coercendis (18 or 17 BCE) (s. ch. 34.1)

excuso (1) excuse, justify

sane ... commissa pred. acc. ff. *excusantes* (AG #393), "as committed"; sane (adv.): certainly, to be sure; libido, -inis (f.): desire, lust; committo, committere, commisi, commissum: commit, perpetrate (<con- + mitto)

quo facilius ... exquireret relat. cl. of purp. w/ compar. (AG #531.2a); consilium, -(i)i (n.): plan; aduersarius, -(i)i (m.): adversary, opponent; mulier, -eris (f.): woman, a wife or mistress; exquiro, exquirere, exquisiui, exquisitum: find out, discover (<ex- + quaero)

festinatas Liuiae nuptias festino (1): hurry through; *festinatas*: "hasty," ppp. as attrib. adj. (AG #494); nuptiae, -arum (f. pl.): wedding; for the wedding to Livia, s. ch. 62.2

feminam ... abductam the charges leveled by Antonius against Augustus are reported in summary form as a list of three ptc. phr. ff. *obiecit*; as Antonius is the source, the events must date to the late 40s or 30s BCE; femina, -ae (f.): woman, wife; consularis, -e: of consular rank; triclinium, -(i)i (n.): dining-room; coram (adv.): openly, publicly; abduco, abducere, abduxi, abductum: lead off, carry away (<ab- + duco)

rursus in conuiuium rubentibus auriculis incomptiore capillo reductam; dimissam Scriboniam quia liberius doluisset nimiam potentiam paelicis; condiciones quaesitas per amicos, qui matres familias et adulta aetate uirgines denudarent atque perspicerent tamquam Thoranio mangone uendente. 2. scribit etiam ad ipsum haec familiariter adhuc necdum plane inimicus aut hostis:

quid te mutauit? quod reginam ineo? uxor mea est? nunc coepi an

---

rursus ... reductam a continuation of the ptc. phr.; *rubentibus auriculis incomptiore capillo*: abl. of quality (description) (AG #415); rubeo, rubere: be (become) red; auricula, -ae (f.): ear (dim. <auris, a form favored by Suet.); incomptus, -a, -um: disheveled (compar. = -ior); capillus, -i (m.): hair; reduco, reducere, reduxi, reductum: bring back (<re- + duco)

dimissam Scriboniam ptc. phr. ff. *obiecit*; for Scribonia (*OCD* 1331), s. ch. 62.2

quia ... doluisset ... potentiam paelicis causal cl. w/ subjv. (AG #540); libere (adv.): openly, freely (compar. = -ius); doleo, dolere, dolui, dolitum: be grieved at; nimius, -a, -um: too great, excessive; potentia, -ae (f.): power, influence; paelex, -icis (f.): rival

condiciones quaesitas per amicos ptc. phr. ff. *obiecit*; condicio, -onis (f.): liaison, affair; quaero, quaerere, quaes(i)i (-siui), quaesitum: seek; in this third and final example Augustus' friends are also attacked for procuring the women for Augustus' affairs

qui ... denudarent atque perspicerent subord. subjv. cl. in informal indir. disc. (AG #592); mater familias: matron, a respectable woman married to the head of a household; adultus, -a, -um: adult, full-grown; *adulta aetate*: abl. of quality (AG #415); uirgo, -inis (f.): virgin; denudo (1): strip (<de- + nudo); perspicio, perspicere, perspexi, perspectum: inspect (<per- + specio)

tamquam Thoranio mangone uendente condit. abl. abs. (AG #420.4); tamquam (conj.): just as, as if; Thoranius should probably be identified as Toranius Flaccus, a well-known slave-dealer of the time; mango, -onis (m.): dealer in slaves; uendo, uendere, uendidi, uenditum: sell

69.2

scribit etiam ad ipsum (= Augustum) Marcus Antonius continues as the subj.; below, Suet. quotes an extended portion of a letter dating to 33 BCE

familiariter (adv.) familiarly, in the manner of close friends

necdum (conj.) not yet

plane (adv.) plainly, clearly

inimicus aut hostis "a personal or state enemy"; inimicus, -a, -um: (subst.) personal opponent; hostis, -is (m.): enemy of the state

muto (1) change

regina, -ae (f.) queen (here = Cleopatra)

ineo, inire, inii (-iui), initum enter, mount, copulate with (a term usu. applied to animals) (<in- + eo)

uxor mea est? at the time Antonius was still married to Augustus' sister Octavia; his question here in the context of this letter shows that he considers his affair with Cleopatra to be similar to Augustus' many extramarital liaisons

coepi, coepisse, coeptum begin (defect. vb., AG #205)

abhinc annos nouem? tu deinde solam Drusillam inis? ita ualeas, uti
tu hanc epistulam cum leges non inieris Tertullam aut Terentillam
aut Rufillam aut Saluiam Titiseniam aut omnes. an refert ubi et in
qua arrigas?

70 Cena quoque eius secretior in fabulis fuit, quae uulgo
δωδεκάθεος uocabatur, in qua deorum dearumque habitu discubuisse conuiuas et ipsum pro Apolline ornatum non Antoni
modo epistulae singulorum nomina amarissime enumerantis
exprobrant sed et sine auctore notissimi uersus:

cum primum istorum conduxit mensa choragum,

---

an abhinc annos nouem "or did I begin nine years ago?"; *abhinc* (adv.): back from the present, ago; *annos nouem*: acc. distance of time before (AG #424f)
Drusilla Livia Drusilla (*OCD* 851), Augustus' wife
ita ualeas "good for you" (lit., "may you be well"); opt. subjv. used for an assertion (AG #441)
uti tu ... non inieris "that you will not have slept with"; *inieris*: fut. pf. indic. affirming the stmt. (with strong irony)
hanc epistulam cum leges tmp. cum cl. w/ fut. indic. (AG #547)
Tertullam ... aut omnes Antonius provides a list of specific women with whom Augustus was carrying on affairs, using dim. forms for their names (Tertulla, Terentilla, Rufilla) to mock affection (for dim., s. AG #243); of the four women named, only Terentilla can perhaps be identified, probably as Maecenas' wife Terentia (s. ch. 66.3)
refert, referre, retulit (impers.) it makes a difference, it is of importance (<re- + fero); *an refert*: "does it matter"
ubi et in qua arrigas indir. quest. (AG #574) ff. *refert*; arrigo, arrigere, arrexi, arrectum: become sexually excited, have an erection (<ad- + rego)

70.1
secretus, -a, -um special, private (compar. = -ior)
in fabulis fuit "was much talked about"; fabula, -ae (f.): talk, conversation
quae (relat. pron.) anteced. *cena*, nom. w/ *uocabatur*
uulgo (adv.) publicly, commonly
δωδεκάθεος "of The Twelve Gods," pred. nom. (AG #284)
in qua ... discubuisse conuiuas et ipsum ... ornatum [esse] Suet. switches to indir. disc. (AG #580) ff. *exprobrant* to report the evidence from Antonius' letters; *qua* (relat. pron.): anteced. *cena*; dea, -ae (f.): goddess; habitus, -us (m.): style of dress; *habitu*: abl. of quality (description) (AG #415); discumbo, discumbere, discubui, discubitum: recline (at table) (<dis- + cumbo); conuiua, -ae (m.): dinner guest; *ipsum* = Augustum; orno (1): dress
non ... modo ... sed et "not only ... but also"
Antoni ... enumerantis ptc. phr., gen. sg. w/ epistulae; amare (adv.): with bitterness, spitefully (superl.= -issime); enumero (1): enumerate, list
exprobro (1) bring up as a reproach; *exprobrant*: w/ two subj., *epistulae* and *uersus*
notissimi uersus nom. pl.; notus, -a, -um: well-known, familiar (superl.= -issimus); Suet. quotes the verses in elegiac couplets from the unknown author (for meter, AG #616)
cum ... mensa ... conduxit tmp. cum cl. w/ indic. (AG #545); conduco, conducere, conduxi, conductum: hire (<con- + duco); mensa, -ae (f.): table; *istorum mensa*: "the table of those people," by METONYMY (AG #641) = "those dinner guests"; choragus, -i (m.): choragus, a production manager

> sexque deos uidit Mallia sexque deas,
> impia dum Phoebi Caesar mendacia ludit,
> dum noua diuorum †cenat† adulteria:
> omnia se a terris tunc numina declinarunt,
> fugit et auratos Iuppiter ipse thronos.

2. auxit cenae rumorem summa tunc in ciuitate penuria ac fames, adclamatumque est postridie omne frumentum deos comedisse et Caesarem esse plane Apollinem, sed Tortorem, quo cognomine is deus quadam in parte urbis colebatur. notatus est et ut pretiosae supellectilis Corinthiorumque praecupidus

---

sex (indecl. adj.) six

Mallia f. nom. sg. proper name, either referring to the woman who hosted the party, or perhaps to the house in which the party was held

dum ... Caesar ... ludit dum w/ pres. indic. denoting continued action in past (AG #556); impius, -a, -um: impious, showing no regard for the gods; Phoebus, -i (m.): Phoebus Apollo; mendacium, -(i)i (n.): lie, false appearance, representation

dum ... cenat a second dum cl. (AG #556); ceno (1): dine on, enact while dining; adulterium, -(i)i (n.): adultery; the text here is corrupt: if *cenat* is correct it must be tr. w/ dir. obj. *adulteria*

numen, -inis (n.) deity, god

declino (1) turn away; *declinarunt* = contr. form of declinauerunt (AG #181)

fugio, fugere, fugi flee, desert

auratus, -a, -um gilded, adorned with gold

thronus, -i (m.) throne

70.2

rumor, -oris (m.) gossip, ill repute

summa ... penuria ac fames two nom. subj. w/ sg. vb. *auxit* (AG #317b); summus, -a, -um: extreme, greatest; penuria, -ae (f.): scarcity, shortage; fames, famis (f.): lack of food, famine; during the years of civil strife from 41–36 BCE, Rome experienced almost continuous food shortages

adclamo (1) shout in protest (<ad- + clamo); *adclamatum est*: (impers.) "it was shouted in protest" (AG #582a)

postridie (adv.) on the following day

omne frumentum deos comedisse et Caesarem esse ... Tortorem indir. disc. (AG #580) ff. *adclamatum est*; frumentum, -i (n.): grain; comedo, comesse, comedi, comesum: eat up, consume (<con- + edo); plane (adv.): clearly; Tortor, -oris (m.): torturer; the epithet "the Torturer" for Apollo is not mentioned in other sources

quo cognomine is deus ... colebatur relat. cl. in indir. disc. w. indic. for factual stmt. (AG #583); *quo cognomine*: relat. pron. w/ anteced. in relat. cl. (AG #307b); colo, colere, colui, cultum: worship

noto (1) censure, criticize, charge; *notatus est*: Augustus returns as the unexpressed subj.

et ut "also as [being]"

pretiosae supellectilis Corinthiorumque objv. gen. w/ *praecupidus* (AG #349a); pretiosus, -a, -um: expensive, precious; supellex, -ectilis (f.): furniture; Corinthius, -a, -um: Corinthian, (n. pl. subst.) Corinthian bronze vessels; Corinthian bronze was a prized alloy of bronze, gold, and silver

praecupidus, -a, -um very covetous of, overly fond of (an unusual adj. <prae- + cupidus)

et aleae indulgens. nam et proscriptionis tempore ad statuam
eius ascriptum est, 'pater argentarius, ego Corinthiarius', cum
existimaretur quosdam propter uasa Corinthia inter proscriptos
curasse referendos, et deinde bello Siciliensi epigramma uulga-
tum est,

    postquam bis classe uictus naues perdidit,
    aliquando ut uincat, ludit assidue aleam.

71   Ex quibus siue criminibus siue maledictis infamiam impudicitiae facillime refutauit et praesentis et posterae uitae castitate,

---

alea, -ae (f.) gaming, gambling
indulgens, -ntis addicted to, partial to (w/ dat.)
proscriptionis tempore "at the time of the proscriptions," abl. of time when (AG #423.1); proscriptio, -
    onis (f.): proscription, the publication of names of citizens who were declared outlaws; the proscriptions
    date to 43–42 BCE (s. ch. 27.1–2)
ascribo, ascribere, ascripsi, ascriptum add in writing, insert (<ad- + scribo); *ascriptum est*: impers.;
    writing graffiti on statues was a common form of protest
argentarius, -(i)i (m.) banker, moneylender (s. ch. 2.3)
Corinthiarius, -(i)i (m.) dealer in Corinthian bronze
cum existimaretur causal cum cl. (AG #549), "since he was thought"; *existimaretur* introd. pers. indir. disc.
    (AG #582) w/ pf. inf. *curasse*; *curasse* = contr. form of curauisse (AG #181)
quosdam . . . inter proscriptos . . . referendos [esse] subst. cl. of purp. w/ acc. + inf. (AG #563) ff. *curasse*,
    "that certain men be listed among the proscribed"; propter (prep. + acc): on account of; uas, uasis
    (uasum, -i) (n.): vessel; proscribo, proscribere, proscripsi, proscriptum: proscribe, outlaw (<pro- +
    scribo); *referendos* [*esse*]: gerv. w/ esse (AG #196, 500.2)
bello Siciliensi abl. of time when (AG #424d); on the Sicilian War, s. ch. 16
epigramma, -atis (n.) short poem, epigram; Suet. quotes the epigram written in six-foot iambic meter
    (AG #618a)
uulgo (1) make widely known, spread widely
postquam . . . perdidit tmp. cl. (AG #543); postquam: after; *classe*: by sea, in a naval battle; uinco, uincere,
    uici, uictum: conquer; nauis, -is (f.): ship, warship; perdo, perdere, perdidi, perditum: destroy, lose
    (troops) (<per- + do); Augustus is the unexpressed subj.
aliquando ut uincat purp. cl. (AG #531); aliquando (adv.): at some time
alea, -ae (f.) game of dice; *aleam ludere*: gamble, play dice; the epigram introduces Augustus' fondness for
    gambling that is fully explored in ch. 71, and implies that he even gambled with his ships

71.1
ex quibus siue criminibus siue maledictis "of these, whether considered charges or slanders"; relat. pron.
    as connective (AG #308f) w/ anteced. in relat. cl. (AG #307b); crimen, -inis (n.): charge, accusation;
    maledictum, -i (n.): insult, slander
infamia, -ae (f.) discredit, disgrace, bad reputation
impudicitia, -ae (f.) sexual immorality; *impudicitiae*: objv. gen. (AG #348)
refuto (1) refute (<re- + futo); *refutauit*: Augustus is subj.
praesens, -ntis present, occurring at the time
posterus, -a, -um occurring later, future
castitas, -atis (f.) sexual purity, moral uprightness

item lautitiarum inuidiam, cum et Alexandria capta nihil sibi
praeter unum myrrhinum calicem ex instrumento regio retinuerit et mox uasa aurea assiduissimi usus conflauerit omnia.
circa libidines haesit, postea quoque (ut ferunt) ad uitiandas
uirgines promptior, quae sibi undique etiam ab uxore conquirerentur. aleae rumorem nullo modo expauit lusitque
simpliciter et palam oblectamenti causa etiam senex ac praeterquam Decembri mense aliis quoque festis et profestis diebus.
2. nec id dubium est. autographa quadam epistula, 'cenaui', ait,

---

item lautitiarum inuidiam supply *refutauit*; lautitia, -ae (f.): extravagance, luxury; *lautitiarum*: objv. gen. (AG #348); inuidia, -ae (f.): jealousy, odium

cum et ... retinuerit causal cum cl. (AG #549) w/ pf. subjv. (for seq. of tenses, AG #485); *Alexandria capta*: tmp. abl. abs. (AG #420.1); myrrhinus, -a, -um: (made of) agate; calix, -icis (m.): drinking cup; instrumentum, -i (n.): furnishings; regius, -a, -um: royal

et ... conflauerit causal cl. continues; uas, uasis (uasum, -i) (n.): vessel; assiduus, -a, -um: regular, ordinary (superl. = -issimus); conflo (1): melt down (<con- + flo); from the melted down gold wares Augustus minted gold coins for distribution

circa libidines haesit "he clung to his sexual desires"; libido, -inis (f.): desire, lust; circa (prep. + acc.): concerning, with regard to; haereo, haerere, haesi, haesum: cling, be tied or glued to (an activity) (*OLD* 6b)

ut ferunt "as they say"

ad uitiandas uirgines gerv. w/ ad to show purp. (AG #506); uitio (1): corrupt, deflower; uirgo, -inis (f.): virgin; engaging in sex with freeborn virgins was a crime (stuprum)

promptus, -a, -um inclined to, eager to (compar: -ior)

quae ... conquirerentur subord. subjv. cl. in informal indir. disc. (AG #592); *quae* (relat. pron): anteced. *uirgines*; undique (adv.): from everywhere; conquiro, conquirere, conquisiui (-sii), conquisitum: search out, collect (<con- + quaero); Livia thus reportedly acted as a procuress, a crime under the Lex Iulia de adulteriis coercendis

alea, -ae (f.) gambling, game of dice

rumor, -oris (m.) rumor, ill repute

expauesco, expauescere, expaui become frightened at (<ex- + pauesco)

simpliciter (adv.) without reserve, candidly

palam (adv.) openly, without concealment

oblectamentum, -i (n.) amusement, delight

etiam senex "even as an old man", pred. appos. (AG #282); senex, senis (m.): old man

praeterquam (conj.) apart from, beyond; Augustus' gambling was a regular habit, not just an indulgence during holidays

Decembri mense abl. of time when or within which (AG #423); December, -bris, -bre: of December; the Saturnalia festival in December was a traditional time for gaming, when the usual prohibition was lifted

aliis quoque festis et profestis diebus abl. of time when (AG #423); dies festus: holiday; dies profestus: ordinary day, a day not kept as a holiday

71.2

dubius, -a, -um uncertain, doubtful

autographa quadam epistula abl.; "in a certain letter that he wrote himself"; autographus, -a, -um: written with one's own hand (a Gk. wd. w/ Latinized spelling); quoting directly from a letter that he himself has consulted, Suet. cites Augustus' own wd. as evidence of his fondness for gambling

ait "he says" (for forms, AG #206a)

'mi Tiberi, cum isdem, accesserunt conuiuae Vinicius et Silius
pater. inter cenam lusimus geronticos et heri et hodie. talis
enim iactatis, ut quisque canem aut senionem miserat, in singulos talos singulos denarios in medium conferebat quos tollebat uniuersos qui Venerem iecerat'.   3. et rursus aliis litteris,
'nos, mi Tiberi, Quinquatrus satis iucunde egimus: lusimus
enim per omnis dies forumque aleatorum calfecimus. frater
tuus magnis clamoribus rem gessit, ad summam tamen per-

---

mi Tiberi voc. (AG #49c)
accedo, accedere, accessi, accessum come (<ad- + cedo)
conuiua, -ae (m.) dinner guest; *conuiuae*: pred. appos., "as dinner guests" (AG #282)
Vinicius et Silius pater "Vinicius and the elder Silius"; the exact identities of the two is uncertain
geronticos (adv.) in the manner of an old man (a Gk. wd. w/ Latinized spelling)
heri (adv.) yesterday
hodie (adv.) today
talis enim iactatis abl. abs. (AG #419); talus, -i (m.): knucklebone, a four-sided rectangular die with
    rounded ends used for gaming; the sides of a talus were numbered one, three, four, or six; iacto
    (1): toss, throw
ut quisque ... miserat tmp. cl. (AG #543); canis, -is (m./f.): dog, the lowest throw at dice (a roll of a one);
    senio, -onis (f.): six (roll of six in dicing)
in singulos talos singulos denarios "individual silver coins for each of the dice"; denarius, -ii (m.): silver
    coin; the stakes on the table would grow a few coins at a time until someone threw a winning roll
medium, -ii (n.) the middle
quos (relat. pron.) anteced. *denarios*
tollo, tollere, sustuli, sublatum pick up, take, remove
qui (relat. pron.) anteced. is the unexpressed subj. of *tollebat*
Venus, -eris (f.) Venus, the best throw in dicing (when all four dice show different numbers)
iacio, iacere, ieci, iactum throw, toss

71.3

Quinquatrus, -uum (f. pl.) the Quinquatria, a five-day festival of Minerva in March; *Quinquatrus*: acc.
    obj. w/ *egimus*
iucunde (adv.) pleasantly, agreeably
ago, agere, egi, actum spend (time)
forum aleatorum "the gamblers' forum"; aleator, -oris (m.): gambler, dice-player; "forum" is a playful
    way to describe the gaming board (tabula), suggesting the seriousness of the business for some of the
    players; Augustus describes the game using business and military terminology
calfacio, calfacere, calfeci, calfactum make hot, heat (<caleo + facio)
frater, -tris (m.) brother (here, Tiberius' brother Drusus); the reference to Drusus indicates that the letter
    was written before 9 BCE, the year of Drusus' death
clamor, -oris (m.) shout, outcry
rem gessit "he conducted the campaign"; *rem gerere*: transact business or military affairs (*OLD* 9)
ad summam "in the end"
perdo, perdere, perdidi, perditum lose, destroy (a common military expression) (<per- + do)

didit non multum, sed ex magnis detrimentis praeter spem
paulatim retractum est. ego perdidi uiginti milia nummum
meo nomine, sed cum effuse in lusu liberalis fuissem, ut soleo
plerumque. nam si quas manus remisi cuique exegissem aut
retinuissem quod cuique donaui, uicissem uel quinquaginta
milia. sed hoc malo. benignitas enim mea me ad caelestem
gloriam efferet'.   4. scribit ad filiam, 'misi tibi denarios ducentos quinquaginta quos singulis conuiuis dederam, si uellent
inter se inter cenam uel talis uel par impar ludere'.

---

detrimentum, -i (n.) harm, loss, military reversal
praeter spem "surpassing his hopes"
paulatim (adv.) little by little, by degrees, gradually
retraho, retrahere, retraxi, retractum win back (<re- + traho); *retractum est*: impers.
uiginti milia nummum "20,000 sesterces"
cum . . . fuissem causal cum cl. (AG #549); *effuse* (adv.): freely, lavishly; *lusus, -us* (m.): game; *liberalis, -e*: generous
plerumque (adv.) on most occasions, mostly, often
si . . . exegissem aut retinuissem . . ., uicissem past C-to-F condit. (AG #517) w/ two relat. cl. in prot.; *si . . . cuique exegissem*: "if I had demanded from each"; *cuique*: dat. of separ. (AG #381); *quas manus remisi*: relat. cl. w/ anteced. in cl. (AG #307b); *manus*: "stakes" (gambling wagers) (*OLD* 26); remitto, remittere, remisi, remissum: let go (<re- + mitto); *quod cuique donaui*: relat. cl. w/out anteced. (AG #307c); uinco, uincere, uici, uictum: win; *uel quinquaginta milia*: "perhaps 50,000"; if Augustus had not let some of the players reclaim wagers he had won and provided the stakes for others, he would have made a tidy sum
malo, malle, malui prefer
benignitas, -atis (f.) friendliness, generosity
ad caelestem gloriam HYPERBOLE (AG #641) demonstrating Augustus' humor; *caelestis, -e*: celestial, heavenly; *gloria, -ae* (f.): honor, glory
effero, efferre, extuli, elatum lift, raise (<ex- + fero)

71.4
filiam = Julia; this letter must date before Julia's banishment in 2 BCE (s. ch. 65.1)
denarios ducentos quinquaginta "250 denarii"; *denarius, -ii* (m.): denarius, a silver coin
conuiua, -ae (m.) dinner guest
si uellent impf. subjv. in prot. of (mixed) past gener. condit. (AG #518c)
par impar "odds or evens," a game involving guessing whether the opponent holds an odd or even number of objects
ludere compl. inf. w/ *uellent* (AG #456)

72 In ceteris partibus uitae continentissimum constat ac sine
suspicione ullius uitii. habitauit primo iuxta {Romanum} forum
supra Scalas anularias, in domo quae Calui oratoris fuerat,
postea in Palatio, sed nihilo minus aedibus modicis Hortensianis
{et} neque laxitate neque cultu conspicuis, ut in quibus porticus breues essent Albanarum columnarum et sine marmore
ullo aut insigni pauimento conclauia. ac per annos amplius
quadraginta eodem cubiculo hieme et aestate mansit <et>
quamuis parum salubrem ualitudini suae urbem hieme experi-

Examples of self-restraint (*continentissimum*). Suetonius shifts from discussing Augustus' vices to cataloging his virtues in other parts of his life. *Continentissimum*, very self-restrained, serves as the emphatic heading for chapters 72–78.

72.1

continens, -ntis self-restrained, moderate (superl. = -ntissimus); *continentissimum* [*eum esse*]: indir. disc. (AG #580) ff. *constat*

consto, constare, constiti (impers.) it is known, it is agreed (*OLD* 9) (<con- + sto)

suspicio, -onis (f.) suspicion, inkling, suggestion

uitium, -(i)i (n.) fault, defect of character, vice

habito (1) live, dwell (in a place)

iuxta (prep. w/ acc.) in the vicinity of, next to

supra (prep. w/ acc.) above, on top of

Scalae Anulariae "Steps of the Ringmakers"; scalae, -arum (f. pl.): stairs, steps; anularius, -a, -um: connected with ringmakers; the area was home to the shops of many jewelers

quae (relat. pron.) anteced. *domo*

C. Licinius Caluus (*OCD* 832), a noted Roman orator and poet

orator, -oris (m.) an orator

Palatium, -(i)i (n.) the Palatine Hill; the precise location of Augustus' house on the Palatine remains disputed

nihilo minus no less

aedibus modicis ... conspicuis abl. of place where (AG #426.3); aedes, -is (f.): (pl.) a house; Hortensianus, -a, -um: of Hortensius, Q. Hortensius Hortalus, the noted orator (*OCD* 708); *laxitate ... cultu*: abl. of specif. (AG #418); laxitas, -atis (f.): spaciousness, size; cultus, -us (m.): adornment, finery; conspicuus, -a, -um: remarkable, notable

ut in quibus porticus breues essent ... et ... conclauia "as there were in the house short porticoes ... and rooms"; relat. cl. of char. expressing cause (AG #535e); *quibus* (relat. pron.): anteced. *aedibus*; porticus, -us (f.): portico, colonnade; breuis, -e: short, small; Albanus, -a, -um: of Alban stone (peperino, a utilitarian local stone); columna, -ae (f.): column, pillar; marmor, -oris (n.): marble; insignis, -e: notable; pauimentum, -i (n.): paved floor, pavement; conclaue, -is (n.): room or suite locked with a key

quadraginta (indecl. adj.) forty

eodem cubiculo hieme et aestate mansit "in winter and in summer he remained in the same bedroom"; Suet. emphasizes that Augustus did not change bedrooms with the season as was common for wealthy Romans; *hieme et aestate*: abl. of time when (AG #423); hiems, -mis (f.): winter; aestas, -atis (f.): summer

quamuis ... experiretur conces. cl. (AG #527), "although he found"; saluber, -bris, -bre: healthy; *parum salubrem*: LITOTES (AG #641); experior, experiri, expertus sum: find by experience (w/ pred. acc., AG #393)

retur assidue in urbe hiemauit. **2.** si quando quid secreto aut sine interpellatione agere proposuisset, erat illi locus in edito singularis, quem Syracusas et τεγύφιον uocabat. huc transibat aut in alicuius libertorum suburbanum, aeger autem in domo Maecenatis cubabat. ex secessibus praecipue frequentauit maritima insulasque Campaniae aut proxima urbi oppida, Lanuuium, Praeneste, Tibur, ubi etiam in porticibus Herculis templi persaepe ius dixit. **3.** ampla et operosa praetoria grauabatur, et neptis quidem suae Iuliae profuse ab ea extructa etiam diruit ad solum, sua uero quamuis modica non tam

---

hiemo (1) pass the winter

72.2
si quando ... proposuisset condit. tmp. cl. w/ plupf. subjv. (AG #542, 518c), "if ever he intended"; *si quando*: if ever; *quid* = aliquid; secreto (adv.): in private; interpellatio, -onis (f.): interruption; *agere*: compl. inf. (AG #456) w/ *proposuisset*

erat illi locus ... singularis "he had a special place"; *illi*: dat. of poss. (AG #373); editus, -a, -um: high, lofty, (n. subst.) a high position; singularis, -e: special, specific (to a person)

quem (relat. pron.) anteced. *locus*

Syracusae, -arum (f. pl.) Syracuse (a city in Sicily)

τεγύφιον "little chamber"

huc (adv.) to this place

transeo, transire, transiui (-ii), transitum proceed, come (<trans- + eo)

suburbanum, -i (n.) country house (n. of adj. used as subst., *OLD* 2)

aeger, -gra, -grum unwell, sick

Gaius Maecenas (*OCD* 883), an eques and close friend of Augustus

secessus, -us (m.) retreat, a secluded place; Augustus owned many villas along the coast

maritima, -orum (n. pl.) coastal areas

Campania, -ae (f.) Campania (a region of Italy south of Latium)

Lanuuium, Praeneste, Tibur three towns a short distance from Rome

Hercules, -is (m.) Hercules; the temple of Hercules Victor at Tibur (modern Tivoli) was an important religious sanctuary

persaepe (adv.) very often

ius dicere administer justice, give legal decisions

72.3
operosus, -a, -um elaborate, ornate

praetorium, -(i)i (n.) large mansion, palace; the term designated the commander's quarters in a military camp, but was applied to distinguished homes and villas

grauo (1) (pass.) object to

[praetoria] neptis ... extructa ptc. phr., obj. of *diruit*; profuse (adv.): extravagantly, with lavish expenditure; on Julia, s. ch. 64–65

diruo, diruere, dirui, dirutum pull down, demolish (<dis- + ruo)

solum, -i (n.) ground, base, foundation

sua [praetoria] ... modica obj. of *excoluit*

non tam ... quam not as much ... as

statuarum tabularumque pictarum ornatu quam xystis et
nemoribus excoluit rebusque uetustate ac raritate notabilibus,
qualia sunt Capreis immanium beluarum ferarumque membra
praegrandia, quae dicuntur gigantum ossa et arma heroum.

73 instrumenti eius et supellectilis parsimonia apparet etiam nunc
residuis lectis atque mensis, quorum pleraque uix priuatae elegantiae sint. ne toro quidem cubuisse aiunt nisi humili et
modice instrato. ueste non temere alia domestica usus est quam
ab sorore et uxore et filia neptibusque confecta, togis neque

---

tabula picta painting; pingo, pingere, pinxi, pictum: paint
ornatus, -us (m.) ornamentation, adornment
xystus, -i (m.) open-air walkway (a Gk. wd. w/ Latinized spelling)
nemus, -oris (n.) forest, woodlands
excolo, excolere, excolui, excultum decorate, adorn (<ex- + colo)
rebusque ... notabilibus "and with things noted for their age and rarity"; uetustas, -atis (f.): age, old age; raritas, -atis (f.): rarity; notabilis, -e: remarkable, noteworthy for (w/ abl. of specif., AG #418)
qualis, -e (relat.) of which sort, such as
Capreae, -arum (f. pl.) Capri, an island off the coast of Campania; *Capreis*: locat. (AG #427.3)
immanis, -e monstrous, of enormous size, immense
belua, -ae (f.) beast, wild animal, monster
fera, -ae (f.) wild animal, beast
membrum, -i (n.) member, limb
praegrandis, -e exceptionally large, enormous
quae dicuntur ... arma heroum relat. cl.; quae (relat. pron.): n. nom. pl., anteced. *membra*; gigans, -ntis (m.): giant; os, ossis (n.): bone; *ossa et arma*: pred. nom. (AG #284); arma, -orum (n. pl.): arms, weapons; heros, -oos (m.): a hero; *heroum*: gen. pl. (for decl., AG #82)

73
instrumentum, -i (n.) equipment, utensils
supellex, -ectilis (f.) furniture, furnishings of a household
parsimonia, -ae (f.) frugality, economy; *parsimonia*: nom. sg.
appareo, apparere, apparui, apparitum be visible, be found (<ad- + pareo)
residuis lectis atque mensis "from the remaining couches and tables"; lectus, -i (m.): bed, couch; mensa, -ae (f.): table; Suet. himself likely had seen some of Augustus' furnishings which had been preserved
quorum pleraque ... sint explanatory subord. subjv. cl. in informal indir. disc. (AG #592.3); priuatus, -a, -um: private, suitable for an ordinary citizen; elegantia, -ae (f.): refinement, elegance; *priuatae elegantiae*: gen. of quality (AG #345)
[eum] ... cubuisse ... instrato indir. disc. (AG #580) ff. aiunt (they say); torus, -i (m.): bed; *toro*: dat. w/ *cubuisse*; humilis, -e: low, rising only slightly from the ground; modice (adv.): modestly, in a rather poor manner; insterno, insternere, instraui, instratum: cover, spread (<in- + sterno)
ueste ... usus est "rarely did he wear other domestic clothing"; *ueste*: abl. w/ *usus est*; *non temere*: scarcely, rarely; domesticus, -a, -um: for use in the home, domestic
quam ab sorore ... confecta compar. cl. w/ *quam* ff. *alia* (AG #407d), "than clothing made by his sister..."; conficio, conficere, confeci, confectum: make, manufacture (<con- + facio)
togis ... fusis abl. ptc. phr. w/ *usus est*; restrictus, -a, -um: drawn tight (ppp. <restringo); fusus, -a, -um: loose, loosely fitting (ppp. <fundo)

restrictis neque fusis, clauo nec lato nec angusto, calciamentis
altiusculis ut procerior quam erat uideretur. et forensia autem
et calceos numquam non intra cubiculum habuit ad subitos
repentinosque casus parata.

74   Conuiuabatur assidue nec umquam nisi recta, non sine magno
ordinum hominumque dilectu. Valerius Messala tradit neminem
umquam libertinorum adhibitum ab eo cenae excepto Mena,
sed asserto in ingenuitatem post proditam Sexti Pompei
classem. ipse scribit inuitasse se quondam in cuius uilla maneret

---

clauo ... angusto abl. of quality (AG #415); clauus, -i (m.): purple stripe; latus, -a, -um: broad, wide; angustus, -a, -um: narrow, small; a broad purple stripe on the tunic was a sign of senatorial status

calciamentum, -i (n.) shoe; *calciamentis*: abl. w/ *usus est*

altiusculus, -a, -um rather higher than normal (dim. <altus, a form favored by Suet.)

ut ... uideretur purp. cl. (AG #531); procerus, -a, -um: tall (compar. = -ior); *procerior*: pred. nom. (AG #284); *quam erat*: compar. (AG #407)

forensia, -ium (n. pl.) clothes for public occasion

calceus, -i (m.) shoe

intra (prep. w/ acc.) within

ad ... casus parata ptc. phr.; subitus, -a, -um: sudden, arising without warning; repentinus, -a, -um: unexpected; casus, -us (m.): event, situation; paro (1): prepare, make ready, *parata* w/ *forensia et calceos*

74

conuiuor (1) give a dinner party

recta [cena] abl. sg., "with a formal dinner"; rectus, -a, -um: proper; a formal dinner involved nine diners arranged on couches based on their social status and standing with the host

dilectus, -us (m.) process of choosing, distinction

Marcus Valerius Messala Corvinus consul in 31 BCE and a leading public figure (*OCD* 1534–1535), s. ch. 58.1-2

neminem ... adhibitum [esse] indir. disc. (AG #580) ff. *tradit*; nemo, -inis (m.): nobody, no one; libertinus, -i (m.): freedman, former slave (alt. form of libertus); adhibeo, adhibere, adhibui, adhibitum: invite (as a guest) (<ad- + habeo)

excepto Mena abl. abs. (AG #419); Menas, -ae (m.): Menas, a Gk. man who had served as a lieutenant of Sextus Pompey (for decl., AG #44)

sed [Mena] **asserto in ingenuitatem** tmp. abl. abs. (AG #420.1); *asserere in ingenuitatem*: (legal term) "claim as free-born"; assero, asserere, asserui, assertum: claim (<ad- + sero); ingenuitas, -atis (f.): status of a free-born person

post proditam ... classem "after he betrayed the fleet of Sextus Pompeius" (in Sardinia and Corsica in 38 BCE); prodo, prodere, prodidi, proditum: betray (<pro- + do)

ipse = Augustus

inuitasse se (= Augustum) indir. disc. (AG #580) ff. *scribit*; inuito (1): entertain; *inuitasse* = contr. form of inuitauisse (AG #181)

in cuius uilla maneret qui ... fuisset "the man in whose villa he was staying who had been ...," two relat. cl. w/out anteced. (AG #307c), w/ subjv. in indir. disc. (AG #580); uilla, -ae (f.): country house, estate; speculator, -oris (m.): bodyguard (vb. subst. <speculo)

qui speculator suus olim fuisset. conuiuia nonnumquam et
serius inibat et maturius relinquebat, cum conuiuae et cenare
inciperent priusquam ille discumberet et permanerent digresso
eo. cenam ternis ferculis aut cum abundantissime senis prae-
bebat, ut non nimio sumptu, ita summa comitate. nam et ad
communionem sermonis tacentis uel summissim fabulantis
prouocabat et aut acroamata et histriones aut etiam triuiales ex
circo ludios interponebat ac frequentius aretalogos.

75 Festos et sollemnes dies profusissime, nonnumquam tantum
   ioculariter celebrabat. Saturnalibus et si quando alias libuisset

---

sero (adv.) late, tardily (compar. = -ius)
ineo, inire, inii (-iui), initum go into, enter into (<in- + eo)
mature (adv.) early (compar. = -ius)
cum conuiuae ... inciperent ... et permanerent digresso eo circumst. cum cl. (AG #546) w/ two vbs.; conuiua,
   -ae (m.): dinner guest; *cenare*: compl. inf. w/ *inciperent*; incipio, incipere, incepi, inceptum: start, begin (<in- +
   capio); *prius quam ille discumberet*: anticipatory cl. w/ subjv. (AG #551b); discumbo, discumbere, discubui,
   discubitum: recline (at table) (<dis- + cumbo); permaneo, permanere, permansi, permansum: remain (<per- +
   maneo); *digresso eo*: tmp. abl. abs. (AG #420.1); digredior, digredi, digressus sum: depart (<dis- + gradior)
ternis ferculis aut ... senis abl. of quality (description) (AG #415); terni, -ae, -a (pl. adj.): three, three at a
   time; ferculum -i (n.): dish, course (of a meal); *cum abundantissime*: "at the most lavishly," cum w/ superl.
   (*OLD* cum² 13a); abundanter (adv.): lavishly (superl. = -tissime); seni, -ae, -a (pl. adj.): six, six at a time
ut ... ita "while ... yet," correl. conj. (AG #323g)
non nimio sumptu ... summa comitate abl. of quality (description) (AG #415); nimius, -a, -um: too
   much, excessive; sumptus, -us (m.): expenditure, outlay; summus, -a, -um: highest, utmost; comitas, -
   atis (f.): friendliness, courtesy
ad communionem sermonis ... prouocabat "he would draw into the common conversation"; communio,
   -onis (f.): mutual participation, association; *tacentis ... fabulantis*: acc. pl. pres. act. ptc., obj. of
   prouocabat; taceo, tacere, tacui, tacitum: be silent; summissim (adv.): softly; fabulor (1): talk, chat;
   prouoco (1): draw forth (<pro- + uoco)
acroama, -atis (n.) act, item of entertainment (music, etc.) (a Gk. wd. w/ Latinized spelling)
histrio, -onis (m.) actor, performer
triuiales ex circo ludios "street-performers from the circus"; triuialis, -e: appropriate to the street; circus, -i
   (m.): circus; ludius, -ii (m.): stage-performer
interpono, interponere, interposui, interpositum intersperse, include (<inter- + pono)
aretalogus, -i (m.) professional storyteller (a Gk. wd. w/ Latinized spelling)

75
festus, -a, -um festive; dies festus: public holiday
sollemnis, -e celebrated; dies sollemnis: anniversary, annual celebration
profuse (adv.) extravagantly, with lavish expenditure (superl. = -issime, an unusual form)
tantum ioculariter "only in jest"; ioculariter (adv.): in fun, jestingly
celebro (1) observe (a holiday), celebrate
Saturnalia, -ium (n. pl.) the Saturnalia, the festival of Saturn on Dec. 17; *Saturnalibus*: abl. of time when (AG #423)
si quando alias libuisset "whenever he wanted at other times," condit. tmp. cl. w/ plpf. subjv. (AG #542,
   518c); alias (adv.): at other times; libet, libere, libuit: (impers.) it is pleasing

modo munera diuidebat, uestem et aurum et argentum, modo
nummos omnis notae, etiam ueteres regios ac peregrinos,
interdum nihil praeter cilicia et spongias et rutabula et forpices
atque alia id genus titulis obscuris et ambiguis. solebat et
inaequalissimarum rerum sortes et auersas tabularum picturas
in conuiuio uenditare incertoque casu spem mercantium uel
frustrari uel explere, ita ut per singulos lectos licitatio fieret et
seu iactura seu lucrum communicaretur.

76 Cibi—nam ne haec quidem omiserim—minimi erat atque uulgaris fere. secundarium panem et pisciculos minutos et caseum

---

uestem et aurum et argentum appos. w/ *munera*; aurum, -i (n.): gold; argentum, -i (n.): silver
nota, -ae (f.) mark, imprint
regius, -a, -um royal; coins were not minted in Rome until the third century BCE, but Romans credited the king Servius Tullius with the introduction of coinage
peregrinus, -a, -um foreign, alien
cilicium, -(i)i (n.) rug or blanket of goat's hair (from Cilicia)
spongia, -ae (f.) sponge
rutabulum, -i (n.) poker, a long implement
forpex, -icis (f.) pincers, tongs, shears
alia id genus "other things of this type"; *id genus*: adv. acc. (AG #397a)
titulis obscuris et ambiguis "with obscure and ambiguous names," abl. of quality (AG # 415); titulus, -i (m.): name, title; obscurus, -a, -um: obscure, unclear; ambiguus, -a, -um: ambiguous, having more than one meaning; the names of the gifts listed have dbl. meanings which would surprise and amuse the recipient (for example, rutabulum might refer to a fire-poker, and also a penis)
sortes et . . . picturas acc. obj. w/ *uenditare*; inaequalis, -e: unequal, variable (superl. = -issimus), *inaequalissimarum rerum*: objv. gen. (AG #348); sors, -rtis (f.): lottery ticket; auersus, -a, -um: having the back turned, reversed; pictura, -ae (f.): picture, painting; as a form of entertainment, dinner guests would bid on these mystery items
uendito (1) offer for sale; *uenditare*: compl. inf. (AG #456) w/ *solebat*
incertoque casu abl. abs. w/out ptc. (AG #419a); incertus, -a, -um: uncertain; casus, -us (m.): outcome
mercor (1) buy, purchase; *mercantium*: gen. pl. pres. act. ptc., subst. "of the people buying"
uel frustrari uel explere compl. inf. (AG #456) w/ *solebat*; frustror (1): frustrate, disappoint; expleo, explere, expleui, expletum: fill up, satisfy (<ex- + pleo)
ita ut . . . licitatio fieret et . . . communicaretur result cl. (AG #537); lectus, -i (m.): dining couch; licitatio, -onis (f.): bidding; iactura, -ae (f.): loss; lucrum, -i (n.): gain, profit; communico (1): share; dinner guests sharing a couch would participate as a team to bid on items

76.1
cibus, -i (m.) food; *cibi*: gen. of quality (description) (AG #345); note the emphatic placement to mark a new rubric
omiserim "I would omit," potent. subjv. used for modest assertion (AG #447)
minimi . . . uulgaris gen. w/ *cibi*; minimus, -a, -um: smallest, least in amount; uulgaris, -e: ordinary, common, everyday
secundarium panem et . . . ficos uirides biferas obj. of *appetebat*; secundarius, -a, -um: second-grade, second-quality, coarse; panis, -is (f.): bread; pisciculus, -i (m.): small fish (dim. <piscis); minutus, -a, -um: small,

bibulum manu pressum et ficos uirides biferas maxime appetebat uescebaturque et ante cenam quocumque tempore et loco
stomachus desiderasset. uerba ipsius ex epistulis sunt: 'nos in
essedo panem et palmulas gustauimus', **2.** et iterum, 'dum
lectica ex regia domum redeo, panis unciam cum paucis acinis
uuae duracinae comedi', et rursus, 'ne Iudaeus quidem, mi
Tiberi, tam diligenter sabbatis ieiunium seruat quam ego hodie
seruaui, qui in balineo demum post horam primam noctis duas

---

tiny; *caseum ... pressum*: ptc. phr.; caseus, -i (m.): cheese; bibulus, -a, -um: moist, soft; premo, premere, pressi, pressum: press; ficus, -i (f.): fig; uiridis, -e: green, unripe; bifer, -era, -erum: bearing fruit twice a year

appeto, appetere, appetiui (-ii), appetitum strive after, have an appetite for (<ad- + peto)

uescor, uesci eat

quocumque ... stomachus desiderasset "at whatever time or place his stomach desired," past gener. condit. relat. cl. (AG #519, 518c); quicumque, quaecumque, quodcumque: whatever; *tempore et loco*: abl. of time when (AG #423) and place where (AG #429.1); stomachus, -i (m.): stomach; desidero (1): desire; *desiderasset* = contr. form of desiderauisset (AG #181)

uerba ipsius Suet. quotes directly the wd. of Augustus from letters of unknown date

essedum, -i (n.) light traveling-chariot, carriage

palmula, -ae (f.) date, the fruit of a palm (dim. <palma)

gusto (1) taste, have a bite of (food)

76.2

dum ... redeo "while I was returning," dum w/ pres. indic. to denote continued action in past (AG #556); *lectica*: abl. of means (AG #409); regia, -ae (f.): the Regia, the official home of the pontifex maximus in Rome; *domum*: acc. place to which w/out prep. (AG #427.2)

uncia, -ae (f.) ounce, a small portion

cum paucis acinis uuae duracinae "with a few firm grapes"; paucus, -a, -um: few, a small number of; acinus, -i (m.) -um, -i (n.): berry; uua, -ae (f.): bunch of grapes; duracinus, -a, -um: having a hard berry or fruit, firm-fleshed

comedo, comesse, comedi, comesum eat up, consume (<con- + edo)

Iudaeus, -a, -um Judaean, Jewish, (subst.) Jew

mi Tiberi voc. (AG #49c)

tam ... quam "so ... as"; adv. used as correl. conj. (AG #323g)

diligenter (adv.) carefully, scrupulously, thoroughly

sabbata, -orum (n. pl.) the Jewish sabbath; *sabbatis*: abl. of time when (AG #423)

ieiunium, -(i)i (n.) fast, day of fasting; it was a common misunderstanding of the Romans that Jews fasted on the sabbath

seruo (1) keep, observe, maintain

hodie (adv.) today

qui ... manducaui relat. cl.; *qui* (relat. pron.): anteced. *ego*; balineum, -i (n.): bathing room, bath; duo, duae, duo (pl. adj.): two (for decl., AG #134b); bucca, -ae (f.): mouth, mouthful; manduco (1): chew, munch, chomp

buccas manducaui prius quam ungui inciperem'. ex hac inobseruantia nonnumquam uel ante initum uel post dimissum conuiuium solus cenitabat, cum pleno conuiuio nihil tangeret.

77 Vini quoque natura parcissimus erat. non amplius ter bibere eum solitum super cenam in castris apud Mutinam Cornelius Nepos tradit; postea quotiens largissime se inuitaret, senos sextantes non excessit aut, si excessisset, reiciebat. et maxime delectatus est Raetico neque temere interdiu bibit. pro potione sumebat perfusum aqua frigida panem aut cucumeris frustum

---

prius quam ungui inciperem anticipatory cl. implying expectancy in past time (AG #551b); unguo, unguere, unxi, unctum: anoint, rub with oil; *ungui*: compl. inf. (AG #456) ff. *inciperem*; incipio, incipere, incepi, inceptum: start, begin (<in- + capio)

inobseruantia, -ae (f.) failure to observe a routine, irregularity

post dimissum conuiuium "after the dinner party had been dismissed"; *dimissum*: ppp. of dimitto

cenito (1) dine habitually (frequent. <ceno, a vb. form favored by Suet.)

cum . . . tangeret conces. cum cl. (AG #549); *pleno conuiuio*: abl. of time when (AG #424d); plenus, -a, -um: full, crowded; tango, tangere, tetigi, tactum: touch, taste (food or drink)

77

uinum, -i (n.) wine; *uini*: objv. gen. (AG #349); a discussion of drinking habits naturally follows the chapter on food

natura, -ae (f.) temperament, nature; *natura*: abl. of specif. (AG #418)

parcus, -a, -um moderate, restrained (superl. = -issimus)

non amplius . . . eum solitum [esse] **. . . apud Mutinam** indir. disc. (AG #580) ff. *tradit*; ter (adv.): three times; bibo, bibere, bibi: drink; *bibere*: compl. inf. (AG #456) w/ *solitum*; *super cenam* = inter cenam; Mutina, -ae (f.): Mutina, modern Modena (s. ch. 10.3)

Cornelius Nepos Roman writer of biographies in the first century BCE (*OCD* 380)

quotiens . . . inuitaret iterative subjv. w/ *quotiens* (BG #567n); large (adv.): liberally, copiously (superl. = -issime), Suet. commonly uses superl. adv.; inuito (1): entertain, treat

senos sextantes "a pint," lit., six sixths, one sextarius (a unit of liquid measure); seni, -ae, -a (pl. adj.): six; sextans, -ntis (m.): one sixth of a sextarius

excedo, excedere, excessi, excessum go beyond, exceed (<ex- + cedo)

si excessisset past gener. condit. w/ plupf. subjv. indicating repeated or customary action in past (AG #518c)

reicio, reicere, reieci, reiectum throw up, vomit (<re- + iacio)

delecto (1) delight, (pass.) be delighted, take pleasure in (w/ abl.)

Raetico [uino] Raeticus, -a, -um: Raetian, of Raetia, a Roman province in the Alps and Bavaria; "Raetian" was the common name of a wine from the northern Po valley

neque temere "and scarcely"

interdiu (adv.) in the daytime, during the day

potio, -onis (f.) drinking, drink

perfusum . . . panem aut . . . pomum a list of dir. obj. w/ *sumebat*; *perfusum . . . panem*: ptc. phr.; perfundo, perfundere, perfudi, perfusum: wet, drench (<per- + fundo); frigidus, -a, -um: cold, cool; panis, -is (f.): bread; cucumis, -eris (m.): cucumber; frustum, -i (n.): small piece, morsel; lactucula, -ae (f.): small lettuce (dim. <lactuca, a frequent form in Suet.); thyrsus, -i (m.): stem of a plant, sprig;

uel lactuculae thyrsum aut recens aridumue pomum suci uinosioris.

78 Post cibum meridianum, ita ut uestitus calciatusque erat, retectis pedibus paulisper conquiescebat opposita ad oculos manu. a cena in lecticulam se lucubratoriam recipiebat, ibi donec residua diurni actus aut omnia aut ex maxima parte conficeret ad multam noctem permanebat. in lectum inde transgressus non amplius cum plurimum quam septem horas dormiebat, ac ne eas quidem continuas sed ut in illo temporis spatio ter aut

---

recens, -ntis: fresh; aridus, -a, -um: dry, dried; pomum, -i (n.): fruit, apple; *suci uinosioris*: "with rather tart juice," gen. of quality (AG #345); sucus, -i (m.): juice, the liquid of a fruit; uinosus, -a, -um: tasting of wine, having a sharp flavor (compar. = -ior)

In this chapter Suetonius presents an unusually detailed account of Augustus' daily routine. As he has already discussed Augustus' attention to judicial matters (ch. 33.1) and his morning calls and attendance at the senate (ch. 53.2–54), the focus here is on Augustus' personal habits and work routine at home.

78.1
cibus, -i (m.) food, meal
meridianus, -a, -um occurring at midday, noontime; the midday meal, usually held at the sixth hour, was called the prandium
ita ut uestitus calciatusque erat "just as he had been dressed and shod"; uestio, uestire, uestiui (-ii), uestitum: clothe, dress; calcio (1): put shoes on; Augustus did not undress, or even remove his shoes, for his afternoon nap
retectis pedibus abl. abs. (AG #419); retego, retegere, retexi, retectum: uncover (<re- + tego)
paulisper (adv.) for a brief while, for a short time
conquiesco, conquiescere, conquieui rest, go to sleep (<con- + quiesco)
opposita ... manu abl. abs. (AG #419); oppono, opponere, opposui, oppositum: place, cover (w/ ad) (<ob- + pono)
a cena = post cenam
lecticula, -ae (f.) small day-bed (dim. <lectica)
lucubratorius, -a, -um suitable for nocturnal studies (an unusual adj. <lucubro, found only here in Latin literature); Augustus used a day-bed for his evening work
donec ... conficeret impf. subjv. in tmp. cl. implying expectancy (AG #553); donec: until; residuus, -a, -um: left over, remaining; diurnus, -a, -um: daily; actus, -us (m.): business; conficio, conficere, confeci, confectum: complete, finish (<con- + facio)
ad multam noctem "until late in the night," ad (*OLD* 10) expressing limit of time
permaneo, permanere, permansi, permansum remain (<per- + maneo)
in lectum inde transgressus ptc. phr.; lectus, -i (m.): bed; inde (adv.): from that place, from there; transgredior, transgredi, transgressus sum: cross over, move across (<trans- + gradior)
non amplius ... quam septem horas compar. cl. (AG #407); cum plurimum (adv.): at most; *septem horas*: acc. of extent of time (AG #423.2)
dormio, dormire, dormiui (-ii), dormitum sleep
continuas [horas]
sed ut ... expergisceretur "but only with him waking up," result cl. expressing proviso (AG #537b); *in ... spatio*: abl. of time, which normally omits prep. (AG #423.1); spatium, -ii (n.): period,

quater expergisceretur. **2.** si interruptum somnum reciperare,
ut euenit, non posset, lectoribus aut fabulatoribus arcessitis
resumebat producebatque ultra primam saepe lucem. nec in
tenebris uigilauit umquam nisi assidente aliquo. matutina
uigilia offendebatur ac si uel officii uel sacri causa maturius
uigilandum esset, ne id contra commodum faceret, in proximo
cuiuscumque domesticorum cenaculo manebat. sic quoque
saepe indigens somni et cum per uicos deportaretur et deposita
lectica inter aliquas moras condormiebat.

---

space; *ter aut quater*: "three or four times"; expergiscor, expergisci, experrectus sum: become awake, wake up

78.2
si ... non posset gener. condit. showing repeated or customary action in past (AG #518c); interrumpo, interrumpere, interrupi, interruptum: interrupt, cut short (<inter- + rumpo); somnus, -i (m.): sleep; recipero (1): recover, regain; *reciperare*: compl. inf. (AG #456) w/ *posset*; *ut euenit*: "as happens"
lectoribus aut fabulatoribus arcessitis tmp. abl. abs. (AG #420.1); lector, -oris (m.): reader, person employed to read aloud (vb. subst. <lego); fabulator, -oris (m.): storyteller (vb. subst. <fabulor, an unusual wd.); arcesso, arcessere, arcessiui (-ii), arcessitum: summon
resumo, resumere, resumpsi, resumptum pick up again, resume (<re- + sumo)
produco, producere, produxi, productum extend, draw out (<pro- + duco); *somnum* is obj.
ultra (prep. + acc.) beyond
lux, lucis (f.) light, daylight
tenebrae, -arum (f. pl.) darkness
uigilo (1) stay awake, be awake
nisi assidente aliquo abl. abs. as cl. of accompanying circumst. (AG #420.5); assideo, assidere, assedi, assessum: sit near (<ad- + sedeo)
matutina uigilia "by getting up early"; abl. of cause (AG #404); matutinus, -a, -um: of the early morning; uigilia, -ae (f.): being awake, wakefulness
offendo, offendere, offendi, offensum cause pain, upset
si ... uigilandum esset prot. of gener. condit. showing repeated or customary action in past (AG #518c); sacrum, -i (n.): religious observance; mature (adv.): early (compar. = -ius); *uigilandum esset*: impers. gerv. in pass. periphr. (AG #500.3), "he had to get up"; uigilo (1): be awake
ne ... faceret negat. purp. cl. (AG #531), "so that he would not be inconvenienced"; contra (prep. w/ acc.): contrary to, otherwise than
in proximo ... cenaculo prep. phr., quicumque, quaecumque, quodcumque (indef. pron.): anyone, someone; domestici, -orum (m. pl.): members of a household or entourage; cenaculum, -i (n.): small room or apartment
indigeo, indigere, indigui stand in need, require (w/ gen.) (<indu- + egeo)
cum ... deportaretur circumst. cum cl. (AG #546); uicus, -i (m.): neighborhood; deporto (1): convey, carry (<de- + porto)
deposita lectica inter aliquas moras tmp. abl. abs. (AG #420.1); depono, deponere, deposui, depositum: set down (<de- + pono); mora, -ae (f.): delay
condormio, condormire, condormiui (-ii) sleep soundly (<con- + dormio)

79 Forma fuit eximia et per omnes aetatis gradus uenustissima,
quamquam et omnis lenocinii neglegens. in capite comendo
tam incuriosus ut raptim compluribus simul tonsoribus operam
daret ac modo tonderet modo raderet barbam eoque ipso
tempore aut legeret aliquid aut etiam scriberet. uultu erat uel
in sermone uel tacitus adeo tranquillo serenoque ut quidam e
primoribus Galliarum confessus sit inter suos eo se inhibitum
ac remollitum quo minus, ut destinarat, in transitu Alpium
per simulationem conloquii propius admissus in praecipitium

Physical appearance (*forma*). A discussion of Augustus' physical appearance (ch. 79–80) includes remarkable personal details that showcase Suetonius' access to "unofficial" sources and reflect Roman interest in physiognomy.

79.1
forma ... eximia ... uenustissima abl. of quality (description) (AG #415); forma, -ae (f.): appearance, features; eximius, -a, -um: outstanding, exceptional; gradus, -us (m): step or stage, phase; uenustus, -a, -um: attractive (superl. = -issimus)

lenocinium, -(i)i (n.) artificial allurement, cosmetic embellishment

neglego, neglegere, neglexi, neglectum be indifferent to, ignore (w/ gen. *omnis lenocinii*) (<nec- + lego)

in capite comendo "in fixing his hair," in w/ gerv. (AG #507) ff. *incuriosus*; caput, -itis (n.): head; como, comere, compsi, comptum: adorn, dress, arrange

incuriosus, -a, -um indifferent, not concerned

ut ... daret ac ... scriberet result cl. (AG #537) ff. *tam incuriosus* [*fuit*], here with five vbs.; raptim (adv.): hurriedly; tonsor, -oris (m.): barber; tondeo, tondere, (totondi), tonsum: cut (hair); rado, radere, rasi, rasum: shave; barba, -ae (f.): beard

uultu ... adeo tranquillo serenoque abl. of quality (description) (AG #415); uultus, -us (m.): facial expression; tacitus, -a, -um: silent; tranquillus, -a, -um: calm; serenus, -a, -um: unruffled

ut quidam ... confessus sit inter suos result cl. (AG #537); primoris, -e: first, of high rank, (m. pl. subst.) the leading men; Gallia, -ae (f.): Gaul, (pl.) "the Gallic provinces"; confiteor, confiteri, confessus sum: admit, confess (<con- + fateor); *inter suos*: "among his fellow Gauls"

eo [*uultu*] **se inhibitum ac remollitum** [*esse*] indir. disc. (AG #580) ff. *confessus sit*; inhibeo, inhibere, inhibui, inhibitum: restrain, check (<in- + habeo); remollio, remollire, remolliui, remollitum: soften (<re- + mollio)

quo minus ... in praecipitium propelleret "from pushing [Augustus] off a cliff," subjv. cl. w/ quominus ff. vb. of hindering (AG #558b); *ut destinarat*: "as he had intended"; *destinarat* = contr. form of destinauerat (AG #181); note that Suet. here retains indic. vb. in subord. cl. in indir. disc.; transitus, -us (m.): crossing; Alpes, -ium (f. pl.): the Alps; *per simulationem ... admissus*: tmp. ptc. phr. (AG #496), "when he had been admitted closer to him on the pretext of needing to speak with him"; simulatio, -onis (f.): pretense (w/ obj. gen.); conloquium, -ii (n.): conversation; prope (adv.): close (compar. = -ius); praecipitium, -ii (n.): fall from a great height; propello, propellere, propuli, propulsum: push forward (<pro- + pello); the anecdote suggests that Augustus possessed

propelleret. **2.** oculos habuit claros ac nitidos—quibus etiam existimari uolebat inesse quiddam diuini uigoris gaudebatque si qui sibi acrius contuenti quasi ad fulgorem solis uultum summitteret, sed in senecta sinistro minus uidit—dentes raros et exiguos et scabros, capillum leuiter inflexum et subflauum, supercilia coniuncta, mediocres aures, nasum et a summo eminentiorem et ab imo deductiorem, colorem inter aquilum candidumque, staturam breuem—quam tamen Iulius Marathus libertus et a memoria eius quinque pedum et dodrantis fuisse

---

an almost divine countenance as the Gallic chieftain abandoned his plan to kill Augustus once he saw up close his serene expression

79.2
habuit "he [Augustus] had"; *habuit* takes eight obj. *oculos, dentes, capillum . . . staturam*
clarus, -a, -um bright, clear
nitidus, -a, -um radiant, shining
quibus etiam existimari uolebat "in which he even wished it to be thought"; *quibus* (relat. pron.): anteced. *oculos*
inesse quiddam diuini uigoris indir. disc. (AG #580) ff. *existimari*; insum, inesse, infui: be present in (w/ dat. *quibus*) (<in- + sum); diuinus, -a, -um: divine; uigor, -oris (m.): energy, vigor
gaudeo, gaudere, gauisus sum be glad, be pleased
si qui . . . uultum summitteret "if anyone lowered his face to him," prot. of gener. condit. (AG #518c); *qui* = aliqui; *sibi . . . contuenti*: tmp. ptc. phr., "when Augustus was gazing upon him rather forcefully"; dat. w/ compd. vb. *summitteret* (AG #370); acriter (adv.): keenly, forcefully (compar. = -rius); contueor, contueri, contuitus sum: gaze upon (<con- + tueor); fulgor, -oris (m.): radiance; uultus, -us (m.): face; summitto, summittere, summisi, summissum: lower (<sub- + mitto)
senecta, -ae (f.) the period of old age; *in senecta*: abl. of time within which (AG #424a), usu. w/out prep.
sinister, -tra, -trum left, on the left side; *sinistro* [*oculo*]: "with his left eye"
minus (compar. adv.) to a smaller degree, much less
dentes . . . scabros obj. of *habuit*; dens, -ntis (m.): tooth; rarus, -a, -um: spaced apart; exiguus, -a, -um: small in size, small in number; scaber, -bra, -brum: rough, decayed
capillos . . . subflauum obj. of *habuit*; capillus, -i (m.): hair; leuiter (adv.): softly, gently, slightly; inflexus, -a, -um: wavy, curled; subflauus, -a, -um: somewhat blond (an unusual adj. <sub- + flauus)
supercilia coniuncta obj. of *habuit*; supercilium, -(i)i (n.): eyebrow; coniunctus, -a, -um: joined together, connected
mediocres aures obj. of *habuit*; mediocris, -e: of medium size; auris, -is (f.): ear
nasum . . . deductiorem obj. of *habuit*, "a nose both projecting somewhat outward at the top and drawing rather downward at the bottom"; nasus, -i (m.): nose; eminens, -ntis: projecting, standing out (compar. = -ntior); deductus, -a, -um: drawn downward (compar. = -ior); Augustus had a classic "Roman nose"
colorem . . . candidumque obj. of *habuit*; color, -oris (m.): complexion, color of the skin; aquilus, -a, -um: dark-hued, swarthy; candidus, -a, -um: pale, white
staturam breuem obj. of *habuit*; statura, -ae (f.): height, stature; breuis, -e: short, small; s. ch. 73, where Augustus is said to have used platform shoes
quam tamen Iulius Marathus . . . tradit relat. cl. w/ indir. disc. presenting evidence that contradicts Suet.'s assessment of Augustus' height; *quam* (relat. pron.): anteced. *staturam*, acc. subj. of indir. disc. (AG #580) ff. *tradit*; *Iulius Marathus libertus*: Julius Marathus, a freedman of Augustus; *a memoria*: "record-keeper," a position within Augustus' household; *quinque pedum et dodrantis*: "five and three-quarters feet," approximately five foot seven inches today

tradit—sed quae commoditate et aequitate membrorum occuleretur ut non nisi ex comparatione astantis alicuius procerioris
intellegi posset.

80   Corpore traditur maculoso dispersis per pectus atque aluum
genetiuis notis in modum et ordinem ac numerum stellarum
caelestis ursae, sed et callis quibusdam ex prurigine corporis
adsiduoque et uehementi strigilis usu plurifariam concretis ad
impetiginis formam. coxendice et femore et crure sinistro
non perinde ualebat, ut saepe etiam claudicaret, sed remedio
habenarum atque harundinum confirmabatur. dextrae quoque
manus digitum salutarem tam imbecillum interdum sentiebat

---

quae ... occuleretur relat. cl. of char. (AG #535) w/ *staturam* as anteced.; commoditas, -atis
(f.): proportion; aequitas, -atis (f.): evenness, symmetry; *commoditate et aequitate*: HENDIADYS (AG #640); membrum, -i (n.): limb; occulo, occulere, occului, occultum: hide, conceal (<ob- + celo)

ut non ... posset result cl. (AG #537); comparatio, -onis (f.): comparison; asto, astare, astiti: stand near
by (<ad- + sto); *astantis*: gen. sg. pres. act. ptc. w/ *alicuius procerioris*; procerus, -a, -um: tall (compar. = -ior); intellego, intellegere, intellexi, intellectum: discern, recognize (<inter- + lego); *intellegi*: pr. pass. compl. inf. (AG #456) w/ *posset*

80
corpore traditur maculoso "he is said to have had a spot-covered body," the syntax here is much abbrev.; *corpore maculoso*: abl. of quality (description) (AG #415); maculosus, -a, -um: covered with blotches, spotted

dispersis ... genetiuis notis in modum ... caelestis ursae ptc. phr., abl. of quality (AG #415); dispergo, dispergere, dispersi, dispersum: scatter, disperse (<dis- + spargo); pectus, -oris (n.): chest; aluus, -i (f.): belly; genetiuus notus: birthmark; stella, -ae (f.): star; *caelestis ursae*: "of the celestial bear," the constellation Ursa Major; caelestis, -e: celestial, heavenly; ursa, -ae (f.): bear

callis quibusdam ... concretis ad impetiginis formam a second ptc. phr., abl. of quality (AG #415); callum, -i (n.) or -us, -i (m.): callus; prurigo, -inis (f.): itching, irritation; adsiduus, -a, -um: constant, continual; uehemens, -ntis: strenuous; strigilis, -is (f.): strigil, a curved implement used to scrape the body after a bath; plurifariam (adv.): in many places (quantitative adv. in -fariam); concresco, concrescere, concreui/concretus sum: harden, form by hardening (<con- + cresco); impetigo, -inis (f.): a scaly sore on the skin; forma, -ae (f.): form

coxendice et ... crure sinistro abl. of specif. (AG #418); coxendix, -icis (f.): hip; femur, -oris (n.): thigh; crus, -uris (n.): lower leg, shin; *sinistro* is understood w/ all three nouns (AG #287.1)

non perinde (adv.) not particularly

ualeo, ualere, ualui, ualitum be strong, be well

ut ... claudicaret result cl. (AG #537); claudico (1): limp

remedio habenarum atque harundinum "by a treatment of straps and canes," a sort of crutch or cast used for support; remedium, -(i)i (n.): remedy, a treatment for an illness; habena, -ae (f.): strap, cord; harundo, -inis (f.): reed, cane

confirmo (1) strengthen, make robust (<con- + firmo)

dextrae quoque manus digitum salutarem tam imbecillum [esse] indir. disc. (AG #580) ff. *sentiebat*; dexter, -tra, -trum: on the right-hand side, right; *digitum salutarem*: "the index finger"; digitus, -i (m.): finger; salutaris, -e: salutary; imbecillus, -a, -um: feeble, physically weak

sentio, sentire, sensi, sensum perceive, sense

ut torpentem contractumque frigore uix cornei circuli supplemento scripturae admoueret. questus est et de uesica, cuius dolore calculis demum per urinam eiectis leuabatur.

81 Graues et periculosas ualitudines per omnem uitam aliquot expertus est, praecipue Cantabria domita, cum etiam destillationibus iocinere uitiato ad desperationem redactus contrariam et ancipitem rationem medendi necessario subiit, quia calida fomenta non proderant frigidis curari coactus auctore Antonio Musa.
2. quasdam et anniuersarias ac tempore certo recurrentes

---

ut ... admoueret result cl. (AG #537); *torpentem contractumque frigore*: ptc. phr. w/ *digitum*, dir. obj. of *admoueret*; torpeo, torpere: be numb; frigus, -oris (m.): cold; *cornei circuli supplemento*: "with the help of a curved brace made of horn"; corneus, -a, -um: made of horn; circulus, -i (m.): circular object (here a curved finger-brace); supplementum, -i (n.): reinforcement; scriptura, -ae (f.): writing; *scripturae*: dat. of purp. (AG #382), "for writing"; admoueo, admouere, admoui, admotum: move (<ad- + moueo)
uesica, -ae (f.) bladder
cuius ... leuabatur relat. cl.; *cuius* (relat. pron.): anteced. *uesica*; dolor, -oris (m.): pain, distress; *dolore*: abl. of separ. (AG #401) ff. *leuabatur*; *calculis ... eiectis*: tmp. abl. abs. (AG #420.1).; calculus, -i (m.): small stone; urina, -ae (f.): urine; eicio, eicere, eieci, eiectum: discharge, expel (<ex- + iacio); leuo (1): relieve, lighten; Augustus suffered from kidney stones

Illnesses and health (*graues et periculosas ualitudines*). Following naturally from the discussion of Augustus' physical appearance, Suetonius turns to the illnesses that Augustus suffered throughout his life. In these chapters (81–82), we see Augustus enduring his ailments and taking whatever steps necessary to protect his health.

81.1
periculosus, -a, -um full of danger
aliquot (indecl. adj.) a number of, several
experior, experiri, expertus sum experience, undergo
Cantabria domita tmp. abl. abs. (AG #420.1); Cantabria, -ae (f.): country of the Cantabri on the north coast of Spain (s. ch. 21.1); domo, domare, domui, domitum: subdue, bring under control; the date of this illness is likely 26 or 25 BCE
cum ... redactus ... subiit tmp. cl. w/ indic. (AG #543); *destillationibus iocinere uitiato*: abl. abs. (AG #419); destillatio, -onis (f.): discharge, catarrh (the exact nature of this condition is not known); iocer, iocineris (n.): liver; uitio (1): harm, impair; *ad desperationem redactus*: ptc. phr.; desperatio, -onis (f.): despair, hopelessness; redigo, redigere, redegi, redactum: reduce (<re- + ago); *contrariam et ancipitem rationem medendi*: "an unusual and uncertain course of treatment," obj. of *subiit*; contrarius, -a, -um: opposite, different from the norm; anceps, -ipitis: uncertain; medeor, mederi: heal, cure; *medendi*: ger.; necessario (adv.): of necessity; subeo, subire, subii (-iui), subitum: undergo, submit to (<sub- + eo)
quia calida fomenta non proderant causal cl. w/ indic. (AG #540); calidus, -a, -um: hot; fomentum, -i (n.): poultice, compress; prosum, prodesse, profui: be of use, help (<pro- + sum)
frigidis [fomentis] **curari coactus** ptc. phr.; frigidus, -a, -um: cold, cool; *frigidis* [*fomentis*]; curo (1): care for, treat (a sick person); *curari*: compl. inf. (AG #456) ff. *coactus*
auctore Antonio Musa abl. abs. w/out ptc. (AG #419a); on Augustus' physician Antonio Musa, s. ch. 59

81.2
quasdam [ualitudines] **... recurrentes** ptc. phr., obj. of *experiebatur*; anniuersarius, -a, -um: occurring yearly; *tempore certo*: abl. of time when (AG #423); recurro, recurrere, recurri, recursum: come back, recur (<re- + curro)

experiebatur; nam sub natalem suum plerumque languebat,
et initio ueris praecordiorum inflatione temptabatur, austrinis
autem tempestatibus grauedine. quare quassato corpore neque
frigora neque aestus facile tolerabat.

82 Hieme quaternis cum pingui toga tunicis et subucula et thorace
laneo et feminalibus et tibialibus muniebatur, aestate apertis
cubiculi foribus ac saepe in peristylo saliente aqua atque
etiam uentilante aliquo cubabat. solis uero ne hiberni quidem
patiens domi quoque non nisi petasatus sub diuo spatiabatur.

---

sub natalem suum "around his birthday"; natalis, -is (m.): birthday; Augustus had been born in late September (s. ch. 5)
plerumque (adv.) on most occasions, mostly, often
langueo, languere be physically sluggish, be unwell
initio ueris abl. of time when (AG #423); uer, ueris (n.): the season of spring
praecordia, -orum (n. pl.) lower chest, diaphragm, stomach; the description is too vague to offer a precise diagnosis
inflatio, -onis (f.) expansion, swelling
tempto (1) afflict, attack
austrinis ... tempestatibus abl. of time when (AG #423): austrinus, -a, -um: of the south wind; tempestas, -atis (f.): storm; the south wind blew most strongly in the spring, bringing clouds and humidity
grauedo, -inis (f.) cold in the head
quare (relat. adv.) because of which, wherefore, hence
quassato corpore causal abl. abs. (AG #420.2); quasso (1): shake repeatedly, weaken, impair
frigus, -oris (m.) cold
aestus, -us (m.) heat, hot weather
tolero (1) endure, tolerate

82.1
hiems, -mis (f.) winter; *hieme*: abl. of time when (AG #423)
quaternis ... tunicis et ... tibialibus abl. of means (AG #409) w/ *muniebatur*; quaterni, -ae, -a (pl. adj.): four each, four at a time; pinguis, -e: thick; tunica, -ae (f.): tunic, garment worn under a toga; subucula, -ae (f.): an under-tunic, an undershirt; thorax, -acis (m.): vest; laneus, -a, -um: made of wool, woolen; feminalia, -ium (n. pl.): thigh coverings (an unusual wd. <femur); tibiale, -is (n.): leg warmer, a protective covering of the lower leg
munio, munire, muniui (-ii), munitum guard, protect with a covering
aestas, -atis (f.) summer; *aestate*: abl. of time when (AG #423)
apertis ... foribus ac ... saliente aqua atque etiam uentilante aliquo three abl. abs. as cl. of accompanying circumstance (AG #420.5); aperio, aperire, aperui, apertum: open, open up; foris, -is (f.): door; peristylum, -i (n.): inner courtyard, peristyle; salio, salire, salui (-ii), saltum: gush, flow; uentilo (1): fan, ventilate
solis gen. ff. *patiens* (AG #349b)
hibernus, -a, -um of or belonging to winter
petasatus, -a, -um wearing a broad-brimmed hat (a petasus), a hat usually worn for journeys
sub diuo "in the open"; diuum, -i (n.): open sky
spatior (1) walk about, stroll

itinera lectica et noctibus fere eaque lenta ac minuta faciebat,
ut Praeneste uel Tibur biduo procederet, ac si quo peruenire
mari posset, potius nauigabat. 2. uerum tantam infirmitatem
magna cura tuebatur, in primis lauandi raritate. unguebatur
enim saepius aut sudabat ad flammam, deinde perfundebatur
egelida aqua uel sole multo tepefacta. at quotiens neruorum
causa marinis Albulisque calidis utendum esset, contentus

---

itinera acc. pl. obj. of *faciebat*
lectica abl. of means
noctibus abl. of time when or within which (AG #423)
lenta ac minuta w/ *itinera*; lentus, -a, -um: slow, leisurely; minutus, -a, -um: small in length, short
ut ... procederet result cl. (AG #537); *Praeneste uel Tibur*: acc. of place to which (AG #427.2);
  Praeneste, -is (n.): Praeneste, a town twenty miles southeast of Rome; Tibur, -ris (n.): Tibur (modern Tivoli), a town eighteen miles northeast of Rome; biduum, -i (n.): a period of two days; *biduo*: abl. of time when or within which (AG #423); procedo, procedere, processi, processum: move forward, go (<pro- + cedo); one might normally travel to Praeneste or Tibur in just one day
si ... posset prot. of gener. condit. (AG #518c); *quo* = aliquo (adv.): somewhere; peruenio, peruenire, perueni, peruentum: come to, arrive at; *peruenire*: compl. inf. (AG #456) w/ *posset*; *mari*: "by sea"
potius (adv.) preferably, rather
nauigo (1) go by ship, sail

82.2

infirmitas, -atis (f.) weakness, ill health
tueor, tueri, tuitus sum protect, keep in good order, maintain; Suet. emphasizes here the actions Augustus took to maintain and improve his health
in primis (adv.) especially, above all
lauo, lauare, laui, lauatum/lautum wash, bathe; *lauandi*: gen. of ger.; daily bathing was the norm for the elite, but might be avoided by those suffering from a physical weakness
raritas, -atis (f.) rarity
unguo, unguere, unxi, unctum anoint, rub with oil
sudo (1) sweat, perspire
flamma, -ae (f.) flame, fire; rather than visit a laconicum (the sweat-room in a bath), Augustus was warmed by an open flame
perfundo, perfundere, perfudi, perfusum wet, drench (<per- + fundo)
egelida aqua ... tepefacta abl. of means; egelidus, -a, -um: tepid, with the chill taken off; tepefacio, tepefacere, tepefeci, tepefactum: warm, make warm (<tepeo + facio); the use of tepid water was more moderate than the hot and cold treatments at the baths
quotiens ... utendum esse "whenever he had to use," iterative subjv. w/ *quotiens* (BG #567n); *utendum*: n. gerv. impers. (AG #500.3); neruus, -i (m.): muscle; *marinis [aquis]*: "sea water," abl. w/ utor; marinus, -a, -um: of the sea; *Albulis calidis [aquis]*: "hot sulfur baths"; Albula, -ae (f.): the Albula river (an early name for the Tiber), (pl.) the sulfur springs near Tibur (Tivoli); calidus, -a, -um: hot
contentus, -a, -um content with, satisfied (+ abl.)

hoc erat, ut insidens ligneo solio, quod ipse Hispanico uerbo
duretam uocabat, manus ac pedes alternis iactaret.

83 Exercitationes campestres equorum et armorum statim post
ciuilia bella omisit et ad pilam primo folliculumque transiit,
mox nihil aliud quam uectabatur et deambulabat, ita ut in
extremis spatiis subsultim decurreret segestri uel lodicula inuolutus. animi laxandi causa modo piscabatur hamo, modo talis
aut ocellatis nucibusque ludebat cum pueris minutis quos facie
et garrulitate amabilis undique conquirebat, praecipue Mauros

---

ut . . . iactaret subst. cl. of result in appos. w/ *hoc* (AG #570); insideo, insidere, insedi, insessum: sit on (w/
    dat.) (<in- + sedeo); ligneus, -a, -um: wooden; solium, -(i)i (n.): a bathtub; *quod* (relat. pron.): anteced.
    solium; Hispanicus, -a, -um: Spanish; dureta, -ae (f.): "dureta" (Iberian term for a tub, an unusual wd.);
    alternis (adv.): alternately, in turn; iacto (1): toss, plunge (into the water)

Exercise regimen (*exercitationes*). As a coda to the discussion of Augustus' appearance and health, Suetonius
presents his exercise regimen and physical activities at various stages of his life.

83
exercitationes campestres equorum et armorum "military training with horses and weapons"; exercitatio,
    -onis (f.): exercise, practice; campestris, -e: belonging to the Campus Martius; equus, -i (m.): horse;
    arma, -orum (n. pl.): arms, weapons; Roman men traditionally trained for military service until the age
    of forty-six; Augustus gave up training at a younger age, presumably due to poor health
ciuilis, -e civil; for the civil wars, s. ch. 9–18
pila, -ae (f.) ball (a small, hard ball used for exercise)
folliculus, -i (m.) inflated ball (dim. <follis)
transeo, transire, transiui (-ii), transitum move on (to a new practice) (<trans- + eo)
uecto (1) carry, transport; (pass.) ride (a horse) (frequent. <ueho)
deambulo (1) go for a walk (<de- + ambulo)
ita ut . . . decurreret . . . inuolutus result cl. (AG #537); extremus, -a, -um: final, last; spatium, -ii
    (n.): period, space; subsultim (adv.): with frequent jumps (an unusual adv. in -tim found only here
    in Latin literature); decurro, decurrere, de(cu)curri, decursum: run (<de- + curro); segestre, -is
    (n.): traveler's cloak; lodicula, -ae (f.): small blanket (dim. <lodix); inuoluo, inuoluere, inuolui,
    inuolutum: cover, wrap (in) (<in- + uoluo); Augustus' walks ended with more vigorous jumping exercises
animi laxandi causa gerv. w/ *causa* (abl.) to express purp. (AG #504b); laxo (1): relax
piscor (1) fish
hamus, -i (m.) hook, fish-hook
talus, -i (m.) knucklebone (a four-sided die used for gaming); for Augustus' fondness for gambling with
    dice, s. ch. 71
ocellatum, -i (n.) stone with small markings like eyes used for gaming (like a modern marble)
nux, nucis (f.) nut (used as a plaything)
minutus, -a, -um small, little
quos . . . conquirebat . . . et Syros relat. cl.; *quos* (relat. pron.): anteced. *pueris; facie et garrulitate*: abl. of specif.
    (AG #418); facies, -iei (f.): physical appearance, looks; garrulitas, -atis (f.): talkativeness, loquacity; amabilis,
    -e: amiable, appealing; *amabilis*: acc. pl. w/ *quos*; undique (adv.): from everywhere; conquiro, conquirere,

et Syros. nam pumilos atque distortos et omnis generis eiusdem ut ludibria naturae malique ominis abhorrebat.

84 Eloquentiam studiaque liberalia ab aetate prima et cupide et laboriosissime exercuit. Mutinensi bello in tanta mole rerum et legisse et scripsisse et declamasse cotidie traditur. nam deinceps neque in senatu neque apud populum neque apud milites locutus est umquam nisi meditata et composita oratione, quamuis non deficeretur ad subita extemporali facultate.

2. ac ne periculum memoriae adiret aut in ediscendo tempus

---

conquisiui (-sii), conquisitum: search out, collect (<con- + quaero); *Mauros et Syros*: acc. pl. appos. w/ *quos* [*pueros*]; Mauri, -orum (m. pl.): the Moors (a people of North Africa); Syrus, -i (m.): a Syrian
pumilus, -a, -um of short stature, (subst.) dwarf
distortus, -a, -um misshapen, deformed; *distortos*: m. pl. subst.
omnis generis eiusdem "everyone of this same kind"; *omnis*: acc. pl.
ludibrium, -ii (n.) object of derision, (pl.) insults, affronts
natura, -ae (f.) nature
mali ominis gen. of quality (description) (AG #345); malus, -a, -um: bad, evil
abhorreo, abhorrere, abhorrui shrink back from, shun, recoil from (<ab- + horreo); Augustus' feelings are noteworthy to Suet. as dwarfs were members of the households of later emperors

Intellectual interests and habits (*eloquentiam studiaque liberalia*). In six chapters (ch. 84–89), Suetonius presents a wide-ranging and detailed discussion that touches on Augustus' education and training, the literary works he authored, his style of writing (including vocabulary and orthography), and his study of Greek.

84.1
eloquentia, -ae (f.) the art of public speaking, oratory
studia liberalia "the liberal arts," study focused on works of Latin and Greek literature; studium, -(i)i (n.): study, intellectual activity; liberalis, -e: liberal, worthy of a free man
cupide (adv.) eagerly, zealously
laboriose (adv.) with much labor, with the greatest attention (superl. = -issime); Suet. commonly uses superl. adv.
Mutinensi bello "during the war at Mutina," abl. of time within which (AG #424); s. ch. 10.2–3
in tanta mole rerum "amid such a great pressure of affairs"; moles, -is (f.): large mass, weight
legisse et scripsisse et declamasse cotidie pers. indir. disc. (AG #582) ff. *traditur* ("he is reported"); declamo (1): make speeches, declaim (<de- + clamo); cotidie (adv.): daily
deinceps (adv.) after that, for the future
meditata et composita oratione abl. abs. as cl. of accompanying circumst. (AG #420.5); meditor (1): practice, rehearse; oratio, -onis, (f.): speech
quamuis non deficeretur ... facultate conces. cl. (AG #527a); deficio, deficere, defeci, defectum: be lacking (w/ abl.) (<de- + facio); *ad subita*: "at unexpected times," ad indicating time (*OLD* 21); subitus, -a, -um: happening without warning, (n. subst.) unexpected state of affairs, emergency; *extemporali facultate*: "the skill to speak extemporaneously"; extemporalis, -e: unpremeditated; facultas, -atis (f.): power, skill

84.2
ne ... adiret aut ... absumeret negat. purp. cl. (AG #531); *periculum memoriae*: "the danger of forgetting"; edisco, ediscere, edidici: learn by heart, memorize (<ex- + disco); *ediscendo*: ger. (AG #507)

absumeret, instituit recitare omnia. sermones quoque cum singulis atque etiam cum Liuia sua grauiores non nisi scriptos et e libello habebat, ne plus minusue loqueretur ex tempore. pronuntiabat dulci et proprio quodam oris sono dabatque assidue phonasco operam, sed nonnumquam infirmatis faucibus praeconis uoce ad populum contionatus est.

85 Multa uarii generis prosa oratione composuit, ex quibus nonnulla in coetu familiarium uelut in auditorio recitauit, sicut rescripta Bruto de Catone, quae uolumina cum iam senior ex magna parte legisset fatigatus Tiberio tradidit perlegenda,

---

recitare (1) compl. inf. (AG #457) ff. *instituit*; in contrast to normal speaking practices of the time, Augustus read aloud from a written text

sermones ... grauiores obj. of *habebat*; Suet. presents Augustus as being extraordinarily carefully when discussing weighty matters, even with his wife Livia

ne ... loqueretur negat. purp. cl. (AG #531); *plus minusue*: "more or less," here = "too much or too little"; *ex tempore*: on the spur of the moment, extemporaneously

dulci et proprio ... sono abl. of manner (AG #412); dulcis, -e: sweet; proprius, -a, -um: one's own, individual; os, oris (n.): voice; sonus, -i (m.): sound, oratorical style

dabatque assidue phonasco operam "he constantly worked with a vocal trainer"; operam dare: pay attention to, apply oneself; phonascus, -i (m.): teacher of elocution (a Gk. wd. w/ Latinized spelling)

infirmatis faucibus causal abl. abs. (AG #420.2); infirmo (1): weaken physically; fauces, -ium (f. pl.): throat

praeconis uoce "by the voice of a herald"; praecox, -onis (m.): professional announcer, one who makes public announcements

contionor (1) deliver a public speech

85.1

multa ... oratione *multa*: n. acc. pl.; *uarii generis*: gen. of quality (AG #345); *prosa oratione*: "in prose," abl. of quality (AG #415); prosus, -a, -um: straight; oratio, -onis, (f.): language

ex quibus ... recitauit relat. cl.; *quibus* (relat. pron.): anteced. *multa*; coetus, -us (m.): gathering; familiaris, -e: closely associated by friendship, intimate, (subst.) close friend; uelut (adv.): just as, as if; auditorium, -(i)i (n.): a lecture-room, hall; it was an established custom for literary men to hold readings of their works for their friends

sicut (conj.) for instance

rescripta Bruto de Catone "A Response to Brutus about Cato"; rescriptum, -i (n.): written reply, response; M. Junius Brutus (*OCD* s.v. Iunius Brutus (2), Marcus, 765–766) had written a work praising and defending his father-in-law, M. Porcius Cato (Uticensis) (*OCD* s.v. Porcius Cato (2), Marcus, 1189–1190), the staunch opponent of Julius Caesar; none of Augustus' literary works survive

quae (relat. pron.) anteced. *uolumina* in relat. cl. (AG #307b)

uolumen, -inis (n.) volume, papyrus roll forming part of a book

cum ... legisset circumst. cum cl. (AG #546); senex, -is (m.): old man (compar. = -ior); *ex magna parte*: "to a large extent"

fatigo (1) tire out, exhaust

perlego, perlegere, perlegi, perlectum read through, finish reading (<per- + lego); *perlegenda*: "to finish reading," acc. of gerv. w/ *tradidit* (BG #430)

item hortationes ad philosophiam et aliqua de uita sua, quam
tredecim libris Cantabrico tenus bello nec ultra exposuit.
2. poeticam summatim attigit. unus liber extat scriptus ab eo
hexametris uersibus, cuius et argumentum et titulus est 'Sicilia',
extat alter aeque modicus epigrammatum, quae fere tempore
balinei meditabatur. nam tragoediam magno impetu exorsus
non succedente stilo aboleuit quaerentibusque amicis quidnam
Aiax ageret, respondit Aiacem suum in spongiam incubuisse.

---

hortationes ad philosophiam "Exhortations to Philosophy"; hortatio, -onis (f.): exhortation, encouragement; *hortationes*: acc. pl., continuing the list of titles Augustus read out ff. *sicut*; philosphia, -ae (f.): philosophy

de uita sua "On His Life," Augustus' autobiography, which Suet. has drawn upon as a source

quam ... exposuit relat. cl.; *quam* (relat. pron.): anteced. *uita sua*; tredecim (indecl. adj.): thirteen; liber, -bri (m.): book; tenus (prep. w/ preceding abl.): as far as (here in a tmp. sense); Cantabricum bellum: the Cantabrian War, s. ch. 20; ultra (adv.): beyond, further, more; expono, exponere, exposui, expositum: set out, relate, describe (<ex- + pono); Augustus' autobiography ended with the year 25 BCE

85.2

poetica, -ae (f.) poetry

summatim (adv.) without depth, superficially; Suet. regularly uses adv. in -tim

attingo, attingere, attigi, attactum take up, engage in (<ad- + tango)

hexametris uersibus "in hexameters," abl. of quality (AG #415); hexameter, -tra, -trum: having six metrical feet

cuius (relat. pron.) anteced. *liber*

argumentum, -i (n.) subject or theme (of a literary work)

titulus, -i (m.) title, name

Sicilia, -ae (f.) Sicily; nothing else is known about Augustus' "Sicily"

alter aeque modicus [liber] "another equally short book"

epigramma, -atis (n.) short poem, epigram

quae ... meditabatur relat. cl.; *quae* (relat. pron.): anteced. *epigrammatum*, obj. of *meditabatur*; *tempore balinei*: abl. of time when (AG #423.1), "at bath time"; balineum, -i (n.): act of bathing, bath; meditor (1): think out, plan

tragoediam ... exorsus tmp. ptc. phr. (AG #496); tragoedia, -ae (f.): tragedy (play); impetus, -us (m.): vigorous effort, vigor, ardor; exordior, exordiri, exorsus sum: begin, start (to write)

non succedenti stilo causal abl. abs. (AG #420.2), "since the writing was not turning out well"; succedo, succedere, successi, successum: succeed (<sub- + cedo); stilus, -i (m.): stylus (a writing implement)

aboleo, abolere, aboleui, abolitum destroy, erase

quaero, quaerere, quaes(i)i (-siui), quaesitum inquire, ask a question; *quaerentibus amicis*: dat. w/ *respondit*

quidnam Aiax ageret "what Ajax was up to," indir. quest. ff. *quaerentibus* (AG #574); quisnam, quaenam, quidnam: who/what, pray tell; Aiax, -acis (m.): Ajax; Augustus was apparently writing a Latin version of Sophocles' tragedy "Ajax"

Aiacem ... incubuisse indir. disc. (AG #580) ff. *respondit*; spongia, -ae (f.): sponge (here used as an eraser); incumbo, incumbere, incubui: throw oneself down on (<in- + cumbo); Augustus' Ajax committed suicide by sponge!; Augustus' self-deprecating remark is also reported by Macrobius (*Sat.* 2.4.1-2)

86 Genus eloquendi secutus est elegans et temperatum, uitatis sententiarum ineptiis atque concinnitate et 'reconditorum uerborum', ut ipse dicit, 'fetoribus', praecipuamque curam duxit sensum animi quam apertissime exprimere. quod quo facilius efficeret aut necubi lectorem uel auditorem obturbaret ac moraretur, neque praepositiones urbibus addere neque coniunctiones saepius iterare dubitauit, quae detractae afferunt aliquid obscuritatis etsi gratiam augent. **2.** cacozelos et antiquarios ut diuerso genere uitiosos pari fastidio spreuit exagi-

---

86.1

eloquor, eloqui, elocutus sum express, speak (<ex- + loquor); *eloquendi*: objv. gen. of ger. (AG #504)
elegans, -ntis refined, graceful, elegant
temperatus, -a, -um moderate, restrained
uitatis ... ineptiis ... concinnitate ... fetoribus abl. abs. (AG #419) w/ three nouns; uito (1): avoid; sententia, -ae (f.): moralistic epigram, aphorism; ineptia, -ae (f.): stupidity, (pl.) frivolities, absurdities; concinnitas, -atis (f.): excessive refinement, artificiality; reconditus, -a, -um: obscure, recondite; fetor, -oris (m.): stench, stink; Suet. ends the list by inserting a direct quotation of Augustus' wd.
praecipuamque curam duxit ... exprimere "he showed great care to express"; duco, ducere, duxi, ductum: bring (w/ acc. + compl. inf., AG #457); *sensum animi*: "his meaning"; sensus, -us (m.): sense, meaning; aperte (adv.): openly, clearly (superl. = -issime); *quam* w/ superl. to denote highest possible degree (AG #291c); exprimo, exprimere, expressi, expressum: express (<ex- + premo)
quod (relat. pron.) "this thing" (i.e., to express himself clearly), relat. pron. as connector (AG #308f)
quo facilius efficeret relat. cl. of purp. w/ compar. (AG #531.2); efficio, efficere, effeci, effectum: bring about (<ex- + facio)
necubi ... obturbaret ac moraretur negat. purp. cl. (AG # 531); necubi (adv.): lest at any place, lest on any occasion; lector, -oris (m.): reader (vb. subst. <lego); auditor, -oris (m.): listener (vb. subst. <audio); obturbo (1): confuse (<ob- + turbo); moror (1): check, delay, impede
praepositio, -onis (f.) preposition; the names of cities do not require a prep. (AG #427)
addere compl. inf. (AG #456) w/ *dubitauit*
coniunctio, -onis (f.) conjunction; Augustus did not use ASYNDETON (AG #323b)
itero (1) repeat; *iterare*: compl. inf. (AG #456) w/ *dubitauit*
quae detractae afferunt ... augent relat. cl.; *quae detractae*: "things which, when omitted"; *praepositiones* and *coniunctiones* are anteced. of *quae*; detraho, detrahere, detraxi, detractum: exclude, omit (<de- + traho); affero, afferre, attuli, allatum: bring, offer, contribute (<ad- + fero); obscuritas, -atis (f.): obscurity, lack of clarity; *obscuritatis*: partit. gen. w/ *aliquid* (AG #346a3)

86.2

cacozelos, -on stylistically affected, in bad taste (a Gk. wd. w/ Latinized spelling, for decl., AG #52); *cacozelos*: acc. pl. subst., "affected stylists"; the term applied to the "Asian" style of oratory (*OCD* s.v. Asianism, 184)
antiquarius, -ii (m.) student of the past, antiquarian
ut diuerso genere uitiosos "as flawed in different ways," pred. acc. (AG #393); diuersus, -a, -um: different, differing; uitiosus, -a, -um: flawed, defective, faulty
fastidium, -(i)i (n.) disgust, disdain, contempt
sperno, spernere, spreui, spretum reject with scorn, disdain
exagito (1) pursue with criticism, scold (frequent. <ex- + ago, a vb. form favored by Suet.)

tabatque nonnumquam, in primis Maecenatem suum, cuius
'myrobrechis', ut ait, 'cincinnos' usque quaque persequitur et
imitando per iocum irridet. sed nec Tiberio parcit ut exoletas
interdum et reconditas uoces aucupanti. M. quidem Antonium
ut insanum increpat, quasi ea scribentem quae mirentur potius
homines quam intellegant, deinde ludens malum et inconstans
in eligendo genere dicendi ingenium eius addit haec,

 3. tuque dubitas Cimberne Annius ac Veranius Flaccus imitandi sint tibi,
ita ut uerbis quae Crispus Sallustius excerpsit ex Originibus Catonis

---

in primis Maecenatem suum "especially his [friend] Maecenas"; Gaius Maecenas (*OCD* 883) was an eques and close friend of Augustus (s. ch. 66.3)

cuius (relat. pron.) anteced. *Maecenatem*

myrobrechis ... cincinnos "perfumed locks of hair" (= flowery literary style); myrobreches (adj.): dripping with perfume (a Gk. wd. w/ Latinized spelling); cincinnus, -i (m.): curled lock of hair; Suet. quotes directly Augustus' wd. that parody Maecenas' style

usque quaque (adv.) everywhere, in every possible situation

persequor, persequi, persecutus sum pursue, harass (<per- + sequor)

imitor (1) copy, imitate; *imitando*: abl. of ger. (AG #507.1)

irrideo, irridere, irrisi, irrisum mock, make fun of (<in- + rideo)

parco, parcere, peperci spare (w/ dat. *Tiberio*)

ut ... aucupanti ptc. phr. w/ *Tiberio*, "as hunting after"; exolesco, exolescere, exoleui, exoletum: fade away, be forgotten (<ex- + olesco); reconditus, -a, -um: obscure, recondite; uox, uocis (f.): word (*OLD* 10); aucupor (1): hunt after

insanus, -a, -um demented, mad

increpo, increpare, increpui, increpitum chide, reproach, inveigh against (<in- + crepo)

quasi ea scribentem "as writing things"; quasi (conj.): as, as for example (*OLD* 7)

quae mirentur ... homines ... intellegant relat. cl. of char. (AG #535); *quae* (relat. pron.): n. acc. pl., anteced. *ea*; miror (1): admire, marvel at; potius (adv.): rather (w/ *quam*); intellego, intellegere, intellexi, intellectum: understand (<inter- + lego)

ludo, ludere, lusi, lusum make fun of

malum et inconstans ... ingenium dir. obj. of *ludens*; malus, -a, -um: unpleasant, bad; inconstans, -ntis: inconsistent, changeable; eligo, eligere, elegi, electum: choose, pick out (<ex- + lego); *eligendo*: abl. gerv. w/ *genere* (AG #507.3), "in picking a style"; *dicendi*: objv. gen. of ger. (AG #504); ingenium, -(i)i (n.): inclination, natural disposition

86.3

tuque dubitas the start of dir. quotation from a letter of Augustus to Antony; dubito (1): be in doubt

Cimberne ... imitandi sint tibi indir. quest. (AG #574); *Cimber*: T. Annius Cimber, a writer of the first century BCE and supporter of Antony; Veranius Flaccus, an author of the period whose identity is uncertain; *imitandi sint*: pass. periphr. (AG #196, #500); *tibi*: dat. of agent (AG #374)

ita ut ... utaris result cl. (AG #537) w/ a relat. cl. *quae ... Catonis*; *quae*: anteced. *uerbis*; *Crispus Sallustius*: C. Sallustius Crispus (*OCD* s.v. Sallust, 1310–1311), Roman historian of the first century BCE; excerpo, excerpere, excerpsi, excerptum: pick out, select (<ex- + carpo); *ex Originibus*: "from 'The Origins,'" a second-century BCE work by M. Porcius Cato (*OCD* s.v. Porcius Cato (1), Marcus, 1188–1189) tracing the rise of Rome; origo, -inis (f.): beginnings, origin; Augustus here is making fun of Antony's antiquarian style

utaris, an potius Asiaticorum oratorum inanis sententiis uerborum uolubilitas in nostrum sermonem transferenda?
et quadam epistula Agrippinae neptis ingenium conlaudans, 'sed opus est', inquit, 'dare te operam ne moleste scribas et loquaris'.

87 Cotidiano sermone quaedam frequentius et notabiliter usurpasse eum litterae ipsius autographae ostentant, in quibus identidem, cum aliquos numquam soluturos significare uult, 'ad K(a)l(endas) Graecas soluturos' ait, et cum hortatur ferenda

---

an potius ... uolubilitas ... transferenda [sit] a second indir. quest. (AG #574) ff. *dubitas*; *Asiaticorum oratorum*: "of the Asiatic [school of] orators"; orator, -oris (m.): orator; inanis, -e: empty; *inanis sententiis*: abl. of specif. (AG #418); uolubilitas, -atis (f.): fluency; noster, -tra, -trum: our; *transferenda* [sit]: pass. periphr. (AG #196, 500); here a criticism of Antony's support for "Asiatic" oratory, which was characterized by wordplay and emotional effects (*OCD* s.v. Asianism and Atticism, 184)

Agrippina (*OCD* s.v. Vipsania Agrippina (2), 1554), s. ch. 64.1

ingenium, -(i)i (n.) temperament, disposition, character

conlaudo (1) praise, commend (<con- + laudo)

opus est it is essential, it is necessary; Suet. quotes directly from Augustus' letter

inquit he said (for conj., AG #205b)

dare te operam subst. cl. of purp. w/ subj. acc. + inf. (AG #563) ff. *opus est*; operam dare: "pay attention"

ne moleste scribas et loquaris negat. purp. cl. (AG #531); moleste (adv.): in an annoying way, with affectation (here = "in an Asiatic or antiquarian style")

Drawing upon Augustus' private letters, Suetonius presents in two chapters (87–88) a detailed discussion of favorite and unusual expressions of Augustus, peculiar features of his handwriting and spelling, and the secret code he used for private communications.

87.1
cotidiano sermone ... usurpasse eum indir. disc. (AG #580) ff. *ostentant*; cotidianus, -a, -um: daily; *quaedam*: "certain expressions"; notabiliter (adv.): in a manner worthy of note, strikingly; usurpo (1): make use of (a word, expression), say habitually; *usurpasse* = contr. form of usurpauisse (AG #181)

autographus, -a, -um written with one's own hand; throughout this section Suet. draws upon his personal knowledge of letters written by Augustus himself

ostento (1) exhibit, display

quibus (relat. pron.) anteced. *litterae*

identidem (adv.) again and again, repeatedly

cum ... uult "whenever he wished," tmp. cl. w/ pres. indic. (AG #548); *aliquos numquam soluturos* [esse]: indir. disc. (AG #580) ff. *significare*; soluo, soluere, solui, solutum: pay, make a payment; significo (1): indicate, *significare*: compl. inf. (AG #456) w/ *uult*

ad Kalendas Graecas soluturos [esse eos] indir. disc. (AG #580) ff. *ait*; *ad Kalendas Graecas*: "on the Greek Kalends," *ad* indicating time (*OLD* 21) (for the Roman calendar, AG #631); the Greek calendar did not include the Kalends

ait "he said" (for conj., AG #206a), introd. dir. quotation

cum hortatur "whenever he urged," tmp. cl. w/ pres. indic. (AG #548); hortor (1): urge

ferenda esse praesentia indir. disc. (AG #580) ff. *hortatur*; *ferenda esse*: pass. periphr. (AG #196, 500); praesens, -ntis: present; *praesentia*: (n. pl. subst.) "present affairs"

esse praesentia, qualiacumque sint, 'contenti simus hoc
Catone', et ad exprimendam festinatae rei uelocitatem, 'celerius quam asparagi cocuntur'.   2.   ponit assidue et pro stulto
'baceolum' et pro pullo 'pullaceum' et pro cerrito 'uacerrosum'
et 'uapide' se habere pro 'male' et 'betizare' pro 'languere',
quod uulgo 'lachanizare' dicitur, item 'simus' pro 'sumus' et
'domos' genetiuo casu singulari pro 'domus', nec umquam
aliter haec duo, ne quis mendam magis quam consuetudinem
putet.   3.   notaui et in chirographo eius illa praecipue: non

---

qualiacumque sint "whatever they are," condit. relat. cl. (AG #519); qualiscumque, qualecumque (indef. relat.): of whatever sort

contenti simus "let us be content with" (hort. subjv., AG #439) or "we are content with," as Suet. notes in ch. 87.2 that Augustus regularly used simus in place of sumus; contentus, -a, -um: content with, satisfied (+ abl.)

hoc Catone "this Cato"; Augustus' expression sets up a contrast b/w M. Porcius Cato (the censor) (*OCD* s.v. Porcius Cato (1), Marcus, 1188–1189) and his great-grandson M. Porcius Cato Uticensis (*OCD* s.v. Porcius Cato (2), Marcus, 1189–1190); the meaning is something like "better the devil you know"

ad exprimendam ... uelocitatem ad w/ gerv. to denote purp. (AG #506); exprimo, exprimere, expressi, expressum: express (<ex- + premo); festino (1): hasten, hurry; uelocitas, -atis (f.): speed

celerius quam asparagi cocuntur celeriter (adv.): quickly (compar. = -ius); *quam*: introd. compar. (AG #407e) ff. *celerius*; asparagus, -i (m.): asparagus; coco, cocere, coxi, coctum: prepare, cook

87.2

et pro stulto ... pro 'languere' Suet. provides a list of unusual wd. used by Augustus; stultus, -a, -um: foolish; baceolus, -a, -um: "queer" (an unusual wd. <Gk. term for a eunuch follower of Cybele); pullus, -a, -um: dark, drab; pullaceus, -a, -um: "darkish" (an unusual adj. <pullus); cerritus, -a, -um: demented; uacerrosus, -a, -um: "block-headed" (an unusual adj. <uacerra); *'uapide' se habere*: "to be feeling 'flat'"; uapide (adv.): in a flat or vapid manner (an unusual adv. <uapidus); male (adv.): poorly, badly; betizo (1): be like a beet, be languid (an unusual vb. <beta w/ Gk. vb. ending); langueo, languere: be physically sluggish, be unwell

quod ... dicitur relat. cl.; *quod* (relat. pron.): anteced. *languere*; uulgo (adv.): commonly; lachanizo (1): wilt like a vegetable, droop, vegetate (a Gk. wd. w/ Latinized spelling)

'simus' pro 'sumus' Augustus' spelling reflects the pronunciation of "sumus" at the time

'domos' ... pro 'domus' genitiuus, -a, -um: genitive; casus, -us (m.): ending, grammatical case; singularis, -e: singular; the unusual form of the gen. sg. ending -ōs in place of -ūs may reflect an archaic or regional form

haec duo [uerba] "these two words," here = 'simus' and 'domos'

ne quis ... putet negat. purp. cl. (AG #531); *quis* = aliquis; *mendam ... consuetudinem*: pred. acc. (AG #393); menda, -ae (f.): fault, error; *magis quam*: rather than; consuetudo, -inis (f.): habitual practice, custom; puto (1): think, suppose

87.3

notaui Suet. emphasizes his personal inspection of documents w/ the 1st pers. vb.

chirographum, -i (n.) handwriting (a Gk. wd. w/ Latinized spelling)

illa "the following things" (AG #297b)

diuidit uerba nec ab extrema parte uersuum abundantis litteras
in alterum transfert sed ibidem statim subicit circumducitque.
88 orthographiam, id est formulam rationemque scribendi a
grammaticis institutam, non adeo custodit ac uidetur eorum
potius sequi opinionem qui perinde scribendum ac loquamur
existiment. nam quod saepe non litteras modo sed syllabas
aut permutat aut praeterit communis hominum error est.
nec ego id notarem, nisi mihi mirum uideretur tradidisse
aliquos legato eum consulari successorem dedisse ut rudi et

---

extremus, -a, -um final, last
abundo (1) overflow; *abundantis*: acc. pl. w/ *litteras*
in alterum [uersum]; standard practice was to finish a wd. on the next line
ibidem (adv.) in that very place
subicit circumducitque "he placed (the final letters) underneath and circled them"; circumduco, circumducere, circumduxi, circumductum: make a circle around, draw a line around (<circum- + duco); Augustus' peculiar habit is otherwise unattested

88
orthographia, -ae (f.) art of writing words correctly, orthography (a Gk. wd. w/ Latinized spelling); *orthographiam*: obj. of *custodit*
id est that is, that is to say
formulam rationemque ... institutam ptc. phr. in appos. w/ *orthographiam* (AG #282); formula, -ae (f.): rule, standard pattern; *formulam rationemque*: HENDIADYS (AG #640); *scribendi*: gen. of ger. (AG #504); grammaticus, -i (m.): grammarian, expert on linguistic and literary questions
non adeo custodit "he does not strictly observe"; custodio, custodire, custodiui (-ii), custoditum: preserve, maintain
potius (adv.) rather, instead
sequi pres. act. inf. w/ *uidetur* in pers. indir. disc. (AG #582)
opinio, -onis (f.) opinion, belief
qui ... existiment "who think that we should write as we speak"; subord. relat. cl. w/ subjv. (AG #580); *qui* (relat. pron.): anteced. *eorum*; perinde (adv., correl. w/ ac): as, equally; *scribendum* [*esse*]: impers. pass. periphr. in indir. disc. (AG #500.3); *loquamur*: pres. act. subjv.
quod ... permutat aut praeterit "the fact that he reversed or left out," subst. cl. (AG #572) as subj.; syllaba, -ae (f.): syllable; permuto (1): transpose, switch, reverse (<per- + muto); praetereo, praeterire, praeterii (-iui), praeteritum: omit, pass over (<praeter- + eo)
communis, -e shared, joint, common
error, -oris (m.) error, mistake
nec ego id notarem, nisi ... uideretur pres. C-to-F condit. (AG #517); *notarem*: note 1st pers. sg.; mirus, -a, -um: remarkable, amazing; *uideretur*: (impers.) "it seemed"
tradidisse aliquos indir. disc. (AG #582) ff. *mirum uideretur*
legato eum consulari successorem dedisse indir. disc. (AG #580) ff. *tradidisse*; *eum*: acc. subj.; consularis, -e: of consular rank; successor, -oris (m.): successor, replacement in office; Augustus is reported to have replaced the legate because of his vulgar spelling
ut rudi et indocto "as unrefined and uneducated"; rudis, -e: uncivilized, rude; indoctus, -a, -um: ignorant, unlearned; *rudi et indocto*: dat. w/ *legato consulari*

indocto cuius manu 'ixi' pro 'ipsi' scriptum animaduerterit. quotiens autem per notas scribit, 'B' pro 'A', 'C' pro 'B', ac deinceps eadem ratione sequentis litteras ponit, pro 'X' autem duplex 'A'.

89   Ne Graecarum quidem disciplinarum leuiore studio tenebatur, in quibus et ipsis praestabat largiter magistro dicendi usus Apollodoro Pergameno, quem iam grandem natu Apolloniam quoque secum ab urbe iuuenis adhuc eduxerat, deinde eruditione etiam uaria repletus per Arei philosophi filiorumque eius

---

cuius . . . animaduerterit causal relat. cl. (AG #535e) w/ subjv. in indir. disc. (AG #580); *cuius* (relat. pron.): anteced. *legato consulari*; *'ixi' pro 'ipsi' scriptum*: " 'ixi' written in place of 'ipsi' "; this anecdote offers interesting evidence that legates in the provinces wrote in their own hand to Augustus, and that Augustus read these letters himself

per notas "in code"; nota, -ae (f.): mark, sign; Augustus used a basic cipher where one letter is substituted with another; the standard Latin alphabet in Augustus' day had twenty-one letters, ending with "x" (*OCD*, s.v. alphabets of Italy, 65–66)

deinceps (adv.) in succession, in turn

sequentis acc. pl. w/ *litteras*

duplex, -icis double

The final chapter on Augustus' education and intellectual pursuits addresses his training in and use of Greek, his search for precepts and examples in literary works, and his encouragement of authors of his day.

89.1

Ne Graecarum quidem disciplinarum leuiore studio "by no less enthusiasm even for Greek studies," LITOTES (AG #326c, 641); disciplina, -ae (f.): instruction, training; *disciplinarum*: objv. gen. w/ *studio* (AG #348); studium, -(i)i (n.): enthusiasm, eagerness for

in quibus et ipsis praestabat largiter relat. cl.; "and in these things too he greatly excelled"; *quibus*: relat. pron. as connective (AG #308f), anteced. *disciplinarum*; praesto, praestare, praestiti, praestatum: excel (<prae- + sto); largiter (adv.): greatly, to a great extent

magistro . . . usus Apollodoro Pergameno ptc. phr.; magister, -tri (m.): teacher; *magistro*: abl. w/ *usus*; *dicendi*: objv. gen. of ger. (AG #504); *Apollodoro Pergameno*: Apollodorus Pergamenus (*OCD* s.v. Apollodorus (5), 120)

quem (relat. pron.) anteced. *Apollodoro Pergameno*

grandis, -e mature; *grandem natu*: "elderly"

Apollonia, -ae (f.) Apollonia, city on the southern Illyrian coast across the Adriatic from Italy; *Apolloniam*: acc. of place to which w/out prep. (AG #427.2), s. ch. 8.2; Augustus took his teacher with him even as he prepared for a military campaign

educo, educere, eduxi, eductum lead out (<ex- + duco)

eruditione . . . repletus ptc. phr.; eruditio, -onis (f.): knowledge, learning; repleo, replere, repleui, repletum: fill up (w/ abl.) (<re- + pleo)

per . . . contubernium prep. phr.; Areius: a philosopher from Alexandria, Egypt; philosophus, -i (m.): philosopher; contubernium, -(i)i (n.): association, friendship; *contubernium* suggests that Augustus' relationship with Areius and his sons Dionysius and Nicanor came when Augustus was an adult, in contrast w/ Apollodorus, who was his magister when he was a young man

Dionysi et Nicanoris contubernium—non tamen ut aut loqueretur expedite aut componere aliquid auderet, nam et si quid res exigeret, Latine formabat uertendumque alii dabat. sed plane poematum quoque non imperitus delectabatur etiam comoedia ueteri et saepe eam exhibuit spectaculis publicis.

2. In euoluendis utriusque linguae auctoribus nihil aeque sectabatur quam praecepta et exempla publice uel priuatim salubria, eaque ad uerbum excerpta aut ad domesticos aut ad exercituum prouinciarumque rectores aut ad urbis magistratus plerumque mittebat prout quique monitione indigerent. etiam

---

non tamen ut aut loqueretur ... aut ... auderet   negat. result cl. expressing proviso (AG #537b); *expedite* (adv.): fluently; *componere*: compl. inf. (AG #456) w/ *auderet*; audeo, audere, ausus sum: dare

si quid res exigeret ... formabat ... dabat   past gen. condit. showing repeated action (AG #518c) w/ two cl. in apod.; *quid* = aliquid; *res*: nom. subj., "if the matter demanded something [in Greek]"; Latine (adv.): in Latin; formo (1): compose, write up; uerto, uertere, uerti, uersum: turn, translate; *uertendum*: gerv., "for translating"; *alii*: dat. sg. (AG #113 for decl.)

plane   (adv.) plainly, clearly

poema, -atis   (n.) piece of poetry, poem; *poematum*: objv. gen. w/ *imperitus* (AG #349a)

imperitus, -a, -um   lacking knowledge, ignorant of; *non imperitus*: LITOTES (AG #641)

delecto   (1) delight, (pass.) be delighted, take pleasure in (w/ abl.)

comoedia ueteri   "Old Comedy," the early Gk. comedy of Aristophanes (*OCD* s.v. comedy (Greek), Old, 354–355); comoedia, -ae (f.): comedy (as a form of drama)

exhibeo, exhibere, exhibui, exhibitum   produce, present (<ex- + habeo)

spectaculis publicis   "at the public games," abl. of time when (AG #424d)

89.2

in euoluendis ... auctoribus   "in reading authors," gerv. w/ in (AG #507); euoluo, euoluere, euolui, euolutum: unroll (a scroll), read (<ex- + uoluo); lingua, -ae (f.): tongue, language; *utriusque linguae*: gen. of quality (AG #345)

aeque   (adv.) as much as (w/ *quam*)

sector   (1) search for, hunt out

praeceptum, -i   (n.) piece of advice, precept

exemplum, -i   (n.) example, a model

priuatim   (adv.) privately, personally; Suet. regularly uses adv. in -tim

saluber, -bris, -bre   salutary, beneficial

eaque ... excerpta   ptc. phr., obj. of *mittebat*; *ad uerbum*: "word for word"; excerpo, excerpere, excerpsi, excerptum: pick out, select (<ex- + carpo); excerpting quotations from books was a common practice

domestici, -orum   (m. pl.) members of a household

rector, -oris   (m.) person in charge of others, governor, commander (vb. subst. <rego)

plerumque   (adv.) often, mostly

prout quique ... indigerent   "to the extent that any needed advising"; prout (conj.): to the extent that, inasmuch as; monitio, -onis (f.): advising; indigeo, indigere, indigui: need, require (w/ abl.) (<indu- + egeo); *indigerent*: iterative subjv. (AG #518c) indicating customary action in past time

libros totos et senatui recitauit et populo notos per edictum
saepe fecit, ut orationes Q. Metelli de prole augenda et Rutili de
modo aedificiorum, quo magis persuaderet utramque rem non
a se primo animaduersam sed antiquis iam tunc curae fuisse.
3. ingenia saeculi sui omnibus modis fouit. recitantis et benigne
et patienter audiit nec tantum carmina et historias sed et orationes et dialogos. componi tamen aliquid de se nisi et serio et
a praestantissimis offendebatur admonebatque praetores ne
paterentur nomen suum commissionibus obsolefieri.

---

liber, -bri (m.) a book
totus, -a, -um whole, entire
populo notos [libros] ... **fecit** "he made them known to the people"; notus, -a, -um: known
ut such as
oratio, -onis (f.) speech, oration
Q. Caecilius Metellus Macedonicus (*OCD* 259), censor in 131 BCE
de prole augenda "On Increasing the Number of Children"; proles, -is (f.): offspring, progeny; *augenda*: abl.
of gerv. (AG #507); s. ch. 34 for Augustus' legislation on marriage, which provides a likely context for
sharing Metellus' oration
Rutilius probably P. Rutilius Rufus (*OCD* 1301), consul 105 BCE
de modo aedificiorum "On the Height-Limit of Buildings"; aedificium, -(i)i (n.): building, edifice
quo magis persuaderet relat. cl. of purp. w/ compar. (AG #531.2a); persuadeo, persuadere, persuasi,
persuasum: persuade (<per- + suadeo)
utramque rem non ... animaduersam [esse] **sed ... fuisse** subst. cl. of purp. w/ inf. + acc. subj. (AG #563d)
ff. *persuaderet*; antiquus, -a, -um: ancient, old, (subst.) "men of old"; *antiquis ... curae*: dbl. dat. (purp. and
ref.) w/ *fuisse* (AG #382.1n1); *iam tunc*: "already for a long time"

89.3

ingenium, -(i)i (n.) talent, intellect; by METONOMY (AG #641), a person of talent
saeculum, -i (n.) generation, age
foueo, fouere, foui, fotum foster, nurture, promote
recitantis "men reciting"; acc. pl. subst., obj. of *audiit*
benigne (adv.) in a friendly spirit, generously
patienter (adv.) patiently, with patience
audio, audire, audiui (-ii), auditum hear, listen to
carmina ... dialogos obj. of *recitantis*; carmen, -inis (n.): poem; historia, -ae (f.): historical writing, history;
oratio, -onis (f.): speech, oration; dialogus, -i (m.): dialogue, literary work in dialogue form; Augustus is
known to have attended readings by Vergil; he had personal friendships with Horace and Livy, and likely
attended their readings as well
componi tamen aliquid de se ... a praestantissimis "that anything be written about himself," indir. disc.
(AG #580) ff. *offendebatur*; serio (adv.): seriously; praestans, -ntis: surpassing others, outstanding
(superl. = -ntissimus); *a praestantissimis*: (subst.) "by the most outstanding men"
offendo, offendere, offendi, offensum trouble, upset; (pass.) be displeased, take offence
admoneo, admonere, admonui, admonitum warn, admonish (<ad- + moneo)
ne paterentur negat. subst. cl. of purp. (= indir. comm.) ff. *admonebat* (AG #563);
nomen suum commissionibus obsolefieri subst. cl. of purp. w/ inf. + acc. subj. (AG #563c) ff. *paterentur*;
commissio, -onis (f.): holding of a contest, competition; obsolefio, obsolefieri: make common, lower in dignity;
Augustus did not want to be degraded by the cheap flattery of orators and poets at public performances

90   Circa religiones talem accepimus. tonitrua et fulgura paulo
      infirmius expauescebat, ut semper et ubique pellem uituli
      marini circumferret pro remedio atque ad omnem maioris tem-
      pestatis suspicionem in abditum et concamaratum locum
      se reciperet, consternatus olim per nocturnum iter transcursu
      fulguris, ut praediximus.

91   Somnia neque sua neque aliena de se neglegebat. Philippensi
      acie quamuis statuisset non egredi tabernaculo propter
      ualitudinem, egressus est tamen amici somnio monitus ces-

---

Religious customs and superstitions (*religiones*). Augustus' personal religious views and habits are the final topic. Suetonius uses subheadings to divide the discussion into subsections covering Augustus' response to thunder and lightning (ch. 90), and respect for dreams (ch. 91), auspices and omens (ch. 92), and foreign religious rites (ch. 93). The focus here is on Augustus' personal actions as his public acts had been treated earlier (s. especially ch. 29–31 for the construction of temples in Rome and his actions as pontifex maximus).

90
circa (prep. + acc.) concerning, with regard to
religio, -onis (f.) religious awe, religious customs
talem "the following"; talis, -e: of such kind (referring to what follows)
tonitrus, -us (m. sg., n. pl.) thunder
fulgur, -uris (n.) lightning
paulo infirmius expauescebat "he feared a little too much"; infirme (adv.): faint-heartedly (compar. = -ius); expauesco, expauescere, expaui: take fright at (<ex- + pauesco)
ut ... circumferret ... se reciperet result cl. (AG #537); ubique (adv.): everywhere; pellis, -is (f.): skin, hide (of an animal); uitulus marinus: seal (lit., sea calf); circumfero, circumferre, circumtuli, circumlatum: carry about (<circum- + fero); remedium, -(i)i (n.): remedy, means of protection (seals were believed never to be struck by lightning); tempestas, -atis (f.): storm; suspicio, -onis (f.): suspicion; abditus, -a, -um: hidden; concamaro (1): cover with a vault (an unusual vb. <con- + camaro)
consternatus ... transcursu fulguris causal ptc. phr. (AG #496); consterno (1): unsettle, throw into confusion (<con- + sterno); nocturnus, -a, -um: occurring at night; transcursus, -us (m.): rapid movement across a space, flash (of lightning)
praedico, praedicere, praedixi, praedictum say before (<prae- + dico), s. ch. 29.3

91.1
somnium, -(i)i (n.) dream
alienus, -a, -um of others, belonging to others
neglego, neglegere, neglexi, neglectum disregard, ignore, fail to respect (<nec- + lego)
Philippensi acie abl. of time when (AG #424d), "at the battle of Philippi"; acies, -ei (f.): a battle line; s. ch. 13.1
quamvis statuisset ... ualitudinem conces. cl. w/ subjv (AG #527a); statuo, statuere, statui, statutum: decide, resolve to (w/ inf.); egredior, egredi, egressus sum: come out from, leave (<ex- + gradior); tabernaculum, -i (n.): tent; *tabernaculo*: abl. of separ. w/ out prep. (AG #402); propter (prep. + acc): on account of
amici somnio monitus causal ptc. phr.; moneo, monere, monui, monitum: warn, advise
cessitque res prospere "and the matter turned out well"; cedo, cedere, cessi, cessum: (w/ adv.) turn out; prospere (adv.): successfully

sitque res prospere quando captis castris lectica eius, quasi
ibi cubans remansisset, concursu hostium confossa atque lacerata est. ipse per omne uer plurima et formidulosissima sed
uana et irrita uidebat, reliquo tempore rariora et minus uana.
2. cum dedicatam in Capitolio aedem Tonanti Ioui <populus>
assidue frequentaret, somniauit queri Capitolinum Iouem cultores sibi abduci seque respondisse Tonantem pro ianitore
ei appositum ideoque mox tintinnabulis fastigium aedis redimiit, quod ea fere ianuis dependebant. ex nocturno uisu etiam

---

quando ... lectica eius ... confossa atque lacerata est "since his litter was run through and torn to shreds"; causal cl. w/ indic. introd. a reason given on the authority of the author (AG #540a); *captis castris*: tmp. abl. abs. (AG #420.1); *quasi ibi cubans remansisset*: "as if he had remained lying there," condit. cl. of compar. (AG #524); remaneo, remanere, remansi: remain (<re- + maneo); concursus, -us (m.): attack; confodio, confodere, confodi, confossum: run through, stab (<con- + fodio); lacero (1): tear to shreds

uer, ueris (n.) season of spring; for Romans dreams might fluctuate seasonally

plurima et ... irrita [somnia] formidulosus, -a, -um: fearful, alarming (superl. = -issimus); uanus, -a, -um: empty; irritus, -a, -um: unrealized, ineffectual

reliquo tempore "for the rest of the time," abl. of time when (AG #423)

rariora ... uana [somnia] rarus, -a, -um: infrequent, rare (compar. = -ior); minus (compar. adv.): to a smaller extent, less

91.2

cum ... populus ... frequentaret causal cum cl. (AG #549); Iuppiter Tonans: Jupiter the Thunderer; tono (1): thunder; the temple to Jupiter Tonans had been dedicated by Augustus in 22 BCE (s. ch. 29.3)

somnio (1) dream

queri Capitolinum Iouem indir. disc. (AG #580) ff. *somniauit*; Capitoline Jupiter was the chief god of the Roman state, whose temple stood on one summit of the Capitoline Hill

cultores sibi abduci seque respondisse indir. disc. (AG #580) ff. *queri*; cultor, -oris (m.): worshipper (vb. subst. <colo); *sibi* = Ioui Capitolino: dat. of separ. (AG #381); abduco, abducere, abduxi, abductum: lead away (<ab- + duco)

seque respondisse indir. disc. (AG #580) ff. *somniauit*; *se* = Augustum (for reflex. pron. in subord. cl., AG #300)

Tonantem ... appositum [esse] indir. disc. conveying Augustus' wd. (AG #580) ff. *respondisse*; ianitor, -is (m.): door-keeper; *ei* = Ioui Capitolino; appono, apponere, apposui, appositum: assign, appoint (<ad- + pono)

ideo (adv.) for that reason

tintinnabulum, -i (n.) bell

fastigium, -(i)i (n.) pediment, gable, rooftop

redimio, redimire, redimii, redimitum encircle, surround (with decoration)

quod ea [tintinnabula] **... dependebant** causal cl. w/ indic. (AG #540); ianua, -ae (f.): door; dependeo, dependere, dependi: hang down from (<de- + pendeo)

ex nocturno uisu "because of a nocturnal vision," (*OLD ex* 18); nocturnus, -a, -um: occurring at night; uisus, -us (m.): sight, vision, supernatural vision (in a dream)

stipem quotannis die certo emendicabat a populo cauam
manum asses porrigentibus praebens.

92 Auspicia et omina quaedam pro certissimis obseruabat. si mane
sibi calceus perperam ac sinister pro dextro induceretur, ut
dirum, si terra mariue ingrediente se longinquam profectionem
forte rorasset, ut laetum maturique et prosperi reditus. sed et
ostentis praecipue mouebatur. enatam inter iuncturas lapidum
ante domum suam palmam in conpluuium deorum Penatium

---

stips, stipis (f.) small coin
quotannis (adv.) every year
die certo abl. of time when (AG #423)
emendico (1) obtain by begging (<ex- + mendico)
cauam manum ... praebens ptc. phr.; cauus, -a, -um: curved, cupped (hand); *asses porrigentibus*: "to those offering coins"; as, assis (m.): copper coin; porrigo, porrigere, porexi, porectum: offer (<por- + rego); *porrigentibus*: dat. pl. pres. act. ptc., subst.

92.1

auspicia et omina auspicium, -(i)i (n.): auspices, a sign taken from birds; Suet. employs technical terminology here
pro certissimis "as most reliable"
obseruo (1) respect, recognize, observe (<ob- + seruo)
si ... calceus ... induceretur prot. of gener. condit. showing repeated action in the past (AG #518c); mane (adv.): in the morning; calceus, -i (m.): shoe; perperam (adv.): incorrectly; sinister, -tra, -trum: left; dexter, -tra, -trum: right; induco, inducere, induxi, inductum: put on (<in- + duco)
ut dirum [obseruabat] "he regarded it as a dire sign"; dirus, -a, -um: awful, dire; dirum is a technical term referring to a sign portending disaster
si ... rorasset prot. of gener. condit. showing repeated action in the past (AG #518c); *terra mariue*: "on land or sea," abl. of place where w/out prep. (AG #429); *ingrediente se ... profectionem*: tmp. abl. abs. (AG #420.1); ingredior, ingredi, ingressus sum: embark on (<in- + gradior); *longinquam profectionem*: "a journey to a far-off place"; longinquus, -a, -um: far-off; profectio, -onis (f.): departure, setting out on a journey; roro (1): (impers.) drizzle; *rorasset*: = contr. form of rorauisset (AG #181)
ut laetum [obseruabat] "he regarded it as a favorable sign"; laetus, -a, -um: happy
[omen] maturique et prosperi reditus "and as a sign of an early and successful return," obj. gen. (AG #348); maturus, -a, -um: early; prosperus, -a, -um: successful, favorable; reditus, -us (m.): return
moueo, mouere, moui, motum move, stir up, disturb
enatam ... palmam ptc. phr., obj. of *transtulit*; enascor, enasci, enatus sum: arise out of, sprout (<ex- + nascor); iunctura, -ae (f.): joint, point where parts are joined; lapis, -idis (m.): stone, rock; palma, -ae (f.): palm tree; the palm was a sign of victory
conpluuium, -ii (n.) the inward sloping roof (of an atrium), here = "courtyard" by METONOMY (AG #641)
Penates, -ium (m. pl.) the household gods, the Penates; the palm was brought into the atrium of the house where the Penates had a shrine

transtulit utque coalesceret magno opere curauit. **2.** apud insulam Capreas ueterrimae ilicis demissos iam ad terram languentisque ramos conualuisse aduentu suo adeo laetatus est ut eas cum re p. Neapolitanorum permutauerit Aenaria data. obseruabat et dies quosdam, ne aut postridie nundinas quoquam proficisceretur aut Nonis quicquam rei seriae incohaeret, nihil in hoc quidem aliud deuitans, ut ad Tiberium scribit, quam δυσφημίαν nominis.

93 Peregrinarum caerimoniarum sicut ueteres ac praeceptas reue-

---

utque coalesceret purp. cl. (AG #531); coalesco, coalescere, coalui, coalitum: grow strong (<con- + alesco); palma is subj.
magno opere (adv.) greatly, strongly, especially
curauit Augustus is subj.

92.2
apud insulam ... ramos conualuisse aduento suo indir. disc. (AG #580) ff. *laetatus est*; Capreae, -arum (f. pl.): Capri, an island off the coast of Campania; ilex, -icis (f.): oak tree; demitto, demittere, demisi, demissum: send down, lower (<de- + mitto); langueo, languere: droop, wilt; *languentis*: acc. pl. w/ *ramos*; ramus, -i (m.): branch; *ramos*: acc. subj.; conualesco, conualescere, conualui: grow strong again, recover (<con- + ualesco); *aduento suo*: "at his arrival"; aduentus, -us (m.): arrival; this sign held special meaning as the corona ciuica, which Augustus had received in 27 BCE for saving the state, is fashioned from oak (ilex)
laetor (1) rejoice, be delighted
ut ... permutauerit result cl. ff. *adeo laetatus est* (AG #537); *eas* = Capreas; *re p[ublica] Neapolitanorum*: "the city of Naples"; permuto (1): exchange (<per- + muto); *permutauerit*: pf. subjv. in result cl. in secondary seq. (AG #485c); *Aenaria data*: abl. abs. (AG #419); Aenaria, -ae (f.): Ischia, an island off the coast of Campania; in 29 BCE Augustus traded Ischia for Capri, which became his private possession
ne ... proficisceretur negat. purp. cl. (AG #531); postridie (adv.): on the day after (w/ acc.); nundinae, -arum (f. pl.): market-day (occurring every eight days); quoquam (adv.): to any place, anywhere; proficiscor, proficisci, profectus sum: start a journey, set out
aut ... incoharet a second negat. purp. cl. (AG #531); Nonae, -arum (f. pl.): the Nones (the ninth day before the Ides of each month); *Nonis*: abl. of time when (AG #423.1); *quicquam rei seriae*: "any serious business"; *rei seriae*: partit. gen. (AG #346a3); serius, -a, -um: weighty, important; incoho (1): start, initiate
nihil ... aliud obj. of *deuitans*
deuito (1) avoid, keep clear of (<de- + uito)
ut ... scribit Suet. again cites Augustus' private correspondence as his source
quam "than," intro. compar. ff. *nihil ... aliud*
δυσφημίαν nominis "the evil-sound of the name"; Augustus considered inauspicious the "non" sound of "nundinae" and "Nonae"

93
peregrinus, -a, -um foreign, alien
caerimonia, -ae (f.) religious rites, ceremonies (usu. pl.)
sicut ... ita (correl. conj.) "just as ... so"
ueteres ac praeceptas [caerimonias] "the ancient and previously established rites"; praecipio, praecipere, praecepi, praeceptum: give instruction in, ordain beforehand (<prae- + capio)
reuerenter (adv.) respectfully, with reverence (superl. = -issime); Suet. commonly uses superl. adv.

rentissime coluit, ita ceteras contemptui habuit. namque Athenis
initiatus, cum postea Romae pro tribunali de priuilegio sacerdotum Atticae Cereris cognosceret et quaedam secretiora proponerentur, dimisso consilio et corona circumstantium solus
audiit disceptantes. at contra non modo in peragranda Aegypto
paulo deflectere ad uisendum Apin supersedit sed et Gaium
nepotem, quod Iudaeam praeteruehens apud Hierosolyma non
supplicasset, conlaudauit.

---

colo, colere, colui, cultum cultivate, worship
ceteras [caerimonias] **contemptui habuit** "the other rites he held in contempt"; contemptus, -us
   (m.): contempt; *contemptui*: dat. of purp. (AG #382.1)
Athenis initiatus causal ptc. phr. (AG #496); Athenae, -arum (f.): Athens; *Athenis*: locat. (AG #427.3);
   initio (1): initiate; Augustus had been initiated into the Eleusinian mysteries, probably during a visit
   to Athens in 31 BCE
cum . . . cognosceret et quaedam secretiora proponerentur circumst. cum cl. (AG #546);
   Romae: locat. (AG #427.3); tribunal, -alis (n.): platform, tribunal (used for judicial purposes);
   priuilegium, -(i)i (n.): special right, privilege; sacerdos, -otis (m./f.): priest, priestess; Atticus, -
   a, -um: Attic, Athenian; Ceres, -eris (f.): Ceres, the goddess of grain, identified with the Greek
   goddess Demeter; secretus, -a, -um: secret, private (compar. = -ior); *secretiora*: n. nom. pl. w/
   quaedam
dimisso consilio et corona circumstantium tmp. abl. abs. (AG #420.1); *dimisso* w/ *consilio* and *corona*
   (AG #287); consilium, -(i)i (n.): advisory council; corona, -ae (f.): circle (of spectators); circumsto,
   circumstare, circumsteti (-iti): stand around (<circum- + sto); *circumstantium*: pres. act. ptc., subst.,
   "of those standing around"
audio, audire, audiui (-ii), auditum hear, listen to; as Augustus had been initiated into the cult, he
   could hear the details of the dispute while maintaining the secrets of the cult
discepto (1) dispute, debate (<dis- + capto); *disceptantes*: pres. act. ptc., subst.
contra (adv.) conversely, on the other hand
in peragranda Aegypto gerv. w/ in (AG #507); peragro (1): travel around; Aegyptus, -i (f.): Egypt;
   Augustus' travels in Egypt date to 30 BCE
deflecto, deflectere, deflexi, deflexum change one's course, deviate (<de- + flecto); *deflectere*: compl.
   inf. (AG #456) ff. *supersedit*
ad uisendum Apin ad + gerv. denoting purp. (AG #506); uiso, uisere, uisi: go and see, visit; Apis, -is
   (m.): Apis, the sacred bull of Egypt worshipped at Memphis
supersedeo, supersedere, supersedi, supersessum refrain from (w/ inf.) (<super- + sedeo)
Gaium nepotem acc. obj. of *conlaudauit*; Gaius traveled past Judaea in 1 CE
quod . . . non supplicasset causal cl. w/ subjv. relying on the authority of another pers. (AG #540);
   Iudaea, -ae (f.): Judaea; praeterueho, praeteruehere, praeteruexi, praeteruectum: pass by, travel past
   (<praeter- + ueho); Hierosolyma, -orum (n. pl.): Jerusalem; supplico (1): make an offering, do
   worship; *supplicasset* = contr. form of supplicauisset (AG #181)
conlaudo (1) praise, commend (<con- + laudo); Suet. is likely drawing upon private letters as
   his source

94   Et quoniam ad haec uentum est, non ab re fuerit subtexere quae ei prius quam nasceretur et ipso natali die ac deinceps euenerint quibus futura magnitudo eius et perpetua felicitas sperari animaduertique posset.

2. Velitris antiquitus tacta de caelo parte muri responsum est eius oppidi ciuem quandoque rerum potiturum. qua fiducia Veliterni et tunc statim et postea saepius paene ad exitium sui cum populo R. belligerauerant. sero tandem documentis apparuit ostentum illud Augusti potentiam portendisse.

Signs foretelling Augustus' greatness and good fortune. The discussion of religious matters leads to a detailed account of the divine signs that foretold Augustus' future greatness. As a transition, Suetonius presents his plan to discuss the signs in chronological order. The longest chapter of the biography (ch. 94) is filled with signs that occurred before Julius Caesar's death.

94.1
quoniam ... uentum est   causal cl. (AG #540a); *quoniam* (conj.): since, seeing that; *uenio, uenire, ueni, uentum*: come; *uentum est*: (impers. pass.) "it has come"

non ab re fuerit subtexere   "it would not be off topic to add"; *fuerit*: potent. subjv. (AG #447.3); *subtexo, subtexere, subtexui, subtextum*: add as a supplement (<sub- + texo)

quae ... euenerint   "the things which happened," relat. cl. of char. (AG #535) with indef. anteced. omitted (AG #307c); *ei*: dat. of ref. (AG #376); *prius quam nasceretur*: anticipatory cl. implying expectancy in past time (AG #551b); *dies natalis*: day of one's birth; *natali die*: abl. of time when (AG #423.1); *deinceps* (adv.): after that, in turn; *euenio, euenire, eueni, euentum*: happen (<ex- + uenio)

quibus ... magnitudo ... et ... felicitas ... posset   "by which his greatness and good fortune are able," a second relat. cl. of char. (AG #535) with indef. anteced. omitted (AG #307c); *futurus, -a, -um*: future; *magnitudo, -inis* (f.): greatness; *felicitas, -atis* (f.): good fortune; *spero* (1): look forward to, hope; *sperari animaduertique*: compl. inf. (AG #456) w/ *posset*

94.2
Velitrae, -arum (f. pl.) modern Velletri, the hometown of the Octavii (s. ch. 1.1); *Velitris*: locat. (AG #427.3)

antiquitus (adv.) long ago

tacta de caelo parte muri   tmp. abl. abs. (AG #420.1); *tacta de caelo*: "struck by lightning"; *tango, tangere, tetigi, tactum*: touch; *murus, -i* (m.): city wall; *muri*: partit. gen. (AG #346a.1); the phr. *de caelo* marks the event as an omen

responsum est   (impers.) "a response was given"; a religious official interpreted the meaning of the sign

eius oppidi ciuem ... potiturum   [esse] indir. disc. (AG #580) ff. *responsum est*; *ciuis, -is* (m.): citizen; *quandoque* (adv.): at some time, some day; *potior, potiri, potitus sum*: take possession of, control (w/ gen.); *potiri rerum*: control affairs (AG #410a)

qua fiducia Veliterni ... belligerauerant   "trusting in this, the people of Velletri waged wars," relat. cl. w/ anteced. in cl. (AG #308f); *fiducia, -ae* (f.): trust, (abl.) with trust (in); *Veliterni, -orum* (m. pl.): the people of Velletri; *ad exitium sui*: "to the point of their own destruction"; *exitium, -(i)i* (n.): destruction, disaster; *sui*: objv. gen. of reflex. pron.; *cum populo R[omano]*; *belligero* (1): wage war (<bellum + gero); Velletri was at war with Rome for much of the fourth century BCE

sero (adv.) late

documentum, -i (n.) example, evidence

appareo, apparere, apparui, apparitum   appear, be clear (<ad- + pareo); *apparuit*: (impers.) "it was clear"

ostentum illud ... portendisse   indir. disc. (AG #580) ff. *apparuit*; *potentia, -ae* (f.): power, influence; *portendo, portendere, portendi, portentum*: indicate (a future event), portend (<por- + tendo)

3. Auctor est Iulius Marathus ante paucos quam nasceretur menses prodigium Romae factum publice quo denuntiabatur regem p. R. naturam parturire, senatum exterritum censuisse ne quis illo anno genitus educaretur, eos qui grauidas uxores haberent, quod ad se quisque spem traheret, curasse ne senatus consultum ad aerarium deferretur.

4. In Asclepiadis Mendetis Theologumenon libris lego Atiam,

94.3

auctor est be on record as saying (*OLD* 9b)

Iulius Marathus freedman and record-keeper of Augustus (s. ch. 79.2)

ante paucos quam nasceretur menses "a few months before he was born," tmp. cl. w/ impf. subjv. instead of indic. in stmt. of fact (AG #551a); *ante* w/ acc. even though followed by *quam*

prodigium Romae factum [esse] **publice** indir. disc. (AG #580a) ff. *auctor est*; prodigium, -ii (n.): prodigy; *Romae*: locat. (AG #427.3); *factum* [*esse*] *publice*: occurred publicly (it was accepted as a formal sign related to the Roman state); in 63 BCE the prodigy was likely seen to relate to the conspiracy of Catiline

quo denuntiabatur relat. cl.; *quo*: anteced. *prodigium*; denuntio (1): announce (by prophecy), signify (<de- + nuntio); indic. vb. emphasizes the fact (AG #583a)

regem p[opulo] **R**[omano] **naturam parturire** indir. disc. ff. *denuntiabatur*; rex, regis (m.): king; *regem*: acc. dir. obj. in emphatic position; *p*[*opulo*]: dat.; natura, -ae (f.): nature; parturio, parturire, parturiui: be pregnant with, be ready to give birth to

senatum exterritum censuisse indir. disc. continues ff. *auctor est* (AG #580a); exterreo, exterrere, exterrui, exterritum: terrify (<ex- + terreo); censeo, censere, censui, censum: decide, decree

ne quis … genitus educaretur negat. subst. cl. of purp. (= indir. comm.) (AG #563); *quis* = aliquis; *illo anno*: abl. of time within which (AG #423); gigno, gignere, genui, genitum: produce, (pass.) be born; educo (1): bring up, rear, raise

eos … curasse indir. disc. ff. *auctor est* (AG #580a), interrupted by relat. cl. and causal cl.; *qui … haberent*: subord. relat. cl. w/ subjv. in indir. disc. (AG #580); grauidus, -a, -um: pregnant; *quod … traheret*: subord. causal cl. (AG #580, #540); traho, trahere, traxi, tractum: assign, attribute to (*OLD* 20); *curasse* = contr. form of curauisse (AG #181)

ne senatus consultum … deferretur negat. subst. cl. of purp. (= indir. comm.) (AG #563) ff. *curasse*; consultum, -i (n.): resolution; *senatus consultum*: a decree of the senate; defero, deferre, detuli, delatum: transfer, convey (<de- + fero); a decree of the senate had to be filed with the urban quaestors in the treasury to become official

94.4

Aesclepiadis Mendetis "of Asclepiades from Mendes"; an author from the Nile Delta in Egypt, he was perhaps a freedman of Augustus

Theologumena, -on (n. pl.) "Discourses on the Gods" (the title of a book) (for Gk. decl., AG #52c); the work does not survive

liber, -bri (m.) book

lego Suet. inserts himself into the narrative, emphasizing his research into obscure sources

Atiam … obdormisse indir. disc. (AG #580) ff. *lego*, interrupted by cum cl., abl. abs., and dum cl.; Atia: Augustus' mother (s. ch. 4.1); *cum … uenisset*: circumst. cum cl. (AG #546); sollemne, -is (n.): religious ceremony; sacer, -cra, -crum: sacred, holy; *media nocte*: abl. of time when (AG #423); uenio, uenire, ueni, uentum: come; *posita … lectica*: tmp. abl. abs. (AG #420.1); *dum ceterae matronae dormirent*: subord. cl. in indir. disc. w/ subjv. (AG #580, 556); dum: while; matrona, -ae (f.): matron, married woman; dormio, dormire, dormiui (-ii), dormitum: sleep; obdormio, obdormire, obdormiui (-ii), obdormitum: fall asleep (<ob- + dormio)

cum ad sollemne Apollinis sacrum media nocte uenisset, posita in templo lectica, dum ceterae matronae dormirent, obdormisse; draconem repente irrepsisse ad eam pauloque post egressum; illam expergefactam quasi a concubitu mariti purificasse se, et statim in corpore eius extitisse maculam uelut picti draconis nec potuisse umquam exigi, adeo ut mox publicis balineis perpetuo abstinuerit; Augustum natum mense decimo et ob hoc Apollinis filium existimatum. eadem Atia, prius quam pareret, somniauit intestina sua ferri ad sidera explicarique per omnem terrarum et caeli ambitum. somniauit et pater Octauius utero Atiae iubar solis exortum.

5. Quo natus est die, cum de Catilinae coniuratione ageretur in curia et Octauius ob uxoris puerperium serius affuisset,

---

draconem ... irrepsisse ... egressum [esse] indir. disc. (AG #580) continues ff. *lego*; draco, -onis (m.): snake; irrepo, irrepere, irrepsi: crawl, creep along (<in- + repo); egredior, egredi, egressus sum: leave (<ex- + gradior)

illam ... purificasse se indir. disc.; *illam* = Atiam; expergefacio, expergefacere, expergefeci, expergefactum: wake up (<expergo + facio); concubitus, -us (m.): sexual intercourse; maritus, -i (m.): husband; purifico (1): cleanse, make ceremonially pure; *purificasse* = contr. form of purificauisse (AG #181)

et statim ... extitisse maculam ... nec potuisse umquam exigi indir. disc.; exsto, exstare, extiti: be found (<ex- + sto); macula, -ae (f.): mark on the skin, blemish; pictus, -a, -um: painted, colored; *exigi*: pres. pass. compl. inf. (AG #456) w/ *potuisse*

adeo ut ... abstinuerit result cl. (AG #537); balineum, -i (n.): bath, act of bathing; perpetuo (adv.): permanently; abstineo, abstinere, abstinui, abstentum: keep distant, keep away from (w/ abl.) (<ab- + teneo)

Augustum natum [esse] **... existimatum** [esse] indir. disc.; *mense decimo*: abl. of time when; decimus, -a, -um: tenth; the claim of Augustus' divine parentage parallels accounts of Alexander the Great and Scipio Africanus

prius quam pareret tmp. cl. w/ impf. subjv. instead of indic. in stmt. of fact (AG #551a); pario, parere, peperi, partum: give birth

somnio (1) dream

intestina sua ferri ... explicarique per ... ambitum indir. disc. (AG #580) used to report the content of Atia's dream; intestinum, -i (n.): (pl.) intestines, internal organs; sidus, -eris (n.): star; explico (1): spread out (<ex- + plico); ambitus, -us (m.): circuit, expanse

utero Atiae iubar solis exortum [esse] indir. disc. (AG #580) reporting the content of Octavius' dream; uterus, -i (m.): womb; *utero*: abl. of source w/ *exortum* (AG #403.2a); iubar, -aris (n.): radiance, brightness; exorior, exoriri, exortus sum; arise from (<ex- + orior)

94.5

quo natus est die "on the day he was born"; *die*: abl. of time when (AG #423.1); the discussion of signs continues in chronological order

cum ... ageretur ... et Octauius ... affuisset circumst. cum cl. (AG #546); *Catilinae*: L. Sergius Catilina (*OCD* 1353), Roman nobleman and senator who led an unsuccessful conspiracy against the state in 63 BCE; coniuratio, -onis (f.): conspiracy; *ageretur*: impers. pass. w/ de, "the conspiracy of Catiline was being discussed" (lit., "it was being discussed concerning the conspiracy"); puerperium, -(i)i (n.): childbirth, delivery; sero (adv.): late (compar. = -ius); *serius*: "rather late"; adsum (assum), adesse, adfui (affui): be present (<ad- + sum); Suet. is the only source to report a senate meeting on September 23, 63 BCE

nota ac uulgata res est P. Nigidium comperta morae causa,
ut horam quoque partus acceperit, affirmasse dominum terrarum orbi natum. Octauio postea, cum per secreta Thraciae
exercitum duceret, in Liberi patris luco barbara caerimonia
de filio consulenti idem affirmatum est a sacerdotibus quod infuso super altaria mero tantum flamma emicuisset ut supergressa fastigium templi ad caelum usque ferretur, unique
omnino Magno Alexandro apud easdem aras sacrificanti simile
prouenisset ostentum. 6. atque etiam sequenti statim nocte
uidere uisus est filium mortali specie ampliorem cum fulmine

- **nota ac uulgata res est** "it is an established and well-known fact"; nosco, noscere, noui, notum: know; uulgo (1): make widely known
- **P[ublium] Nigidium ... affirmasse** indir. disc. (AG #580) interrupted by an abl. abs. and tmp. cl.; Publius Nigidius Figulus (*OCD* 1016) was a senator and scholar of the first century BCE; *comperta morae causa*: tmp. abl. abs. (AG #420.1); comperio, comperire, comperi, comperitum: find out, learn (a fact); mora, -ae (f.): delay; *ut ... acceperit*: tmp. cl. w/ subjv. in indir. disc. (AG #580, #543); partus, -us (m.): birth; affirmo (1): assert positively, affirm (<ad- + firmo)
- **dominum ... natum** [esse] indir. disc. (AG #580) ff. *affirmasse*; *terrarum orbi*: "for the world"; *orbi*: dat. of ref. (advantage) (AG #376); orbis, -is (m.): circular object, disk; orbis terrarum: the world
- **Octauio ... consulenti** tmp. ptc. phr. (AG #496), indir. obj. of *affirmatum est*; *cum ... duceret*: circumst. cum cl. (AG #546); secretum, -i (n.): remote place; Thracia, -ae (f.): Thrace; Liber, -eri (m.): the god Liber (Liber Pater), identified with Dionysus/Bacchus; lucus, -i (m.): sacred grove; *barbara caerimonia*: abl. of means (AG #409); barbarus, -a, -um: foreign; caerimonia, -ae (f.): religious rites; for Octavius' campaign in Thrace, s. ch. 3.2; a well-known oracle was located in the area
- **idem affirmatum est** *idem* (the fact that a "master for the earth" was born) is subj.
- **sacerdos, -otis** (m./f.) priest, priestess
- **quod ... flamma emicuisset** causal cl. w/ subjv. relying on the authority of another pers. (AG #540); *infuso ... mero*: tmp. abl. abs (AG #420.1); infundo, infundere, infudi, infusum: pour (<in- + fundo); altaria, -ium (n. pl.): altar; merum, -i (n.): unmixed wine; flamma, -ae (f.): flame; emico, emicare, emicui, emicatum: shoot forth (<ex- + mico)
- **ut [flamma] supergressa ... ferretur** result cl. (AG #537); supergredior, supergredi, supergressus sum: pass beyond (<super- + gradior); fastigium, -(i)i (n.): pediment
- **unique ... simile prouenisset ostentum** a second causal cl. w/ subjv. (AG #540); *uni*: dat. sg. w/ *Magno Alexandro sacrificanti*, indir. obj. of *prouenisset*; omnino (adv.): altogether, in all (emphasizing the rarity of the event); sacrifico (1): perform a sacrifice; prouenio, prouenire, proueni, prouentum: be produced, turn up (<pro- + uenio); Alexander the Great (*OCD* s.v. Alexander (3) III, 56–58) had campaigned in the same area in 335 BCE

94.6

- **sequenti ... nocte** abl. of time when (AG #423.1)
- **uidere uisus est** "he seemed to see"; Octavius is the subj.
- **mortali specie** abl. of compar. ff. *ampliorem* (AG #406); mortalis, -e: mortal; species, -ei (f.): appearance
- **cum fulmine ... ac radiata corona** fulmen, -inis (n.): lightning, thunderbolt; sceptrum, -i (n.): scepter, a royal staff; exuuiae, -arum (f. pl.): special attributes (of gods); Jupiter Optimus Maximus was the chief

et sceptro exuuiisque Iouis Optimi Maximi ac radiata corona, super laureatum currum bis senis equis candore eximio trahentibus. infans adhuc, ut scriptum apud C. Drusum extat, repositus uespere in cunas a nutricula loco plano, postera luce non comparuit diuque quaesitus tandem in altissima turri repertus est iacens contra solis exortum.

7. Cum primum fari coepisset in auito suburbano obstrepen-

---

    god of the Roman state, whose temple was on the Capitoline Hill; radiatus, -a, -um: furnished with rays, radiant; corona, -ae (f.): crown; the detailed description here and following likens the apparition of Augustus to a triumphant general and to the gods Jupiter and Apollo

laureatus, -a, -um adorned with laurel

currus, -us (m.) chariot

bis senis equis ... trahentibus abl. abs. (AG #419); seni, -ae, -a (pl. adj.): six; equus, -i (m.): horse; *candore eximio*: abl. of quality (AG #415); candor, -oris (m.): whiteness; eximius, -a, -um: outstanding, exceptional; traho, trahere, traxi, tractum: move by pulling

infans, -ntis (m./f.) infant, small child (who does not yet talk)

ut scriptum apud C. Drusum extat "as is found in the writings of Gaius Drusus," ut w/ indic. vb. introd. case or example; scriptum, -i (n.): writing, written record; apud: "in the writings of" (w/ acc.); Gaius Drusus' identity is uncertain

repositus ... loco plano tmp. ptc. phr. (AG #496); repono, reponere, reposui, repositum: put down, place, set in position (<re- + pono); uespera, -ae (f.): evening; *uespere* (locat.): "in the evening" (AG #427.3a); cunae, -arum (f. pl.): cradle; nutricula, -ae (f.): child's nurse, wet-nurse (dim. <nutrix, a form favored by Suet.); planus, -a, -um: flat, on the ground level; *loco plano*: abl. of place where w/out prep. (AG #429.1)

postera luce "the next morning," abl. of time when (AG #423.1); posterus, -a, -um: occurring later, future; lux, lucis (f.): light, daylight

compareo, comparere, comparui be seen, appear, show oneself (<con- + pareo)

quaero, quaerere, quaes(i)i (-siui), quaesitum seek, inquire about

altus, -a, -um tall, high (superl. = -issimus)

turris, -is (f.) tower

reperio, reperire, repperi, repertum find, discover (<re- + pario)

iacens contra solis exortum ptc. phr.; iaceo, iacere, iacui: recline, lie down; contra (prep. w/ acc.): facing; exortus, -us (m.): rising, appearance; the point of this elaborate tale is that the infant Augustus was drawn toward his true father, the sun god Apollo

94.7

cum primum fari coepisset circumst. cum cl. (AG #546); Suet. uses subjv. where indic. vb. might be expected to define time when (AG #545); for, fari, fatus sum: speak, talk; *fari*: compl. inf. (AG #456) w/ *coepisset*; coepi, coepisse, coeptum: begin (defect. vb., AG #205); note the careful chronological progression from ch. 94.6, when Augustus was *infans adhuc*

auitus, -a, -um of or belonging to a grandfather, ancestral

suburbanum, -i (n.) country house (n. of adj. used as subst., OLD 2)

obstrepentis forte ranas silere subst. cl. of purp. w/ acc. subj. + inf. (AG #563a) ff. *iussit*; obstrepo, obstrepere, obstrepui, obstrepitum: make a loud noise (<ob- + strepo); *obstrepentis*: acc. pl. pres. act. ptc. w/ *ranas*; rana, -ae (f.): frog; sileo, silere, silui: be silent

tis forte ranas silere iussit atque ex eo negantur ibi ranae coaxare. ad quartum lapidem Campanae uiae in nemore prandenti
ex inprouiso aquila panem ei e manu rapuit et, cum altissime
euolasset, rursus ex inprouiso leniter delapsa reddidit.

8. Q. Catulus post dedicatum Capitolium duabus continuis
noctibus somniauit, prima Iouem Optimum Maximum e praetextatis compluribus circum aram ludentibus unum secreuisse
atque in eius sinum signum rei p. quod manu gestaret reposuisse, at insequenti animaduertisse se in gremio Capitolini Iouis
eundem puerum, quem cum detrahi iussisset, prohibitum

---

ex eo "after this"
coaxo, coaxare croak (a Gk. wd. w/ Latinized spelling); *coaxare*: compl. inf. w/ *negantur* (AG #456); a similar story is told of Hercules, who silenced crickets
lapis, -idis (m.) stone, milestone
Campana uia the Campanian road, the road from Rome south to Capua; Campanus, -a, -um: Campanian; uia, -ae (f.): road
nemus, -oris (n.) forest, grove
prandenti ... ei (= Augusto) dat. of separ. w/ *rapuit* (AG #381); prandeo, prandere, prandi, pransum: eat lunch
ex inprouiso unexpectedly, suddenly
aquila, -ae (f.) eagle; the bird of Jupiter, the eagle was a sign of power
panis, -is (f.) bread
cum altissime euolasset circumst. cum cl. (AG #546); alte (adv.): high, to a great height (superl. = -issime); Suet. commonly uses superl. adv.; euolo (1): fly away (<ex- + uolo); *euolasset* = contr. form of euolauisset (AG #181)
leniter (adv.) gently, with a gentle movement
delabor, delabi, delapsus sum descend, drop down (<de- + labor); *delapsa* w/ *aquila*
reddidit [panem ei]

94.8

Q[uintus] Lutatius Catulus (*OCD* s.v. Lutatius Catulus (2), Quintus, 867–868), consul 78 BCE, who restored the Temple of Jupiter on the Capitoline Hill
post dedicatum Capitolium prep. phr. w/ ppp. (BG #437n2); Capitolium, -(i)i (n.): the Temple of Jupiter Optimus Maximus on the Capitoline Hill; the restored temple was rededicated in 69 BCE and Catulus probably died in 60 BCE, providing a terminus ante quem for the story
duabus continuis noctibus abl. of time when (AG #423.1)
somnio (1) dream
prima [nocte] abl. of time when (AG #423.1)
Iouem ... secreuisse atque ... reposuisse indir. disc. (AG #580) used to report the dream; *e praetextatis ... ludentibus*: ptc. phr.; praetextatus, -a, -um: wearing the toga praetexta (the toga worn by boys before manhood), (m. subst.) "boys"; circum (prep. w/ acc.): around; secerno, secernere, secreui, secretum: separate off (<se- + cerno); *eius* = "the boy's"; sinus, -us (m.): fold (of a toga) used as a pocket; signum, -i (n.): small statue; *signum rei p[ublicae]* was likely a statue of the goddess Roma; *quod manu gestaret*: "which he was carrying in his hand," relat. cl. w/ subjv. in indir. disc. (AG #580); *quod* (relat. pron.): anteced. *signum*; repono, reponere, reposui, repositum: put away (<re- + pono)
insequenti [nocte] abl. of time when (AG #423.1)
animaduertisse se [Catulum] **... prohibitum** [esse] **monitu dei** indir. disc. (AG #580) used to report the dream on the second night; gremium, -ii (n.): lap; *quem cum detrahi iussisset*: "when he had ordered him

monitu dei, tamquam is ad tutelam rei p. educaretur. ac die
proximo obuium sibi Augustum, cum incognitum alias haberet, non sine admiratione contuitus simillimum dixit puero
de quo somniasset. quidam prius somnium Catuli aliter
exponunt, quasi Iuppiter compluribus praetextatis tutorem a
se poscentibus unum ex eis demonstrasset ad quem omnia desideria sua referrent eiusque osculum delibatum digitis ad os
suum rettulisset.

9. M. Cicero C. Caesarem in Capitolium prosecutus somnium

  "to be removed," circumst. cum cl. (AG # 546) w/ subst. cl. of purp.; *quem:* relat. pron. as connective (AG #308f), acc. subj. w/ inf. (*detrahi*) in subst. cl. of purp. (AG #563a) ff. *iussisset;* detraho, detrahere, detraxi, detractum: remove (<de- + traho); prohibeo, prohibere, prohibui, prohibitum: prevent (<pro- + habeo); monitus, -us (m.): warning, command

tamquam is ... educaretur "that he was being raised," *tamquam* w/ subjv. to express a belief or rumor, not necessarily untrue (AG #524, BG #602n4); tutela, -ae (f.): protection, defence; *rei p[ublicae]*; educo (1): bring up, raise

die proximo abl. of time when (AG #423.1)

obuium sibi Augustum acc. obj. of *contuitus;* obuius, -a, -um: laying in the path of (w/ dat.)

cum ... haberet conces. cum cl. (AG #549), "although he didn't know him previously"; incognitus, -a, -um: unknown, not recognized; alias (adv.): at other times, previously

admiratio, -onis (f.) wonder, astonishment, admiration

contueor, contueri, contuitus sum look at, gaze on (<con- + tueor); Catulus is subj.

[Augustum] simillimum ... puero [esse] indir. disc. (AG #580) ff. *dixit*

de quo somniasset relat. cl. w/ subjv. in indir. disc. (AG #580); *somniasset* = contr. form of somniauisset

quidam ... exponunt Suet. sets out an alternative account of Catulus' first dream; prior, prius: earlier, first (compar. adj.); somnium, -(i)i (n.): dream; expono, exponere, exposui, expositum: set out, relate, describe (<ex- + pono)

quasi Iuppiter ... demonstrasset *quasi* w/ subjv. to express a belief or rumor (AG #524, BG #602n4); *compluribus praetextatis ... poscentibus*: abl. abs. (AG #419); tutor, -oris (m.): guardian; posco, poscere, poposci: ask for, demand; demonstro (1): point to (<de- + monstro); *demonstrasset* = contr. form of demonstrauisset (AG #181); this alternate version focuses on the selection of Augustus from among the group of boys who were themselves asking Jupiter for a guardian (of the state)

ad quem ... referrent relat. cl. of purp. (AG #531.2), "to whom they might bring all of their requests"; desiderium, -(i)i (n.): desire, expressed request

eiusque osculum ... rettulisset continuation of *quasi* cl. w/ subjv.; *eius osculum delibatum digitis*: "his [the boy Augustus'] lips touched by his (Jupiter's) fingers"; osculum, -i (n.): mouth, lips; delibo (1): touch lightly (<de- + libo); digitus, -i (m.): finger; os, oris (n.): mouth; Jupiter showed his approval of the young Augustus by touching the boy's lips, then bringing his fingers up to his own mouth as if to accept the kiss

94.9

M. Cicero ... prosecutus tmp. ptc. phr. (AG #496); M. Tullius Cicero was consul in 63 BCE (*OCD* s.v. Tullius Cicero (1), Marcus, 1514–1519); *C[aium] Caesarem* = Gaius Julius Caesar (*OCD* s.v. Iulius Caesar (2), Gaius, 757–760), Augustus' great-uncle and (later) adoptive father; the report of Cicero's dream adds special weight to the prophecies as Cicero was a noted republican; the reported encounter must have occurred before October of 48 BCE (s. ch. 94.10)

somnium, -(i)i (n.) a dream

pristinae noctis familiaribus forte narrabat, puerum facie liberali demissum e caelo catena aurea ad fores Capitoli constitisse
eique Iouem flagellum tradidisse. deinde repente Augusto uiso,
quem ignotum plerisque adhuc auunculus Caesar ad sacrificandum acciuerat, affirmauit ipsum esse cuius imago secundum
quietem sibi obuersata sit.

    10. Sumenti uirilem togam tunica lati claui resuta ex utraque
parte ad pedes decidit. fuerunt qui interpretarentur non aliud
significare quam ut is ordo cuius insigne id esset quandoque ei
subiceretur.

---

pristinus, -a, -um previous
familiaris, -e closely associated by friendship, intimate, (subst.) close friend
narro (1) relate, tell, talk about
puerum ... constitisse Cicero's dream is reported in indir. disc. (AG #580); *facie liberali*: abl. of quality
    (AG #415); facies, -ei (f.): physical appearance, looks; liberalis, -e: noble, befitting a free man; demitto,
    demittere, demisi, demissum: send down, lower (<de- + mitto); catena, -ae (f.): chain; *catena aurea*: abl.;
    foris, -is (f.): door; consto, constare, constiti: stand (<con- + sto)
eique Iouem ... tradidisse indir. disc. continues with *Iouem* as acc. subj.; flagellum, -i (n.): whip, lash
Augusto uiso tmp. abl. abs. (AG #420.1)
quem (relat. pron.) anteced. *Augusto*, obj. of *acciuerat*
ignotum plerisque adhuc "as yet unknown to most people"; ignotus, -a, -um: unfamiliar, unknown
auunculus, -i (m.) uncle (great-uncle)
sacrifico (1) perform a sacrifice; *ad sacrificandum*: ger. w/ ad to show purp. (AG #506)
accio, accire, acciui (-ii), accitum send for, invite (<ad- + ci(e)o)
affirmo (1) affirm, confirm (<ad- + firmo)
ipsum (= Augustum) **esse** "that it was Augustus," indir. disc. (AG #580) ff. *affirmauit*
cuius imago ... obuersata sit relat. cl. in indir. disc. w/ subjv. (AG #580); *cuius*: anteced. *ipsum* (= Augustum);
    imago, -inis (f.): image, likeness; *secundum quietem*: "in a dream"; secundum (prep. + acc.); quies, -ietis
    (f.): calm, the rest of sleep; *sibi* = Ciceroni, dat. of agent (AG #375); obseruo (1): observe (<ob- + seruo)

94.10

sumenti [Augusto] **uirilem togam** tmp. ptc. phr. (AG #496); *sumenti*: dat. of separ. w/ *decidit* (AG #381);
    the event dates to October of 48 BCE
tunica ... resuta ex utraque parte tmp. ptc. phr. (AG #496); *tunica*: subj.; tunica, -ae (f.): tunic, garment
    worn under a toga; *lati claui*: "with a broad purple stripe" (a mark of senatorial rank), gen. of quality
    (AG #345); latus, -a, -um: broad; clauus, -i (m.): purple stripe; resuo, resuere, resui, resutum: undo the
    stitching of (an unusual vb. <re- + suo found only here in Latin literature); this story is anachronistic, as
    the children of senators were only granted the right to wear the latus clauus later in the Augustan period
decido, decidere, decidi fall down, drop down (<de- + cado)
fuerunt qui interpretarentur "there were those who interpreted," relat. cl. of char. after gener. expression
    (AG #535a); interpretor (1): explain, interpret, understand
non aliud significare "that it indicated nothing other," indir. disc. w/ subj. acc. omitted (AG #581n1) ff.
    interpretarentur; significo (1): indicate
quam ut is ordo ... subiceretur compar. cl. of result (AG #535c); *is ordo*: i.e., the senate; *cuius insigne*
    id esset: relat. cl. w/ subjv. by attraction (AG #593); insigne, -is (n.): emblem or symbol; quandoque
    (adv.): at some time, some day; *ei* = Augusto

11. Apud Mundam Diuus Iulius castris locum capiens, cum siluam caederet, arborem palmae repertam conseruari ut omen uictoriae iussit. ex ea continuo enata suboles adeo in paucis diebus adoleuit ut non aequiperaret modo matricem uerum et obtegeret frequentareturque columbarum nidis, quamuis id auium genus duram et asperam frondem maxime uitet. illo et praecipue ostento motum Caesarem ferunt ne quem alium sibi succedere quam sororis nepotem uellet.

12. In secessu Apolloniae Theogenis mathematici pergulam

94.11
Munda, -ae (f.) Munda, a town in Hispania Baetica where Julius Caesar won a victory in 45 BCE (s. ch. 8.1)

Diuus Iulius Suet. here refers to Julius Caesar by the divine title he assumed after his death, stressing that the omen was received by a god (s. ch. 2.1 for use of Diuus Julius; ch. 8, 10, etc. for Caesar)

cum siluam caederet circumst. cum cl. (AG #546); silua, -ae (f.): forest, wood; caedo, caedere, cecidi, caesum: cut down

arborem ... conseruari subst. cl. of purp. w/ acc. subj. + inf. (AG #563a) ff. *iussit*; arbor, -oris (f.): tree (w/ type in gen., AG #342); palma, -ae (f.): palm (the palm was a sign of victory); reperio, reperire, repperi, repertum: find, discover (<re- + pario): conseruo (1): preserve, keep unharmed (<con- + seruo)

ut omen uictoriae "as an omen of victory"

ex ea [palma] **continuo enata suboles** ptc. phr., subj. of *adoleuit*; continuo (adv.): without delay, immediately; enascor, enasci, enatus sum: sprout, grow forth from (<ex- + nascor); suboles, -is (f.): offspring

in paucis diebus in w/ abl. of time for emphatic precision (AG #424a)

adolesco, adolescere, adoleui (-ui), adultum grow up, mature

ut ... aequiperaret ... obtegeret frequentareturque columbarum nidis result cl. (AG #537); aequipero (1): become equal with (w/ acc.); matrix, -icis (f.): parent tree; obtego, obtegere, obtexi, obtectum: cover, hide from view (<ob- + tego); columba, -ae (f.): dove; nidus, -i (m.): nest

quamuis id auium genus ... uitet conces. cl. w/ subjv. (AG #527); auis, -is (f.): bird; durus, -a, -um: hard; asper, -era, -erum: rough; frons, -ndis (f.): foliage; uito (1): avoid

illo ... motum [esse] **Caesarem** indir. disc. (AG #580) ff. *ferunt*; moueo, mouere, moui, motum: move, stir up

ne ... uellet negat. purp. cl. (AG #531.1); *quem alium ... succedere*: subst. cl. of purp. w/ acc. + inf. ff. *uellet* (AG #563b.2); *quem* = aliquem; succedo, succedere, successi, successum: succeed, be successor to (w/ dat.) (<sub- + cedo); this story of the portent received by Caesar while in Spain echoes Suet.'s earlier statement (ch. 8.1) that Augustus won his great-uncle's favor when he joined him on his Spanish campaign

94.12
secessus, -us (m.) withdrawal into seclusion, retirement (from Rome)

Apollonia, -ae (f.) Apollonia, city on the southern Illyrian coast across the Adriatic from Italy; *Apolloniae*: locat. (AG #427.3); the event dates to 44 BCE (s. ch. 8.2)

Theogenes, -is Theogenes, otherwise unknown (for Gk. decl., AG #82)

mathematicus, -i (m.) astrologer

pergula, -ae (f.) attachment to a building used for commercial purposes, study, studio

comite Agrippa ascenderat. cum Agrippae, qui prior consulebat,
magna et paene incredibilia praedicerentur, reticere ipse geni-
turam suam nec uelle edere perseuerabat metu ac pudore ne
minor inueniretur. qua tamen post multas adhortationes uix et
cunctanter edita exiliuit Theogenes adorauitque eum. tantam
mox fiduciam fati Augustus habuit ut thema suum uulgauerit
nummumque argenteum nota sideris Capricorni, quo natus
est, percusserit.

95 Post necem Caesaris reuerso ab Apollonia et ingrediente eo

---

comite Agrippa abl. abs. (AG #419a); M. Vipsanius Agrippa (*OCD* 1554–1555) was the lifelong friend of Augustus

ascendo, ascendere, ascendi, ascensum go up to, ascend to (<ad- + scando)

cum . . . magna et paene incredibilia praedicerentur circumst. cum cl. (AG #546); prior, prius: earlier, first; incredibilis, -e: incredible, unbelievable; *incredibilia*: n. pl. as subst., "unbelievable things"; praedico, praedicere, praedixi, praedictum: predict, prophesy (<prae- + dico)

reticeo, reticere, reticui refrain from speaking, keep silent (<re- + taceo); *reticere*: compl. inf. w/ *perseuerabat* (AG #456)

ipse (= Augustus)

genitura, -ae (f.) hour of birth, a technical term in astrology (<gigno)

uelle edere compl. inf. (AG #456)

perseuero (1) persist, continue resolutely (<per- + seuero)

metu ac pudore abl. of cause (AG #404b); pudor, -oris (m.): feeling of shame

ne minor inueniretur negat. purp. cl. (AG #531), "lest he be found to be inferior"; inuenio, inuenire, inueni, inuentum: find, discover (<in- + uenio)

qua [genitura] . . . edita tmp. abl. abs. (AG #420.1); adhortatio, -onis (f.): appeal, exhortation; cunctanter (adv.): with delay, with hesitation

exilio, exilire, exilui leap up, jump up (<ex- + salio)

adoro (1) do homage or obeisance to, treat with religious reverence (<ad- + oro); this final sign in the chapter is the greatest as Theogenes' actions indicate that he considered Augustus to be a god

fiducia, -ae (f.) trust, faith in (w/ gen.)

fatum, -i (n.) fate, destiny

ut . . . uulgauerit . . . percusserit result cl. w/ pf. subjv. (AG #485c, #537); thema, -atis (n.): horoscope (a Gk. wd. w/ Latinized spelling); uulgo (1): make widely known, spread widely; argenteus, -a, -um: silver; nota, -ae (f.): mark, imprint; *nota*: abl. of quality (AG #415); sidus, -eris (n.): star; Capricornus, -i (m.): Capricorn; *quo natus est*: "under which he was born"; percutio, percutere, percussi, percussum: strike, stamp (a coin) (<per- + quatio); numerous coin types bearing the image of Capricorn survive; the calculation by which Augustus' birth date falls under Capricorn remains obscure

The next chapter continues in chronological order the discussion of signs that foretold Augustus' greatness, here recounting signs after Caesar's death and at the start of Augustus' first consulship.

95

post necem Caesaris nex, necis (f.): murder; the date is 44 BCE

reuerso . . . et ingrediente eo urbem tmp. abl. abs. (AG #420.1); reuertor, reuerti, reuersus sum: return, come back (<re- + uertor); *ab Apollonia*: "from the vicinity of Apollonia" (AG #428a)

urbem repente liquido ac puro sereno circulus ad speciem
caelestis arcus orbem solis ambiit ac subinde Iuliae Caesaris
filiae monimentum fulmine ictum est. primo autem consulatu
et augurium capienti duodecim se uultures ut Romulo
ostenderunt et immolanti omnium uictimarum iocinera replicata intrinsecus ab ima fibra paruerunt, nemine peritorum
aliter coiectante quam laeta per haec et magna portendi.

---

liquido ac puro sereno conces. abl. abs. w/out ptc. (AG #419a, 420.3); liquidus, -a, -um: clear, unclouded; purus, -a, -um: free from mist or clouds, clear; serenum, -i (n.): clear sky, blue sky
circulus, -i (m.) circle, ring
ad speciem caelestis arcus "in the likeness of a rainbow"; species, -ei (f): appearance; caelestis, -e: celestial, heavenly; arcus, -us (m.): bow, rainbow
orbis, -is (m.) circular object, orb
ambio, ambire, ambiui (-ii), ambitum surround, encircle (<ambi- + eo)
subinde (adv.) immediately, shortly afterward
Iulia Julia, the daughter of Julius Caesar (OCD s.v. Iulia (2), 753), who had died in 54 BCE
monimentum, -i (n.) tomb, sepulchral monument; Julia's tomb was in the Campus Martius
fulmen, -inis (n.) lightning, thunderbolt
icio, icere, ici, ictum strike; the lightning strike indicated Jupiter's support for a member of Caesar's family
primo ... consulatu abl. of time when (AG #423.1)
augurium capienti [Augusto] augurium, -(i)i (n.): taking of auguries, augury; *capienti*: dat. indir. obj. of *ostenderunt*
duodecim (indecl. adj.) twelve
uultur, -uris (m.) vulture
ut Romulo "just as to Romulus"; when founding Rome, twelve vultures had appeared to Romulus (cf. Livy 1.7.1)
immolanti [Augusto] dat. indir. obj. of *paruerunt*; immolo (1): offer in sacrifice
uictima, -ae (f.) animal offered in sacrifice
iocinera replicata ... ab ima fibra ptc. phr. reflecting technical language of sacrifice, subj. w/ *paruerunt*; iocer, -ineris (n.): liver; replico (1): turn back on itself, fold back, bend back (<re- + plico); intrinsecus (adv.): inward, toward the inside; imus, -a, -um: lowest, bottommost; fibra, -ae (f.): lobe (of the liver); the livers of sacrificial victims might be studied by haruspices, specially trained Etruscan priests
pareo, parere, parui, paritum be visible, be seen
nemine peritorum aliter coiectante quam abl. abs. (AG #419) w/ compar., "with none of the experts interpreting it otherwise than"; nemo, neminis (m.): nobody, no one; Suet. uses *nemine* in place of the more common nullo (AG #314a); peritus, -a, -um: having knowledge, (m. subst.) "an expert"; coicio, coicere, coieci, coiectum: interpret (OLD 14) (<con- + iacio)
laeta ... et magna portendi indir. disc. (AG #580) ff. *coiectante*; laetus, -a, -um: happy; *laeta*: n. pl. subst., "happy things"; *per haec*: "through these [inward-curved livers]"; portendo, portendere, portendi, portentum: indicate (a future event), portend (<por- + tendo); *portendi*: pres. pass. inf.

96 Quin et bellorum omnium euentus ante praesensit. contractis
ad Bononiam triumuirorum copiis aquila tentorio eius super-
sedens duos coruos hinc et inde infestantis afflixit et ad terram
dedit, notante omni exercitu futuram quandoque inter collegas
discordiam talem qualis secuta est atque exitum praesagiente.
<aduenienti> Philippos Thessalus quidam de futura uictoria
nuntiauit auctore Diuo Caesare, cuius sibi species itinere

The final chapter recounting signs of Augustus' greatness links back to the discussion of wars, the first of the topics covered by Suetonius (ch. 9). The use of ring composition here signals that the end of the biography is approaching.

96.1
quin (adv.) indeed, in fact

euentus, -us (m.) outcome

ante praesensit PLEONASM (AG #640); ante (adv.): beforehand, in advance; praesentio, praesentire, praesensi, praesensum: apprehend beforehand, know in advance (<prae- + sentio); Augustus is the unexpressed subj.

contractis ... copiis tmp. abl. abs. (AG #420.1); *ad Bononiam*: "near Bononia" (AG #428d); Bononia, -ae (f.): Bononia (modern Bologna); triumuir, -i (m.): triumvir, (pl.) the triumvirs Augustus, Antony, and Lepidus; the occasion was the reconciliation of Augustus with Antony and Lepidus in late 43 BCE (s. ch. 13.1)

aquila, -ae (f.) eagle

tentorium, -ii (n.) tent

supersedeo, supersedere, supersedi, supersessum sit on top of (w/ dat.) (<super- + sedeo)

duos coruos ... infestantis ptc. phr., obj. of *afflixit* and *dedit*; coruus, -i (m.): raven; infesto (1): harass; the eagle is the implied obj. of *infestantis*

affligo, affligere, afflixi, afflictum strike down, crush (<ad- + fligo)

notante omni exercitu ... atque exitum praesagiente abl. abs. (AG #419) w/ two ptc.; *futuram ... discordiam*: ptc. phr., obj. of *notante*; quandoque (adv.): at some time, some day; discordia, -ae (f.): discord, a disagreement; *talem qualis secuta est*: "such discord as actually followed"; talis, -e: such; qualis, -e (relat.): of which sort, such as; exitus, -us (m.): outcome; praesagio, praesagire, praesagiui: have a presentiment of, sense in advance; the army correctly interpreted the sign: the eagle (Augustus), at first harassed by the two crows (Antony and Lepidus), would ultimately prevail

aduenienti [Augusto] **Philippos** ptc. phr., dat. indir. obj. ff. *nuntiauit*; aduenio, aduenire, adueni, aduentum: arrive at, reach (w/ acc.) (<ad- + uenio); Philippi, -orum (m. pl.): Philippi, town in eastern Macedonia that was site of the battle of 42 BCE (s. ch. 13)

Thessalus, -a, -um Thessalian, of Thessaly, (m. subst.) "a Thessalian man"

futurus, -a, -um future, coming, imminent

nuntio (1) announce

auctore Diuo Caesare abl. abs. w/out ptc. (AG #419a)

cuius ... species ... occurrisset relat. cl. w/ subjv. expressing a reason (AG #592.3); species, -ei (f.): phantom, supernatural apparition (*OLD* 9); *itinere auio*: abl. of place where w/out prep. (AG #429); auius, -a, -um: remote, unfrequented; occurro, occurrere, occurri, occursum: meet, encounter (w/ dat.)

auio occurrisset. **2.** circa Perusiam sacrificio non litante, cum
augeri hostias imperasset ac subita eruptione hostes omnem rei
diuinae apparatum abstulissent, constitit inter haruspices quae
periculosa et aduersa sacrificanti denuntiata essent cuncta in
ipsos recasura qui exta haberent, neque aliter euenit. pridie
quam Siciliensem pugnam classe committeret, deambulanti in
litore piscis e mari exiliuit et ad pedes iacuit. apud Actium
descendenti in aciem asellus cum asinario occurrit: homini

(<ob- + curro); the appearance of Divus Julius at this time has special significance as Caesar had just recently been deified in Rome and the battle at Philippi was fought against his assassins

96.2
circa Perusiam sacrificio non litante abl. abs. (AG #419); Perusia, -ae (f.): Perusia (modern Perugia); sacrificium, -(i)i (n.): sacrifice; lito (1): give favorable omens; s. ch. 14 for the war at Perusia against L. Antonius

cum ... imperasset ac ... hostes ... abstulissent circumst. cum cl. (AG #546); *augeri hostias*: subst. cl. of purp. (AG #563a) ff. *imperasset*; hostia, -ae (f.): sacrificial animal; impero (1): command, give orders; *imperasset* = contr. form of imperauisset (AG #181); subitus, -a, -um: sudden; eruptio, -onis (f.): sudden rush of troops; *rei diuinae* = sacrificii (cf. ch. 1.1); apparatus, -us (m.): equipment, apparatus; aufero, auferre, abstuli, ablatum: take away (<ab- + fero)

consto, constare, constiti stand, (impers.) it is agreed (<con- + sto)

haruspex, -icis (m.) diviner, an Etruscan soothsayer who interprets the entrails of sacrificial victims

quae ... denuntiata essent "the dangerous and unfavorable things which had been announced," relat. cl. w/ subjv. in indir. disc. (AG #580) ff. *constitit*; periculosus, -a, -um: dangerous; aduersus, -a, -um: unfavorable, hostile; sacrifico (1): perform a sacrifice; *sacrificanti*: dat. subst., "to the one sacrificing"; denuntio (1): announce (by prophecy) (<de- + nuntio)

cuncta ... recasura [esse] indir. disc. (AG #580) ff. *constitit*; cunctus, -a, -um: all; recido, recidere, rec(c)idi, recasum: fall back on, rebound (<re- + cado)

qui exta haberent relat. cl. w/ subjv. in indir. disc. (AG #580); qui: anteced. *ipsos*; exta, -orum (n. pl.): organs of the upper torso of an animal, heart, lungs, and liver (of a sacrificial animal)

euenio, euenire, eueni, euentum turn out, happen (<ex- + uenio); *euenit*: impers. (s. ch. 15)

pridie quam ... committeret anticipatory cl. implying expectancy (AG #551b); pridie (adv.): on the day before (w/ *quam*); Siciliensis, -e: Sicilian; pugna, -ae (f.): fight, battle; *classe*: "with his fleet"; committo, committere, commisi, commissum: join, engage in (<con- + mitto); the campaign in Sicily against Sextus Pompey dates to 36 BCE (s. ch. 16)

deambulanti [Augusto] **in litore** tmp. ptc. phr. (AG #496); deambulo (1): go for a walk (<de- + ambulo); *deambulanti*: dat. indir. obj.; litus, -oris (n.): seashore, coast

piscis ... exiliuit et ... iacuit piscis, -is (m.): fish; mare, -is (n.): sea; exilio, exilire, exilui: leap up, jump up (<ex- + salio); iaceo, iacere, iacui: lie down, be deposited; Pliny (*NH* 9.55) offers an expanded account of the same event, spelling out the meaning—that Sextus Pompey, who controlled the seas, would soon be at Augustus' feet

apud Actium "at Actium"; the battle dates to 31 BCE (s. ch. 17.2)

descendenti [Augusto] **in aciem** tmp. ptc. phr. (AG #496); descendo, descendere, descendi, descensum: descend, come down (<de- + scando); *descendenti*: dat. indir. obj. w/ *occurrit*; acies, -ei (f.): battle line, battle

asellus, -i (m.) ass, donkey (dim. <asinus)

asinarius, -(i)i (m.) donkey-driver

homini ... bestiae ... erat nomen *homini ... bestiae*: dat. of poss. (AG #373a); Eutychus: a Gk. name, "Lucky"; bestia, -ae (f.): animal, beast; Nicon: a Gk. name, "Victor"

Eutychus, bestiae Nicon erat nomen, utriusque simulacrum aeneum uictor posuit in templo in quod castrorum suorum locum uertit.

97 Mors quoque eius, de qua dehinc dicam, diuinitasque post mortem euidentissimis ostentis praecognita est. cum lustrum in campo Martio magna populi frequentia conderet, aquila eum saepius circumuolauit transgressaque in uicinam aedem super nomen Agrippae ad primam litteram sedit. quo animaduerso uota quae in proximum lustrum suscipi mos est collegam suum

---

simulacrum, -i (n.) image, statue
aeneus, -a, -um bronze, made of bronze
uictor, -oris (m.) victor; *uictor*: "as victor," pred. appos. (AG #282)
in quod ... locum uertit "into which he transformed ..."; *quod* (relat. pron.): anteced. *templo*; uerto, uertere, uerti, uersum: turn, transform; on the founding of the city of Nicopolis at Actium, s. ch. 18.2; the statues and the tale of their origin are recorded in several other sources

Death and burial (*mors eius*). This section marks a transition as Suetonius first sets out signs foretelling Augustus' death and posthumous deification before concluding the biography with a narrative account of Augustus' final days and death.

97.1
qua (relat. pron.) anteced. *mors*
dehinc (adv.) after this, then
diuinitas, -atis (f.) divinity; Augustus was not formally consecrated as a god until after his death, but the signs Suet. recounts indicate that his deification was preordained
evidens, -ntis clear, obvious (superl. = -ntissimus)
praecognosco, praecognoscere, praecognoui, praecognitum know beforehand, have foreknowledge of (<prae- + cognosco)
cum lustrum ... conderet circumst. cum cl. (AG #546), "when he was concluding the census"; lustrum, -i (n.): lustrum, a purification ceremony performed at the conclusion of the census; Campus Martius: the "Field of Mars" in Rome; frequentia, -ae (f.): crowd; Suet. uses the technical language to mark the conclusion of the census; the date is 14 CE
aquila, -ae (f.) eagle
circumuolo (1) fly around (<circum- + uolo)
transgressaque in uicinam aedem tmp. ptc. phr. (AG #496); transgredior, transgredi, transgressus sum: cross over, move across (<trans- + gradior); uicinus, -a, -um: neighboring; *aedem* (sg.): temple, shrine
super nomen Agrippae the eagle perched above a shrine constructed by Agrippa that bore his name on an inscription, likely Agrippa's Pantheon; by perching on the letter "A," the eagle singled out Augustus
quo animaduerso abl. abs.; *quo*: "this thing," relat. pron. as connective (AG #308f), referring to the actions of the eagle; Augustus recognized this as a sign of his impending death
uota ... collegam suum Tiberium nuncupare subst. cl. of purp. w/ subj. acc. + inf. (AG #563a) ff. *iussit*; uotum, -i (n.): vow; *uota*: acc. pl. obj. of *nuncupare*; *quae ... suscipi mos est*: "which it is customary to take up"; *in proximum lustrum*: "for the next census"; nuncupo (1): declare, solemnly pronounce; Tiberius had been appointed as Augustus' colleague for carrying out the census (s. ch. 27.5)

Tiberium nuncupare iussit, nam se, quamquam conscriptis paratisque iam tabulis, negauit suscepturum quae non esset soluturus.   2. sub idem tempus ictu fulminis ex inscriptione statuae eius prima nominis littera effluxit. responsum est centum solos dies posthac uicturum, quem numerum C littera notaret, futurumque ut inter deos referretur, quod aesar, id est reliqua pars e Caesaris nomine, Etrusca lingua deus uocaretur.   3. Tiberium igitur in Illyricum dimissurus et Beneuentum usque prosecuturus, cum interpellatores aliis atque aliis causis

---

se ... suscepturum [esse] indir. disc. (AG #580) ff. *negauit*; *quamquam conscriptis ... tabulis*: conces. abl. abs. (AG #420.3); conscribo, conscribere, conscripsi, conscriptum: write down (<con- + scribo); paro (1): prepare; written tablets contained the vows made on behalf of Rome

quae non esset soluturus relat. cl. w/ subjv. in indir. disc. (AG #580); *quae*: anteced. *uota*; soluo, soluere, solui, solutum: discharge, fulfill (a vow); *soluturus esset*: 1st (act.) periphr. (AG #194); Augustus would not make vows that he knew he would not live to honor

97.2

sub idem tempus "at about the same time"; this incident should be dated to May 11, 14 CE

ictu fulminis "by a stroke of lightning"; ictus, -us (m.): blow, stroke; fulmen, -inis (n.): lightning, thunderbolt

inscriptio, -onis (f.) inscription; Dio (56.29.4) reports that the statue was on the Capitoline Hill

effluo, effluere, effluxi melt away (<ex- + fluo); *prima littera* is subj. of *effluxit*

responsum est (impers.) "a response was given"; Suet. uses religious terminology here, indicating that the Etruscan priests, the haruspices, were consulted about the matter and formally reported their findings

centum solos dies posthac uicturum [esse] indir. disc. ff. *responsum est* (AG #582a) w/ Augustus as implied acc. subj.; *centum solos dies*: acc. of extent of time (AG #423.2), centum (indecl. adj.): a hundred; uiuo, uiuere, uixi, uictum: live

quem numerum C littera notaret relat. cl. in indir. disc. w/ subjv. (AG #580); for Roman numerals, s. AG #133; the "C" had melted away from the name CAESAR

futurumque [esse] **ut inter deos referretur** "and he was going to be numbered among the gods"; continuation of indir. disc. ff. *responsum est* (AG #582a) w/ a subst. cl. of result (AG #569a)

quod aesar ... deus uocaretur "because a god is called 'aesar' "; causal cl. w/ subjv. relying on the authority of another pers. (AG #540); *aesar*: pred. nom. (AG #283); *Caesaris*: appos. gen. (AG #343d); Etruscus, -a, -um: Etruscan; lingua, -ae (f.): tongue, language; "aisar" is the pl. form of "ais" (god) in Etruscan

97.3

Tiberium ... dimissurus et ... prosecuturus tmp. ptc. phr. (AG #496), Augustus is subj.; Illyricum, -i (n.): territory of the Illyrians, east of the Adriatic Sea; Beneuentum, -i (n.): city in Samnium (modern Benevento); *Beneuentum*: acc. of place to which w/out prep. (AG #427.2)

cum interpellatores ... detinerent circumst. cum cl. (AG #546); interpellator, -oris (m.): petitioner (vb. subst. <interpello); *aliis atque aliis causis*: "with more and more cases"; *in iure dicendo*: "in giving legal judgments"; detineo, detinere, detinui, detentum: detain, keep from going (<de- + teneo); Augustus is understood as obj.

in iure dicendo detinerent, exclamauit—quod et ipsum mox inter omina relatum est—non si omina morarentur amplius se posthac Romae futurum. atque itinere incohato Asturam perrexit et inde praeter consuetudinem de nocte ad occasionem aurae euectus causam ualitudinis contraxit ex profluuio alui.

98 Tunc Campaniae ora proximisque insulis circuitis Caprearum quoque secessui quadriduum impendit remississimo ad otium et ad omnem comitatem animo. **2.** forte Puteolanum sinum

---

exclamo (1) cry out, exclaim (<ex- + clamo)
quod et ipsum ... relatum est "a thing which itself was soon recorded among the omens," an explanatory relat. cl. that builds suspense for Augustus' wd. of exclamation
si omina morarentur prot. of fut. condit. in indir. disc. (AG #589.3) ff. *exclamauit*; moror (1): delay
non ... amplius se ... futurum [esse] apod. in indir. disc. (AG #580) ff. *exclamauit*; *Romae*: locat. (AG #427.3); these prophetic wd. of Augustus mark a transition in the narrative as Suet. shifts from a discussion of omens to an account of Augustus' final days
itinere incohato abl. abs. (AG #419); incoho (1): start
Astura, -ae (f.) Astura, a small island off the coast of Latium; *Asturam*: acc. of place to which w/out prep. (AG #427.2)
pergo, pergere, perrexi, perrectum proceed, make one's way (<per- + rego)
praeter consuetudinem "contrary to custom"; consuetudo, -inis (f.): habit, custom
de nocte ... euectus causal ptc. phr. (AG #496); *de nocte*: "by night"; *ad occasionem aurae*: "at the opportunity of a wind," ad w/ an occurrence indicating time (*OLD* 21); occasio, -onis (f.): opportunity, circumstance; aura, -ae (f.): wind, breeze; eueho, euehere, euexi, euectum: (pass.) be carried, sail (<ex- + ueho)
ex "starting from" (*OLD* 6)
profluuium, -(i)i (n.) discharge, looseness
aluus, -i (f.) stomach, bowels

98.1
Campaniae ora proximisque insulis circuitis tmp. abl. abs. (AG #420.1); Campania, -ae (f.): Campania (a region of Italy south of Latium); ora, -ae (f.): coast; *ora*: abl.; circueo, circuire, circuii, circuitum: go around, skirt (<circum- + eo)
Caprearum secessui "for rest on Capri"; Capreae, -arum (f. pl.): Capri, an island off the coast of Campania; *Caprearum*: appos. gen. (AG #343d); secessus, -us (m.): withdrawal into privacy, private retreat; Capri and other areas on the Campanian coast were favorite retreats for Augustus (s. ch. 72.2-3, 92.2)
quadriduum, -i (n.) period of four days
impendo, impendere, impendi, impensum spend, devote (w/ acc. dir. obj. + dat. indir. obj., AG #370) (<in- + pendo)
remississimo ... animo abl. abs. w/out ptc. (AG #419a); remissus, -a, -um: relaxed (superl. = -issimus) (<ppp. of remitto, AG #494a); otium, -(i)i (n.): leisure; comitas, -atis (f.): friendliness, social interaction

98.2
Puteolanum sinum praeteruehenti tmp. ptc. phr. (AG #496); Puteolanus, -a, -um: of Puteoli (a coastal town near Naples); sinus, -us (m.): bay, recess in the coastline: praeterueho, praeteruehere, praeteruexi, praeteruectum: pass by, travel past (<praeter- + ueho); *praeteruehenti* [*Augusto*]: dat. indir. obj. w/ *congesserant*

praeteruehenti uectores nautaeque de naue Alexandrina, quae
tantum quod appulerat, candidati coronatique et tura libantes
fausta omina et eximias laudes congesserant, per illum se
uiuere, per illum nauigare, libertate atque fortunis per illum
frui. qua re admodum exhilaratus quadragenos aureos comitibus diuisit iusque iurandum et cautionem exegit a singulis non
alio datam summam quam in emptionem Alexandrinarum
mercium absumpturos.   3.   sed et ceteros continuos dies inter
uaria munuscula togas insuper ac pallia distribuit, lege proposita ut Romani Graeco, Graeci Romano habitu et sermone ute-

---

uector, -oris (m.) passenger (on a ship) (vb. subst. <ueho)
nauta, -ae (m.) sailor
nauis, -is (f.) ship
Alexandrinus, -a, -um Alexandrian, from Alexandria in Egypt
quae ... appulerat relat. cl.; *quae* (relat. pron.): anteced. *naue*; tantum quod: "only just"; appello, appellere,
    appuli, appulsum: put in (to port) (<ad- + pello)
candidati ... libantes nom. pl. w/ *uectores nautaeque*; candidatus, -a, -um: dressed in white; coronatus, -a, -
    um: adorned with wreaths, garlanded; tus, turis (n.): incense, frankincense; libo (1): make an offering of
fausta omina et eximias laudes acc. obj. of *congesserant*; faustus, -a, -um: fortunate, bringing good fortune;
    eximius, -a, -um: outstanding, exceptional; laus, laudis (f.): praise, commendation
congero, congerere, congessi, congestum heap up (<con- + gero)
per illum se uiuere ... nauigare ... frui indir. disc. (AG #580) is used to report the wd. of praise;
    illum = Augustum; uiuo, uiuere, uixi, uictum: live, be alive; nauigo (1): sail; fortuna, -ae (f.): good
    fortune; fruor, frui, fructus sum: enjoy (+ abl.); the praise of the Alexandrians reflects the worship of
    Augustus in Egypt, where the living ruler was a god
qua re "by this"; *qua*: relat. pron. as connective (AG #308f)
admodum (adv.) to a great extent, very much
exhilaro (1) cheer, gladden (<ex- + hilaro)
quadrageni, -ae, -a (pl. adj.) forty each
aureus, -i (m.) gold coin
ius iurandum oath
cautio, -onis (f.) written pledge
non alio datam summam ... absumpturos [esse] indir. disc. (AG #580a) records the term of the pledge; alio
    (adv.): for another purpose (intro. compar. w/ *quam*); emptio, -onis (f.): purchasing; merx, -cis (f.): commodity,
    (pl.) goods, merchandise; absumo, absumere, absumpsi, absumptum: spend (money) (<ab- + sumo)

98.3
ceteros continuos dies acc. of extent of time (AG #423.2)
munusculum, -i (n.) small gift, favor
insuper (adv.) in addition, as well
pallium, -ii (n.) pallium, a draped outer garment (the Gk. himation)
distribuo, distribuere, distribui, distributum divide up, distribute (<dis- + tribuo)
lege proposita abl. abs. (AG #419)
ut Romani ... uterentur subst. cl. of purp. (AG #563d); habitus, -us (m.): style of dress; the festive atmosphere
    was marked by the change of traditional clothing that marked one as Gk. or Roman; Capri and the city of
    Naples, to which it had belonged until 29 BCE, had substantial Gk. populations (s. ch. 92.2)

rentur. spectauit assidue exercentes ephebos, quorum aliqua
adhuc copia ex uetere instituto Capreis erat. isdem etiam epulum
in conspectu suo praebuit permissa, immo exacta iocandi
licentia diripiendique pomorum et obsoniorum rerumque
<uariarum> missilia. nullo denique genere hilaritatis abstinuit.

4. Vicinam Capreis insulam Apragopolim appellabat a desidia
secedentium illuc e comitatu suo. sed ex dilectis unum Masgaban
nomine quasi conditorem insulae κτίστην uocare consueuerat.
huius Masgabae ante annum defuncti tumulum cum e triclinio

---

ephebus, -i (m.) ephebe, a Gk. adolescent; the training of ephebes was a traditional practice in Gk. states
quorum aliqua adhuc copia ... erat relat. cl.; *quorum* (relat. pron.): anteced. *ephebos*, partit. gen. (AG #346) w/ *copia*; institutum, -i (n.): an established practice, custom; *Capreis*: locat. (AG #427.3); the training of ephebes prepared the young men for membership in the citizen body
epulum, -i (n.) public feast, banquet
conspectus, -us (m.) sight, view
permissa ... iocandi licentia diripiendique ... missilia abl. abs. (AG #419), "with license given for joking and snatching up gifts"; immo: rather, more correctly; iocor (1): jest, joke; *iocandi*: objv. gen. of ger. (AG #504) w/ *licentia*; licentia, -ae (f.): license, unruly behavior; deripio, deripere, deripui, dereptum: grasp, snatch up (<de- + rapio); *deripiendi*: objv. gen. of ger. w/ dir. obj. *missilia* (AG #504a); *pomorum ... rerum*: appos. gen. (AG #343d) w/ *missilia*; pomum, -i (n.): fruit; obsonium, -(i)i (n.): provisions (for a meal); missile, -is (n.): missile, projectile, (pl.) gifts thrown to a crowd
denique (adv.) finally, indeed
hilaritas, -tatis (f.) lightheartedness, gaiety, amusement
abstineo, abstinere, abstinui, abstentum keep distant, abstain from (w/ abl.) (<ab- + teneo)

98.4

uicinam Capreis insulam "an island near Capri"; uicinus, -a, -um: neighboring; the identity of the island is uncertain
Apragopolis "Leisure-city," a pun on two Gk. wd.; *Apragopolim*: acc. sg. (AG #75a.1)
desidia, -ae (f.) idleness, inactivity
secedo, secedere, secessi, secessum withdraw, retire (<se- + cedo); *secedentium*: gen. pl. pres. act. ptc., subst., "of those retiring"
illuc (adv.) to that place
comitatus, -us (m.) entourage, attendant crowd
dilectus, -a, -um beloved, dear; *ex dilectis*: "from his favorites"
Masgaba a name of north African origin; Masgaba may be one of the pueri who entertained Augustus (s. ch. 83)
conditor, -ris (m.) founder (vb. subst. <condo)
κτίστην "city founder," Gk. wd., pred. acc. (AG #393); Gk. colonies revered their founders; that Augustus would name his favorite Masgaba a "city founder" here pokes fun at his laziness
consuesco, consuescere, consueui, consuetum become accustomed to (w/ inf.) (<con- + suesco)
huius Masgabae ... defuncti ptc. phr.; *ante annum*: a year before (AG #424f)
tumulum, -i (m.) burial mound, tomb
cum e triclinio animaduertisset circumst. cum cl. (AG #546); triclinium, -(i)i (n.): dining-room

animaduertisset magna turba multisque luminibus frequentari, uersum compositum ex tempore clare pronuntiauit,

κτίστου δὲ τύμβον εἰσορῶ πυρούμενον,

conuersusque ad Thrasyllum Tiberi comitem contra accubantem et ignarum rei interrogauit cuiusnam poetae putaret esse. quo haesitante subiecit alium,

ὁρᾷς φάεσσι Μασγάβαν τιμώμενον;,

ac de hoc quoque consuluit. cum ille nihil aliud responderet quam cuiuscumque essent optimos esse, cachinnum sustulit atque in iocos effusus est. **5.** mox Neapolim traiecit quamquam etiam tum infirmis intestinis. morbo uariante tamen et

---

tumulum ... frequentari indir. disc. (AG #580) ff. *animaduertisset*; lumen, -inis (n.): light, lamp or torch
ex tempore on the spur of the moment
clare (adv.) out loud
κτίστου δὲ τύμβον εἰσορῶ πυρούμενον "I see the tomb of the city founder on fire," a line of Gk. iambic trimeter (AG #618); Augustus' use of Gk. is fitting for the setting at Capri
conuersusque ad Thrasyllum ... accubantem et ignarum rei ptc. phr. w/ prep. phr.; conuerto, conuertere, conuerti, conuersum: turn, turn toward (w/ ad) (<con- + uerto); Ti. Claudius Thrasyllus (*OCD* 329) was an astrologer and friend of Tiberius; contra (adv.): on the opposite side, facing (him); accubo, accubare: lie, recline (at a table) (<ad- + cubo); ignarus, -a, -um: having no knowledge (w/ gen.)
cuiusnam poetae putaret esse indir. quest. (AG #574) ff. *interrogauit* w/ *putaret* introd. indir. disc., "what poet's work he thinks it is"; quinam, quaenam, quodnam (interrog. adj.): what?; poeta, -ae (m.): poet; puto (1): think, suppose
quo haesitante abl. abs. (AG #419); *quo* (relat. pron.): anteced. *Thrasyllum*; haesito (1): hesitate, be uncertain
alium [uersum]
ὁρᾷς φάεσσι Μασγάβαν τιμώμενον; "Do you see Masgaba being honored with torches?," a second line of Gk. iambic trimeter (AG #618)
cum ille ... responderet circumst. cum cl. (AG #546)
[uersus] cuiuscumque essent optimos esse "whosoever they were, the verses were very good," indir. disc. (AG #580) ff. *responderet* w/ relat. cl.; quicumque, quaecumque, quodcumque (indef. relat. pron.): whoever; optimus, -a, -um: best, very good
cachinnus, -i (m.) laugh
tollo, tollere, sustuli, sublatum raise, send up
effundo, effundere, effudi, effusum let loose, break out into (pass. w/ in) (<ex- + fundo)

98.5
Neapolis, -is (f.) Naples, a city in Campania; *Neapolim*: acc. of place to which w/out prep. (AG #427.2)
traicio, traicere, traieci, traiectum cross over (<trans- + iacio)
infirmis intestinis abl. of quality (AG #415a); infirmus, -a, -um: weak, frail; intestinum, -i (n.): (pl.) guts, intestines
morbo uariante conces. abl. abs. (AG #420.3); morbus, -i (m.): illness, sickness; uario (1): fluctuate, change

quinquennale certamen gymnicum honori suo institutum perspectauit et cum Tiberio ad destinatum locum contendit. sed
in redeundo adgrauata ualitudine tandem Nolae succubuit
reuocatumque ex itinere Tiberium diu secreto sermone detinuit
neque post ulli maiori negotio animum accommodauit.

99   Supremo die identidem exquirens an iam de se tumultus foris
esset, petito speculo capillum sibi comi ac malas labantes corrigi
praecepit et admissos amicos percontatus ecquid iis uideretur
mimum uitae commode transegisse adiecit et clausulam,

---

quinquennale certamen ... institutum ptc. phr., obj. of *perspectauit*; quinquennalis, -e: occurring every five years (four years in modern reckoning); certamen, -inis (n.): contest, competition; gymnicus, -a, -um: gymnastic; the athletic competition at Naples had been established in 2 CE on the model of the Gk. games at Olympia
perspecto (1) watch to the end (<per- + specto); Augustus watched the entire competition which lasted several days
contendo, contendere, contendi, contentum hasten, press on (<con- + tendo); Augustus accompanied Tiberius as he set off for Illyricum (s. ch. 97.3); they parted ways at Beneventum in Samnium (central Italy)
in redeundo "in returning"; *redeundo*: ger. (AG #507)
adgrauata ualitudine causal abl. abs. (AG #420.2); adgrauo (1): increase, aggravate (<ad- + grauo)
Nola, -ae (f.) Nola, a town in the interior of Campania; *Nolae*: locat. (AG #427.3)
succumbo, succumbere, succubui, succubitum lie down, collapse; *succubuit*: "he took to his bed"
reuocatum ... Tiberium tmp. ptc. phr. (AG #496); reuoco (1): call back, summon (<re- + uoco); the account presented by Suet. differs from that of Tacitus (*Ann.* 1.5.3) and Dio (56.31.1) in significant ways, reporting Tiberius' return and conversation with Augustus before Augustus' death (cf. Vell. Pat. 2.123.1)
secretus, -a, -um secret, private
detineo, detinere, detinui, detentum detain (<de- + teneo)
accommodo (1) make available for (w/ acc. and dat.) (<ad- + commodo)

Augustus' final day is recorded under the rubric *supremo die*. Even at the end of his life, Augustus is devoted to the Roman people, his friends, and family members, and concerned that he presents himself as a good example.

99.1
supremo die abl. of time when (AG #423.1); supremus, -a, -um: last, final
identidem (adv.) again and again, repeatedly
exquiro, exquirere, exquisiui, exquisitum ask about, inquire into (<ex- + quaero)
an ... tumultus foris esset indir. quest. (AG #574) ff. *exquirens*; *an* = num; foris (adv.): outside
petito speculo tmp. abl. abs. (AG #420.1); speculum, -i (n.): mirror
capillum sibi comi ac malas labantes corrigi subst. cl. of purp. w. acc. subj. + inf. ff. *praecepit* (AG #563a); capillus, -i (m.): hair; como, comere, compsi, comptum: arrange; mala, -ae (f.): (usu. pl.) jaws; labo (1): be unsteady, be loose; corrigo, corrigere, correxi, correctum: make straight, straighten out (<con- + rego)
praecipio, praecipere, praecepi, praeceptum give instruction, give as a command (<prae- + capio)
percontor (1) interrogate, question
ecquid iis uideretur "whether he seemed to them," indir. quest. (AG #574) ff. *percontatus*; ecquid: whether
mimum uitae commode transegisse pers. indir. disc. ff. *uideretur* (AG #582); mimus, -i (m.): mime, farcical play; commode (adv.): properly, agreeably; transigo, transigere, transegi, transactum: carry through to the end, complete (<trans- + ago); *transegisse*: pf. act. inf.
clausula, -ae (f.) tag line, conclusion of a verse

ἐπεὶ δὲ †ΤΙΑΧΟΙ† καλῶς τὸ παίγνιον,
δότε κρότον καὶ πάντες ἡμᾶς μετὰ χαρᾶς προπέμψατε.
omnibus deinde dimissis, dum aduenientes ab urbe de Drusi
filia aegra interrogat, repente in osculis Liuiae et in hac uoce
defecit, 'Liuia, nostri coniugii memor uiue ac uale!', sortitus
exitum facilem et qualem semper optauerat. 2. nam fere quotiens audisset cito ac nullo cruciatu defunctum quempiam, sibi
et suis εὐθανασίαν similem—hoc enim et uerbo uti solebat—
precabatur. unum omnino ante efflatam animam signum alienatae mentis ostendit, quod subito pauefactus a quadraginta se

---

ἐπεὶ δὲ †ΤΙΑΧΟΙ† καλῶς τὸ παίγνιον, / δότε κρότον καὶ πάντες ἡμᾶς μετὰ χαρᾶς προπέμψατε "Since ... well the play, give applause and send us all joyfully on our way"; the text of the two lines of Gk. verse is corrupted, but the sentiment is clear: Augustus' final pronouncement mimics the ending of a play

omnibus deinde dimissis tmp. abl. abs. (AG #420.1)

dum ... interrogat tmp. dum cl. w/ pres. indic. to denote continued past action (AG #556); dum: "while"; aduenio, aduenire, adueni, aduentum: arrive (<ad- + uenio); *aduenientes*: (subst.) "those arriving"; *Drusi filia*: "the daughter of Drusus" = Livia Julia (*OCD* s.v. Livia Iulia, 851), Augustus' step-granddaughter, often called "Livilla"; aeger, -gra, -grum: unwell, sick

in osculis Liuiae lit.: "on the lips of Livia," i.e., while she was kissing him; osculum, -i (n.): mouth, lips

deficio, deficere, defeci, defectum pass away, die (<de- + facio)

Liuia ... uiue et uale Suet. quotes directly Augustus' final wd.; noster, -tra, -trum: our; coniugium, -(i) i (n.): marriage; memor, -oris: mindful, having in memory (w/ gen.); uiuo, uiuere, uixi, uictum: live; *uiue*: sg. impv.; ualeo, ualere, ualui, ualitum: farewell

sortitus exitum facilem ptc. phr.; sortior, sortiri, sortitus sum: acquire, receive as one's lot; exitus, -us (m.): conclusion, end of one's life; facilis, -e: easy, easy to bear

qualis, -e (relat. adj.) of which sort, such as; *qualem* [*exitum*]

opto (1) wish for, desire

99.2

quotiens audisset iterative subjv. w/ *quotiens* (BG #567n); audio, audire, audiui (-ii), auditum: hear; *audisset*: contr. form of audivisset (AG #181)

cito ac nullo cruciatu defunctum [esse] quempiam indir. disc. (AG #580) ff. *audisset*; cito (adv.): quickly; cruciatus, -us (m.): severe pain; quispiam, quaepiam, quippiam: someone, anybody

sibi et suis "for himself and his loved ones," indir. obj. w/ *precabatur*

εὐθανασίαν "euthanasia," Gk. wd., acc. dir. obj. of *precabatur*

hoc enim et uerbo uti solebat "for he was accustomed to use this word," an aside; *uti*: compl. inf. w/ *solebat* (AG #456)

precor (1) ask for, pray for

ante efflatam animam "before he died"; efflo (1): breathe out (<ex- + flo); anima, -ae (f.): breath; animam efflare: expire, die

signum, -i (n.) sign

alienatae mentis "of having lost his sanity"; alieno (1): lose possession of; mens, -tis (f.): mind

quod ... questus est causal cl. w/ indic. showing the reason is given on the authority of the author (AG #540); subito (adv.): suddenly; pauefacio, pauefacere, pauefeci, pauefactum: terrify, alarm;

iuuenibus abripi questus est. id quoque magis praesagium quam mentis deminutio fuit, siquidem totidem milites praetoriani extulerunt eum in publicum.

100 Obiit in cubiculo eodem quo pater Octauius, duobus Sextis, Pompeio et Appuleio, cons. XIIII. Kal. Septemb., hora diei nona, septuagesimo et sexto aetatis anno, diebus V et XXX minus.
  2. corpus decuriones municipiorum et coloniarum a Nola

---

a quadraginta se iuuenibus abripi: indir. disc. ff. *questus est*; quadraginta (indecl. adj.): forty; abripio, abripere, abripui, abreptum: carry away (<ab- + rapio)
magis (compar. adv.) more; introd. compar. w/ *quam* (AG #407)
praesagium, -(i)i (n.) presage, portent
deminutio, -onis (f.) diminution, loss
siquidem (causal conj.) seeing that, inasmuch as
totidem (indecl. adj.) the same number, as many
praetorianus, -a, -um of the praetorian guards (elite soldiers in Rome)
effero, efferre, extuli, elatum carry out, bring out (<ex- + fero)
in publicum in public, into the open; the praetorian guardsmen must have moved Augustus' body outside the house after he died; the full details of the transfer of his body to Rome are set out below

Augustus dies (*obiit*). Suetonius carefully recounts the place and time of Augustus' death, the special arrangements made for transporting his body to Rome, and the honors proposed for him.

100.1
obeo, obire, obii, obitum die (<ob- + eo)
quo pater Octauius [obierat] relat. cl. (AG #308i); quo (relat. adv.): in which place, where
duobus Sextis ... cons[ulibus] tmp. abl. abs. w/out ptc. (AG #419a, 420.1); the year was 14 CE
XIIII [ante] **Kal**[endas] **Septemb**[ris] "fourteen days before the kalends of September" = August 19 (for Roman dates, AG #424g, 631)
hora ... nona abl. of time when (AG #423); nonus, -a, -um: ninth
septuagesimo et sexto aetatis anno "in the seventy-sixth year of life," abl. of time when
diebus V et XXX abl. of deg. of diff. ff. *minus* (AG #414); minus (compar. adv.): less

100.2
corpus "the body of Augustus"; note the emphatic placement of corpus: in this section corpus appears as the obj. or subj., much like Augustus had been throughout the life; Romans who died away from the city were usually cremated wherever they died and their ashes were transferred to Rome for burial; the transport of Augustus' body was exceptional
decurio, -onis (m.) member of the municipal senate, town councillor
municipiorum et coloniarium municipium, -(i)i (n.): self-governing city, municipality; colonia, -ae (f.): settlement, colony; the route took Augustus' body through a dozen towns, with the leaders of each town playing a prominent role
a Nola abl. of place from which (AG #426) (usu. w/out prep. w/ name of city); Nola, -ae (f.): Nola, a town in the interior of Campania

Bouillas usque deportarunt noctibus propter anni tempus, cum
interdiu in basilica cuiusque oppidi uel in aedium sacrarum
maxima reponeretur. a Bouillis equester ordo suscepit urbique
intulit atque in uestibulo domus conlocauit. senatus et in
funere ornando et in memoria honoranda eo studi certatim
progressus est ut inter alia complura censuerint quidam funus
triumphali porta ducendum praecedente Victoria quae est in
curia, canentibus neniam principum liberis utriusque sexus,
alii exequiarum die ponendos anulos aureos ferreosque sumen-

Bouillae, -arum (f. pl.) Bovillae, a town in Latium twelve miles from Rome; *Bouillas*: acc. of place to which w/out prep. (AG #427.2)
deporto (1) convey, carry (<de- + porto); *deportarunt* = contr. form of deportauerunt (AG #181)
noctibus "by night," abl. of time when (AG #423); temperatures were too high to transport the body in the daytime
propter (prep. + acc) on account of
cum ... reponeretur causal cum cl. (AG #549); interdiu (adv.): during the day; basilica, -ae (f.): colonnaded hall, basilica; *in aedium sacrarum maxima*: "in the greatest of the temples"; sacer, -cra, -crum: sacred; *sacrarum aedium*: partit. gen. (AG #346a.2); repono, reponere, reposui, repositum: place (<re- + pono)
infero, inferre, intuli, illatum carry into (w/ acc. and dat.) (<in- + fero); supply corpus as dir. obj.
uestibulum, -i (n.) forecourt, entranceway
conloco (1) put in a particular place, set up (<con- + loco); the body arrived in Rome during the night of September 2–3, two weeks after his death
in funere ornando abl. of gerv. w/ in (AG #507.3); funus, -eris (n.): funeral, funeral procession; orno (1): arrange
in memoria honoranda abl. of gerv. w/ in (AG #507.3); honoro (1): honor, celebrate
eo studi "to such a degree of enthusiasm"; eo (adv.): to such a point or degree; studium, -(i)i (n.): enthusiasm, eagerness; *studi*: partit. gen. (AG #346a.4)
certatim (adv.) with rivalry, in competition; Suet. regularly uses adv. in -tim
progredior, progredi, progressus sum go forward, advance (<pro- + gradior)
ut ... censuerint quidam result cl. (AG #537) divided into three cl.: *quidam ... alii ... nonnulli*, each followed by a subst. cl. of purp.; censeo, censere, censui, censum: recommend; Suet. provides details of three sets of proposals that illustrate the high regard of the senate for Augustus before noting (100.3) that strict limits were set on the honors
funus ... ducendum [esse] subst. cl. of purp. w/ acc. subj. + inf. ff. *censuerint* (AG #563d); porta triumphalis: the triumphal gate; *triumphali porta*: abl. of way by which (AG #429a); *ducendum* [*esse*]: 2nd (pass.) periphr. (AG #194b, 196)
praecedente Victoria abl. abs. (AG #419); praecedo, praecedere, praecessi, praecessum: go in front (<prae- + cedo); Victoria: the statue of the goddess of Victory, dedicated by Augustus in the Curia Julia in 29 BCE
canentibus ... liberis utriusque sexus abl. abs. (AG #419); cano, canere, cecini: sing, chant; nenia, -ae (f.): song sung at a funeral, dirge; *utriusque sexus*: gen. of quality (AG #345); sexus, -us (m.): sex
alii [censuerint]
exequiarum die ponendos [esse] **anulos aureos fereosque sumendos** [esse] subst. cl. of purp. w/ acc. subj. + inf. ff. *censuerint* (AG #563d); *exequiarum die*: abl. of time when (AG #423); exequiae, -arum (f. pl.): funeral procession, obsequies; *ponendos* [*esse*]: 2nd (pass.) periphr. (AG #194b, 196); anulus, -i (m.): a ring; ferreus, -a, -um: made of iron; *fereos* [*anulos*]; *sumendos* [*esse*]: 2nd (pass.) periphr.; taking off one's gold ring was a sign of great distress; iron rings were associated with slaves

dos, nonnulli ossa legenda per sacerdotes summorum collegiorum.   **3.** fuit et qui suaderet appellationem mensis Augusti in Septembrem transferendam, quod hoc genitus Augustus, illo defunctus esset, alius ut omne tempus a primo die natali ad exitum eius saeculum Augustum appellaretur et ita in fastos referretur. uerum adhibito honoribus modo bifariam laudatus est, pro aede Diui Iuli a Tiberio et pro rostris ueteribus a Druso Tiberi filio, ac senatorum umeris delatus in Campum crematusque.   **4.** nec defuit uir praetorius qui se effigiem

---

nonnulli [censuerint]
ossa legenda [esse] **per sacerdotes summorum collegiorum** subst. cl. of purp. w/ acc. subj. + inf. ff. *censuerint* (AG #563d); os, ossis (n.): bone; ossa legere: to collect the bones from a pyre (after cremation); *legenda* [*esse*]: 2nd (pass.) periphr. (AG #194b, 196); sacerdos, -otis (m./f.): priest, priestess; summus, -a, -um: greatest; collegium, -(i)i (n.): college or board (of priests); the "summa collegia" were the pontifs, augurs, quindecemviri, and septemviri.

100.3
fuit subst. vb. (AG #284b), "there was"
qui suaderet relat. cl. of char. (AG #535a); suadeo, suadere, suasi, suasum: recommend, advocate
appellationem ... transferendam [esse] subst. cl. of purp. w/ acc. subj. + inf. ff. *suaderet* (AG #563d); appellatio, -onis (f.): name; *transferendam* [*esse*]: 2nd (pass.) periphr. (AG #194b, 196); for the renaming of the month Sextilis for Augustus in 8 BCE, s. ch. 31.2
quod ... genitus ... defunctus esset causal cl. w/ subjv. providing the reasons given for the proposed change (AG #540); *hoc* [*mense*] ... *illo*: abl. of time when or within (AG #423); gigno, gignere, genui, genitum: produce, (pass.) be born
alius [suaderet]
ut omne tempus ... appellaretur et ... referretur subst. cl. of purp. w/ subjv. (AG #563); dies natalis: day of one's birth; exitus, -us (m.): end of one's life; *saeculum Augustum*: "the Augustan age," pred. nom. w/ *appellaretur* (AG #284); saeculum, -i (n.): human lifetime, age; fasti, -orum (m. pl.): the calendar
adhibito honoribus modo abl. abs. (AG #419); adhibeo, adhibere, adhibui, adhitum: set (a limit) (w/ dat.) (<ad- + habeo)
bifariam (adv.) in two places (numeral adv. in -fariam)
laudo (1) praise, deliver a funerary eulogy of; Augustus is subj.
aedes Diui Iuli the Temple of Divus Julius, at the southeast end of the Roman Forum, which included a new speaker's platform adorned with the beaks of ships (rostra) captured at Actium
rostra uetera "the old rostra," the speaker's platform at the northwest end of the Forum
umerus, -i (m.) shoulder
defero, deferre, detuli, delatum transfer, convey (<de- + fero); *delatus* [*est*]
Campus [Martius] the "Field of Mars" in Rome
cremo (1) burn, cremate; *crematus* [*est*]

100.4
nec defuit LITOTES (AG #326c); desum, deesse, defui: be lacking (<de- + sum); Suet. here highlights that this was an unusual and special occurrence
praetorius, -a, -um of praetorian rank; Dio (56.46.2) identifies the former praetor as Numerius Atticus
qui ... iuraret relat. cl. of char. (AG #535a) or purp. (AG #531.2) w/ indir. disc. (AG #580c) ff. *iuraret*; *se ... uidisse*: indir. disc.; effigies, -ei (f.): ghost or spirit; *cremati* [*Augusti*]; eo, ire, ii (iui), itum: go,

cremati euntem in caelum uidisse iuraret. reliquias legerunt
primores equestris ordinis tunicati et discincti pedibusque nudis
ac Mausoleo condiderunt. id opus inter Flaminiam uiam ripam-
que Tiberis sexto suo consulatu extruxerat circumiectasque
siluas et ambulationes in usum populi iam tum publicarat.

101 Testamentum L. Planco C. Silio cons. III. Non. Apriles ante
annum et quattuor menses quam decederet factum ab eo ac
duobus codicibus partim ipsius partim libertorum Polybi et
Hilarionis manu scriptum depositumque apud se uirgines

---

proceed; iuro (1): swear, affirm by oath; the testimony of a witness to Augustus' ascent to heaven mirrors the story of Romulus' deification; Suet. does not report the subsequent actions of the senate to deify Augustus

reliquiae, -arum (f. pl.) the remains (of Augustus' body)

primoris, -e first, of high rank, (m. pl. subst.) "the leading men"

tunicati et discincti w/ *primores*; tunicatus, -a, -um: wearing a tunic; discinctus, -a, -um: not wearing a belt; the senior equites were dressed for mourning

pedibus nudis abl. of quality (AG #415a); nudus, -a, -um: bare

Mausoleum, -i (n.) the Mausoleum of Augustus; *Mausoleo*: abl. of place where ff. *condiderunt* (AG #430); the name Mausoleum comes from the tomb of the fourth-century BCE King Mausolus of Halicarnassus in Caria

Flaminia uia the Flaminian Way, the main road leading north from Rome

ripa, -ae (f.) bank (of a river)

Tiberis, -is (m.) the river Tiber

sexto suo consulatu abl. of time when (AG #423.1), 28 BCE

circumicio, circumicere, circumieci, circumiectum place round, surround (<circum- + iacio)

silua, -ae (f.) forest, wood

ambulatio, -onis (f.) promenade, place for walking

publico (1) make public property; *publicarat* = contr. form of publicauerat (AG #181)

Augustus' will (*testamentum*). For Romans, the will presented an individual's final judgments and offered a last view of his character. As such this is a fitting concluding chapter for Suetonius' *Life of Augustus*, as we see Augustus once again display care for his family and the Roman people.

101.1

testamentum ... factum ab eo ptc. phr., dir. obj. of *protulerunt*; *L. Planco C. Silio cons.*: abl. abs. expressing time (AG #419a, 424g) = 13 CE; *III Non. Apriles*: "on the third day before the Nones of April" = April 3 (for the calendar, AG #631); *ante ... quam decederet*: anticipatory cl. implying expectancy in past time (AG #551b); *annum et quattuor menses*: distance of time before (AG #424f); quattuor (indecl. adj.): four; decedo, decedere, decessi, decessum: depart, die (<de- + cedo)

ac ... scriptum second ptc. phr. w/ *testamentum*; codex, -icis (m.): book; partim (adv.): in part, partly; Augustus' freedmen Polybius and Hilarion are otherwise unknown

depositum apud se third ptc. phr. w/ *testamentum*; depono, deponere, deposui, depositum: deposit, put aside for safe keeping (<de- + pono); *se* (reflex.) = uirgines Vestales

uirgines Vestales subj. of *protulerunt*; Vestal Virgins, priestesses of Vesta (*OCD* s.v. Vesta, Vestals, 1544–1545); uirgo, -inis (f.): virgin; the wills of elite Romans were often entrusted to the Vestals

Vestales cum tribus signatis aeque uoluminibus protulerunt,
quae omnia in senatu aperta atque recitata sunt. **2.** heredes
instituit primos Tiberium ex parte dimidia et sextante, Liuiam
ex parte tertia, quos et ferre nomen suum iussit, secundos
Drusum Tiberi filium ex triente, ex partibus reliquis
Germanicum liberosque eius tres sexus uirilis, tertio gradu propinquos amicosque compluris. legauit populo R. quadringenties, tribubus tricies quinquies sestertium, praetorianis militibus
singula milia nummorum, cohortibus urbanis quingenos,
legionaris trecenos nummos. quam summam repraesentari

---

signo (1) sign, affix a seal to
uolumen, -inis (n.) roll of papyrus
profero, proferre, protuli, prolatum bring forth, carry out (<pro- + fero)
quae omnia "all of which," namely the will plus the three papyrus scrolls
aperio, aperire, aperui, apertum open; *aperta* [*sunt*]

101.2
heres, -edis (m./f.) heir; primary heirs were first to receive the inheritance
instituit Augustus is subj.
ex parte dimidia et sextante one-half and one-sixth part (= 2/3)
ex parte tertia one-third part; it was a unique honor to recognize Livia with such a large bequest
quos et ferre nomen suum subst. cl. of purp. ff. *iussit* w/ inf. + subj. acc. (AG #563a); *quos* (relat. pron.): anteced. *Tiberium* and *Liuiam*; Livia became Julia Augusta and Tiberius received the name Augustus, which he used sparingly (s. Suet. *Tib.* 26.2)
secundos [heredes] secondary heirs came into an inheritance only if the primary heirs refused or were unable to take up the inheritance; s. introduction for family tree
triens, -ntis (m.) third part
Germanicum liberosque eius tres Germanicus Iulius Caesar (*OCD* 760–761) and his three sons, Nero, Drusus, and Gaius (Caligula)
sexus uirilis "of the male sex," gen. of quality (AG #345)
gradus, -us (m) step or stage, position
propinquos amicosque propinquus, -i (m.): kinsman; only the future emperor Claudius is known to have been among these heirs
legauit populo R. quadringenties ... nummos Suet. carefully enumerates the bequests made to the people and soldiers; lego (1): bequeath; *populo R*[*omano*]; quadringenties: 40 million (sesterces); tribus, -us (m.): tribe (a voting group in Rome); tricies quinquies sestertium: 3.5 million sesterces; praetorianus, -a, -um: praetorian, of the praetorian guards (the elite soldiers in Rome); milia, -ium (pl.): thousands; cohors, -rtis (f.): armed force, cohort; urbanus, -a, -um: urban, connected with the city (Rome); *quingenos*: 500; legionarius, -a, -um: legionary, (m. subst.) a legionary solider; *trecenos*: 300
quam summam repraesentari subst. cl. of purp. w/ acc. subj. + inf. ff. *iussit* (AG #563a); repraesento (1): pay at once (<re- + praesento)

iussit, nam et confiscatam semper repositamque habuerat.
3. reliqua legata uarie dedit perduxitque quaedam ad uicena sestertia, quibus soluendis annuum diem finiit, excusata rei familiaris mediocritate nec plus peruenturum ad heredes suos quam milies et quingenties professus, quamuis uiginti proximis annis quaterdecies milies ex testamentis amicorum percepisset, quod paene omne cum duobus paternis patrimoniis ceterisque hereditatibus in rem p. absumpsisset. Iulias filiam neptemque, si quid iis accidisset, uetuit sepulcro suo inferri.   **4.** tribus uoluminibus

---

[summam] **confiscatam ... repositamque habuerat** confisco (1): lay up in a treasury, keep in store; repono, reponere, reposui, repositum: put away, stored (<re- + pono); Suet. emphasizes that Augustus had set aside the funds in his personal treasury to ensure that the legacies could be paid right away

101.3
legatum, -i (n.) bequest, legacy; it was traditional for Romans to recognize friends and relatives with bequests, and Augustus himself had benefitted from such recognition (s. below)
uarie (adv.) variously, in different ways
perduco, perducere, perduxi, perductum bring up to (a specified amount) (<per- + duco)
uicena sestertia 20,000 sesterces
quibus soluendis "for paying these bequests"; *quibus* (relat. pron.): anteced. *legata*; soluo, soluere, solui, solutum: pay; *soluendis:* dat. of gerv. (AG #505)
annuum diem "a day a year away"; by delaying the payment of these bequests, Tiberius was given time to assemble the sums and the would-be recipients were bound in support of Augustus' heir
finio, finire, finiui (-ii), finitum specify, appoint (a date)
excusata ... mediocritate abl. abs. (AG #419); excuso (1): plead in excuse; res familiaris: one's private property; mediocritas, -atis (f.): smallness, moderateness of the amount
nec plus peruenturum [esse] **... quam milies et quingenties** indir. disc. (AG #580) ff. *professus*; peruenio, peruenire, perueni, peruentum: come to (<per- + uenio); *milies et quingenties*: 150 million
quamuis ... percepisset conces. cl. w/ subjv. (AG #527a); *uiginti proximis annis*: abl. of time within which (AG #423.1); quaterdecies milies: 1,400,000,000; percipio, percipere, percepi, perceptum: acquire, receive (<per- + capio)
quod paene omne ... absumpsisset "almost all of which he had spent"; relat. cl. w/ subjv. by attraction (AG #593); paternus, -a, -um: paternal; patrimonium, -(i)i (n.): estate, fortune (Augustus had received inheritances from his father Octavius and from Julius Caesar); hereditas, -atis (f.): inheritance; *in rem p[ublicam]*: "on the state"; in the *Res Gestae*, Augustus also highlighted his many expenditures on behalf of the state
Iulias filiam neptemque ... inferri subst. cl. of purp. w/ acc. subj. + inf. (AG #563a) ff. *uetuit*; *si quid iis accidisset*: prot. of gener. condit. w/ plupf. subjv. (AG #518c); *quid* = aliquid, subj.; accido, accidere, accidi: happen to, befall (<ad- + cado); ueto, uetare, uetui, uetitum: forbid, prohibit; sepulcrum, -i (n.): tomb; *sepulcro*: dat. w/ *inferri* (AG #370); infero, inferre, intuli, illatum: carry in, bury (<in- + fero); a Roman testator retained the right to exclude others from burial in his tomb; for Augustus' falling-out with the Julias, s. ch. 65

101.4
tribus uoluminibus "in three rolls", abl. w/ *complectus est* (AG #430); uolumen, -inis (n.): roll of papyrus; Suet. discusses each roll in turn: *uno ... altero ... tertio*

uno mandata de funere suo complexus est, altero indicem
rerum a se gestarum, quem uellet incidi in aeneis tabulis quae
ante Mausoleum statuerentur, tertio breuiarium totius imperii,
quantum militum sub signis ubique esset, quantum pecuniae in
aerario et fiscis et uectigaliorum residuis. adiecit et libertorum
seruorumque nomina a quibus ratio exigi posset.

---

mandatum, -i (n.) an order

funus, -eris (n.) a funeral

complector, complecti, complexus sum include in (<con- + plecto); *complectus est* has three dir. obj. setting out the contents of each of the three scrolls: *mandata . . . indicem . . . breuiarium*; note that Augustus is subj. of the final sentences of the life

index, -icis (m.) summary, catalogue; the index rerum gestarum is the famous *Res Gestae*, copies of which survive in inscriptions from Asia Minor

quem uellet incidi in aeneis tabulis subord. subjv. cl. in informal indir. disc. (AG #592) w/subst. cl. of purp. ff. *uellet* (AG #563b), "which he wished to be inscribed"; incido, incidere, incidi, incisum: incise, inscribe (<in- + caedo); *incidi:* pres. pass. inf.; aeneus, -a, -um: bronze

quae . . . statuerentur relat. cl. w/ subjv. by attraction (AG #593), "which were to be set up"; *quae* (relat. pron.): anteced. *tabulis*; statuo, statuere, statui, statutum: set up, erect

breuiarium, -(i)i (n.) brief account, summary statement (an unusual wd. <breuis)

totus, -a, -um whole, entire (for decl., AG #113)

quantum militum . . . ubique esset, quantum pecuniae in . . . residuis indir. quest. (AG #574) summarizing the contents of the third volume; quantum (interrog.): how much (how many), w/ partit. gen. (AG #346); signum, -i (n.): military standard; fiscus, -i (m.): imperial treasury; *in uectigaliorum residuis*: "in outstanding tax revenues"; uectigal, -alis (n.): taxes; residuus, -a, -um: outstanding, yet to be paid

a quibus ratio exigi posset subord. subjv. cl. in informal indir. disc. (AG #592), "from whom an account could be exacted"